# INTRODUCING CICERO

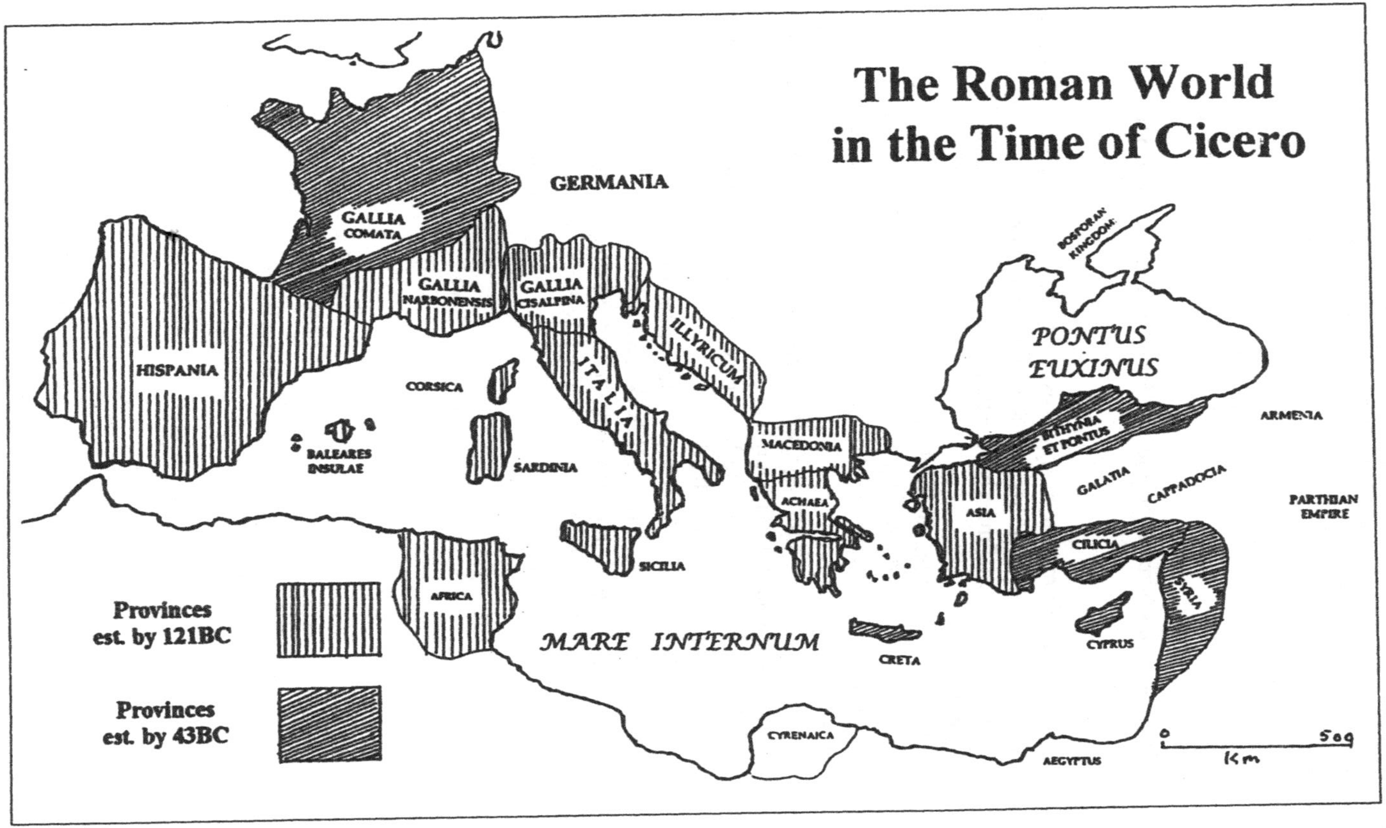
The Roman World
in the Time of Cicero
GERMANIA
GALLIA COMATA
GALLIA NARBONENSIS
GALLIA CISALPINA
HISPANIA
CORSICA
BALEARES INSULAE
SARDINIA
ITALIA
ILLYRICUM
SICILIA
MACEDONIA
ACHAEA
BOSPORAN KINGDOM
PONTUS EUXINUS
BITHYNIA ET PONTUS
ARMENIA
GALATIA
CAPPADOCIA
PARTHIAN EMPIRE
ASIA
CILICIA
SYRIA
CYPRUS
CRETA
MARE INTERNUM
AFRICA
CYRENAICA
AEGYPTUS
0 500
Km
Provinces est. by 121BC
Provinces est. by 43BC

This reader was prepared by the following members of the Scottish Classics Group:

Mary S.R. Burns, formerly Assistant Deputy Principal and Principal Teacher of Classics, The Mary Erskine School, Edinburgh.

Iain R. Macaskill, formerly Principal Teacher of Classics, Knox Academy, Haddington.

M. Barclay Miller, formerly Deputy Rector and Principal Teacher of Classics, Perth Academy.

Richard M. Orr, formerly Adviser in Classics in Strathclyde Region and the City of Glasgow.

Henry L. Philip, formerly HM Inspector of Schools and Headmaster, Liberton High School, Edinburgh.

William F. Ritchie, formerly Deputy Rector and Principal Teacher of Classics, Arbroath High School.

Kenneth G. Silver, formerly Rector of Jedburgh Grammar School and Principal Teacher of Classics, Falkirk High School.

Geoffrey Suggitt, formerly Headmaster, Stratton School, Biggleswade, and Principal Teacher of Classics, George Watson's College, Edinburgh.

# INTRODUCING CICERO

A selection of passages from the writings of
Marcus Tullius Cicero

With notes on his life and times

**Prepared by The Scottish Classics Group**

**Bristol Classical Press**

This impression 2004
First published in 2002 by
Bristol Classical Press
an imprint of
Gerald Duckworth & Co. Ltd.
90-93 Cowcross Street, London EC1M 6BF
Tel: 020 7490 7300
Fax: 020 7490 0080
inquiries@duckworth-publishers.co.uk
www.ducknet.co.uk



A catalogue record for this book is available from the British Library

ISBN 1 85399 637 8

Cover illustration: Cicero, from a portrait bust, Vatican Museums, Rome.

# Contents

# List of Maps



# List of Illustrations

# Notes for the Student

In this book, we offer a selection of relatively short excerpts from Cicero's speeches, letters and philosophical writings, covering a range of styles: rhetorical, narrative, epistolary and dialectic. The passages also offer interesting contemporary comment on one of the most important periods in Roman history, and they are linked to and supplemented by an English commentary designed to give you some understanding of Cicero's career and of the eventful times and political climate in which he lived. These historical links provide a continuous account of the whole period and give enough background to allow each passage to be read on its own. The passages appear chronologically and not in a graded order of difficulty.

Because of the variety of topics, the vocabulary is extensive; and so, since our aim is to help you to read the text as quickly as possible, we have provided within each chapter very full lists of words, giving only the forms required to understand that passage. The Select Vocabulary at the end of the book has been restricted mainly to words which are not in the special vocabularies or are given only in the notes at the point where they occur in the text.

The notes are more extensive than would normally be the case. Mostly, we have explained the meaning of difficult phrases by a literal translation rather than by a grammatical explanation. However, for those who wish to analyse the grammar and syntax, we have provided references to the relevant sections in *The Latin Language* (Oliver and Boyd — Eighth Impression), a streamlined grammar book prepared by the Scottish Classics Group (referred to as 'See LL' in the notes).

It is important for you to take the Latin words in the order in which they occur. The illogicality of approaching a Latin passage using the 'Find the subject, find the verb, etc' method is surely nowhere more clearly illustrated than in a speech, where the Roman audience had no option but to take in the words in the order in which they were spoken! Besides, unless you learn to read Latin in the order in which it appears, you will fail to appreciate the power of Cicero's oratory, achieved by such techniques as the balancing of words, phrases and clauses, the skilful positioning of words to produce a particular effect, and the overall sound-pattern of the words themselves. To help you to deal with complex sentences, we strongly urge you to study the 'Overview' notes and exercises on pages 121-31 of *The Latin Language*, and pages xii-xiv of this book.

Finally, in *Points for Discussion*, there are only a few comprehension questions. We have chosen instead to concentrate on two elements which, we think, provide the main justification for reading Cicero today. The first of these relates to points of style, a knowledge of which is basic to an appreciation of Cicero's artistry as orator and writer. [See Appendix 1 'Cicero and Oratory' — shortened to CAO in the notes on the Latin text.] The second concerns the relevance of ancient writings to the modern world. We believe that lessons can still be learned from events long past; indeed, the lessons may be all the clearer from being studied objectively at a distance. We believe that every opportunity should be taken to use Latin authors like Cicero to show the universality of many of these issues and their continuing relevance for us today.

# Marcus Tullius Cicero (106-43 BC)

| BC | Cicero's Life | Other Important Events |
|---|---|---|
| 106 | Born at Arpinum on 3 January. [Marius was born there in 157 BC.] | Marius consul six times between 107 and 100 BC. |
| 90 | Receives toga praetexta (age 16). | Rivalry growing between Marius and Sulla. |
| 89 | Serves in the army of Pompey's father (age 17). | |
| 88 | Studies literature, politics and philosophy in Rome. | Civil war. Sulla captures Rome. Marius flees. |
| 86 | | Marius dies. Sulla in the East fighting Mithridates. |
| 83 | | Sulla returns to Rome to fight and defeat the followers of Marius. |
| 81 | First public speech: *Pro Quinctio*: a civil action (age 25). | Sulla becomes dictator. Introduces new legislation to amend constitution. |
| 80 | First political speech. Defends Roscius on murder charge (Chap.1). | |
| 79-77 | Studies rhetoric in Athens and Rhodes (Chap.3) (age 27-29). | Sulla gives up the dictatorship. |
| 78 | | Death of Sulla. |
| 77 | Returns to Rome and marries Terentia (age 29). | Pompey given command in Spain. |
| 75-74 | Quaestor in Sicily (Chap.2) and thus gains entry to the Senate (age 31). | Pompey in Spain fighting against Sertorius (76-71 BC). |
| 70 | Prosecutes Verres (Chap.4-6). Now leading advocate in Rome. Begins to support Pompey (age 36). | First consulship of Pompey and Crassus. |
| 69 | Serves as curule aedile (age 37). | Caesar elected quaestor for 68 BC. |
| 67 | Writes his first letters to Atticus. | Pompey clears the seas of pirates. |
| 66 | Praetor in Rome. Supports giving Pompey the command against Mithridates (Chap.7) (age 40). | |
| 65 | His son Marcus is born. Prepares to stand for the consulship (Chap.8). | Caesar serves as aedile. |
| 63 | As consul thwarts Catiline (Chap.9). Executes conspirators (age 43). | Caesar elected praetor for 62 BC. |
| 62 | Pompey still his idol (Chap 10). | Clodius profanes the mysteries of the Bona Dea. |
| 61 | Destroys Clodius' alibi in the Bona Dea scandal. | Pompey finally defeats Mithridates and returns to Rome. Caesar propraetor in Spain. Clodius becomes a tribune. |

| BC | Cicero's Life | Other Important Events |
|---|---|---|
| 60 | Adopts a neutral stance towards the Triumvirs. | First Triumvirate of Caesar, Pompey and Crassus.Pompey marries Julia, Caesar's daughter. |
| 59 | | First consulship of Caesar. He is made governor of Narbonensis, Cisalpine Gaul and Illyricum for five years. |
| 58 | Clodius accuses Cicero of executing citizens without trial. Cicero driven into exile (Chap.11-12) (age 48). | Caesar takes over his province and begins campaigns to conquer Gaul and increase his province. |
| 57 | Recalled from exile. Returns to Rome in triumph (Chap.13). Tullia's first husband (Piso) dies. | Pompey becomes food-controller in Italy because of threat to corn-supply. |
| 56 | Defends Sestius against charge of violence in gang warfare in 59 BC. Tullia marries and soon divorces her second husband. | The Triumvirs (Caesar, Pompey and Crassus) renew their pact at Luca. |
| 55 | Busy in the courts, but not active politically. | Second consulship of Pompey and Crassus. Caesar's command in Gaul extended. First invasion of Britain. |
| 54 | | Crassus governor of Syria; Pompey governor of Spain but stays in Rome. Julia dies. |
| 53 | Cicero enters the college of augurs. | Crassus defeated by the Parthians and then murdered. |
| 52 | Clodius killed in gang fight; Milo is accused. Cicero fails in his defence. Cicero made governor of Cilicia. | Rioting in Rome. Pompey appointed sole consul and allies himself with Senate to undermine Caesar's position. |
| 51-50 | Cicero governor of Cilicia (age 55) (Chap.14-15). Tullia marries her third husband, Dolabella. | |
| 49 | Caesar tries to win Cicero over but he joins Pompey in Greece. Cicero has marriage difficulties (Chap 17). | Caesar crosses the Rubicon and civil war between Caesar and Pompey begins (Chap. 16). |
| 48 | After the defeat at Pharsalus, Cicero returns to Italy. Concentrates on philosophical writings (Chap18-20). (age 58). | Pompey defeated at Pharsalus in Greece. Flees to Egypt where he is murdered. |
| 47 | Cicero is pardoned by Caesar but still keeps out of politics. | Caesar returns to Rome after victories over Pompey's followers. |
| 46 | Cicero divorces Terentia and marries his young ward, Publilia (age 60). | Caesar mops up Pompeians in various parts of Mediterranean. Carries out reform of the calendar. |
| 45 | Cicero grief-stricken over the death of his daughter, Tullia. | Caesar finally defeats Pompeians and becomes dictator in Rome. |
| 44 | After the murder of Caesar, Cicero attacks the consul Antony in *The Philippics* (Chap.21-2) (age 62). | Antony seizes control of Rome and the conspirators flee to Greece. Octavian comes to Rome to stake his claim. |
| 43 | Delivers *Philippics 5-14*. Put on proscription list and murdered on 7th December (Chap.24) (age 63). | Octavian seizes the consulship in August. Forms Second Triumvirate with Antony and Lepidus in November. |

# Overview

When we are reading a piece of English or listening to someone speaking, we can often anticipate how a sentence will develop. For example, we often start laughing before a comedian reaches the end of a joke. Of course, this does not happen all the time, but it happens more frequently than we sometimes realise. In fact, clues abound in English. For example, in a sentence which begins 'He prevented ...', we can be almost certain that it will continue '... something' or '... someone from doing something.' In the same way, 'we decided ...' will usually continue ' ... to do something'; and 'they interrogated ...' is likely to continue ' ... someone about something'. Similarly, 'I wondered ...' could be followed by a variety of words (*who*, *what*, *where*, *when*, *why*, etc), but these words all have one thing in common — they are all question words. There are countless clues like these in English, which help us to anticipate how a sentence is likely to develop.

English relies heavily on word order for its meaning. Latin is much more flexible in its word order and relies on a different and distinctive system of clues to prepare the listener/reader for what is coming, e.g. verb endings, case endings of nouns, agreement of adjectives, etc. Using these clues the Romans built up the meaning of a sentence as it unfolded. They did not 'jump about' in the sentence, picking out first the subject, then the verb, then the object, and so on. If the Romans had thought in that way, they would have put the words in that order. This point becomes very obvious in the case of a speech. Cicero's audience did not have a written text in front of them. They listened to the words as he spoke them and built up the meaning of what he was saying as he was saying it. It is important that we too should try to read Latin in the order in which it appears, building up information as we go through the sentence.

We realise that, when reading Cicero, you will not always understand immediately the meaning of what he has said. Having the text in front of you gives you the advantage of re-reading each sentence. We recommend, therefore, that you should 'suspend judgement' about the final translation until you have reached the end of the sentence. This will be particularly necessary where there are words whose case you cannot immediately determine or conjunctions that could have more than one meaning. When you have 'completed' the sentence in this way, it is likely that (not being a native Latin speaker) you will have to go back to the beginning and go through it again, before putting the translation into a natural English order. The longer and more complex a sentence is, the more important it is to tackle the Latin in this way. Those who adopt the 'hit or miss' (Find the subject, find the verb, etc.) method are in danger of picking the wrong subject, verb, etc. from the wrong clause when there are several clauses in the sentence.

We recommend that you tackle a Latin sentence in a systematic, analytical way, using a technique which we call Overview. The aim of this technique is to reduce the sentence to smaller, more manageable units before completing the translation. When subordinate clauses or phrases are clearly recognisable, it is often possible to deal with them one by one and to set them aside for the moment, until only the main clause remains. It is then far easier to understand the sentence as a whole. For a fuller treatment of this technique and for practice exercises, you should study pages 121-31 of *The Latin Language* (Eighth Impression), published by Oliver and Boyd. However, to illustrate the technique, we give you two examples of how Overview would help you to tackle two complicated sentences in this book:

## Example 1 (This is the opening sentence of Chapter 1)

**credo ego vos, iudices, mirari quid sit quod, cum tot summi oratores hominesque nobilissimi sedeant, ego potissimum surrexerim, qui neque aetate neque ingenio neque auctoritate sim cum his qui sedeant comparandus.**

**credo ego**: *I believe.* This must be followed by either the dative of a person or an Accusative and Infinitive clause. **vos** is accusative and therefore points forward to an infinitive.

**iudices**: *members of the jury.* Because this is a speech and **iudices** is flanked by commas, it is likely to be vocative.

**mirari**: This is the infinitive linked to the accusative **vos** — *that you are wondering.*

**quid sit**: Introduces an Indirect Question (the clue is **mirari**). At this stage, we do not know whether **quid** means *what* or *why*? [Suspend judgement.]

**quod**: Does this word mean *because* or *which* or *that*? [Suspend judgement.]

**cum**: Is this the preposition meaning *with* or the conjunction meaning *when*, *since* or *although*? [Suspend judgement.]

**cum tot summi oratores hominesque nobilissimi sedeant**: Since there is no ablative with **cum**, it must be a conjunction introducing a subordinate clause — *when/since/although so many outstanding orators and men of the noblest rank are remaining seated.* [Lay this subordinate clause aside for the moment and you will see that **quod ego potissimum surrexerim** forms a clause.]

You can now answer the questions on which you suspended judgement. *Why it is that* clearly makes most sense for **quid sit quod** — *why it is that I in particular have risen.* All three translations of **cum** are just possible, but *when* is probably the most natural.

**qui** is a relative pronoun, but what is its antecedent? It is likely to be **ego.**

**neque aetate neque ingenio neque auctoritate**: These are balanced ablative phrases. [Suspend judgement on how to translate them.]

**sim**: This confirms that the antecedent of **qui** is **ego**.

**cum**: The ablative **his** clearly identifies **cum** as the preposition meaning *with.* Translate *with these (men).*

**qui sedeant**: a relative clause whose antecedent is **his**. [Leave aside **cum his qui sedeant**, *with these men who are sitting.* This leaves **qui sim comparandus,** *who am to be compared.*

It should now be clear that the balanced ablative phrases may be translated as *neither in age nor in ability nor in influence.*

The whole sentence means:
*I suppose that you, members of the jury, are wondering why it is that, when so many outstanding orators and men of the noblest rank remain seated, I rather than anyone else should have got to my feet, I who am to be compared neither in age nor in ability nor in influence with these men who remain seated.*

## Example 2 (Lines 68-72 of Chapter 9)

**cum haesitaret, cum teneretur, quaesivi quid dubitaret proficisci eo quo iam pridem pararet, cum arma, cum secures, cum fasces, cum tubas, cum signa militaria, cum aquilam illam argenteam, cui ille etiam sacrarium domi suae fecerat, scirem esse praemissam.**

**cum haesitaret, cum teneretur**: The verbs immediately establish that **cum** is a conjunction — *when/since/although he hesitated and was held in check.*

**quaesivi**: *I asked.* Expect either a noun in the accusative, **ab** + an ablative, or an Indirect Question.

**quid** must introduce an Indirect Question. Does it mean *what* or *why*? [Suspend judgement.]

**dubitaret**: Does the verb mean *to doubt* or *to hesitate* here?

**proficisci**: The use of the infinitive indicates that **dubitaret** means *he hesitated.*

**quid dubitaret proficisci** therefore means *why he hesitated to set out.*

**eo**: To translate **eo** as *I go* would produce nonsense in this context. **eo** must therefore mean *to that place.*

**quo**, following immediately after **eo**, must be introducing a relative clause (**quo iam pridem pararet**) amplifying **eo** — *to that place to which he had been preparing (to set out) for a long time.*

| | | |
|---|---|---|
| **cum arma** | ) | Since **cum** is not followed by an ablative, |
| **cum secures** | ) | it must be a conjunction meaning *when* or |
| **cum fasces** | ) | *since* or *although*; and **tubas** and **aquilam** |
| **cum tubas** | ) | show that all of these balanced nouns are |
| **cum signa militaria** | ) | in the accusative case. Why accusative? |
| **cum aquilam illam argenteam** | ) | Suspend judgement for the moment. |

**cui** is the dative of the relative pronoun (antecedent **aquilam**) introducing the relative clause **cui ille etiam sacrarium domi suae fecerat** — *for which he had even made a shrine in his home.*

**scirem** is the verb of the **cum** clause — *when/since/although I knew.* With the verb **scire**, you should expect either a direct object or an Accusative and Infinitive clause. The accusatives listed above would not make sense as direct objects of **scirem** and must therefore form part of an Accusative and Infinitive clause.

**esse praemissam** completes the Accusative and Infinitive clause. Here, **praemissam** agrees with the nearest accusative (**aquilam**), but it is to be taken with all the accusatives listed above.

Translate: *Since (or when) he was hesitating and was trapped, I asked (him) why he hesitated to leave for that place to which he had long intended to go, since I knew that arms, axes and rods* (i.e. the consul's symbols of power), *trumpets, military standards and that silver eagle, for which he had even set up a shrine in his home, had been sent ahead.*

For other examples of how to use Overview, see pages 28, 78 and 86 of this book.

**nescire quid antequam natus sis acciderit, id est semper esse puerum.**
*To be ignorant of what happened before you were born is to remain a child for ever.*
Orator xxxiv.120

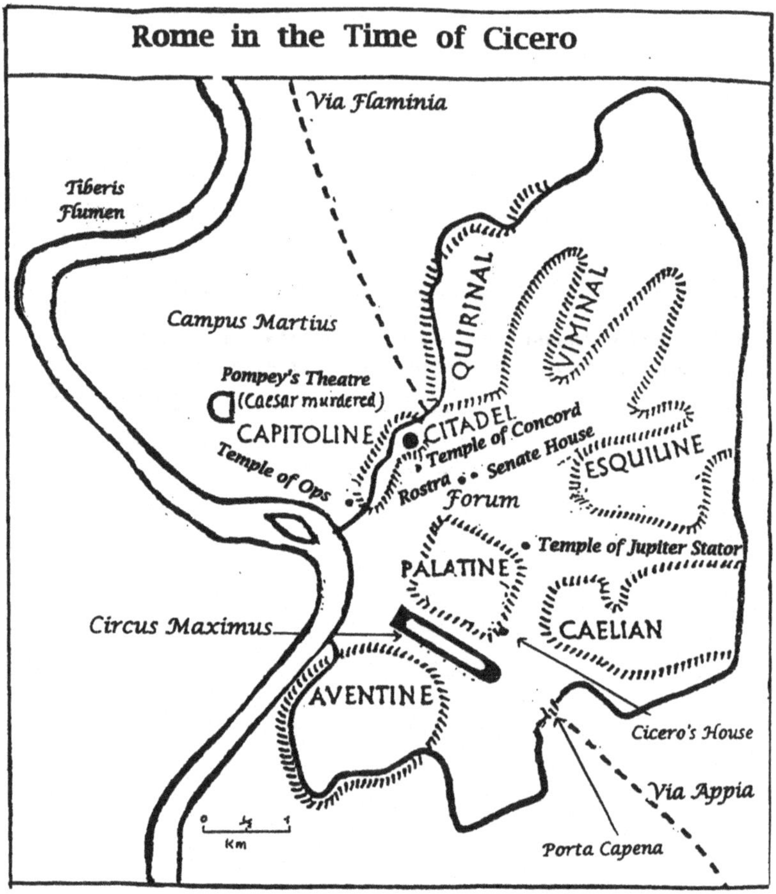
Rome in the Time of Cicero
Via Flaminia
Tiberis
Flumen
Campus Martius
QUIRINAL
VIMINAL
Pompey's Theatre
(Caesar murdered)
CAPITOLINE
CITADEL
Temple of Concord
Senate House
ESQUILINE
Temple of Ops
Rostra
Forum
Temple of Jupiter Stator
PALATINE
Circus Maximus
CAELIAN
AVENTINE
Cicero's House
Via Appia
Porta Capena
Km

# Marius and Sulla

The decade 90-80 BC was a troubled period in Roman history, marked by the struggle for power between Sulla, leader of the **Optimates** (a group broadly composed of senators and aristocratic families), and Marius, leader of the **Populares** (those who challenged the controlling power of the Senate by championing the interests of the common people, often for their own selfish ends).

Having defeated the Marians, Sulla began a reign of terror in which he proscribed his opponents, i.e. he published (**proscribere,** *to publish*) lists of their names and accused them of being enemies of the state. Anyone proscribed in this way could be murdered with impunity and have all his possessions confiscated by the state. Sulla gathered round him several unscrupulous men who used the proscriptions to build up a fortune for themselves. They were even prepared to accuse some Romans who had not opposed Sulla but who had possessions which those fortune-hunters coveted. One such fortune-hunter was the freedman Chrysogonus, a favourite henchman of Sulla, who became a much-feared man because of the influence he could wield.

On one occasion, it is likely that he arranged for the proscription and murder of Sextus Roscius, who had actually been a supporter of the **Optimates**. At the state auction, Chrysogonus paid only 2,000 sesterces for Roscius' estates although they were worth 6,000,000. To divert attention from himself, he then arranged for Roscius' son to be accused of his father's murder.

During this period, Cicero had little opportunity to demonstrate his oratorical skills in public, as the law courts had virtually closed down. In the savage proscriptions, thousands of people had been executed without trial; and so, in 80 BC, when the case of Roscius came up in the recently reconstituted courts, no one was willing to defend young Roscius against the charge of killing his father, as it was known that Chrysogonus was behind the charge. After all, an opponent of Chrysogonus might well find his name posted in the next proscription list! With ten years of arduous training behind him, Cicero was well equipped to undertake this task; but it required great courage for him to appear for the defence, as the fact that he was still politically unknown could not ensure his safety, despite what he says in the opening paragraph of Chapter 1. Not for the last time, however, Cicero took a calculated risk and decided to undertake Roscius' defence. Later in his life, he derived great pleasure and pride from reminding the Romans repeatedly of that brave decision.

**Pro Roscio Amerino:** Roscius was a citizen of Ameria, a town 50 miles (80 km) north of Rome, which had been granted citizenship rights ten years before this speech.

1 **quid sit quod**: *why it is that*. The phrase is more emphatic than **cur** or **quare** on its own.

1 **summi oratores, homines nobilissimi**: Note how the nouns and adjectives are positioned. (For Chiasmus, see CAO on page 237.) Since Sulla had put the aristocracy back in power, it might have been expected that men of the noblest rank would have been prepared to defend Roscius. They showed some measure of support for him by being in court, but they did not have the nerve to speak up in his defence.

3 **aetate**: *in age*. Cicero was only 26 at the time. This ablative and the ablatives **ingenio** (*ability*) and **auctoritate** (*influence*) are to be taken with **sim comparandus** (*am to be compared*). (For Gerundive of Obligation, see LL p. 61.)

4 **omnes hi**: Cicero at this point would actually gesture towards them.

5 **iniuriam novo scelere conflatam**: *an injustice inspired by a new (kind of) villainy*.

5 **iniuriam oportere defendi**: *that an injustice must be resisted*. The Accusative and Infinitive **iniuriam ... defendi** is the subject of **oportere**, and the whole expression depends on **putant**. (For **oportet**, see LL p. 58.)

5 **defendi, defendere**: Note the deliberate juxtaposition of these words. To bring out the contrast, English would insert *but* between the clauses.

6 **propter iniquitatem temporum**: *because of the uncertainty* (literally *unevenness*) *of the times*. Men feared what might happen to them if they offended Sulla and his friends in any way.

7 **officium**: *duty*. When someone was involved in a trial, it was expected that those with whom he had strong ties would come to court to try to influence the jury in his favour by their very presence. Such supporters were called **advocati** but, unlike advocates in modern times, they did not usually speak.

9 **quid ergo?**: *why then (is this so)?* Cicero uses these words to introduce a series of questions which he will immediately answer himself.

9 **tanto officiosior**: *so much more attentive to my duties*. Note that **officiosus** does not mean *officious*, which implies that someone pays excessive attention to his duties. (For the ablative **tanto**, see LL p. 16.)

10 **ne istius quidem laudis ita sum cupidus**: *I am not so eager for even that fame (that you are thinking of)*.

10 **ut aliis eam praereptam velim**: *that I would wish other people to have been deprived of it*, literally *that I would wish it to have been snatched away beforehand from others*. (For the dative used with verbs of 'Taking Away', see LL p. 10.)

11 **me:** Note how this word is given added emphasis by allowing it to displace **igitur** as the second word in the sentence.

12 **quia**: *because*. Note that this word begins a series of replies to the question posed in lines 11-12. **quia ... putaretur** (lines 12-15) discusses the effect likely to be produced if the distinguished men speak out, while **ego ... poterit** (lines 15-17) contrasts the effect of a speech by himself.

13 **si verbum fecisset**: *if he had said anything* (literally *made a word*). This clause amplifies **si dixisset** (*if he had spoken*) in line 12.

14 **de re publica**: *of a political nature*, literally *concerning the state*.

14 **fieri necesse est**: *is inevitable*, literally *is necessary to happen*.

# *1. Cicero's First Important Case*

*(Pro Roscio Amerino 1-5)*

*Why do you think that I am here defending Roscius when there are so many other orators, much abler than I, who might have been expected to undertake the task? It would really be quite dangerous for them to do so because of the importance that would be attached to their words. An unknown speaker like myself does not suffer from such a disadvantage. Consequently, I have taken up the case, having been chosen only as a last resort.*

credo ego vos, iudices, mirari quid sit quod, cum tot summi oratores hominesque nobilissimi sedeant, ego potissimum surrexerim, qui neque aetate neque ingenio neque auctoritate sim cum his qui sedeant comparandus. omnes hi, quos videtis adesse, in hac causa iniuriam novo scelere conflatam putant oportere defendi, defendere ipsi propter iniquitatem temporum non audent. ita fit ut adsint propterea quod officium sequuntur, taceant autem idcirco quia periculum vitant.

quid ergo? audacissimus ego ex omnibus? minime. an tanto officiosior quam ceteri? ne istius quidem laudis ita sum cupidus ut aliis eam praereptam velim. quae me igitur res praeter ceteros impulit ut causam Sex.Rosci reciperem? quia, si quis istorum dixisset quos videtis adesse, in quibus summa auctoritas est atque amplitudo, si verbum de re publica fecisset (id quod in hac causa fieri necesse

**credo** (3), to believe, imagine
**iudices** (*m.pl*), members of the jury
**miror** (1), to wonder, marvel
**summus, -a ,-um**, eminent
**sedeo** (2), to sit, stay seated
**potissimum**, rather than any other
**surgo** (3), **surrexi**, to rise, stand up
**comparo** (1), to compare
**adsum, adesse**, to be present
**causa, -ae** (*f*), case, trial, cause
**audeo** (2), to dare
**fit ut** (+ subj.), it happens that
**propterea quod**, because
**taceo** (2), to be silent
**autem**, however, but
**idcirco quia**, for the reason that
**vito** (1), to avoid
**audax, -acis**, bold, rash, foolhardy
**minime**, no, not at all
**an**, or
**praeter** (+ acc.), more so than
**ceteri, -ae, -a**, the rest, the others
**impello** (3), **-puli**, to drive on
**recipio** (3), to undertake
**si quis/quid**, if anyone/anything
**iste, ista, istud**, that
**amplitudo, -inis** (*f*), dignity, status, importance
**id quod**, something which

15 **multo plura**: Today we are well aware of how the media can exaggerate or distort even the most innocent remarks of prominent people. (For the ablative used with a comparative, see LL p. 16.)

15 **putaretur**: *he would be thought.* (For this type of Conditional, see LL p. 54.)

16 **occultum esse**: Both this infinitive and **ignosci** (line 17) depend on **poterit**.

16 **nondum ad rem publicam accessi**: *I have not yet entered politics*, literally *I have not yet approached affairs of state*. This (in 80 BC) was Cicero's first appearance in a criminal case. It was not until 75 BC that he assumed public office (the quaestorship).

17 **ignosci adulescentiae:** *to excuse it because of my youth*, literally *for my youth to be pardoned.* **ignosci** is present infinitive passive used impersonally.

18 **his de causis**: *for these reasons*. **causae** (three words later) means *case*. The juxtaposition of these words in the sentence is quite deliberate.

18 **patronus exstiti**: *I have come forward as defence counsel*. The **patronus** actually spoke in court for the accused, whereas the **advocatus** (see note on line 7) merely attended to give him moral support.

18 **unus**: *(as) the only one.*

19 **qui maximo ingenio**: Supply **possem dicere** from line 20. (For Generic clauses, see LL p. 103.)

20 **neque uti defensus**: *and not so that* (Roscius) *might be defended.* **uti** (another form of **ut**) and **uti ne** (a survival from earlier Latin usage for the more usual **ne**) both introduce Purpose clauses. (For Purpose clauses, see LL p. 44.) Supply **esset** with **defensus** to balance **desertus esset** at the end of the sentence.

## Points for Discussion

1. In lines 1, 2, 9, 13 and 19, Cicero uses several superlatives. In each case, what effect do you think he is trying to achieve?
2. Orators rely a great deal on balanced expressions (see CAO page 237). List one example from each of the three paragraphs.
3. Why do you think Cicero repeats **quos videtis adesse** (lines 4 and 12) and also uses **adsint** in line 6?
4. List the points which Cicero makes in explaining why he, rather than the more experienced orators, is defending Roscius. Which of these do you find convincing and which not? Do you think it really was safer for him than for them?
5. Cicero makes a very strong assertion in the final sentence of the speech (translated on the opposite page): *For when, at every hour of the day, ... all feeling of humanity*. Do you agree with Cicero? Discuss his claim in the context of media coverage of events in modern times.
6. What modern parallels to the proscriptions can you think of?

est), multo plura dixisse quam dixisset putaretur: ego autem si quid liberius dixero, vel occultum esse propterea quod nondum ad rem publicam accessi vel ignosci adulescentiae poterit.

his de causis ego huic causae patronus exstiti, non electus unus qui maximo ingenio sed relictus ex omnibus qui minimo periculo possem dicere, neque uti satis firmo praesidio defensus Sex. Roscius verum uti ne omnino desertus esset.

**liberius**, rather freely, too freely
**vel ... vel ...**, either ... or ...
**occultus, -a, -um**, hidden,
**ignosco** (3) (+ dat.), to forgive, pardon
**eligo** (3), **elegi, electum**, to choose, select
**ingenium, -i** (*n*), ability
**relinquo** (3), **-liqui, -lictum**, to leave
**firmus, -a, -um**, strong
**praesidium, -i** (*n*), defence
**verum**, but
**omnino**, altogether
**desero** (3), **-ui, -sertum**, to abandon

The above extract is less than 3% of the whole speech. For Cicero, this speech was more than just a defence of Roscius, as can be seen from the passionate appeal he made at the end of it:

*Wise men who have the authority and power that you possess, members of the jury, must do all that they can to remedy the evils which are seriously affecting the Republic. You are all well aware that the Roman people, which in former times was thought to be very merciful to enemies, is at the present time suffering from the cruelty inflicted on its own citizens. Remove this cruelty from the lives of our citizens, and do not allow it to haunt this country of ours. Its intrinsic evil has not only exterminated ever so many citizens in the most horrendous way, but it has robbed even the most moderate men of their capacity for compassion because they have grown accustomed to the occurrence of misfortune. For when, at every hour of the day, we see or hear that some atrocity has occurred, even the most gentle of us cannot withstand the effect of a never-ending succession of calamities and we lose all feeling of humanity.*

The speech was, in fact, a thinly veiled attack on the tyranny of Sulla, and it voiced a yearning for peace and personal security which many would probably have liked to express, but did not dare. The fact that Roscius was acquitted was a triumph in itself. No reprisals were taken against Cicero, and Sulla died two years later. By this speech, Cicero established himself as one of the ablest advocates in Rome.

# The Cursus Honorum

In Republican times, public officials in Rome were elected annually and held office for one year only. These offices came in a recognised sequence, forming a ladder of advancement which the Romans called **cursus honorum**. There was a lower age-limit for each office, and Cicero attained each of these offices at the minimum age:

| | |
|---|---|
| quaestor | 31 |
| aedile | 37 |
| praetor | 40 |
| consul | 43 |

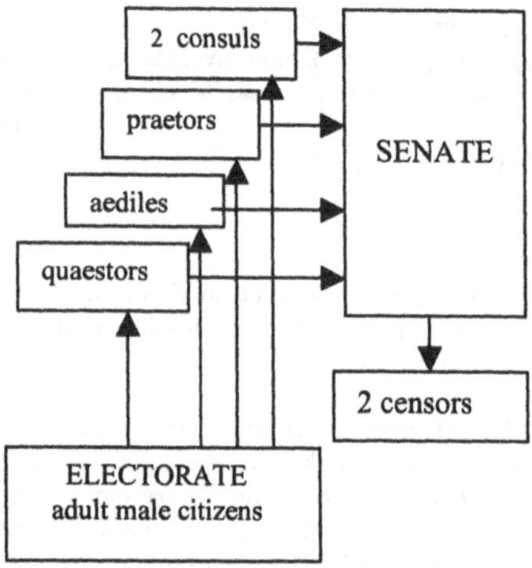


Apart from the consulship, where there were always two, the number of these officials varied at different times in history, but there were never fewer than two at each level. The tyranny which the Romans experienced under the last of the kings, Tarquinius Superbus, convinced them that no one should have supreme power in the city. The one exception to that rule was the constitutional dictatorship: during a national emergency, one man could be appointed **dictator** for up to six months. In the political struggles of the last century BC, however, there were several occasions when a general used his military power to bypass the **cursus honorum**.

The **Quaestors** were in charge of finance, and often assisted governors of provinces.

The **Aediles** directed city services such as maintenance of public buildings, street cleaning, weights and measures, policing, and the presentation of public games.

The **Praetors** were law officials and were responsible for the proclamation of laws and the running of the courts in which they often acted as judges. At the end of their year of office, they could serve as provincial governors with the title of **propraetor**.

The **Consuls**, broadly speaking, combined the responsibilities that would in modern times be associated with a president and a prime minister. They initiated business in the Senate and chaired its meetings; they commanded the army in time of war. At the end of their term of office, they normally became governors of the more important provinces with the rank of **proconsul**.

Two **Censors** (usually ex-consuls) were appointed every five years to carry out a census of the people. During their 18-month period of office, they gathered such information as the age of each citizen and the amount of property he held; they awarded contracts for public buildings; they also supervised the roll of the Senate and could remove any senators guilty of misconduct.

These offices continued under the Empire, but they were largely honorary as the effective control of government lay in the hands of the Emperor. However, **proconsuls** and **propraetors** still carried out the important task of governing provinces.

# Cicero's First Office

Cicero's political career began at the elections held in 76 BC when he secured the quaestorship (**quaestura**), the lowest ranking office in the **cursus honorum** and one in which aspiring politicians spent a kind of apprenticeship under an experienced general or governor. The quaestor had two main tasks — looking after the financial arrangements of his superior and acting as quartermaster in charge of stores.

Cicero spent his quaestorship (75 BC) as assistant to the governor of Sicily, the praetor Sextus Peducaeus. Because Sicily was one of the main sources for Rome's corn supply, it was of such importance that two quaestors were sent there annually, one to deal with the area around Syracuse, the other with the district of Lilybaeum (the modern town of Marsala) in the western part of the island. It was to the latter that Cicero was sent.

1 **mihi aliquid adrogare**: *to be too boastful*, literally *to claim something for myself.* The verb **adrogare** means *to claim as one's own something which does not belong to oneself.*

2 **dixero**: For the use of the future perfect indicative in Conditional clauses, see LL p. 54.

2 **ullius:** *of anyone.* Take with **quaesturam**.

4 **mehercule!**: *by Hercules!* — a mild oath used by Roman men, whereas women were inclined to say **mecastor!** (*by Castor!*).

4 **sic existimabam**: *what I was thinking was*, literally *thus I was thinking.* **sic** points forward to the Accusative and Infinitive clause which reveals what his thoughts were.

5 **in summa caritate**: *when corn was very dear*, i.e. because it was so scarce.

6 **negotiatoribus ... mercatoribus ... mancipibus**: *bankers ..., merchants ..., tax-gatherers.* The contracts to collect the taxes from the provinces were auctioned by the state. The large companies which bought these contracts then had to recover their money and make a profit by collecting as much money as they could from the people in the province. The contracts for most provinces were auctioned in Rome, but the Sicilian contracts were auctioned on the island under the supervision of the quaestors. It was not unknown for the quaestors to make some money for themselves out of these transactions.

7 **sociis abstinens**: *not enriching myself at the expense of our allies*, literally *keeping away from (the possessions of) our allies.* Roman governors and their staff frequently abused their power by extorting money and other possessions from the people in the province.

9 **in me**: *for me.*

9 **hac spe decedebam ut**: *I was on my way home from the province confident that*, literally *I was leaving in this hope that.* The verb **decedere** is the technical expression used for a magistrate leaving a province after completing his term of office there. Cicero uses the **ut** clause to explain **hac spe** —— a technique he frequently employs.

10 **omnia**: *all (kinds of honours)*, literally *all things.*

10 **delaturum**: Supply **esse**.

11 **diebus eis**: *at the time*, literally *in those days.* The phrase is explained by the **cum** clause in line 12.

11 **itineris faciendi causa**: *intending to make the journey (overland from there to Rome).* (For this use of the Gerundive, see LL p. 61.)

# 2. *A Useful Lesson*

(Pro Plancio 64-66)

*The trial of Gnaeus Plancius on a charge of bribery took place in 54 BC. In the following short extract from his speech in defence of Plancius (a digression which has nothing to do with the charge), Cicero describes the high expectations he had had twenty years earlier on returning from what he had considered a most distinguished quaestorship at Lilybaeum in Sicily.*

non vereor ne mihi aliquid, iudices, videar adrogare si de quaestura mea dixero. nec vereor ne quis audeat dicere ullius in Sicilia quaesturam aut gratiorem aut clariorem fuisse.

vere mehercule hoc dicam: sic tum existimabam, nihil homines aliud Romae nisi de quaestura mea loqui. frumenti in summa caritate maximum numerum miseram; negotiatoribus comis, mercatoribus iustus, mancipibus liberalis, sociis abstinens, omnibus eram visus in omni officio diligentissimus: excogitati quidam erant a Siculis honores in me inauditi. itaque hac spe decedebam ut mihi populum Romanum ultro omnia delaturum putarem.

*His dreams were rudely shattered when he reached a health resort on his way home to Rome. The incident taught him a very important lesson which he never forgot.*

at ego, cum casu diebus eis itineris faciendi causa decedens e provincia

**vereor** (2), to fear
**iudices** (*m.pl*), members of the jury
**videor** (2), **visus sum**, to seem
**sed tamen**, and yet, yet
**quis**, someone, anyone
**audeo** (2), to dare
**gratus, -a, -um**, popular
**clarus, -a, -um**, distinguished
**vere**, truly, frankly
**tum**, then, at that time
**existimo** (1), to think
**alius, alia, aliud**, other
**loquor** (3), to speak
**frumentum, -i** (*n*), corn
**numerus, -i** (*m*), quantity
**comis, -is, -e**, courteous, civil
**iustus, -a, -um**, just, fair
**liberalis, -is, -e**, generous
**officium, -i** (*n*), duty, official duty
**diligens, -entis**, diligent, efficient
**excogito** (1), to think out, devise
**Siculus, -i** (*m*), a Sicilian
**honos, -oris** (*m*), honour, distinction
**inauditus, -a, -um**, unheard of
**ultro**, unasked, spontaneously
**defero, -ferre, -tuli, -latum**, to grant
**puto** (1), to think
**at**, but

12 **Puteolos**: At this time, Puteoli, situated just north of the Bay of Naples, was the nearest reasonably good harbour to the south of Rome. Besides being a good emporium for foreign goods, it was a fashionable resort for the aristocracy of Rome. From there, Cicero would travel by land to Rome itself. Note how Cicero uses both **casu** (*by chance*) and **forte** (*as it so happened*) to emphasise that it was sheer chance that he arrived there at the height of the season, and not a deliberate decision on his part in the hope of having a bigger audience to cheer him.

13 **concidi paene**: *I almost collapsed.*

13 **quaesisset** is a contracted form of **quaesi(vi)sset**. Compare **exissem** = **exiissem** in line 14.

14 **quidnam novi**: *any news*. (For Partitive Genitive, see LL p. 9.)

15 **cui**: For Linking Relative, see LL p. 26.

15 **etiam mehercule**: *yes, by Hercules*. (For the use of words like **etiam** (*yes*) and **immo** (*no*) as answers to direct questions, see LL p. 38.)

18 **quasi qui omnia sciret**: *one of those know-alls*, literally *as if (someone) who knew everything*. The subjunctive **sciret** is Generic (see LL p. 103).

18 **hunc**: *this (fellow)*. **quaestorem** (line 19) is used predicatively.

20 **me unum ex eis feci**: *I posed as one of those*, literally *I made myself one of those*.

20 **ad aquas**: *for the waters*. Puteoli was a spa which was famous for its health-giving mineral waters and hot baths.

21 **ea res**: *that incident.*

21 **haud scio an**: *I rather think that*, literally *I do not know if*. The statement is expressed in such a doubtful way that it is treated as an Indirect Question with its verb in the subjunctive.

23 **aures hebetiores**: Supply **esse** – *(that) the ears were rather dull.*

24 **audituri**: *likely to hear*, a common meaning of the future participle.

24 **feci ut**: *I made (sure) that.*

25 **in oculis**: *in the public eye.*

25 **pressi forum**: *I haunted the forum*. The verb **premere** suggests that he constantly frequented the forum, forcing himself on the people there.

25 **a congressu meo**: *from a meeting with me.*

26 **ianitor**: *doorkeeper*. Important people placed a slave in charge of their front door to vet those who came to the house asking to see the master. Note that **neque ... neque ...** does not cancel out **neminem**, but reinforces it.

## Points for Discussion

1. In line 2, why do you think **ullius** is placed first in its clause?
2. In lines 6-8, why do you think Cicero chose these particular examples? How do you think Roman officials normally behaved in the provinces?
3. In lines 8-9, what effect does Cicero produce by placing **excogitati** as the first word in the sentence and **inauditi** as the last?
4. Using the above passage, prepare a few words of advice for an up-and-coming politician. In what other careers would the same advice be useful?
5. What do you think the passage tells us about Cicero as a person?

Puteolos forte venissem, cum plurimi et lautissimi in eis locis solent esse, concidi paene, iudices, cum ex me quidam quaesisset quo die Roma exissem et num quidnam esset novi.

cui cum respondissem me e provincia decedere: 'etiam mehercule,' inquit, 'ut opinor, ex Africa.'

huic ego iam stomachans fastidiose 'immo ex Sicilia' inquam.

tum quidam, quasi qui omnia sciret, 'quid? tu nescis' inquit 'hunc quaestorem Syracusis fuisse?'

quid multa? destiti stomachari et me unum ex eis feci qui ad aquas venissent. sed ea res, iudices, haud scio an plus mihi profuerit quam si mihi tum essent omnes gratulati. nam posteaquam sensi populi Romani aures hebetiores, oculos autem esse acres atque acutos, destiti quid de me audituri essent homines cogitare; feci ut postea cotidie praesentem me viderent, habitavi in oculis, pressi forum; neminem a congressu meo neque ianitor meus neque somnus absterruit.

**plurimi, -ae, -a**, very many
**lautus, -a, -um**, fashionable
**soleo** (2), to be accustomed
**quaero** (3), **quaesivi (ex** + abl.), to ask
**exeo, -ire, -ii** (+ abl.), to go out (of), leave
**num**, whether
**respondeo** (2), **-spondi**, to reply
**ut**, as
**opinor** (1), to think, believe
**stomachor** (1), to be irritated, be annoyed
**fastidiose**, scornfully
**inquam**, I say
**nescio** (4), to be unaware, not to know
**Syracusae, -arum** (*f.pl*), Syracuse
**quid multa?** to cut a long story short
**desisto** (3), **-stiti** (+ infinitive), to stop
**plus**, more
**prosum, prodesse, profui** (+ dat.), to benefit, do good to
**gratulor** (1) (+ dat.), to congratulate
**posteaquam**, after
**sentio** (4), **sensi**, to realise
**oculus, -i** (*m*), eye
**autem**, however, but
**acer, acris, acre**, keen, alert
**acutus, -a, -um,** sharp
**cogito** (1), to think about
**cotidie**, daily, every day
**praesens, -entis**, present, in person
**habito** (1), to live, dwell
**somnus, -i** (*m*), sleep
**absterreo** (2), to drive away

1 **nos**: *I.*. Cicero frequently refers to himself as *we*. Compare lines 2, 3, 6, 7, 8, etc.

2 **quantum efficere potuissemus**: *as far as possible*, literally *as much as I had been able to bring about.*

3 **docti**: *already (fully) trained.* The Forum was, of course, the place where public cases were heard.

3 **Moloni dedimus operam**: *I studied under Molo*, literally *I devoted my attention to Molo*. Molo had a school of rhetoric in Rhodes. The dictator Sulla had given Rhodes control over neighbouring communities and, when these communities later appealed against having to pay taxes to Rhodes, Molo was one of the envoys sent to Rome in 81 BC to plead Rhodes' case.

4 **dictatore Sulla**: *while Sulla was dictator*. (For this type of Ablative Absolute, see LL p. 30.)

4 **legatus**: *as envoy*, i.e. it is used predicatively.

4 **de Rhodiorum praemiis**: *concerning the taxes imposed by the Rhodians.*

5 **causa** is nominative case, and the perfect participle passive (**dicta**) agrees with it.

6 **tantum commendationis habuit**: *won such acclaim*. (For Partitive Genitive, see LL p. 9.) In defending Roscius, Cicero risked incurring the wrath of Sulla. [See Chapter 1 for more information.]

6 **non ulla**: Supply **causa. non ulla** is more emphatic than **nulla**. Translate *not a single case.*

6 **non digna nostro patrocinio**: *beyond my competence as a defence counsel,* literally *not suitable for my defending.*

7 **multae**: Supply **erant causae**.

8 **tamquam elucubratas**: *a product, as it were, of the midnight-oil*, literally *as if composed by lamplight.* He had worked hard on these speeches until well into the night.

9 **non naevo aliquo aut crepundiis**: *not by some birthmark or child's rattles*. In Roman comedies, the plot of the play often revolved round the identification of a long-lost son or daughter (now grown-up) by the father, who recognised his offspring by a birthmark or by toys which had been given to the child.

9 **corpore omni**: *by my entire person.*

10 **videris**: Remember that, throughout this passage, Cicero is speaking to Brutus.

10 **non nulla**: *some (particulars).*

# *3. Training for Oratory*

(Brutus 311-319)

The following extract is taken from a work on the art of public speaking which Cicero wrote towards the end of his life. He imagines he is having a conversation with Marcus Junius Brutus and, in this passage, he looks back on the time when he delivered the speech in defence of Roscius. He admits that there were flaws in his oratorical style in those days and says that he recognised even then how hard he would have to work if he was to achieve his ambition of becoming a truly great orator. He then describes the intensive course of training he undertook under some of the greatest teachers of oratory in order to eliminate his faults and perfect his technique.

*Cicero describes his early efforts at speech-making.*

tum primum nos ad causas et privatas et publicas adire coepimus, non ut in foro disceremus, quod plerique fecerunt, sed ut, quantum nos efficere potuissemus, docti in forum veniremus. eodem tempore Moloni dedimus operam; dictatore enim Sulla, legatus ad senatum de Rhodiorum praemiis venerat. itaque prima causa publica pro Sex.Roscio dicta tantum commendationis habuit ut non ulla esset quae non digna nostro patrocinio videretur. deinceps inde multae, quas nos diligenter elaboratas et tamquam elucubratas afferebamus.

*He gives a pen-picture of his physical appearance and initial oratorical deficiencies.*

nunc, quoniam totum me, non naevo aliquo aut crepundiis, sed corpore omni videris velle cognoscere, complectar non nulla etiam quae fortasse videantur minus necessaria.

**primum**, for the first time
**causa, -ae** (*f*), case
**et ... et ...**, both ... and ...
**adeo, -ire** (**ad** + acc.), to undertake
**coepi**, I began
**disco** (3), to learn
**plerique**, most, the majority
**dico** (3), **dixi, dictum**, to say, speak
**deinceps inde**, one after another
**elaboratus, -a, -um**, elaborate
**affero, -ferre**, to bring to court
**quoniam**, since
**totus, -a, -um**, complete, whole
**videor** (2), to seem
**cognosco** (3), to get to know
**complector** (3), to include
**fortasse**, perhaps
**minus**, less

13 **qui habitus et quae figura putatur**: *an appearance and physique which are considered.* As usual in this type of expression, the antecedents (**habitus** and **figura**) are attracted into the relative clause (see LL p. 26). **putatur** agrees with the nearer of its two subjects.

13 **non procul abesse a vitae periculo**: *to be likely to lead to an early death*, literally *to be not far from a danger to life.*

15 **hoc**: *this*, which is explained in more detail in the **quod** clause which follows (*the fact that ...*).

15 **sine remissione sine varietate**: *without lowering (of the voice and) without any variation (in tone)*. Note that there is no connecting word between the two phrases. (For Asyndeton, see CAO on page 238.)

16 **vi summa vocis**: *by forcing my voice*, literally *with very great force of voice.* This can seriously damage the vocal cords.

19 **quodvis potius periculum mihi adeundum (esse) quam discedendum (esse)**: *I should run any risk rather than abandon*, literally *that any risk whatsoever should be approached by me rather than that I should withdraw.* (For Dative of Agent with a Gerundive, see LL p. 62.)

19 **a sperata dicendi gloria**: *my ambition to be a distinguished orator*, literally *from my hoped-for glory of speaking.*

22 **temperatius dicere**: *to speak in a more restrained way.*

22 **ut consuetudinem dicendi mutarem**: *to change my style of speaking.* This Purpose clause depends on and explains **ea causa mihi fuit**, *this was my reason.*

23 **cum essem versatus**: *after I had been involved.*

26 **veteris Academiae**: *of the Old Academy.* This was the school which the Greek philosopher Plato had founded in Athens at the beginning of the fourth century BC. The main subjects studied there were philosophy, mathematics, science and astronomy.

28 **summo auctore**: *under an excellent tutor.*

29 **apud Demetrium Syrum**: *under Demetrius the Syrian.* Nothing further is known about this man.

29 **non ignobilem**: *not undistinguished.* The double negative produces a fairly strong positive statement of praise. (For Litotes, see CAO on page 235.)

30 **studiose exerceri solebam**: *I put a great deal of effort into practising (oratory)*, literally *I was accustomed to practise conscientiously.*

erat eo tempore in nobis summa gracilitas et infirmitas corporis, procerum et tenue collum, qui habitus et quae figura non procul abesse putatur a vitae periculo, si accedit labor et laterum magna contentio. eoque magis hoc eos quibus eram carus commovebat, quod omnia sine remissione sine varietate, vi summa vocis et totius corporis contentione dicebam.

itaque cum me et amici et medici hortarentur ut causas agere desisterem, quodvis potius periculum mihi adeundum quam a sperata dicendi gloria discedendum putavi. sed cum censerem remissione et moderatione vocis et commutato genere dicendi me et periculum vitare posse et temperatius dicere, ut consuetudinem dicendi mutarem, ea causa mihi in Asiam proficiscendi fuit. itaque cum essem biennium versatus in causis et iam in foro celebratum meum nomen esset, Roma sum profectus.

*First of all, I studied under the foremost teachers in Athens.*

cum venissem Athenas, sex menses cum Antiocho veteris Academiae nobilissimo et prudentissimo philosopho fui, studiumque philosophiae rursus summo auctore et doctore renovavi. eodem tamen tempore Athenis apud Demetrium Syrum veterem et non ignobilem dicendi magistrum studiose exerceri solebam.

**gracilitas, -atis** (*f*), slenderness
**infirmitas, -atis** (*f*), weakness
**procerus, -a, -um**, long
**tenuis, -is, -e**, thin
**collum, -i** (*n*), neck
**accedo** (3), **accessi**, to be added
**labor, -oris** (*m*), hard work, exertion
**latus, -eris** (*n*), lung
**contentio, -onis** (*f*), straining
**eo magis**, all the more
**carus, -a, -um**, dear
**commoveo** (2), to move, cause concern to
**amicus, -i** (*m*), friend
**medicus, -i** (*m*), doctor
**hortor** (1), to urge
**causam agere**, to plead a case
**desisto** (3) (+ infin.), to desist (from), stop (doing)
**censeo** (2), to think, conclude
**moderatio, -onis** (*f*), moderation
**commuto** (1), to change
**genus, -eris** (*n*), style, kind
**vito** (1), to avoid
**proficiscor** (3), **-fectus sum**, to set out, leave
**biennium, -i** (*n*), (period of) two years
**celebratus, -a, -um**, well-known, talked about, on everyone's lips
**mensis, -is** (*m*), month
**nobilis, -is, -e**, famous, celebrated
**prudens, -entis**, wise, shrewd
**rursus**, again
**doctor, -oris** (*m*), teacher
**renovo** (1), to resume, take up again
**vetus, -eris**, old, experienced
**exerceor** (2), to exercise, practise

31 **a me Asia tota peragrata est**: *I travelled over the whole of Asia (Minor)*, literally *the whole of Asia was travelled through by me.*

31 **cum summis quidem oratoribus**: *with really outstanding orators.* He met up with these orators during his travels and learned a great deal from listening to them delivering speeches and from practising with them.

32 **ipsis libentibus**: *with their willing co-operation*, literally *themselves being willing.* (For Ablative Absolute, see LL p. 30.)

32 **quibus**: *with them.* (For Linking Relative, see LL p. 26.)

34 **is dedit operam**: *he devoted his efforts.*

34 **ut nimis redundantes nos iuvenili quadam dicendi impunitate et licentia reprimeret**: *to restraining an over-elaborateness in my style of speaking characterised by a certain youthful indiscipline and lack of control,* literally *to restrain us* (i.e. *me*) *overflowing too much with a certain youthful recklessness of speaking and lack of restraint.*

35 **diffluentes**: Supply **nos (= me)**. (cf. line 1.)

37 **prope mutatus**: *well-nigh transformed.*

38 **quasi deferverat oratio**: *my style of speaking* (literally *my speech*) *had, as it were, cooled down.*

39 **lateribus vires et corpori mediocris habitus accesserat**: *my lungs had grown stronger and I had become a person of average appearance*, literally *strength (had been added) to my lungs and an ordinary appearance had been added to my body.* Although the verb **accesserat** has two subjects (**vires** and **habitus**), it agrees with the nearer one, as often happens.

## Points for Discussion

1 Write down two examples of balance in the first sentence (lines 1-3).
2. What effect does **tamquam** produce in line 8, and **quasi** in line 38? Comment on the appropriateness of the simile **quasi extra ripas diffluentes** (line 35). What effect do you think Cicero is trying to achieve?
3. Study lines 12-25 and list examples of balanced phrases and clauses.
4. From the information provided by Cicero in this passage, list the qualities which he says were required in an effective Roman orator.

*After that, I studied under several leading orators in Asia Minor, before going on to Rhodes, where the best orator of all brought about a complete transformation in my technique.*

post a me Asia tota peragrata est, fuique cum summis quidem oratoribus, quibuscum exercebar ipsis libentibus. quibus non contentus, Rhodum veni meque ad eundem quem Romae audiveram Molonem applicavi. is dedit operam ut nimis redundantes nos iuvenili quadam dicendi impunitate et licentia reprimeret et quasi extra ripas diffluentes coerceret.

ita recepi me biennio post non modo exercitatior sed prope mutatus. nam et contentio nimia vocis resederat et quasi deferverat oratio, lateribusque vires et corpori mediocris habitus accesserat.

**post**, afterwards
**contentus, -a, -um**, content, satisfied
**Rhodus, -i** (*f*), Rhodes
**applico** (1), to attach
**ripa, -ae** (*f*), bank (of a river)
**diffluo** (3) to spread
**coerceo** (2), to check, stop, restrain
**se recipere**, to return
**biennio post**, two years later
**exercitatus, -a, -um**, trained
**nimius, -a, -um**, excessive
**resido** (3), **-sedi**, to settle down, subside

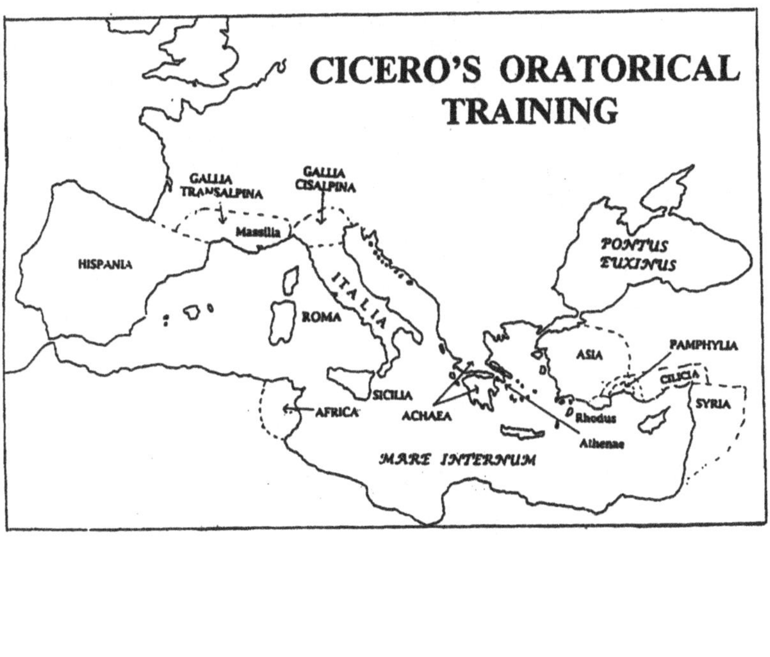

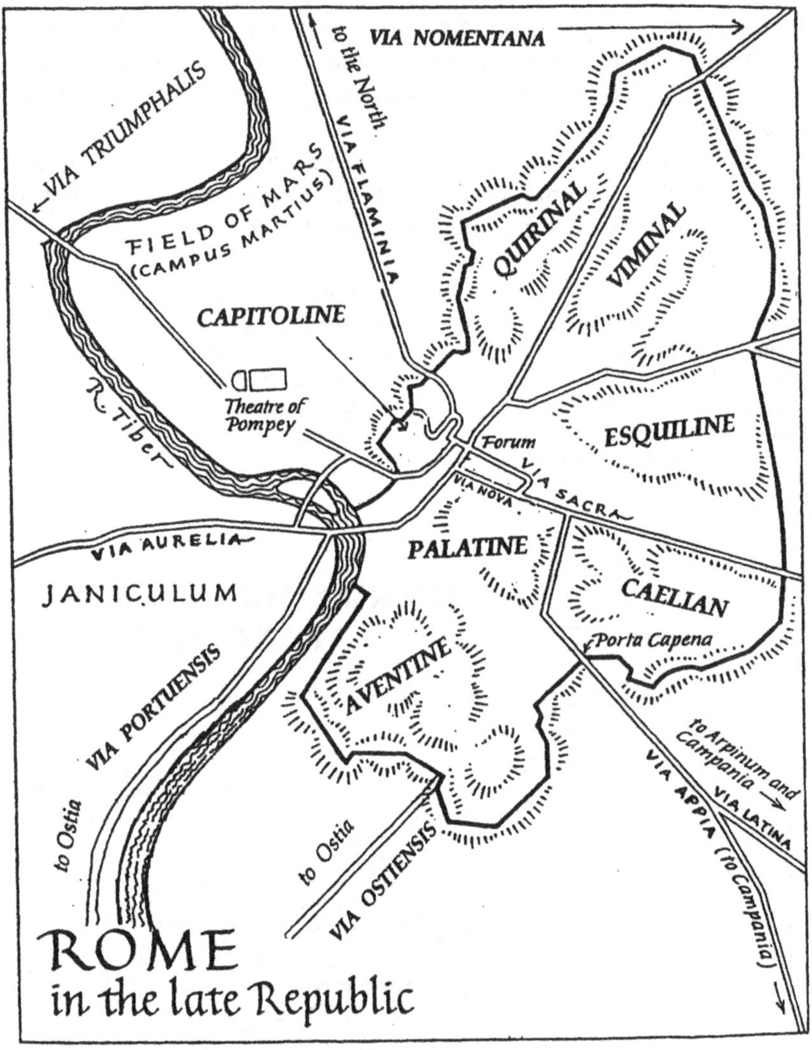
VIA NOMENTANA
to the North
VIA TRIUMPHALIS
VIA FLAMINIA
FIELD OF MARS
(CAMPUS MARTIUS)
QUIRINAL
VIMINAL
CAPITOLINE
Theatre of Pompey
R. Tiber
Forum
ESQUILINE
VIA SACRA
VIA NOVA
VIA AURELIA
PALATINE
JANICULUM
CAELIAN
Porta Capena
AVENTINE
VIA PORTUENSIS
to Arpinum and Campania
VIA LATINA
VIA APPIA (to Campania)
to Ostia
to Ostia
VIA OSTIENSIS
ROME
in the late Republic

# Selecting a Prosecutor

As quaestor in 75 BC, Cicero was given the task of assisting the governor of Sicily in the day-to-day administration of the western part of the island. He was distinctly proud of having carried out his duties there in a scrupulously fair way during his year of office. From 73-71 BC, however, the province was governed by the propraetor Gaius Verres, and under him the Sicilians suffered from extortion and physical violence.

Nothing could be done about this as long as Verres held the office of propraetor, since the governor's power was such that no one could dispute his authority. However, as soon as Verres became a private citizen again, the Sicilians sent a deputation to Rome to see if they could have Verres prosecuted for maladministration and extortion.

The Romans did not have a public prosecution service but left it to individuals to bring to trial anyone suspected of wrong-doing. The Sicilians appealed to Cicero to undertake this task for them; but Verres used his wealth and influence to persuade Caecilius, a friend of his family, to apply to become the prosecutor, thereby hoping to increase his chances of acquittal by having his 'own man' prosecute him.

His chances were further improved when the task of deciding which of the two, Cicero or Caecilius, should be selected was given to a special court consisting entirely of senators, the social group from which Verres could expect most sympathy and support. Each of the 'applicants' made a speech to this court, trying to convince it that he would make the better prosecutor, and the court was expected to reach its decision entirely on the basis of these speeches. The wishes of the Sicilians were not taken into consideration. This sort of hearing was called a **divinatio** (*divinely inspired prediction*) because the judges had to rely solely on their own subjective judgement and impressions (little more than a hunch), rather than on the evidence submitted, as would have happened in a trial.

The following passage is taken from the speech in which Cicero attacked Caecilius' claim to become prosecutor. It was delivered in 70 BC, roughly four months before the actual trial of Verres began.

1 **itaque**: This is not used in the sense of *therefore*: it is **ita** + **que**, meaning *and ... in such a way.*

1 **ex ea provincia decessissem**: *I had discharged my duties in that province*, literally *I had left that province.* **decedere** is the technical term for leaving a province at the end of one's term of office.

3 **factum est uti**: *the result was that.* Cicero often uses the variant form **uti** instead of **ut**. Sometimes he seems to do this because he is fond of using old forms of the language; at other times, the sound of **uti** may suit the rhythm of the words better.

3 **cum ... tum ...**: *while ... also ...* : Although this basically means *both ... and ...*, the part introduced by **tum** is given much more emphasis than if **et ... et ...** had been used.

3 **summum ... nonnullum praesidium suis fortunis**: *the main (protection for their interests) ... some protection for their interests.* The use of **nonnullum** (contrasted with **summum**) is mock modesty on Cicero's part.

3 **in veteribus patronis**: *in their ancient patrons.* Just as individuals (**clientes**) would look to important men (**patroni**) for help in times of trouble, so cities and communities would often have a special relationship (possibly extending back through several generations) with certain influential families.

5 **constitutum esse**: *lay*, literally *was based.*

6 **cuncti**: *all*, used instead of **omnes** to indicate that they took this action as a united group.

8 **si quod tempus accidisset quo tempore**: *if any occasion arose on which*, literally *if any time happened at which time.*

10 **me non defuturum (esse)**: *that I would not fail (to support).* This Accusative and Infinitive clause depends on **(me) ostendisse**.

11 The colon after **defenderem** in our text indicates that the indirect speech is continuing, without any introductory word of speaking. English would tend to insert something like *they said that.*

12 **ad quos confugerent**: For relatives used in Purpose clauses, see LL pp. 44-5.

# 4. *Who Should Prosecute Verres?*

(in Q. Caecilium 2-5, 20-21, 37-43, 71-73)

*Cicero explains why, having been counsel for the defence in all of his previous cases, he has decided to undertake the prosecution of Verres. He is only fulfilling a promise he made to the Sicilians. They have now approached him and given him details of the many injustices and hardships they suffered at the hands of Verres.*

cum quaestor in Sicilia fuissem, iudices, itaque ex ea provincia decessissem ut Siculis omnibus iucundam diuturnamque memoriam quaesturae nominisque mei relinquerem, factum est uti cum summum in veteribus patronis multis, tum nonnullum etiam in me praesidium suis fortunis constitutum esse arbitrarentur.

quare nunc populati atque vexati cuncti ad me publice saepe venerunt ut suarum fortunarum omnium causam defensionemque susciperem. me saepe esse pollicitum, saepe ostendisse dicebant, si quod tempus accidisset quo tempore aliquid a me requirerent, commodis eorum me non defuturum. venisse tempus aiebant, non iam ut commoda sua, sed ut vitam salutemque totius provinciae defenderem: sese iam ne deos quidem in suis urbibus ad quos confugerent habere, quod eorum

**iudices, -um** (*m.pl*), members of the jury
**Siculus, -i** (*m*), a Sicilian
**iucundus, -a, -um,** pleasant, agreeable
**diuturnus, -a, -um,** (long) lasting
**quaestura, -ae** (*f*), quaestorship
**nomen, -inis** (*n*), name
**relinquo** (3), to leave behind
**arbitror** (1), to think
**quare**, therefore
**populo** (1), to plunder
**vexo** (1), to harass, plague
**publice**, officially
**causa, -ae** (*f*), cause, case
**suscipio** (3), **-cepi**, to undertake
**polliceor** (2), **-icitus sum**, to promise
**ostendo** (3), **-tendi**, to show, make clear
**aliquis, -quid**, anyone, anything, someone, something
**requiro** (3), to need
**commodum, -i** (*n*), interest
**desum, deesse** (+ dat.), to be lacking, fail
**aio**, I say
**vita, -ae** (*f*), life
**salus, -utis** (*f*), safety
**totus, -a, -um**, whole
**sese = se**
**ne ... quidem**, not even
**deus, dei** (*m*), god
**confugio** (3), to flee for refuge

14 **quas res ... eas omnes**: *all the things which*, literally *what things ... all those things*. By placing the relative clause at the beginning of the sentence, Cicero gives much greater emphasis to the accusation contained in **eas omnes sese ... pertulisse**. (See LL p. 26 for the reversal of clauses.) The Accusative and Infinitive (**sese pertulisse**) again has no introductory word of speaking. Note also how, by placing **omnes** between **eas** and **sese**, Cicero probably wants his audience to take **omnes** with both words, thus making the accusation even more emphatic.

15 **hoc uno praetore**: *in the praetorship of this one man*. Note the emphatic position of **uno**. (For this type of Ablative Absolute, see LL pp. 30-1.)

16 **rogare et orare**: *they earnestly begged (me)*, literally *they asked and begged (me)*. These infinitives are not a continuation of the indirect speech but Historic Infinitives (see LL p. 32) which are used to indicate a sense of urgency.

16 **illos supplices**: *an appeal for help from those*, literally *those suppliants*. The word **supplex** is used of someone who goes down on his/her knees, as a sign of complete surrender to the mercy and protection of another.

17 **quos nemini supplices esse oporteret**: *who ought to have been suppliants to no one*. They said that they should not have had to ask for help because Cicero was under an obligation to come to their aid automatically.

17 **me incolumi**: *as long as I was alive*, literally *me (being) safe*. (For this type of Ablative Absolute, see LL pp. 30-1.)

18 **tuli graviter et acerbe**: *I found it extremely distressing*, literally *I bore heavily and bitterly*. The Accusative and Infinitive **me adduci** (*that I was being brought*) is the object of **tuli**.

18 **in eum locum ut**: *into such a situation that.*

18 **eos homines spes falleret**: *(that) those men should be disappointed*, literally *(that) hope should fail those men.*

20 **ad defendendos homines**: *to (the task of) defending people*. (For this use of the Gerundive, see LL p. 61.)

20 **ab ineunte adulescentia**: *from my earliest youth*, literally *from youth beginning*. The Romans regarded men as being **adulescentes** roughly from their late teens up to their early thirties.

21 **tempore**: *by circumstances.*

21 **traducerer**: *I should transfer*. Besides having an Active and a Passive Voice, ancient Greek had a Middle Voice which was used when the action affected the subject itself. Latin has no Middle Voice but uses Passive forms for this purpose. For example, the Active form **traduco** is transitive (*I transfer something*); **traducor** used as a true Passive means *I am transferred*; the form **traducor**, used in the Middle sense, is intransitive — *I transfer*, literally *I transfer myself.*

22 **habere eos actorem Q.Caecilium**: *(that) they (already) had someone to act for them (in) Quintus Caecilius*. The position of **habere** gives it extra emphasis. **Q. Caecilium** is used in apposition to the object **actorem**.

22 **qui praesertim**: *especially since he*. (For Causal **qui**, see LL p. 103.)

24 **quo ego adiumento sperabam, id**: *that means of support by which I was hoping*. When the relative clause precedes its antecedent, the antecedent noun is usually attracted into the relative clause and made to agree with the relative pronoun (see LL p. 26). By proposing that Caecilius should represent the Sicilians, Cicero had hoped to be freed from his obligation to them.

simulacra sanctissima C.Verres ex delubris religiosissimis sustulisset; quas res luxuries in flagitiis, crudelitas in suppliciis, avaritia in rapinis, superbia in contumeliis efficere potuisset, eas omnes sese hoc uno praetore per triennium pertulisse. rogare et orare ne illos supplices aspernarer quos me incolumi nemini supplices esse oporteret.

*The Sicilians reject Cicero's attempts to excuse himself and convince him that he should undertake the case.*

tuli graviter et acerbe, iudices, in eum me locum adduci ut aut eos homines spes falleret qui opem a me atque auxilium petissent, aut ego, qui me ad defendendos homines ab ineunte adulescentia dedissem, tempore atque officio coactus ad accusandum traducerer. dicebam habere eos actorem Q.Caecilium, qui praesertim quaestor in eadem provincia post me quaestorem fuisset.

quo ego adiumento sperabam hanc a me posse molestiam demoveri,

**simulacrum, -i** (*n*), statue, image
**sanctus, -a, -um**, holy, sacred
**delubrum, -i** (*n*), shrine, temple
**religiosus, -a, -um**, holy
**tollo** (3), **sustuli**, to carry off, steal
**luxuries, -ei** (*f*), over-indulgence
**flagitium, -i** (*n*), shameful act
**crudelitas, -atis** (*f*), cruelty
**supplicium, -i** (*n*), punishment
**avaritia, -ae** (*f*), greed, avarice
**rapina, -ae** (*f*), plundering, robbery
**superbia, -ae** (*f*), arrogance, insolence
**contumelia, -ae** (*f*), insult, affront
**efficio** (3), to bring about, inflict
**triennium, -i** (*n*), (period of) three years
**perfero, -ferre, -tuli**, to endure
**aspernor** (1), to spurn, reject
**opem** (acc.), help, support
**auxilium, -i** (*n*), help
**peto** (3), **-ivi**, to ask for, request
**petissent = petivissent**
**do** (1), **dedi**, to give, devote
**officium, -i** (*n*), duty, sense of duty
**cogo** (3), **coegi, coactum**, to compel
**molestia, -ae** (*f*), disagreeable task
**demoveo** (2), to remove

25 **adversarium maxime**: *completely the opposite*. The placing of **maxime** after the adjective strengthens the superlative meaning.

25 **illi mihi hoc remisissent**: *they would have released me from this obligation*. (For this type of Conditional sentence, see LL p. 54.) The verb **remittere** takes the accusative of the thing from which someone is excused and the dative of the person who is excused (see LL p. 10).

26 **istum**: *that fellow*, a derogatory term.

26 **nossent** is a contracted form of **novissent**, *they had known*.

28 **vetere consuetudine institutoque maiorum**: *by the established tradition of our ancestors*, literally *by the old custom and practice of our ancestors*.

29 **ex meo tempore**: *to suit my own circumstances*. (cf. line 21 for this use of **tempus**.)

30 **mihi**: *by me*. (For Dative of Agent with a Gerundive, see LL pp. 11 and 62.)

32 **sine nos**: *allow us*. **sine** is imperative of **sino**.

33 **id quod cuivis probare deberent**: *what ought to seem reasonable to everyone*, literally *that for which they ought to win approval from anyone*.

33 **dicerent**: *they would be saying*. This is, in effect, the main clause following **si dicerent** in line 31. (For this type of Conditional, see LL p. 54.)

34 **nunc**: *as things stand*, literally *now*.

34 **utrumque se nosse**: *(they are saying) that they know both (of us)*. **nosse** is a contracted form of **novisse**. (cf. line 26.)

36 **satis dicunt**: *they are saying (clearly) enough*. Note how Cicero places the Indirect Question before this for emphasis.

36 **tamen**: *in spite of this*, i.e. the clear message that they are giving. Note the repetition of **tamen** in the next few lines. (For Anaphora, see CAO on page 238.)

36 **his invitissimis**: *to these men despite their very strong opposition*, literally *to these very unwilling (men)*.

37 **te offeres?**: *will you push yourself forward?*, literally *will you offer yourself?*

37 **aliena** means literally *that which properly belongs to another*, i.e. to Cicero in this case.

37 **loquere = loqueris** (future tense). Compare **pollicebere** in line 39.

38 **desertos**: Supply **esse**.

39 **velle**: Understand a phrase such as **operam dare** with both **velle** and **posse**.

39 **sua causa**: *for their sakes*.

id mihi erat adversarium maxime; nam illi multo mihi hoc facilius remisissent, si istum non nossent aut si iste apud eos quaestor non fuisset. adductus sum, iudices, officio, fide, misericordia, multorum bonorum exemplo, vetere consuetudine institutoque maiorum ut onus hoc laboris atque officii non ex meo sed ex meorum necessariorum tempore mihi suscipiendum putarem.

In the next section of the speech (not included here), Cicero underlines how important it is for Rome's moral status that the Extortion Law should be strictly enforced, since it is the only safeguard which non-Romans have against provincial maladministration. He then states that, in making their choice of prosecutor, the court should bear in mind two main points: which man would the plaintiffs most want to speak on their behalf, and which would the accused least want? In this case, there should be no doubt since delegates from virtually every community in Sicily have requested that Cicero should act for them against Verres, who has stripped their communities of all their precious possessions and maltreated many of their citizens.

*If it was possible for them to speak for themselves, this is what the Sicilians would like to say to Caecilius in their rejection of him as prosecutor.*

si tibi, Q.Caecili, hoc Siculi dicerent: ‘te non novimus, nescimus qui sis, numquam te antea vidimus. sine nos per eum nostras fortunas defendere cuius fides est nobis cognita’; nonne id dicerent quod cuivis probare deberent? nunc hoc dicunt: utrumque se nosse, alterum se cupere defensorem esse fortunarum suarum, alterum plane nolle.

cur nolint, etiamsi tacent, satis dicunt. verum non tacent: tamen his invitissimis te offeres? tamen in aliena causa loquere? tamen eos defendes qui se ab omnibus desertos potius quam abs te defensos esse malunt? tamen iis operam tuam pollicebere qui te neque velle sua causa

**adduco** (3), **-duxi, ductum**, to induce, prompt, persuade
**fides, -ei** (*f*), good faith, trustworthiness
**misericordia, -ae** (*f*), pity
**exemplum, -i** (*n*), example
**onus, oneris** (*n*), burden
**labor, -oris** (*m*), hard work, trouble
**necessarius, -i** (*m*), friend
**puto** (1), to think
**nescio** (4), to be ignorant, not to know
**cognitus, -a, -um**, recognised
**quivis**, anyone
**alter, altera, alterum**, the one, the other
**cupio** (3), to wish, desire
**nolo, nolle**, to refuse, reject
**plane**, clearly, definitely
**etiamsi**, even although
**taceo** (2), to be silent, say nothing
**verum**, but
**loquor** (3), to speak
**desero** (3), **-ui, -sertum**, to desert, abandon
**potius**, rather
**abs = ab**
**malo**, to prefer, like better
**opera, -ae** (*f*), support, assistance

40 **si cupias**: *(even) if you wanted (to)*. (For this type of Conditional, see LL p. 54.)

40 **reliquarum fortunarum**: *of (retaining) what remains of their fortunes.*

41 **quam habent in legis et in iudicii severitate positam**: *(the hope) which they have (and which is) based on the strictness of both the law and the court.* The repetition of **in** before the genitives justifies the use of *both* in our translation.

42 **de quibus non optime es meritus, eos**: *those whom you did not treat at all well.* Again, the relative clause precedes its antecedent. (cf. lines 14 and 24.)

44 **persequendi iuris sui**: *of pursuing their rights.* This Gerundive phrase and **deplorandae calamitatis** (*of bewailing their misfortune*) both depend on **potestatem**. (For this use of the Gerundive, see LL p. 61.)

45 **de te**: This phrase belongs to the Indirect Question **quemadmodum existimes**, *your own thoughts about yourself* (line 46). In this sentence, Cicero uses one of his favourite debating techniques. In the parenthesis, he tries to show that he is a reasonable person by pretending to be his opponent's friend; and, while he is apparently asking his opponent to think things out for himself, he is actually in a subtle way getting the jury to follow the argument without feeling that a conclusion is being forced upon them. Note the emphatic position of **de te**, and how it is followed (after the parenthesis) by the emphatic **tu ipse vide**.

45 **mehercule!**: *by Hercules!* – a mild oath used by Roman men, whereas women were inclined to say **mecastor!** (*by Castor!*).

47 **tu te collige**: *concentrate on the issue*, literally *collect yourself.*

47 **qui sis**: *what sort of person you are.*

49 **de**: *when it comes to dealing with*, literally *about.*

51 **tot res, tam graves, tam varias**: Another of Cicero's favourite oratorical devices. Instead of making one point, he reinforces it and makes it sound more important by using a list of similar points. Compare **causam ... fortunasque, ... ius, ... gravitatem** earlier in the sentence, and **voce, memoria, consilio, ingenio** immediately after this; also the repetition of **quae**, as well as the list **Achaea, Asia Pamphyliaque** in the next sentence; and, in addition, the triple use of **putasne** in lines 49, 52 and 55. (For **congeries verborum**, see CAO on page 237.)

52 **quae ... quae ... quae ...**: See note on line 54 on page 28.

52 **in quaestura**: Verres had been quaestor in Cisalpine Gaul in 84 BC under Cn.Papirius Carbo, a supporter of Marius. Verres himself, however, was a supporter of Sulla and, according to Cicero, he had deserted Carbo and had taken with him all the money entrusted to him as quaestor. Cicero claims that none of this money ever reached Sulla.

53 **in legatione**: *when he was acting as deputy-governor* (**legatus**) in Cilicia in 80-79 BC.

nec, si cupias, posse arbitrantur? cur eorum spem exiguam reliquarum fortunarum, quam habent in legis et in iudicii severitate positam, vi extorquere conaris? cur, de quibus in provincia non optime es meritus, eos nunc plane fortunis omnibus conaris evertere? cur iis non modo persequendi iuris sui sed etiam deplorandae calamitatis adimis potestatem?

The Sicilians clearly do not wish Caecilius to plead their case; but Hortensius, who is defending Verres, certainly wishes this because his task will be very much easier if he has to contend with such an inexperienced opponent. There is a strong suspicion that, far from being hostile to Verres, as he claims, Caecilius is keen to undertake the case so that he may be able to suppress certain evidence which could implicate himself. After all, he himself probably profited from Verres' corrupt practices while he was handling financial matters as Verres' quaestor.

*Cicero next deals with Caecilius' lack of experience. Speaking to him as one friend to another, he asks Caecilius whether he thinks he has the ability and experience to take on such an important and complicated case in which it is vital that the advocate has a complete grasp of the issues and can put them over convincingly to the jury.*

de te, Caecili (iam mehercule hoc extra hanc contentionem certamenque nostrum familiariter tecum loquar), tu ipse quemadmodum existimes vide etiam atque etiam, et tu te collige, et qui sis et quid facere possis considera!

putasne te posse de maximis acerbissimisque rebus, cum causam sociorum fortunasque provinciae, ius populi Romani, gravitatem iudicii legumque susceperis, tot res tam graves, tam varias, voce, memoria, consilio, ingenio sustinere? putasne te posse, quae C.Verres in quaestura quae in legatione, quae in praetura, quae Romae, quae in Italia, quae in

**spes, spei** (*f*), hope
**exiguus, -a, -um**, small, slender
**vis, vim, vi**, force
**extorqueo** (2), to tear away
**conor** (1), to try, attempt
**bene mereor de** (+ abl.), to treat well, behave well towards
**everto** (3) (+ abl.), to deprive (of)
**adimo** (3) (+ dat.), to take away (from)
**potestas, -atis** (*f*), power
**contentio, -onis** (*f*), contest, rivalry
**certamen, -inis** (*n*), contest, competition
**familiariter**, in a friendly way, as one friend to another
**video** (2), to see, look at, reflect upon
**etiam atque etiam**, again and again, earnestly
**acerbus, -a, -um**, bitter, painful
**socius, -i** (*m*), ally
**ius, iuris** (*n*), rights
**gravitas, -atis** (*f*), dignity, authority
**suscipio** (3), **-cepi**, to undertake
**gravis, -is, -e**, serious, important
**varius, -a, -um**, varied, complex
**vox, vocis** (*f*), voice
**consilium, -i** (*n*), thought, thinking powers
**ingenium, -i** (*n*), intelligence
**sustineo** (2), to sustain, support

54 **quae peccarit (= peccaverit)**: *the crimes he committed*, literally *what he has done wrong*. As in lines 14, 24 and 42, the relative clauses precede the antecedent (**ea**, in line 54). The technique is very useful in such a long sentence. As his audience may have lost the thread of so many clauses introduced by **quae**, Cicero pulls everything together by providing **ea** as a simple object for **distinguere**. The Overview technique (see pages xii-xiv of this book and LL pp. 121-31) is invaluable in unravelling a long, complicated sentence such as this:

**putasne te posse**
    **quae C.Verres in quaestura** (peccarit)
    **quae** (C.Verres) **in legatione** (peccarit)
    **quae** (C.Verres) **in praetura** (peccarit)
    **quae** (C.Verres) **Romae** (peccarit)
    **quae** (C.Verres) **in Italia** (peccarit)
    **quae** (C.Verres) **in Achaea, Asia Pamphyliaque peccarit**
        **ea** (quemadmodum locis temporibusque divisa sint)
        **sic criminibus et oratione distinguere?**

54 **quemadmodum locis temporibusque divisa sint, sic**: *in the same way as they are distinct in the places and times (in which they occurred)*, literally *just as they were separated in places and times, so ...* (For Correlatives, see LL pp. 63-4.)

55 **criminibus et oratione**: *in the way you deal with the charges*, literally *in the charges and in the speech.*

56 **ea**: Again, the antecedent **ea** sums up the preceding list of **quae** clauses. (cf. line 54.)

57 **aeque ... atque**: *just as* (literally *equally*) ... *as*. (For Correlatives, see LL pp. 63-4.)

59 **magna**: *important.*

60 **dicenda**: *must be stated.* (For Gerundives, see LL p. 61.)

63 **in quo si te multum natura adiuvaret**: *(even) if you were naturally gifted in this direction*, literally *if nature were helping you greatly in this.*

63 **si ... si ... si ...**: The use of the subjunctive in all of these Conditional clauses suggests that none of this is true (see LL pp. 54-5), as does **tamen esset** in line 66.

65 **elaborasses = elaboravisses**: *you had worked hard (at them).*

65 **litteras Graecas**: *Greek literature*, the study of which formed an important element in Roman education generally, but particularly in the training of an orator.

65 **Lilybaei**: Caecilius, a Sicilian, was educated in the Sicilian town of Lilybaeum, whereas Cicero had gone to Athens, a much more fashionable centre of learning, for his advanced education. Cicero here appeals to the snobbishness of the senators, implying that Caecilius was not a true-blue Roman. (For Locatives, see LL p. 20.)

66 **esset magnum**: *it would be difficult.*

66 **tam exspectatam**: *so (eagerly) awaited.*

67 **et ... et ... et ... et ...** : Note again how Cicero piles one idea upon another — four infinitives each linked to an ablative noun (indeed, two ablatives in the final example). (For **congeries verborum**, see CAO on page 237.)

69 **quid ergo?**: *what (of it) then?*

70 **ut esse possent**: *in order to acquire those qualities*, literally *so that those things could be (in me)*, referring back to **haec in te sunt omnia?** Note that **haec** (ll. 69 and 71), **rerum** (l. 71), **his rebus** (l. 72) and **quas** (l. 73) all refer to the qualities mentioned in lines 67-8.

70 **mihi est elaboratum**: *I have worked hard.* (For verbs used impersonally in the passive, see LL p. 57; and for Dative of Agent, see LL p. 11.)

Achaea, Asia Pamphyliaque peccarit, ea, quemadmodum locis temporibusque divisa sint, sic criminibus et oratione distinguere? putasne te posse facere ut, quae ille libidinose, quae nefarie, quae crudeliter fecerit, ea aeque acerba et indigna videantur esse his qui audient atque illis visa sunt qui senserunt?

magna sunt ea quae dico, mihi crede. noli haec contemnere! dicenda, demonstranda, explicanda sunt omnia. causa non solum exponenda sed etiam graviter copioseque agenda est. perficiendum est, si quid agere aut perficere vis, ut homines te non solum audiant verum etiam libenter studioseque audiant. in quo si te multum natura adiuvaret, si optimis a pueritia disciplinis atque artibus studuisses et in his elaborasses, si litteras Graecas Athenis (non Lilybaei), Latinas Romae (non in Sicilia) didicisses, tamen esset magnum tantam causam, tam exspectatam et diligentia consequi et memoria complecti et oratione exponere et voce ac viribus sustinere.

*Cicero admits that even he feels a certain apprehension about tackling this case, despite all his experience of the law-courts; and he wonders if he can produce a speech which will do justice to the Sicilians' cause. Caecilius, on the other hand, seems completely unconcerned about the immensity of the task that is facing him — hardly surprising, since this lack of concern is brought about by his inexperience.*

fortasse dices 'quid ergo? haec in te sunt omnia?' utinam quidem essent! verum tamen ut esse possent magno studio mihi a pueritia est elaboratum.

**divido** (3), **-visi, -visum**, to separate
**distinguo** (3), to keep distinct
**facere ut** (+ subj.), to bring it about that
**libidinose**, wantonly, in a lustful way
**nefarie**, wickedly, in a criminal way
**crudeliter**, cruelly
**indignus, -a, -um** (+ abl.), unworthy
**sentio** (4), **sensi**, to experience
**credo** (3), (+ dat.), to believe
**contemno** (3), to despise, minimise
**demonstro** (1), to show, establish
**explico** (1), to explain
**expono** (3), to set out, mention
**copiose**, in great detail
**ago** (3), **egi, actum**, to do, discuss, present
**perficio** (3), to bring about, achieve
**quis, quid**, anyone, anything
**libenter**, willingly
**studiose**, eagerly, attentively
**pueritia, -ae** (*f*), boyhood
**disciplina, -ae** (*f*), training, teaching
**ars, artis** (*f*), skill
**studeo** (2) (+ dat.), to study, practise
**Athenae, -arum** (*f.pl*), Athens
**disco** (3), **didici**, to learn
**consequor** (3), to follow through, master
**complector** (3), to embrace, retain
**oratio, -onis** (*f*), eloquence
**vires, -ium** (*f.pl*), strength, vigour
**fortasse**, perhaps
**utinam** (+ subj.), I wish that, would that
**quidem**, indeed
**verum tamen**, nevertheless
**studium, -i** (*n*), study, zeal, effort

71 **propter magnitudinem rerum ac difficultatem**: *because of the immense difficulty of (acquiring) them*, i.e. these qualities. (For Hendiadys, see CAO on page 234.)

73 **cogitasti = cogitavisti**: *you have considered.*

73 **ne nunc quidem**: *not even now*, i.e. when you are about to tackle a task in which you will really need them.

74 **quae et quantae sint**: *their nature and importance*, literally *what and how big they are.*

75 **quae studia**: *what excitement.* This introduces the first of a series of five Indirect Questions, all depending on **prospicio**.

76 **futuri**: *likely to be.* (For future participles, see LL p. 29.) This agrees with **concursus** but applies also to **studia**.

79 **quae**: *(all of) this*, referring to all the thoughts he expressed in the previous sentence. (For Linking Relative, see LL p. 26.)

79 **timeo quidnam pro offensione hominum eloqui possim**: *I am anxious (about) what on earth I can say which will do justice to the indignation of the people*, literally *I am fearful what on earth I can say in proportion to the indignation of men.* In **quidnam**, the suffix **-nam** adds emphasis. The ablatives **exspectatione** and **magnitudine** are governed by **dignum** (*worthy of*).

80 **illi**: *to him*, i.e. Verres.

80 **inimici infensique**: The basic meaning of both words is *hostile*. Orators frequently repeat ideas in this way to emphasise what they are saying. (cf. **rogare et orare** in line 16.) (For Paired Words, see CAO on page 236.)

81 **nihil ... nihil ... nihil ...**: For Anaphora, see CAO on page 238.

82 **laboras**: *you are anxious about.*

82 **si quid ediscere potueris**: *if you have been able to learn anything by heart.* The quotations within the dashes are examples of the kind of stock expression with which Cicero says Caecilius will fill out his speech. It was part of an orator's training to learn phrases, and even whole speeches, by heart.

82 **Iovem ego Optimum Maximum**: *(I appeal to) Jupiter, the Best and Greatest.* The abbreviation **IOM** frequently appears in Latin inscriptions.

83 **vellem, si fieri potuisset**: *I would have liked, if only it had been possible.*

84 **venturum**: Supply **esse**. The infinitive agrees with **te**.

quodsi ego haec propter magnitudinem rerum ac difficultatem assequi non potui, qui in omni vita nihil aliud egi, quam longe tu te ab his rebus abesse arbitrare, quas non modo antea numquam cogitasti, sed ne nunc quidem cum in eas ingrederis quae et quantae sint suspicari potes?

iam nunc mente et cogitatione prospicio quae tum studia hominum, qui concursus futuri sint; quantam exspectationem magnitudo iudicii sit allatura; quantam auditorum multitudinem C.Verris infamia concitatura; quantam denique audientiam orationi meae improbitas illius factura sit.

quae cum cogito, iam nunc timeo quidnam pro offensione hominum qui illi inimici infensique sunt et exspectatione omnium et magnitudine rerum dignum eloqui possim. tu horum nihil metuis, nihil cogitas, nihil laboras. si quid ex vetere aliqua oratione — '*Iovem ego Optimum Maximum*' aut '*vellem, si fieri potuisset, iudices*' aut aliquid huius modi — ediscere potueris, praeclare te paratum in iudicium venturum arbitraris.

**quodsi**, and if
**assequor** (3), to attain, master
**quam!**, how!
**longe**, far, much
**absum, -esse**, to be distant, fall short
**arbitrare = arbitraris**
**antea**, before, previously
**ingredior** (3), to enter, embark upon
**suspicor** (1), to suspect, conjecture
**mens, mentis** (*f*), mind
**cogitatio, -onis** (*f*), imagination
**prospicio** (3), to foresee, picture
**concursus, -us** (*m*), crowd
**exspectatio, -onis** (*f*), expectation, interest
**iudicium, -i** (*n*), trial
**affero, -ferre, attuli, allatum**, to bring
**auditor, -oris** (*m*), hearer, listener
**multitudo, -inis** (*f*), crowd
**infamia, -ae** (*f*), ill-repute, notoriety
**concito** (1), to excite, attract
**denique**, in short, to sum up
**audientia, -ae** (*f*), attention, attentiveness
**improbitas, -atis** (*f*), wickedness, depravity
**metuo** (3), to fear
**vetus, veteris**, old
**aliqui, -qua, -quod**, some, any
**modus, -i** (*m*), way, kind
**praeclare**, brilliantly, splendidly

Caecilius is so naive that he does not even realise that he will be up against a very skilled advocate. His lack of professional experience in the courts will be his undoing when he comes face to face with Hortensius, who is representing Verres. Cicero, however, knows Hortensius' methods well, since they have already appeared in the same cases, sometimes on the same side, sometimes on opposing sides. Caecilius is the sort of weak prosecuting counsel that any accused person would wish to have against him. Little credence can be put in Caecilius' assertion that he hates Verres because he was wronged by him. It is highly likely that Caecilius himself profited from Verres' corrupt practices while serving as quaestor under Verres. There is also no precedent for the prosecution of a senior official by one of his subordinates. If Rome's reputation for dealing fairly with its allies is to be preserved, it is vital that the best man should be appointed as prosecutor in cases of extortion.

86 **hoc**: *this* is explained by the Accusative and Infinitive clause which follows.

86 **de quo nulla umquam opinio fuerit**: *whom no one has ever held in high regard*, literally *about whom no opinion has ever been*. In other words, he has never seemed good enough even to merit an opinion being formed about him.

88 **ut** introduces a Purpose clause depending on **laborat** (line 89), as does **uti** (= **ut**) in line 88. For the form **uti**, compare line 3.

88 **ante collectam**: *previously won*.

88 **reliqui temporis spem**: *hope for the future*, literally *hope of the remaining time*.

89 **non nimis ... non nimis ... non nimis ...** : For Anaphora, see CAO on page 238.

89 **nimis severe**: *too rigorously*.

90 **acturum** (**esse**): *will conduct*. This infinitive completes the Accusative and Infinitive clause which began at **Q.Caecilium** in line 86.

90 **nihil quod deperdat**: *nothing to lose*. (For Generic Subjunctive, see LL p. 103.)

90 **in offensione**: *if he fails*, literally *in misfortune*.

91 **ut discedat**: *even though he may emerge (from this case)*, literally *though he may go away*.

91 **turpissime flagitiosissimeque**: As in line 80, Cicero drives home his point by using two words with the same basic meaning (here *disgracefully*), but he adds even greater emphasis by using the superlative forms. (For Paired Words, see CAO on page 236.)

93 **a nobis**: Cicero often refers to himself as *we*.

93 **obsides**: *hostages (to fortune)*. He lists these in lines 95 ff.

93 **quos ut**: *and so that ... them*. (For Linking Relative, see LL p. 26.)

94 **erit dimicandum**: *I will have to fight*. (For verbs used impersonally in the passive, see LL pp. 57 and 62.)

95 **spem quam propositam nobis habemus**: *the hope which we keep* (literally *hold placed*) *in front of us*. Cicero again uses the plural *we/us* when referring to himself. Note that the perfect participle + **habere** is different from the 'have' form of the perfect indicative: *I have placed* refers to an action in the past, whereas *I have* or *hold (it) placed* describes the state of something in the present.

96 **labore vigiliisque**: *by working hard day and night*, literally *by labour and wakeful nights*.

97 **ut**: *with the result that*.

98 **haec quae dixi**: *those things which I have mentioned*, i.e. the hostages to fortune (**honorem**, **spem** and **existimationem**).

98 **per populum Romanum**: *by (the favour of) the Roman people*.

98 **incolumia ac salva**: Again, Cicero uses two words with the same basic meaning (cf. lines 80 and 91). (For Paired Words, see CAO on page 236.)

99 **si tantulum offensum titubatumque sit**: *(but) if I blunder or stumble ever so little*. (For verbs used impersonally in the passive, see LL p. 57.)

99 **ut**: *the effect will be*, another Result clause balancing the one which began in line 97.

*To conclude, Caecilius has no reputation to lose and nothing to gain by this prosecution, and so he is unlikely to throw himself wholeheartedly into it. On the other hand, if they choose Cicero, they can rely on his doing his utmost to succeed, since one false step or failure at this stage would imperil his whole future career.*

quam ob rem hoc statuere, iudices, debetis: Q.Caecilium, de quo nulla umquam opinio fuerit nullaque in hoc ipso iudicio exspectatio futura sit, qui neque ut ante collectam famam conservet neque uti reliqui temporis spem confirmet laborat, non nimis hanc causam severe, non nimis accurate, non nimis diligenter acturum. habet enim nihil quod in offensione deperdat; ut turpissime flagitiosissimeque discedat, nihil de suis veteribus ornamentis requiret.

a nobis multos obsides habet populus Romanus, quos ut incolumes conservare, tueri, confirmare ac recuperare possimus, omni ratione erit dimicandum. habet honorem quem petimus, habet spem quam propositam nobis habemus, habet existimationem multo sudore, labore vigiliisque collectam ut, si in hac causa nostrum officium ac diligentiam probaverimus, haec quae dixi retinere per populum Romanum incolumia ac salva possimus; si tantulum offensum titubatumque sit, ut ea quae singillatim ac diu collecta sunt uno tempore universa perdamus.

quapropter, iudices, vestrum est deligere quem existimetis facillime posse magnitudinem causae ac iudicii sustinere fide, diligentia, consilio, auctoritate. vos si mihi Q.Caecilium anteposueritis, ego me dignitate

**quam ob rem**, therefore
**statuo** (3), to decide
**debeo** (2), I ought, owe
**fama, -ae** (*f*), reputation
**conservo** (1), to preserve
**confirmo** (1), to establish, justify
**accurate**, accurately, carefully
**ornamentum, -i** (*n*), distinction
**requiro** (3), to lose
**incolumis, -is, -e**, safe, unharmed
**tueor** (2), to protect
**recupero** (1), to recover, redeem
**ratio, -onis** (*f*), means, way
**honos, -oris** (*m*), honour, office
**existimatio, -onis** (*f*), reputation
**sudor, -oris** (*m*), sweat
**colligo** (3), **-legi, -lectum**, to collect, gather, win
**probo** (1), to prove
**retineo** (2), to retain, keep
**salvus, -a, -um**, safe and sound, sound
**singillatim**, one by one
**diu**, for a long time
**universus, -a, -um**, all together
**perdo** (3), to lose
**quapropter**, therefore
**vestrum est**, it is up to you
**deligo** (3), to choose
**existimo** (1), to think
**sustineo** (2), to sustain, bear the weight of
**fides, -ei** (*f*), integrity
**consilium, -i** (*n*), judgement
**auctoritas, -atis** (*f*), authority, prestige
**antepono** (3), **-posui**, to prefer
**dignitas, -atis** (*f*), worth, merit

104 **populus Romanus ne arbitretur, providete**: *see to it that the Roman people does not think.* Although **populus Romanus** belongs to the **ne** clause, Cicero places these words before the conjunction to increase their impact.

104 **tam honestam accusationem**: *(to have) such an upright prosecutor (as myself)*, literally *such an honourable prosecution.* By using *prosecution* instead of *prosecutor*, Cicero tones down the element of self-praise.

105 **neque ordini vestro placere**: and *is not what your order wants*, literally *and does not please your order*. Roman citizens were classified according to rank or 'order' (**ordo**). The members of the court which was hearing this speech were all drawn from the senatorial order. The distinction between **placuisse** and **placere** is important. The perfect infinitive refers to the decision to be taken by the jurors in this particular case; the present infinitive generalises the issue, suggesting that, if the jury corruptly tries to ensure Verres' acquittal by choosing the weaker prosecuting counsel, the Roman people may come to the conclusion that this decision reflects the general attitude of senators to prosecutions brought against any of their own members. This concluding sentence is, of course, a form of blackmail.

## Points for Discussion

1. It has been said that Cicero will not use one word if he can use two. Study lines 1-17 and produce lists of pairs of words linked by the Latin equivalent of *and* (lines 2, 3, 6, 7, 11 and 16). In how many of these do you think something is added by the second word, and in how many is Cicero striving only after sound effect?
2. Comment on the repeated use of **tamen** in lines 36-9, and of **cur** in lines 40-3.
3. Lines 49-68 are very carefully constructed to produce the maximum effect. List examples of the following rhetorical techniques (see CAO pp. 236 and 238):
   (a) A series of balanced phrases beginning with the same word (lines 52-3, 56 and 63-5).
   (b) Balanced contrasts (lines 60-1 and 62-3).
   (c) The use of the same opening words in the three sentences in lines 49-55.
   What overall effect do you think Cicero is trying to produce? Do you think he succeeds?
4. In lines 101-6, comment on the way Cicero uses the words **vestrum, vos, mihi, ego, me, populus Romanus, vobis, vestro.**
5. Lines 1-30 are largely a narrative description which sets the scene of the speech. In line 31, Cicero switches to a conversational dialogue with his opponent. Do you think this is more effective or less effective than a straight narrative would have been?
6. List the factors which Cicero claims have influenced him in deciding to represent the Sicilians.
7. Summarise the main reasons why, according to Cicero, the jury should reject Caecilius.

superatum non arbitrabor: populus Romanus ne tam honestam, tam severam diligentemque accusationem neque vobis placuisse neque ordini vestro placere arbitretur, providete!

**supero** (1), to defeat, beat, overcome
**severus, -a, -um**, strict
**diligens, -entis**, conscientious, thorough

# Cicero Attacks Verres

Cicero succeeded in persuading the preliminary hearing that he, rather than Caecilius, should be appointed prosecutor of Verres (see Chapter 4). He then asked for 110 days to gather his evidence and prepare his case. He went immediately to Sicily and, in less than two months, he had amassed a huge amount of evidence despite the obstruction of the new governor who was a friend of Verres.

Having failed in their efforts to have a sympathetic prosecutor appointed, Verres and his influential friends next tried to obstruct the trial by arranging for the ex-governor of another province to be tried for extortion, the case to begin in the same court on the day before the date fixed by Cicero for the opening of Verres' trial.

The court did not become available until 5 August 70 BC and, if the proceedings of the trial could be prolonged to the end of the year, a fresh trial would have to be begun, by which time Hortensius (the defence counsel) would be one of the consuls, and another supporter of Verres would be the praetor appointed to preside over the court which handled extortion cases. The chances of completing the trial before the end of 70 BC were further reduced by the fact that the court would not meet on the numerous (often long) public holidays which occurred in the latter part of the year.

Normally, trials were divided into two main sections. In the **actio prima**, the prosecuting counsel delivered a long introductory speech in which he explained the case for the prosecution in great detail, supported by the reading of various relevant documents. The defence counsel then made a long speech in which he refuted the accusations. Next, the witnesses were heard and cross-examined, after which both counsel debated the points raised by the witnesses. Following the **actio prima** there had to be an interval of at least one day before the start of the **actio secunda**, in which each counsel summed up all the evidence in a further long speech.

Realising that time was against him, Cicero abandoned the normal procedure. Instead of spending time on a long introductory speech, he delivered a series of short speeches, each of which dealt with a specific charge, and then began to call his witnesses. This tactic not only denied Hortensius the opportunity of prolonging the proceedings by making his own long introductory speech; it also meant that he was completely unprepared for cross-examining the witnesses brought by Cicero.

So devastating was the evidence of the stream of witnesses that, when the **actio prima** ended on the ninth day, Hortensius did not even attempt to reply to Cicero's summation. On the following day, Verres left Rome and went into exile, leaving the court to pass a formal 'Guilty' verdict. He had already taken the precaution of removing most of the stolen art treasures to Massilia (Marseilles), his chosen place of exile; and so, the compensation that the Sicilians received was limited to the property which he could not take with him. In exile, he continued his dissolute living for some twenty-six years. Ironically, his love of art treasures brought about his death. In 43 BC, Mark Antony, one of the Triumvirs who seized power after the assassination of Julius Caesar, asked him to hand over some Corinthian bronzes which he wanted for himself. When Verres refused, Antony had him proscribed and killed. [For 'proscription', see page 1.]

The **actio secunda** of Verres' trial never took place, but Cicero later published the speeches which he would have delivered if the trial had continued. Chapters 5 and 6 are two short excerpts from this devastating indictment of Verres.

# Sicily and Segesta

The strategic position and fertile soil of Sicily made it throughout the centuries a magnet for invaders and settlers of many races. According to legend, Aeneas and his followers in their wanderings after the fall of Troy were hospitably entertained in Sicily by Acestes, a ruler of Trojan descent. When Aeneas later sailed on to Italy, some of his followers did not accompany him but stayed behind in Sicily and founded a city of their own which they called Segesta.

When we study historical times, we find that, by the 9th century BC, Sicily's indigenous inhabitants (about whom we know little except for their tribal names) were dominated by invading settlers of Phoenician, Carthaginian or Greek origin. Roman domination of Sicily did not begin until Rome won the island from Carthage in the First Punic War (264-241BC) and Sicily became Rome's first province. Sicily was of vital importance to Rome since it was one of the main suppliers of corn to feed the city's vast population.

Diana (Artemis) as a huntress,
*National Museum, Naples.*
*Rex Features/Mansell Collection*

Diana (Artemis) holding a torch,
*Vatican Museum, Rome.*
*Rex Features/Mansell Collection*

2 **loca**: *area*, literally *places*. The plural of **locus** is commonly neuter.

4 **cognatione**: *by a blood-relationship*. In ancient times, it was considered very important to be able to trace one's lineage as far back as possible, even to legendary figures. This claim was based on the fact that Aeneas, the mythical ancestor of the Romans, is supposed to have left some of his followers behind in Sicily (see page 37).

5 **suo nomine ac sua sponte**: *on its own account and of its own accord*, i.e. Segesta had not been dragged into the war to support Rome or any other city.

6 **captum atque deletum est**: This is historically inaccurate. The Carthaginians did not capture and destroy Segesta. They did, however, carry off its treasures.

7 **ornamento urbi esse**: *to beautify the city*. (For Predicative Dative, see LL p. 13.)

7 **possent**: For Generic Subjunctive, see LL p. 103.

7 **sunt**: Take with **deportata**.

9 **ex aere simulacrum**: *a statue (made) of bronze*.

9 **cum ... tum ...** : *both ... and ...* This is more emphatic than **et ... et ....**

9 **summa atque antiquissima praeditum religione**: *regarded as one of their most sacred objects from ancient times*, literally *invested with the greatest and most ancient sanctity*. In this phrase, the literal translation of **religione** is *with sanctity*. However, the noun **religio** has a wide range of meanings and, throughout this passage, it will be necessary to choose the most appropriate one in each context: *reverence for the gods*, *fear of the gods*, *religious awe*, *religious scruples*, *conscience*, *holiness*, *religious aura*, *sanctity*, *an object of worship*, *a holy object*, *a holy place*, *religious beliefs*, *religious practice*, *religion*.

10 **singulari opere artificioque perfectum**: *a work of the most exquisite skill and craftsmanship*, literally *completed with unique work and craftsmanship*.

12 **mutarat = mutaverat**: *had changed*, i.e. it was in a different place, and different people were looking at it.

13 **digna quam sanctissime colerent videbatur**: *she seemed worthy of their most devout worship* (literally *whom they should worship most devoutly*). (For **dignus** followed by a relative clause in the subjunctive, see LL p. 103.)

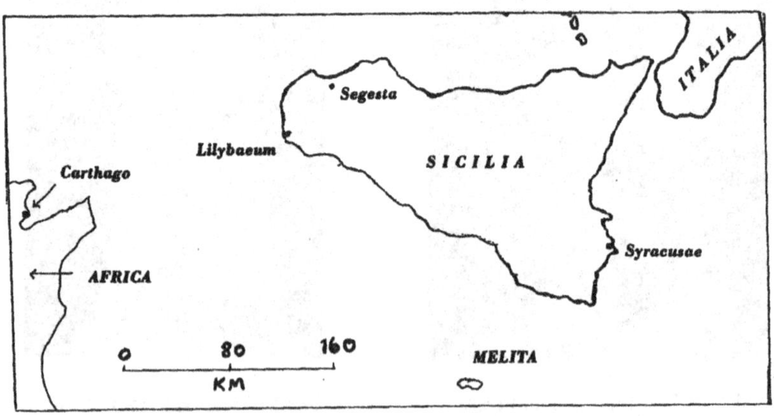

# 5. *Theft from Segesta*

(In Verrem II.iv.72, 74-80)

*When the Carthaginians gained control of Segesta, they carried off all its art treasures, among which was a bronze statue of Diana, so beautiful that even they held it in awe.*

Segesta est oppidum pervetus in Sicilia, iudices, quod ab Aenea fugiente a Troia atque in haec loca veniente conditum esse demonstrant. itaque Segestani non solum perpetua societate atque amicitia verum etiam cognatione se cum populo Romano coniunctos esse arbitrantur. hoc quondam oppidum, cum illa civitas cum Poenis suo nomine ac sua sponte bellaret, a Carthaginiensibus vi captum atque deletum est, omniaque quae ornamento urbi esse possent Carthaginem sunt ex illo loco deportata.

fuit apud Segestanos ex aere Dianae simulacrum, cum summa atque antiquissima praeditum religione, tum singulari opere artificioque perfectum. hoc translatum Carthaginem locum tantum hominesque mutarat, religionem quidem pristinam conservabat; nam propter eximiam pulchritudinem etiam hostibus digna quam sanctissime colerent videbatur.

**oppidum, -i** (*n*), town
**pervetus, -eris**, very old
**iudices, -um** (*m.pl*), members of the jury
**fugio** (3), to flee
**condo** (3), **-didi, -ditum**, to found (a city)
**demonstro** (1), to point out, assert, claim
**non solum ... verum etiam ...**, not only ... but also ...
**perpetuus, -a, -um**, permanent
**societas, -atis** (*f*), alliance
**verum**, but
**coniungo** (3), **-iunxi, -iunctum**, to bind together
**quondam**, long ago, in times past
**civitas, -atis** (*f*), state, community
**Poeni, -orum** (*m.pl*), Carthaginians
**bello** (1), to be at war
**deleo** (2), **-evi, -etum**, to destroy
**deporto** (1), to carry off
**apud** (+ acc.), among
**perficio** (3), **-feci, -fectum**, to finish
**transfero, -ferre, -tuli, -latum**, to carry across, transfer, move
**tantum**, only, merely
**quidem**, but
**pristinus, -a, -um**, former
**conservo** (1), to preserve, keep
**eximius, -a, -um**, excellent, outstanding
**pulchritudo, -inis** (*f*), beauty
**etiam**, even
**sancte**, religiously, devoutly

17 **sane excelsa in basi**: *on a very high pedestal.*

18 **eumque restituisse perscriptum (erat)**: *and there was an inscription which recorded in detail (the fact) that he had restored.* This inscription would have been in smaller letters than the name **P.Africanus**. Note that the prefix **per-** intensifies the meaning of **perscriptum**, signifying that the inscription *recorded in detail* what happened. This was Publius Scipio Africanus, the victor in the Third Punic War which ended in 146 BC. He was the adopted grandson of the Scipio Africanus who had ended the Second Punic War by defeating Hannibal and the Carthaginians at Zama in 202 BC.

20 **cum quaestor essem**: Cicero was quaestor in the western part of Sicily in 75 BC.

20 **nihil est demonstratum prius**: *this was the first thing that was shown*, literally *nothing was shown before.* Note the considerable emphasis given to both **nihil** and **prius** by placing the one first in the clause and the other last.

21 **admodum amplum et excelsum signum**: *a colossal statue*, literally *a very large and tall statue.* (For the use of Paired Words, see CAO on page 236.)

22 **cum stola**: *draped in* (literally *with*) *a long flowing robe.* Most illustrations of Diana depict her as a lively, athletic huntress dressed in a short skirt. In archaic art, however, she is the cold, austere goddess of nature dressed in long robes. (See illustrations on page 37.) At several points in this speech, Cicero reveals that, despite his protestations to the contrary, he was really quite knowledgeable about art.

22 **verum tamen inerat in illa magnitudine aetas atque habitus virginalis**: literally *but yet there was in that large size a girl's age and dress*, i.e. in spite of its vast size, the statue still managed to convey the impression that it was the figure of a young girl.

24 **arcum**: *bow.* The torch (**fax**) and the bow exemplify the two main functions of Diana as the goddess of the moon (bringing *light*) and of hunting (inflicting *death).*

25 **iste** agrees with **hostis praedoque**. Cicero regularly uses **iste** (*that man, the accused*) to refer to the person on the opposite side in the case. The very sound of this pronoun enables him to spit out his contempt.

25 **sacrorum omnium et religionum**: *of all sacred things and holy objects.*

26 **illa ipsa face**: *by that very torch*, which the statue was holding (see line 24).

26 **cupiditate atque amentia**: *with uncontrollable craving*, literally *with desire and madness.* (For Hendiadys, see CAO on page 234.)

29 **illi dicere**: *they* (i.e. the magistrates) *said.* **dicere** is a Historic Infinitive (see LL p. 32), as are **petere, minari** and **ostendere** (lines 30-1). On the other hand, **esse** and **teneri** belong to the two Accusative and Infinitive clauses which depend on **dicere**.

29 **religione**: See note on line 9.

*Years later, when he had defeated the Carthaginians in the Third Punic War, Publius Scipio had restored all the stolen treasures to the various Sicilian towns. At the same time, the magnificent statue of Diana was returned to the people of Segesta.*

illo tempore Segestanis maxima cum cura haec ipsa Diana redditur. reportatur Segestam, in suis antiquis sedibus summa cum gratulatione civium et laetitia reponitur. haec erat posita Segestae sane excelsa in basi, in qua grandibus litteris P.Africani nomen erat incisum eumque Carthagine capta restituisse perscriptum. colebatur a civibus, ab omnibus advenis visebatur. cum quaestor essem, nihil mihi ab illis est demonstratum prius. erat admodum amplum et excelsum signum cum stola; verum tamen inerat in illa magnitudine aetas atque habitus virginalis. sagittae pendebant ab umero, sinistra manu retinebat arcum, dextra ardentem facem praeferebat.

*As soon as Verres set eyes on the statue, he demanded that it be handed over. The leaders of Segesta continued to refuse, even when he threatened them.*

hanc cum iste sacrorum omnium et religionum hostis praedoque vidisset, quasi illa ipsa face percussus esset, ita flagrare cupiditate atque amentia coepit. imperat magistratibus ut eam demoliantur et sibi dent; nihil sibi gratius ostendit futurum.

illi vero dicere sibi id nefas esse seseque cum summa religione tum summo metu legum et iudiciorum teneri. iste tum petere ab illis, tum

**cura, -ae** (*f*), care
**reddo** (3), to give back, return
**reporto** (1), to carry back
**sedes, -um** (*f.pl*), home
**gratulatio, -onis** (*f*), public thanksgiving
**laetitia, -ae** (*f*), joy
**grandis, -is, -e**, large
**littera, -ae** (*f*), letter
**incido** (3), **-cidi, -cisum**, to cut, inscribe
**advena, -ae** (*m*), stranger, visitor
**viso** (3), to visit, go and see
**sagitta, -ae** (*f*), arrow
**pendeo** (2), to hang
**umerus, -i** (*m*), shoulder
**sinister, -tra, -trum**, left
**retineo** (2), to hold (close to oneself)
**ardens, -entis**, burning
**praefero, -ferre**, to hold out in front
**praedo, -onis** (*m*), robber, plunderer
**quasi**, as if
**percutio** (3), **-cussi, -cussum**, to smite, strike
**flagro** (1), to be aflame, burn
**coepi**, I began
**demolior** (4), to dismantle, take down
**gratus, -a, -um**, pleasing
**ostendo** (3), to show, indicate
**vero**, but
**nefas** (indeclinable), sinful, against divine law
**sese = se**
**metus, -us** (*m*), fear
**lex, legis** (*f*), law
**iudicium, -i** (*n*), law-court
**teneo** (2), to hold, bind
**peto** (3) (**a** + abl.), to ask, request

31 **tum spem, tum metum ostendere**: *he played on their hopes and fears*, literally *at one time he showed hope, at another time fear.*

31 **opponebant illi nomen interdum P.Africani**: *they* (**illi**) *countered every now and again* (**interdum**) *with the name of Publius Africanus*, literally *now and again they put the name of Publius Africanus in the way (of his demands).*

32 **populi Romani**: *(the property) of the Roman people.*

32 **nihil se in eo potestatis habere quod**: *(they said that) they had no control over a thing which*, i.e. no right to dispose of it. (For Partitive Genitive, see LL p. 9.)

35 **nihilo remissius**: *no less forcefully*, literally *by nothing more mildly.* (For ablative expressing Measure of Difference, see LL p. 16.)

36 **in senatu**: This, of course, refers to the senate in Segesta, not Rome.

36 **reclamatur**: For verbs used impersonally in the passive, see LL p. 57. (cf. **pernegatur** in line 37.)

38 **quidquid erat oneris**: *whatever burden could be imposed* (literally *there was*). (For Partitive Genitive, see LL p. 9.)

38 **in nautis remigibusque exigendis**: *in requisitioning sailors and rowers.* (For this use of the Gerundive, see LL p. 61.) Although Segesta was a **civitas libera** (i.e. a self-governing state, which was free from interference from the governor and paid lower taxes), it was nevertheless required to provide ships and men for the Roman navy and also to supply corn to feed the population of Rome. To increase pressure on the Segestans, Verres demanded much more from them than from the other communities.

39 **aliquanto amplius**: *considerably more.* (cf. the use of **nihilo** and **multo** in line 35; and see LL p. 16.)

40 **evocabat**: *he kept on ordering ... to appear before him.* The verb **evocare** is much stronger than **arcessere** (line 41).

41 **circum omnia fora rapiebat**: *he kept dragging them from one assize town to another.* The assizes, or courts, were held in the **fora** of several towns in Sicily. Because Verres did not explain why he had summoned them, they were obliged to remain constantly on call.

42 **singillatim uni cuique calamitati fore se denuntiabat**: *he gave notice to each one individually that he would ruin (him).* (For Predicative Dative, see LL p. 13.) **fore** is a future infinitive of **esse.**

44 **multis malis magnoque metu**: For Alliteration, see CAO on page 235. Compare also the alliterative sound of **praetoris imperio parendum** (line 45) and **lacrimis et lamentationibus** (line 46).

45 **parendum esse**: For verbs used impersonally in the passive, see LL p. 57.

47 **simulacrum tollendum locatur**: *a contract was issued for taking down the statue*, literally *removing the statue was contracted for.* (For this use of the Gerundive, see LL p. 61.)

minari, tum spem, tum metum ostendere. opponebant illi nomen interdum P.Africani; populi Romani illud esse dicebant; nihil se in eo potestatis habere quod imperator clarissimus urbe hostium capta monumentum victoriae populi Romani esse voluisset.

*Verres then used various other indirect pressures against them until they eventually agreed to hand over the statue to him.*

cum iste nihilo remissius atque etiam multo vehementius instaret cotidie, res agitur in senatu. vehementer ab omnibus reclamatur. itaque illo tempore ac primo istius adventu pernegatur. postea, quidquid erat oneris in nautis remigibusque exigendis, in frumento imperando, Segestanis praeter ceteros imponebat, aliquanto amplius quam ferre possent. praeterea magistratus eorum evocabat, optimum quemque et nobilissimum ad se arcessebat, circum omnia provinciae fora rapiebat, singillatim uni cuique calamitati fore se denuntiabat, universis se funditus eversurum esse illam civitatem minabatur.

itaque aliquando, multis malis magnoque metu victi, Segestani praetoris imperio parendum esse decreverunt. magno cum luctu et gemitu totius civitatis, multis cum lacrimis et lamentationibus virorum mulierumque omnium, simulacrum Dianae tollendum locatur.

**minor** (1), to threaten
**clarus, -a, -um**, illustrious, well-known
**monumentum, -i** (*n*), memorial
**vehementer**, violently, vehemently
**insto** (1), to press, insist, persist
**cotidie**, every day, daily
**ago** (3), to discuss
**reclamo** (1), to cry out against, protest
**adventus, -us** (*m*), arrival, visit
**pernego** (1), to refuse completely
**frumentum, -i** (*n*), corn
**impero** (1), to demand
**praeter** (+ acc.), beyond, more than
**impono** (3) (+ dat.), to impose (on)
**fero, ferre**, to bear, endure
**praeterea**, in addition
**quisque, quidque**, each
**optimus quisque**, all the best men
**nobilis, -is, -e**, notable, well-known
**arcesso** (3), to summon
**universi, -ae, -a**, all together, collectively
**funditus**, utterly, completely
**everto** (3), **-verti, -versum**, to overturn, destroy
**aliquando**, eventually
**malum, -i** (*n*), calamity
**vinco** (3), **vici, victum**, to conquer, overcome
**pareo** (2) (+ dat.), to obey
**decerno** (3), **-crevi**, to decide
**luctus, -us** (*m*), grief, sorrow
**gemitus, -us** (*m*), groan, cry of grief
**totus, -a, -um**, all, whole
**lacrima, -ae** (*f*), tear
**mulier, -eris** (*f*), woman
**tollo** (3), **sustuli, sublatum**, to carry off, remove

49 **scitote**: This is the imperative of **scire**, *be assured*, literally *know*. Note the emphasis given to the Accusative and Infinitive clause by reversing the positions of **repertum esse** and **neminem**.

50 **auderet**: For Generic Subjunctive, see LL p. 103.

50 **barbaros**: *barbarians*, the word regularly used by Greeks when referring to non-Greeks. These were native Sicilians who remained in the west of the island when the Greeks established their colonies there. They were regarded by the new settlers as less civilised.

51 **operarios**: *as workmen*.

53 **quod**: *it*. (For Linking Relative, see LL p. 26.)

53 **quem conventum mulierum factum esse arbitramini?**: *can you imagine the huge number of women who gathered (to watch)?*, literally *what a gathering of women do you think was made?*

54 **quorum nonnulli**: *some of them*. (For Linking Relative, see LL p. 26.)

56 **nuntiasset** is a contracted form of **nuntiavisset** (*announced*). (cf. **complesse** in line 64.)

60 **turpissimus atque impurissimus**: For the use of Paired Words, see CAO on page 236.

62 **hoc**: *than this*. (For Ablative of Comparison, see LL p. 16.) The word *this* is explained in the four Accusative and Infinitive clauses which are introduced by **quam**, *than (the fact) that*.

62 **tota Sicilia**: *in the whole of Sicily*. The ablative expressing Place Where is regularly used without the preposition **in** when the adjective **totus** appears in the phrase (see LL p. 15).

63 **unxisse**: The object of this infinitive (and of **complesse** and **prosecutas esse**) is **Dianam** (understood).

*Even then, the people of Segesta refused to carry out the actual dismantling of this sacred statue, and workmen from outside the city had to be employed to carry out the task. Its removal from the city was accompanied by emotional scenes involving the whole population.*

videte quanta religio fuerit. apud Segestanos repertum esse, iudices, scitote neminem, neque liberum neque servum neque civem neque peregrinum, qui illud signum auderet attingere. barbaros quosdam Lilybaeo scitote adductos esse operarios; ii denique illud ignari totius negotii ac religionis mercede accepta sustulerunt.

quod cum ex oppido exportabatur, quem conventum mulierum factum esse arbitramini, quem fletum maiorum natu? quorum nonnulli etiam illum diem memoria tenebant cum illa eadem Diana Segestam Carthagine revecta victoriam populi Romani reditu suo nuntiasset. quam dissimilis hic dies illi tempori videbatur! tum imperator populi Romani, vir clarissimus, deos patrios reportabat Segestanis ex urbe hostium recuperatos; nunc ex urbe sociorum praetor eiusdem populi Romani turpissimus atque impurissimus eosdem illos deos nefario scelere auferebat.

quid hoc tota Sicilia est clarius, quam omnes Segestae matronas et virgines convenisse, cum Diana exportaretur ex oppido, unxisse unguentis, complesse coronis et floribus, ture, odoribus incensis usque ad agri fines prosecutas esse?

**reperio** (4), **repperi, repertum**, to find
**liber, -eri** (*m*), free man
**peregrinus, -i** (*m*), foreigner
**audeo** (2), to dare
**attingo** (3), to touch, lay hands on
**denique**, finally, eventually
**ignarus, -a, -um**, ignorant
**negotium, -i** (*n*), business, affair
**merces, -edis** (*f*), fee, wages
**fletus, -us** (*m*), weeping
**maiores natu**, older people
**memoria tenere**, to remember
**reveho** (3), **-vexi, -vectum**, to bring back
**reditus, -us** (*m*), return
**quam!**, how!
**dissimilis, -is, -e**, dissimilar, unlike, different
**clarus, -a, -um**, famous, distinguished
**patrius, -a, -um**, ancestral
**recupero** (1), to recover
**turpis, -is, -e**, loathsome, unscrupulous
**impurus, -a, -um**, filthy, vile
**nefarius, -a, -um**, heinous
**scelus, -eris** (*n*), crime
**aufero, -ferre**, to carry off
**matrona, -ae** (*f*), married woman
**convenio** (4), **-veni**, to gather
**ungo** (3), **unxi**, to anoint
**unguentum, -i** (*n*), perfume
**compleo** (2), **-evi**, to cover, shower
**corona, -ae** (*f*), garland
**flos, floris** (*m*), flower
**tus, turis** (*n*), incense, frankincense
**odor, -oris** (*m*), spice
**incendo** (3), **-ndi, -nsum**, to burn
**usque ad** (+ acc.), right up to
**ager, agri** (*m*), land, territory
**finis, -is** (*m*), boundary
**prosequor** (3), **-secutus sum**, to escort

66 **hanc tantam religionem**: *this very strong religious feeling*. By putting this phrase first in the sentence, outside the **si** clause, Cicero gives it tremendous emphasis since it places the crucial issue immediately before his audience. For **religio**, see the note on line 9.

66 **in imperio**: *when you were governor*, literally *(when) in command*.

67 **ne nunc quidem**: *not even now*, contrasting with **tum** in line 66.

67 **in tanto tuo liberorumque tuorum periculo**: *when you and your children are in such danger*, literally *in your and your children's so great danger*. The phrase **in periculo** has to be taken with both the adjective **tuo** and the genitive **liberorum tuorum**. If Verres were to be found guilty, any penalty imposed on him would automatically affect the inheritance of his children.

68 **quem** (*which*) has to be taken with both **aut hominem** and **aut deum**, and both of these form Accusative and Infinitive clauses with **futurum (esse)**. (For the Predicative Dative **auxilio**, see LL p. 13.)

69 **aut vero**: *or indeed*, leading on to the more important of the two alternatives.

69 **tantis eorum religionibus violatis**: *when such sacrilege has been committed against them*. The plural noun **religionibus** includes not only the sacred objects and places of the gods but also the beliefs of the worshippers which had been outraged. (See note on line 9.)

70 **in pace atque in otio**: *in the settled times of peace*, literally *in peace and calm*. The statue survived two wars but not the governorship of Verres in peacetime. (For the use of Paired Words, see CAO on page 236.)

71 **quae**: a Linking Relative, referring to Diana. (See LL p. 26.)

72 **quae**: Again, this Linking Relative refers to Diana. It introduces two clauses, the second of which begins at **P.Africani**. There is no linking word in the Latin, but English would probably insert a conjunction such as *but*. (For Asyndeton, see CAO on page 238.) For Publius Scipio Africanus, see the note on line 18.

73 **loco mutato**: *although its location was changed*. The word **tamen** indicates that this Ablative Absolute should be translated concessively.

73 **religionem**: The word **religio** is used in two slightly different senses in this sentence. Although the statue was not worshipped by the Carthaginians, they were nonetheless affected by its *religious aura* (line 73). To the Segestans, however, it was an object of true reverence. When it was returned to them, therefore, it recovered its *sanctity* (line 74).

76 **res indigna atque intoleranda videbatur**: *it seemed scandalous and intolerable*. The adjectives are used predicatively. (For the use of Paired Words, see CAO on page 236.)

76 **non solum ... verum etiam ...**: The Accusative and Infinitive clauses (**religiones esse violatas** and **C.Verrem sustulisse**) which accompany these words explain **res**. The order of the Latin is important. Having carefully built up an impressive picture of the magnificence of what Africanus did for the Segestans, Cicero reserves the final three words (**C.Verrem sustulisse**) to show how Africanus' efforts were all undone in a moment by Verres. For the same effect to be produced in English, the passive might have to be used to translate the verb.

80 **quod**: For Linking Relative, see LL p. 26.

80 **isti**: *to the accused*. (cf. line 25.)

81 **tamquam indicem**: *(which was) as it were a witness*. An **index** was an informer who pointed the finger of accusation at someone, hence our 'index' finger.

*Cicero turns his attention to Verres and accuses him of having no religious scruples whatsoever. He then tells the jury of how Verres completely ignored the outrage which his action had aroused, hoping that, in time, people would forget about it.*

hanc tu tantam religionem si tum in imperio propter cupiditatem atque audaciam non pertimescebas, ne nunc quidem in tanto tuo liberorumque tuorum periculo perhorrescis? quem tibi aut hominem invitis dis immortalibus aut vero deum tantis eorum religionibus violatis auxilio futurum putas? tibi illa Diana in pace atque in otio religionem nullam attulit? quae cum duas urbes in quibus locata fuerat captas incensasque vidisset, bis ex duorum bellorum flamma ferroque servata est; quae Carthaginiensium victoria loco mutato religionem tamen non amisit, P.Africani virtute religionem simul cum loco recuperavit. quo quidem scelere suscepto, cum inanis esset basis et in ea P.Africani nomen incisum, res indigna atque intoleranda videbatur omnibus non solum religiones esse violatas verum etiam P.Africani, viri fortissimi, rerum gestarum gloriam, memoriam virtutis, monumenta victoriae C.Verrem sustulisse.

quod cum isti renuntiaretur de basi ac litteris, existimavit homines in oblivionem totius negotii esse venturos si etiam basim tamquam indicem

**audacia, -ae** (*f*), brazenness
**pertimesco** (3), to fear greatly
**perhorresco** (3), to shudder and tremble (at)
**invitus, -a, -um**, unwilling
**di immortales**, the immortal gods
**affero, -ferre, attuli**, to bring to, bring about
**loco** (1), to place
**bis**, twice
**ferrum, -i** (*n*), sword
**servo** (1), to save, preserve
**amitto** (3), **amisi**, to lose
**virtus, -utis** (*f*), uprightness, integrity
**simul cum**, at the same time as, along with
**recupero** (1), to recover, regain
**quidem**, indeed, in fact
**suscipio** (3), **-cepi, -ceptum**, to perpetrate
**inanis, -is, -e**, empty
**res gestae** (*f.pl*), achievements
**renuntio** (1), to bring back word
**existimo** (1), to think, reckon
**oblivio, -onis** (*f*), forgetfulness

82 **tollendam locaverunt**: Supply **basim**. (For this use of the Gerundive, compare line 47 and see LL p. 61.) Again, the Segestans had to carry out an unenviable task on Verres' instructions.

83 **ex publicis litteris**: *from the public records*. The contract had been read to the court during the first part of the trial (**prior actio**). (See the article 'Cicero Attacks Verres' on page 36.)

84 **P. Scipio**: This was Publius Cornelius Scipio Nasica, who was present in court to support Verres. By all accounts, he hardly merited the superlative epithets applied to him by Cicero.

85 **officium tuum debitum**: *the loyalty which you owe*, literally *your duty owed*.

86 **vestrae**: The change from **tuum** (line 85) to **vestrae** in line 86 is interesting. In the latter case, Cicero is probably thinking not only about Nasica but also of the whole Scipio family, past and present.

87 **tuas partes**: *your rôle*. Cicero means that Scipio should be the prosecutor. The metaphor (see CAO on page 235) is from the stage.

89 **requirit**: *reclaim*, literally *ask back*. The strong contrast between the two questions, **cur M.Tullius ... requirit** and **(cur) P.Scipio ... defendit**, is emphasised by the lack of a connective. (For Asyndeton, see CAO on page 238.) English would probably insert a linking word such as *whereas*.

89 **quisnam**: *who, pray tell me*.

90 **mortui**: *since he is no longer alive (amongst us)*, i.e. to defend it himself.

90 **quis monumenta**: Supply **tuebitur**.

92 **spoliata illa patieris**: *you will allow them (to remain) with the plunderer* (literally *plundered*). The perfect participle describes the state that they are now in. (Compare **mortui** in line 90 and **defensum esse vis** in line 87.)

93 **defendis**: At first sight, the present tense seems strange after the series of futures (**relinques**, **deseres** and **patieris**). The futures refer to actions which Scipio may deny will happen; but he cannot deny that he is at that moment in court defending Verres.

94 **clientes**: *clients*. These were people who looked to others for protection. In Rome, they were men who attached themselves as followers to rich citizens, especially powerful politicians; in this case, they were people from a small community looking for support from the more powerful Roman state.

97 **dedicatum fuisse** is used rather than **dedicatum esse** because the statue is no longer in the place where it was dedicated.

97 **hoc Verrem ...**: As often happens in Latin, no new verb is used to introduce this Accusative and Infinitive clause, since the force of **certiorem te faciunt** still continues.

sui sceleris sustulisset. itaque tollendam istius imperio locaverunt; quae vobis locatio ex publicis litteris Segestanorum priore actione recitata est.

*Cicero now appeals to the family loyalty of Publius Scipio, who is supporting Verres. How can he leave it to someone else to defend the honour of his ancestor, preferring instead to defend the man who has dishonoured that ancestor?*

te nunc, P.Scipio, te, inquam, lectissimum ornatissimumque adulescentem, appello; abs te officium tuum debitum generi et nomini requiro et flagito. cur pro isto, qui laudem honoremque familiae vestrae depeculatus est, pugnas? cur eum defensum esse vis? cur ego tuas partes suscipio? cur tuum munus sustineo? cur M.Tullius P.Africani monumenta requirit, P.Scipio eum qui illa sustulit defendit? quisnam, per deos immortales, tuebitur P.Scipionis memoriam mortui, quis monumenta atque indicia virtutis, si tu ea relinques ac deseres, nec solum spoliata illa patieris sed etiam eorum spoliatorem vexatoremque defendis?

*The witnesses from Segesta have told you how your ancestor Publius Scipio Africanus helped them and how Verres robbed them. They too appeal to your family loyalty.*

adsunt Segestani, clientes tui, socii populi Romani atque amici; certiorem te faciunt P.Africanum Carthagine deleta simulacrum Dianae maioribus suis restituisse, idque apud Segestanos eius imperatoris nomine positum ac dedicatum fuisse: hoc Verrem demoliendum et asportandum nomenque omnino P.Scipionis delendum tollendumque

**loco** (1), to place a contract
**locatio, -onis** (*f*), contract
**recito** (1), to read out
**inquam**, I say
**lectus, -a, -um**, excellent, distinguished
**ornatus, -a, -um**, accomplished
**appello** (1), to call upon, appeal to
**abs = ab**
**genus, -eris** (*n*), family
**flagito** (1), to demand
**laus, laudis** (*f*), praise, reputation
**depeculor** (1), to plunder, detract from
**suscipio** (3), to undertake, take
**munus, -eris** (*n*), task, duty, burden
**sustineo** (2), to bear, support, shoulder
**tueor** (2), to protect
**indicium, -i** (*n*), sign, evidence
**relinquo** (3), to abandon
**desero** (3), to desert
**spoliator, -oris** (*m*), plunderer
**vexator, -oris** (*m*), tormentor
**socius, -i** (*m*), ally
**amicus, -i** (*m*), friend
**certiorem facere** (3), to inform
**restituo** (3), **-ui,** to restore
**imperator, -oris** (*m*), general
**dedico** (1), to dedicate, consecrate
**asporto** (1), to carry off
**omnino**, altogether, completely

99 **curasse = curavisse**: *organised*. (For the Gerundive used with curare, see LL p. 61. Compare lines 47 and 82.)

99 **orant te atque obsecrant**: *they earnestly entreat you*, literally *they beg and beseech you*. For emphasis, Cicero frequently uses two words of similar meaning. (See Paired Words, CAO on page 236.)

99 **religionem**: *the object of (their) worship*. (Compare line 9.)

100 **quod**: As often in Latin, the relative clause is placed in front of its antecedent (**id**, in line 101) to give more emphasis to the main clause (see LL p. 26).

101 **te** refers to Scipio Nasica.

102 **aut illi facere**: Supply **possunt**. The pronouns **his** and **illi** both refer to the Segestans.

102 **nisi ut**: *other than to*.

## Points for Discussion

1. Give the tense of the participles **fugiente** (line 1) and **veniente** (line 2), and explain why this tense is used.
2. Cicero often uses pairs of words to produce a particular effect. Comment on the following pairs, stating what effect you think the addition of the second word produces: **societate atque amicitia** (line 3), **captum atque deletum est** (line 6), **summa atque antiquissima** (line 9), **opere artificioque** (line 10), **amplum et excelsum** (line 21), **hostis praedoque** (line 25), **in pace atque in otio** (line 70), **spoliatorem vexatoremque** (line 92), **orant atque obsecrant** (line 99).
3. Sometimes Cicero deliberately omits conjunctions. Comment on the following, stating what you think is achieved by omitting the conjunctions and also what the effect would be if they were not omitted:
   (a) **colebatur ... visebatur** (lines 19-20)
   (b) **sagittae ... praeferebat** (lines 23-4)
   (c) **praeterea ... minabatur** (lines 40-3)
4. Comment on the effect produced by the positioning of the following words: **fuit** (line 9), **redditur, reportatur** and **reponitur** (lines 15-17), **cotidie** (line 36), **neminem** (line 49), **operarios** (line 51), **tum** and **nunc** (lines 57 and 59), **mortui** (line 90).
5. What effect do you think is produced by the repetition of the word **tum** (line 31), **neque** (line 49), **te** (line 84), **cur** (lines 86-8)?
6. Identify alliterative and vowel patterns (see CAO on page 235) in lines 44-7, and comment on their effectiveness.
7. The word **religio** appears several times in the passage. Use note 9 (page 38) to review its uses in lines 10, 12, 25, 29, 48, 52, 66, 69, 70, 73, 74, 77 and 99.
8. State at least three ways (other than by invoking **religio**) in which Cicero tries to influence the jury by appealing to their respect for history and tradition.
9. Cicero regularly blackens the characters of his opponents, while painting a complimentary picture of those on his own side. In lines 84-93, he seems to mix praise and criticism when addressing Publius Scipio, who is supporting Verres. Why do you think he does this?

curasse. orant te atque obsecrant ut sibi religionem, generi tuo laudem gloriamque restituas ut, quod per P.Africanum ex urbe hostium recuperarint, id per te ex praedonis domo conservare possint. quid aut tu his respondere honeste potes, aut illi facere nisi ut te ac fidem tuam implorent? adsunt et implorant.

**recuperarint = recuperaverint**
**praedo, -onis** (*m*), robber
**conservo** (1), to save
**honeste**, honourably
**fides, -ei** (*f*), good faith, honour
**imploro** (1), to appeal to

**illa vox et imploratio 'civis Romanus sum' quae saepe multis in ultimis terris opem inter barbaros et salutem tulit ...**
*That cry and appeal 'I am a Roman citizen' which has often brought help and safety among barbarians in many distant lands ...*

In Verrem, V.lvii.147

This declaration was of no avail to Verres' victims, but more than a century later it gave St Paul the protection of Roman law (Acts, Chapter 22, verses 25-8).

For the background to this passage, see the articles on pages 19 and 36.

1 **nemini video dubium esse quin**: *I see that you are all convinced that*, literally *I see that it is doubtful to no one that*. (For this use of **quin** with the subjunctive, see LL p. 105.)

2 **sacra profanaque omnia**: *everything, both what was sacred and what was not*, literally *all things (both) sacred and secular* (i.e. not sacred).

2 **privatim**: *from individuals*, literally *privately*. Contrast **publice**, *from communities*.

2 **spoliarit = spoliaverit**: *plundered*.

2 **versatus sit**: *was involved*.

3 **religione**: *religious scruples*. For a full discussion of the various meanings of **religio**, see Note 9 on page 38.

4 **furandi atque praedandi**: For the Gerund, see LL p. 61.

4 **mihi ostenditur**: *is offered (in reply) to me*.

4 **magnifica et praeclara**: *magnificent and splendid*. Cicero, of course, is being sarcastic. He will go on to show how ineffective Verres really was as a general.

4 **eius**: *of him* (i.e Verres).

5 **cui quemadmodum resistam**: *how I am to counter it* (literally *resist it*). (For Linking Relatives, see LL p. 26; for Deliberative Questions, see LL p. 38.) A most powerful oratorical technique is to anticipate what the opposition is going to say and then discredit it before the opposition has a chance to put its case.

5 **multo ante**: *well in advance*, literally *previously by much*. (For the ablative expressing Measure of Difference, see LL p. 16.)

5 **mihi est providendum**: *I must consider*. (For this use of the Gerundive with the Dative of the Agent, see LL p. 62.)

6 **ita causa constituitur**: *the line of defence which is being built up is as follows*, literally *the case is being established in this way*. The Accusative and Infinitive clause which follows gives the details of the defence.

7 **istius**: *of the accused*. Cicero regularly uses the pronoun **iste** (which is much stronger than **is**) for the accused and those supporting him in the case. It is an expression of contempt which relies very much on sound for its effect; and it would probably be accompanied by an aggressive pointing gesture.

7 **dubiis formidolosisque temporibus**: *in times of uncertainty and anxiety*, literally *in uncertain and fearful times*.

7 **a fugitivis**: *from runaway slaves*. Rome's economy relied very heavily on the use of slaves, and the slave population became so large that fear of an insurrection was never far from the forefront of Roman minds. In 73 BC, Verres' first year as governor in Sicily, the gladiator Spartacus had started an armed uprising of slaves and gladiators in the south of Italy; it was so serious that it took two years and the armies of Rome's top two generals, Crassus and Pompey, to put it down. There was also a fear that the revolt would extend to the slaves in Sicily where there had been two previous uprisings (135 BC and 103 BC), both of which had lasted between two and three years. In some respects, a revolt in Sicily was more serious than one in Italy because of the threat to Rome's vital corn supplies. Proving that Verres had, in fact, prevented a slave revolt would provide a strong defence of Verres' governorship.

9 **quid agam?**: *What am I to do?* (cf. **quo conferam?** and **quo vertam?**) (For Deliberative Questions, see LL p. 38.)

# 6. *Verres the General*

(In Verrem II.v. 1-4, 25-32)

*I know that you are convinced that Verres is guilty. However, I rather think that Hortensius, in order to persuade you to acquit him, will now resort to the tactic of painting a glowing picture of Verres' military achievements.*

nemini video dubium esse, iudices, quin apertissime C.Verres in Sicilia sacra profanaque omnia et privatim et publice spoliarit, versatusque sit sine ulla non modo religione verum etiam dissimulatione in omni genere furandi atque praedandi. sed quaedam mihi magnifica et praeclara eius defensio ostenditur; cui quemadmodum resistam multo mihi ante est, iudices, providendum. ita enim causa constituitur, provinciam Siciliam virtute istius et vigilantia singulari dubiis formidolosisque temporibus a fugitivis atque a belli periculis tutam esse servatam.

quid agam, iudices? quo accusationis meae rationem conferam? quo

**iudices, -um** (*m.pl*), members of the jury
**aperte**, openly
**non modo ... verum etiam ...**, not only ... but also ...
**dissimulatio, -onis** (*f*), pretence, attempt at concealment
**genus, -eris** (*n*), kind, type, category
**furor** (1), to steal
**praedor** (1), to plunder
**defensio, -onis** (*f*), defence
**virtus, -utis** (*f*), courage, valour, ability
**vigilantia, -ae** (*f*), vigilance, alertness, watchfulness
**singularis, -is, -e**, exceptional
**tutus, -a, -um**, safe
**servo** (1), to keep, preserve
**quo?**, where (to)?
**ratio, -onis** (*f*), method, line, argument
**confero, -ferre**, to direct

10 **quasi murus quidam**: *like a (defensive) wall.* (For Simile, see CAO on page 235.)

10 **boni nomen imperatoris**: *his reputation as a good general*, literally *the title of good general.* Cicero implies that the description of Verres as **bonus imperator** is an invention of Hortensius.

11 **novi locum**: *I know the script* (literally *place*), i.e. the kind of argument Hortensius, the defence counsel, is going to use. Students in a school of rhetoric had to learn stock expressions and themes, sometimes even whole speeches. They were also taught techniques for developing these in a formal speech.

11 **se iactaturus sit**: *will wax eloquent*, literally *will throw himself around.* Hortensius had a reputation for holding the jury's attention by means of grand gestures and the dramatic way in which he presented his case.

12 **tempora rei publicae**: *the (critical) times for the state.* At the time when Verres was governor of Sicily (73-72 BC), Rome's military resources were considerably stretched. In Spain, Sertorius, one of the Marian faction who had fled from Rome after being proscribed by Sulla (see p.1), successfully resisted several Roman armies for nine years until he was murdered in 72 BC; in the east, the third war against Mithridates broke out in 74 BC and also lasted nine years; the uprising of the slaves and gladiators under Spartacus began in 73 BC and lasted until 71 BC. Meanwhile, pirates were taking advantage of Rome's weakness, not only to attack vital shipping but even to make raids on the Italian coast near Rome.

13 **tum ... tum ...**: Repeating **tum** produces a much more powerful effect than would the use of a connective such as **atque**. (For Anaphora, see CAO on page 238. Compare the repetition of **ne** in lines 14-15.)

13 **pro suo iure**: *as of right.* Hortensius was consul-elect and therefore felt entitled to make such an authoritative demand, since one of the main tasks of the consuls was to see that the state came to no harm.

14 **ne patiamini**: *that you should not allow*, an Indirect Command (see LL p. 41).

14 **Siculorum testimoniis**: *by the evidence of Sicilians.* **testimoniis** is plural, since the Sicilian communities all brought different examples of the crimes that Verres had committed. Note the powerful effect of placing **Romano** and **Siculorum** side by side.

15 **ne obteri velitis**: *that you should not consent to* (literally *wish*) *being destroyed.*

17 **non possum dissimulare**: *I must be honest with you*, literally *I cannot pretend (that something is not the case)*. (cf. **dissimulatione** in line 3.)

18 **eximiam virtutem**: *outstanding ability.* Cicero is being sarcastic.

18 **venit mihi in mentem**: *I remember*, literally *it comes into my mind.*

19 **M'.Aquilii**: As consul in 101 BC, Manius Aquilius had put down the slave uprising in Sicily which had begun in 103 BC (see note on line 7). At the end of his consulship, he stayed on as proconsular governor of Sicily. On his return to Rome, he was accused of extortion. (Note that **M'**. is the abbreviation for **Manius.**)

19 **quantum auctoritatis, quantum momenti**: *how influential, how decisive*, literally *how much influence, how much weight.* (For Partitive Genitive, see LL p. 9.) Note again the use of Anaphora (cf. line 13).

21 **causa prope perorata**: *when he was nearing the end of his closing speech*, literally *the case having been almost completely spoken.* (For Ablative Absolute, see LL p. 30.) The peroration is the concluding part of a speech.

24 **adverso corpore**: *on the front of his body.* This showed he had received the wounds while facing up to the enemy, not running away.

me vertam? ad omnes enim meos impetus quasi murus quidam boni nomen imperatoris opponitur. novi locum; video ubi se iactaturus sit Hortensius. belli pericula, tempora rei publicae, imperatorum penuriam commemorabit. tum deprecabitur a vobis, tum etiam pro suo iure contendet ne patiamini talem imperatorem populo Romano Siculorum testimoniis eripi, ne obteri laudem imperatoriam criminibus avaritiae velitis.

The orator Marcus Antonius successfully employed the same tactic in the trial of Manius Aquilius. By displaying the wounds which Aquilius had received in defence of his country, he convinced the jury that they should not condemn him.

non possum dissimulare, iudices. timeo ne C.Verres propter hanc eximiam virtutem in re militari omnia quae fecit impune fecerit. venit enim mihi in mentem in iudicio M'.Aquilii quantum auctoritatis, quantum momenti oratio M.Antonii habuisse existimata sit; qui, ut erat in dicendo non solum sapiens sed etiam fortis, causa prope perorata ipse arripuit M'.Aquilium constituitque in conspectu omnium, tunicamque eius ab pectore abscidit ut cicatrices populus Romanus iudicesque aspicerent adverso corpore acceptas. simul et de illo vulnere quod ille in

**me verto**, I turn (intransitive)
**impetus, -us** (*m*), attack
**oppono** (3), to oppose, set against, put up as a defence
**penuria, -ae** (*f*), scarcity, shortage
**commemoro** (1), to mention, remind (of)
**deprecor** (1) (**a** + abl.), to beg, implore
**contendo** (3), to demand, insist
**eripio** (3) (+ dat.), **-ripui**, to snatch (from)
**laus, laudis** (*f*), reputation, record
**crimen, -inis** (*n*), accusation, charge
**avaritia, -ae** (*f*), avarice, greed
**propter** (+ acc.), because of
**impune**, without punishment, with impunity
**iudicium, -i** (*n*), trial
**existimo** (1), to think, consider
**ut**, as, insofar as
**sapiens, -entis**, wise, shrewd
**fortis, -is, -e**, forceful, vigorous, powerful
**arripio** (3), **-ripui**, to seize, take hold of
**constituo** (3), **-ui**, to place, make to stand
**conspectus, -us** (*m*), view, sight
**pectus, -oris** (*n*), chest
**abscindo** (3), **-scidi**, to tear away, rip off
**cicatrix, -icis** (*f*), scar
**aspicio** (3), **-spexi**, to see, view, gaze at
**simul**, at the same time
**vulnus, -eris** (*n*), wound

25 **ab hostium duce**: This refers to the slave leader whom Aquilius killed in battle.

25 **eo adduxit ... ut**: *he worked ... up into such a state that.*

26 **vehementer ut vererentur ne**: *that they were absolutely terrified that*, literally *that they vehemently feared that.* (For Fearing clauses, see LL p. 49.) **vehementer** has been placed outside its clause to give it even greater emphasis. Note also the effect of the **v-** sounds, often used by Cicero to describe emotionally charged situations. (For Alliteration, see CAO on page 235.) If you use the Overview technique (see pages viii-x of this book and LL pp. 121-31), you will see that the verb of the **ne** clause is **videretur** in line 28.

26 **quem virum ... , hic**: *the man whom.* When a relative clause is subordinate in importance, it usually follows its antecedent. When, as here, the information it contains is as important as that in the main clause, Latin authors tend to put the relative clause in front of the antecedent, and any noun which would normally have been the antecedent (here, **vir**) is attracted into the relative clause (here, **quem virum**). (See LL p. 26.)

27 **ad laudem**: *for the praise.*

29 **ab illis**: *by my opponents*, literally *by those men over there.*

29 **ratio viaque**: *style and line*, literally *method and way.*

29 **idem quaeritur**: *(and) they are aiming at the same result*, literally *the same thing is being sought.* (For Asyndeton, see CAO on page 238.)

30 **sit fur**: *he may be a thief.* (For this use of the subjunctive, see LL p. 107.) The opposition may argue that, even if all the accusations were true, nevertheless (**at**) all of that would be outweighed by the importance of Verres' success as a general. Note the repetition of **sit** and how this is countered by repeating **at** in line 31. (For Anaphora, see CAO on page 238.)

31 **felix**: *lucky*, i.e. someone whom the gods had clearly marked out to be successful — an important quality in a general, as far as the Romans were concerned.

32 **reservandus**: *(a man who) must be preserved.* (For this use of the Gerundive, see LL p. 61.)

33 **cupio mihi ab illo subici**: *I hope he* (Verres) *will prompt me*, literally *I wish that there be supplied to me by him.* **subici** is present infinitive passive.

34 **si quid forte praetereo**: *if I happen to omit anything*, literally *if by chance I pass anything by.*

35 **quae quidem**: *(all those) at least which.* The clause limits the extent of **omnibus**.

35 **belli fugitivorum suspicionem**: *his claim that there was going to be a slave revolt*, literally *the suspicion of a war of runaway slaves.* By using the word **suspicionem**, Cicero ignores the fact that there had been a real threat of a slave war in Sicily during Verres' praetorship (see lines 7-8) and sarcastically suggests that Hortensius and Verres are making the whole thing up. Cicero's audience, however, would be well aware that Spartacus' revolt had been quashed only the year before this trial.

36 **nihil** is the direct object of **praetermisi**.

36 **habetis hominis consilia**: *you know* (literally *have*) *the fellow's planning ability.* Note the derisory use of the noun **homo**, instead of **vir**.

37 **summa illuc pertinet ut sciatis**: *the main thing is that you should know*, literally *the most important thing relates to this (point)* (**illuc = ad illud**) *that you should know.* The noun **summa** (from which the English word 'sum' is derived) is very close in meaning to the modern expression 'the bottom line'. When adding up numbers, the Romans wrote the total, not at the bottom as we do, but at the top (the highest line).

capite ab hostium duce acceperat multa dixit, eoque adduxit eos qui erant iudicaturi vehementer ut vererentur ne, quem virum fortuna ex hostium telis eripuisset cum sibi ipsi non pepercisset, hic non ad populi Romani laudem sed ad iudicum crudelitatem videretur esse servatus.

eadem nunc ab illis defensionis ratio viaque temptatur, idem quaeritur. sit fur, sit sacrilegus, sit flagitiorum omnium vitiorumque princeps; at est bonus imperator, at felix et ad dubia rei publicae tempora reservandus.

Cicero goes on to maintain that such an argument is, strictly speaking, irrelevant; but, to give Verres the benefit of the doubt, he examines in the next long section of the speech Verres' claims to military fame and, by means of ridicule, demolishes them one by one.

*Having demonstrated the kind of general Verres certainly was not, Cicero says he will now turn to a description of the kind he actually was.*

cupio mihi ab illo, iudices, subici, quoniam de militari eius gloria dico, si quid forte praetereo. nam mihi videor iam de omnibus rebus eius gestis dixisse, quae quidem ad belli fugitivorum suspicionem pertinerent; certe nihil sciens praetermisi. habetis hominis consilia, diligentiam, vigilantiam, custodiam defensionemque provinciae. summa illuc pertinet ut sciatis

**iudico** (1), to judge, pass judgement, decide the verdict
**telum, -i** (*n*), weapon
**parco** (3), **peperci** (+ dat.), to spare
**crudelitas, -atis** (*f*), cruelty, harsh treatment
**tempto** (1), to try
**sacrilegus, -i** (*m*), someone who commits sacrilege, temple-robber
**flagitium, -i** (*n*), shameful act
**vitium, -i** (*n*), vice
**princeps, -ipis** (*m*), instigator, ring-leader
**dubius, -a,** -um, uncertain, critical
**quoniam**, since
**res gestae** (*f.pl*), achievements
**pertineo** (2) (**ad** + acc.), to be concerned with, relate to
**certe**, certainly
**sciens, scientis**, knowingly, consciously
**praetermitto** (3), **-misi**, to pass by, omit, gloss over
**diligentia, -ae** (*f*), thoroughness, meticulous attention to detail
**custodia, -ae** (*f*), guardianship

38 **ne qui**: *so that no one*, literally *lest anyone*.

39 **talem**: *of such quality* — another example of sarcasm (see CAO on page 231).

41 **itinerum laborem**: *(as to) the exertion involved in travelling*, literally *the exertion of journeys*. The size and mountainous nature of Sicily and the remoteness of some of its communities would make this task quite onerous. Although **laborem** is the direct object of **reddiderit**, which appears at the end of the sentence, Cicero has placed it at the head of the sentence to highlight Verres' avoidance of exertion.

41 **primum**: *first of all*. This is an adverb, not an adjective agreeing with **laborem**.

41 **in re militari**: *in the exercise of military duties*. Some provinces had a higher military significance than others, and Sicily was one such province because of the importance of the grain supply.

42 **iste**: *the accused*. (cf. line 7.)

43 **ratione consilioque**: *by calculated planning*, literally *by thinking and planning*. (For Hendiadys, see CAO on page 234.)

44 **temporibus hibernis**: *in winter*, literally *in wintry times*.

44 **ad magnitudinem frigorum**: *against the severity of cold spells*. Note how Cicero uses **et** to link this phrase to the phrase **tempestatum vim ac fluminum**, in which **ac** links the two nouns in the genitive case.

46 **compararat = comparaverat**: *he had provided*.

46 **cuius hic situs atque haec natura esse loci caelique dicitur ut**: *whose location, setting and climate are said to be such that*, literally *of which this is said to be the situation and this (is said to be) the nature of the place and the sky so that* ... The adjectives **hic** and **haec**, when followed by **ut**, have the same force as **talis** (*such that*). The phrase **natura loci** is more specific than **situs** which refers to the area in general.

47 **nullus umquam dies tam magna ac turbulenta tempestate fuerit**: *no day was ever so wild and stormy*, literally *no day was ever with so great and turbulent weather*. (For Ablative of Description, see LL p. 15.)

48 **quin**: *that ... not*. (See LL p. 105.)

49 **iste bonus imperator**: A highly sarcastic description (see CAO on page 231). (cf. lines 10-11.)

50 **eum non facile quisquam videret**: *it was not easy for anyone to see him*, literally *anyone did not easily see him*.

50 **sed ne ... quidem**: *let alone*, literally *but not even*. Note the deliberate play on the rhyming sound of **extra tectum ... extra lectum**. To the Roman, **lectus** could mean either *a bed* to sleep on or *a couch* in the dining room.

53 **cum coeperat**: *whenever (it) began*. The Frequentative Pluperfect Indicative (see LL p. 89) is used to make it clear that this happened more than once.

53 **cuius**: *its*. This Linking Relative (see LL p. 26) introduces an aside in which Cicero pours more scorn on Verres.

53 **cuius initium iste non a Favonio notabat**: *he did not mark its beginning from (the arrival of) the west wind*. Favonius, the west wind (often called Zephyr), brought milder weather (as its derivation from **favere**, *to favour* suggests) — a sure sign that winter was on its way out. (For **iste**, compare line 7.)

(quoniam plura genera sunt imperatorum) ex quo genere iste sit, ne qui diutius in tanta penuria virorum fortium talem imperatorem ignorare possit.

*Governors normally have to spend a great deal of time travelling round their provinces, and this is particularly necessary in Sicily. Verres, however, went to tremendous lengths to ensure that even in winter he had all his home comforts.*

itinerum primum laborem, qui vel maximus est in re militari, iudices, et in Sicilia maxime necessarius, accipite quam facilem sibi iste et iucundum ratione consilioque reddiderit.

primum temporibus hibernis ad magnitudinem frigorum et tempestatum vim ac fluminum praeclarum hoc sibi remedium compararat. urbem Syracusas elegerat, cuius hic situs atque haec natura esse loci caelique dicitur ut nullus umquam dies tam magna ac turbulenta tempestate fuerit quin aliquo tempore eius diei solem homines viderint. hic ita vivebat iste bonus imperator hibernis mensibus ut eum non facile non modo extra tectum sed ne extra lectum quidem quisquam videret. ita diei brevitas conviviis, noctis longitudo stupris et flagitiis continebatur.

*When spring came, he certainly did begin to move about the province, but was it on horseback? No, he was carried everywhere in a litter and took to his bed as soon as he reached his destination. There he held court and issued his decrees, but only briefly, for he did not wish to interrupt for too long his love-making and drinking.*

cum autem ver esse coeperat (cuius initium iste non a Favonio neque ab

**plures, plura**, several
**genus, -eris** (*n*), type, kind
**diutius**, (any) longer
**ignoro** (1), to be unaware of, disregard
**vel**, certainly
**accipio** (3), to hear, learn
**quam**, how
**iucundus, -a, -um**, pleasant, agreeable
**reddo** (3), **-didi**, to render, make
**tempestas, -atis** (*f*), storm
**vis, vim** (acc.), **vi** (abl.), force, violence
**flumen, -inis** (*n*), river, river in spate
**praeclarus, -a, -um**, splendid, admirable
**remedium, -i** (*n*), remedy, solution
**eligo** (3), **elegi**, to choose
**aliqui, -qua, -quod**, some
**sol, solis** (*m*), sun
**vivo** (3), to live
**mensis, -is** (*m*), month
**extra** (+ acc.), outside
**tectum, -i** (*n*), house, dwelling, abode
**brevitas, -atis** (*f*), shortness
**convivium, -i** (*n*), banquet, feasting
**stuprum, -i** (*n*), debauchery, lewd act
**contineo** (2) (+ abl.), to spend (in)
**autem**, but, however, moreover
**ver, veris** (*n*), spring

54 **cum rosam viderat, tum ...** : *it was only when he saw a rose that he ...*, literally *whenever he saw a rose, then ...* The addition of **tum** to the Frequentative use of **cum** (see LL p. 89) stresses that *it was then, and only then (that) ...* The earlier part of the sentence makes it clear that we must not assume that Verres even went outside to see the roses in bloom. Cicero would not need to tell his audience that fashionable Romans frequently arranged for rose-petals to be strewn at their lavish banquets.

55 **labori atque itineribus**: *to the hardship of travel*, literally *to hardship and travels*. (For Hendiadys, see CAO on page 234.)

55 **eo usque patientem**: *so hardy*, literally *capable of enduring to such a degree.*

57 **viderit**: The perfect subjunctive is used to emphasise that this didn't happen even once.

57 **Bithyniae regibus**: By and large, the Romans despised the self-indulgence of rulers in the eastern part of the Roman world. Litters were the only form of transport permitted in Rome itself, and they were used mainly by ladies of rank, elderly people and foppish men. The governor of a province would be expected to present a manly image and not to use such an effeminate form of transport.

57 **lectica octaphoro**: *in a litter carried by eight bearers.*

58 **pulvinus perlucidus Melitensis**: *a cushion covered with very fine Maltese linen*, literally *a transparent Maltese cushion*. Malta was famed for its linen which was so fine that light could shine through it (hence **perlucidus**).

59 **coronam**: *garland*. Garlands were commonly worn round the head at banquets; but, to wear one also round the neck, especially on a journey, was foppish in the extreme.

59 **reticulum tenuissimo lino, minutis maculis**: *a sachet of the finest thread, with tiny meshes*. (For Ablative of Description, see LL p. 15.) The fineness of the material allowed the scent of the rose petals to pass through. Cicero ridicules this as affectation, but it may have been used like a nosegay to counter obnoxious odours.

61 **venerat**: For Frequentative **cum**, see LL p. 89 and compare lines 53 and 54.

62 **usque in cubiculum**: *right into his bedroom*. **usque in** indicates even farther than **usque ad** would have indicated. Cicero piles on the ridicule.

63 **equites**: *knights*. These were businessmen and financiers who, though not of noble rank, through their wealth wielded enormous influence in the running of the state. The imperfect (**veniebant**) indicates that this was the regular practice, and Cicero reinforces the point by repeating the verb.

63 **id quod**: *as*, literally *that thing which.*

64 **secreto deferebantur**: *were submitted* (literally *were brought in*) *secretly*, making it easy for informers to lay false information and make unsubstantiated accusations.

64 **palam auferebantur**: *were openly carried away*. This verb often means *to carry off spoils* or *steal*. This, together with the fact that the hearing was held in secret, gives a strong hint of corruption. Cicero implies that the verdict went to the highest bidder.

65 **pretio, non aequitate iura discripserat**: *he had dispensed justice according to how big a bribe he had received rather than with impartiality*, literally *he had interpreted the laws by price, not by justice*. The verb **discribere** means literally *to divide* or *apportion*. (For Frequentative clauses, see LL pp. 52 and 89.)

66 **Veneri et Libero**: *to love-making and drinking*. Venus was the goddess of love, and Liber (otherwise known as Bacchus) was the god of wine. Names of gods and goddesses were frequently used to indicate the sphere with which they were concerned, e.g. Mars for war, Neptune for the sea.

66 **deberi**: *ought to be devoted*, literally *was owed.*

aliquo astro notabat; sed, cum rosam viderat, tum incipere ver arbitrabatur), dabat se labori atque itineribus; in quibus eo usque se praebebat patientem atque impigrum ut eum nemo umquam in equo sedentem viderit. nam, ut mos fuit Bithyniae regibus, lectica octaphoro ferebatur, in qua pulvinus erat perlucidus Melitensis rosa fartus. ipse autem coronam habebat unam in capite, alteram in collo, reticulumque ad nares sibi admovebat tenuissimo lino, minutis maculis, plenum rosae.

sic confecto itinere, cum ad aliquod oppidum venerat, eadem lectica usque in cubiculum deferebatur. eo veniebant Siculorum magistratus, veniebant equites Romani, id quod ex multis iuratis audistis; controversiae secreto deferebantur, paulo post palam decreta auferebantur. deinde, ubi paulisper in cubiculo pretio non aequitate iura discripserat, Veneri iam et Libero reliquum tempus deberi arbitrabatur.

**astrum, -i** (*n*), star, constellation
**incipio** (3), to begin
**arbitror** (1), to think, believe
**se praebere** (2), to show oneself
**impiger, -gra, -grum**, energetic
**equus, -i** (*m*), horse
**mos, moris** (*m*), custom, habit
**fartus, -a, -um**, stuffed
**collum, -i** (*n*), neck
**nares, -ium** (*f.pl*), nostrils
**admoveo** (2), to apply (to), hold (to)
**plenus, -a, -um** (+ gen.), full (of)
**conficio** (3), **-feci, -fectum**, to finish, complete
**oppidum, -i** (*n*), town
**iuratus, -i** (*m*), person bound by oath, sworn-witness
**audistis = audivistis**
**controversia, -ae** (*f*), legal dispute
**paulo post**, a little later
**decretum, -i** (*n*), decree, decision
**paulisper**, for a short time

**Slaves carrying a lectica**

67 **quo loco**: *in this connection*, literally *at which point*. (For Linking Relative, see LL p. 26.)

67 **mihi non praetermittenda (esse) videtur**: *I feel I ought to mention*, literally *it seems to me (it) ought not to be passed over by me*. (For Dative of Agent with a Gerundive, see LL p. 62.)

68 **scitote**: *let me assure you*, literally *know* (imperative plural).

68 **oppidum nullum ex iis oppidis**: Note the repetition of **oppidum** to emphasise *not a single one of those towns*.

69 **conventum agere**: *to hold assizes*. Instead of bringing all the cases to one central court in the most important city, the governor (**praetor**), like our judges and sheriffs, periodically heard cases in towns that were nearer the people involved in the case.

69 **quo in oppido**: *in which*, referring back to **nullum ex iis oppidis**, which is separated from the relative clause by so many words that the audience may have lost the thread of the sentence. In such a situation, orators frequently repeat the antecedent in the relative clause. We ourselves commonly do this when giving complicated descriptions in conversation.

70 **non isti delecta ad libidinem mulier esset**: *a woman had not been selected for him to gratify* (literally *for*) *his lust*. **ad** expresses Purpose.

70 **non ignobili**: *highly respectable*, literally *not of lowly birth*. Stating it negatively makes the expression much stronger. (For Litotes, see CAO on page 235.)

71 **ex eo numero**: *of them*, literally *from that number*.

72 **palam**: Note the emphatic position of **palam**. By Cicero's time, it was quite respectable for the mistress of the house to take dinner along with her husband's guests. However, being the only female present (for the guests would not bring their wives to the meal), she would sit while the rest of the company reclined, and she would withdraw before the heavy drinking began. It would be considered quite disgraceful therefore for Verres to invite female friends to dinner, especially to the riotous sort of party which Cicero goes on to describe.

72 **si quae castiores erant**: *those who were less brazen*, literally *if any were purer*.

73 **non illo silentio praetorum**: *not characterised by the quiet dignity (expected) of governors*, literally *not with that well-known silence of governors*. (For Ablative of Description, see LL p. 15.) Note this special use of **ille** meaning, according to context, *the famous*, *the well-known*, *the notorious*.

74 **populi Romani** has to be taken with both **praetorum** and **imperatorum**.

75 **cum**: *amidst*, literally *with*.

77 **vocabatur**: *would come*, literally *was called*.

77 **qui** is concessive. Translate *although he*.

78 **illis legibus quae in poculis ponebantur**: *the rules of drinking parties*, literally *those laws which were placed in drinking*. (**poculum** is both the *drinking-cup* and the *drink* that is in it.) One of the guests was normally chosen as **magister** (or **arbiter) bibendi**, and it was he who decided the list of toasts to be drunk and the proportion of water to wine for the drinking-party. It was thought barbarous and harmful to drink unmixed wine, dilution being normally three measures of water to, at most, two of wine.

79 **erant exitus eius modi ut**: *the banquets usually ended up in such a way that*, literally *the outcomes were of such a kind that*. The force of **ut** continues to **iacerent** in line 81.

79 **inter manus auferretur**: *was carried away in the arms (of the other guests)*.

*Verres was punctilious about certain things: he always made sure that he had plenty of female companions, even at his dinner-parties, which were usually riotous affairs where the guests often came to blows. After some dinners the dining-room was like a battlefield.*

quo loco mihi non praetermittenda videtur praeclari imperatoris egregia ac singularis diligentia. nam scitote oppidum esse in Sicilia nullum ex iis oppidis in quibus consistere praetores et conventum agere soleant, quo in oppido non isti ex aliqua familia non ignobili delecta ad libidinem mulier esset. itaque non nullae ex eo numero in convivium adhibebantur palam. si quae castiores erant, ad tempus veniebant, lucem conventumque vitabant. erant autem convivia non illo silentio praetorum populi Romani atque imperatorum, neque eo pudore qui in magistratuum conviviis versari solet, sed cum maximo clamore atque convicio; non numquam etiam res ad pugnam atque ad manus vocabatur. iste enim praetor severus ac diligens, qui populi Romani legibus numquam paruisset, illis legibus quae in poculis ponebantur diligenter obtemperabat. itaque erant exitus eius modi ut alius inter manus

**egregius, -a, -um**, exceptional
**consisto** (3), to halt, stay
**deligo** (3), **-legi, -lectum**, to select, choose
**non nullus, -a, -um**, some
**adhibeo** (2), to invite
**ad tempus**, at an appointed hour, by appointment
**lux, lucis** (*f*), light, (broad) daylight
**conventus, -us** (*m*), assembled company, crowd
**vito** (1), to avoid
**autem**, moreover
**pudor, -oris** (*m*), decorum, propriety, modesty
**versor** (1), to exist, be found
**convicium, -i** (*n*), wrangling, abusive language
**non numquam**, sometimes
**pugna, -ae** (*f*), battle, fighting
**manus, -us** (*f*), hand, blow
**severus, -a, -um**, strict
**diligens, -entis**, punctilious
**pareo** (2) (+ dat.), to obey
**obtempero** (1) (+ dat.), to obey
**alius ... alius ...**, one ... another ...

80 **tamquam occisus**: *for dead*, literally *as if slain*. This phrase is paralleled by **ut fusi**, *sprawling* in line 81.

82 **Cannensem pugnam nequitiae**: *a veritable Cannae of debauchery*. At the battle of Cannae (216 BC) the Roman army was almost annihilated by Hannibal. In lines 77-83, Cicero uses the metaphor of battle to sneer at Verres. What a glorious commander to have lost all his troops in the battlefield of the dining-room! (For Metaphor, see CAO on page 235.)

83 **arbitraretur**: *would have thought*. (For Potential Subjunctive, see LL p. 108.)

84 **cum vero aestas summa esse coeperat**: *but when it was the height of summer*, literally *but whenever the highest (point of) summer began to be*. (For Frequentative clauses, see LL pp. 52 and 89.)

84 **quod tempus**: *the time which*, literally *which time*. (For the attraction of the antecedent into the relative clause, compare line 26; and see LL p. 26.)

85 **consuerunt**: Although the 1st person singular of the perfect tense is **consuevi**, the contracted form **consuerunt** is normally used for the third person plural.

86 **tum obeundam esse maxime provinciam**: *that this is the best time to inspect the province*, literally *that then, most of all, the province requires to be gone round*.

86 **frumenta**: *heaps of grain*, as against corn standing in the fields. The quantity of the grain would be obvious when it was lying on the threshing-floor.

87 **quod**: For emphasis, Cicero repeats the **quod** of line 85.

87 **et ... et ... et ...** : The repetition of **et** tells us that these three statements about the slaves should be taken closely together, whereas the clauses beginning **frumenti** and **tempus** give two other reasons (not connected with the slaves) why governors tour the province at this time of year.

87 **familiae**: *the (complete) households (of slaves)*. The noun **familia** includes not only the master and his family but also all the slaves who served them. In rural districts, slaves would be widely scattered for most of the year and so would present little danger. However, when they brought in the harvest for threshing, there was a danger that they might be encouraged by their large numbers to start a revolt. It was therefore important for the governor to be seen touring the province, to remind the slaves of Rome's power and leave them in no doubt about what would happen if they did revolt.

88 **labor operis maxime offendit**: *the hard work involved in* (literally *of*) *the operation is most irksome (to the slaves)*.

89 **iste novo quodam genere imperator**: *this newfangled sort of general*, literally *this general of a certain new kind*. (For Ablative of Description, see LL p. 15.) The indefinite adjective **quodam** is used to impart an ironical tone. (For Sarcasm and Irony, see CAO p. 231).

90 **stativa castra**: *a permanent camp*. An army on the move built a new camp every night. Permanent camps were established only in areas that had been completely pacified, or where the army dug in for the winter.

91 **in ipso aditu atque ore**: *right at the very entrance*, literally *in the very entrance and mouth*.

91 **ubi primum ex alto sinus ab litore ad urbem inflectitur**: *where the bay begins to curve in from the open sea along the shore-line towards the city*, literally *where the bay from the open sea first bends from the shore to the city*. The passive form **inflectitur** is used since the verb has an intransitive meaning.

92 **tabernacula carbaseis intenta velis**: *canvas marquees*, literally *tents stretched with linen awnings*.

e convivio tamquam e proelio auferretur, alius tamquam occisus relinqueretur, plerique ut fusi sine mente ac sine ullo sensu iacerent, ut quivis, cum aspexisset, non se praetoris convivium sed Cannensem pugnam nequitiae videre arbitraretur.

*At the height of summer, governors in Sicily normally carry out a thorough inspection of the province. Not so Verres. His practice was to set up permanent camp in one of the most pleasant parts of Syracuse. The only people admitted were his lecherous male and female friends — and this was the environment in which his teenage son was brought up! His favourite female companion was Tertia; but the other 'ladies' resented her because she was not in their social class! The townsfolk were delighted by his absence because it gave them a respite from his criminal acts.*

cum vero aestas summa esse coeperat, quod tempus omnes Siciliae semper praetores in itineribus consumere consuerunt, propterea quod tum putant obeundam esse maxime provinciam cum in areis frumenta sunt, quod et familiae congregantur et magnitudo servitii perspicitur et labor operis maxime offendit, frumenti copia commonet, tempus anni non impedit: tum, inquam, cum concursant ceteri praetores, iste novo quodam genere imperator pulcherrimo Syracusarum loco stativa sibi castra faciebat. nam in ipso aditu atque ore portus, ubi primum ex alto sinus ab litore ad urbem inflectitur, tabernacula carbaseis intenta velis collocabat.

**proelium, -i** (*n*), battle
**plerique**, most
**mens, mentis** (*f*), mind, sense
**sensus, -us** (*m*), sensation, consciousness
**iaceo** (2), to lie
**quivis**, anyone
**consumo** (3), to spend, occupy
**consuesco** (3), **-suevi**, to become accustomed
**propterea quod**, for the very reason that
**puto** (1), to think
**area, -ae** (*f*), threshing-floor
**congregor** (1), to assemble, gather together
**servitium, -i** (*n*), slave-class, slave body
**perspicio** (3), to see, perceive
**copia, -ae** (*f*), abundance
**commoneo** (2), to impress, invite attention, make an impression
**impedio** (4), to hinder, make difficult
**inquam**, I say, I tell (you)
**concurso** (1), to move about, travel widely
**Syracusae, -arum** (*f.pl*), Syracuse
**ceteri, -ae, -a**, the other, the rest of
**portus, -us** (*m*), harbour
**altum, -i** (*n*), the deep (sea)
**colloco** (1), to place, position, erect

94 **ex illa domo praetoria**: *from that official residence*, literally *from that praetorian* (i.e. governor's) *home*. Hiero, the ruler of Syracuse, had supported the Carthaginians at the start of the First Punic War (264 BC), but he was defeated by the Romans and then besieged in Syracuse. He surrendered to them in 263 BC and became a faithful ally of Rome until his death in 216 BC.

96 **nemini nisi qui**: *only to someone who*, literally *to no one except (someone) who*.

96 **aut socius aut minister**: **socius** refers to a companion who would share in the lewd acts; **minister** is a servant who would assist Verres in the gratification of his lust.

97 **consuerat = consueverat**: *had had a sexual relationship*.

98 **incredibile est quanta multitudo**: *an unbelievably large number*, literally *it is incredible how big a number*.

99 **digni istius amicitia**: *worthy of that creature's friendship*, i.e. men who were equally corrupt and depraved.

100 **adulta aetate filius**: *his grown-up son*. (For Ablative of Description, see LL p. 15.) The son was about 16 at the time.

100 **etiamsi natura a parentis similitudine abriperet**: *even if he were by nature totally different from his father*, literally *even if nature were tearing him from the likeness to his father*.

103 **Tertia illa**: *the notorious Tertia*. (For **illa**, compare line 73.)

103 **perducta per dolum atque insidias**: *abducted by underhand trickery*, literally *brought across through guile and a plot*.

103 **ab Rhodio tibicine**: We have no way of knowing whether this means *from Rhodius the flute-player* or *from her Rhodian flute-player*.

104 **castris**: The word is used sarcastically, mocking Verres' claim to be a great general.

104 **indigne pateretur**: *were indignant (that)*. Although there are two subjects (**uxor Cleomenis** and **uxor Aeschrionis**), the verb is singular, agreeing with the nearer subject, as often happens in Latin.

106 **honesto loco nata**: *a lady of respectable parentage*, literally *born of honourable rank*.

106 **mimi Isidori filiam venisse**: *that the daughter of Isidorus the comic actor had come*. This Accusative and Infinitive depends on **indigne pateretur** in line 104. The word **mimus** was used both of the actor and of the type of play in which he appeared. Though such plays were highly popular, acting was regarded as a disreputable profession in Roman society. Cicero hints at the irony of these ladies thinking they were superior to an actor's daughter simply because they belonged to upper-class families, even though their own characters were far from respectable.

106 **iste Hannibal**: *that Hannibal over there*, (pointing to Verres). Hannibal was probably the greatest general that the Romans had ever faced and, having suffered several serious defeats at his hands, they had the utmost respect for him. It is said that Hannibal believed that the social background of his soldiers was less important than their fighting ability. In likening Verres to Hannibal, Cicero is being highly sarcastic, since the point of comparison is not Verres' ability as a general but the fact that he was more concerned about the services these women rendered him than about their breeding and character.

107 **qui virtute putaret oportere non genere certari**: *since he thought that the rivalry (between individual women) should be settled by merit rather than by social class*, literally *who thought that it ought to be contested by ability not by birth*. (For Causal **qui**, see LL p. 103; for Impersonal verbs see LL pp. 57-8.)

huc ex illa domo praetoria, quae regis Hieronis fuit, sic emigrabat ut eum per illos dies nemo extra illum locum videre posset. in eum autem ipsum locum aditus erat nemini, nisi qui aut socius aut minister libidinis esse posset. huc omnes mulieres quibuscum iste consuerat conveniebant, quarum incredibile est quanta multitudo fuerit Syracusis. huc homines digni istius amicitia, digni vita illa conviviisque veniebant. inter eius modi viros et mulieres adulta aetate filius versabatur ut eum, etiamsi natura a parentis similitudine abriperet, consuetudo tamen ac disciplina patris similem esse cogeret.

huc Tertia illa perducta per dolum atque insidias ab Rhodio tibicine maximas in istius castris effecisse dicitur turbas, cum indigne pateretur uxor Cleomenis Syracusani, nobilis mulier, itemque uxor Aeschrionis, honesto loco nata, in conventum suum mimi Isidori filiam venisse. iste autem Hannibal, qui in suis castris virtute putaret oportere non genere

**huc**, here, to this spot
**emigro** (1), to move house
**aditus, -us** (*m*), access, admittance
**libido, -inis** (*f*), lust, debauchery
**vita, -ae** (*f*), life, life-style
**versor** (1), to move about (among), associate (with), spend time (with)
**consuetudo, -inis** (*f*), background, environment, association
**disciplina, -ae** (*f*), training, upbringing
**similis, -is, -e** (+ gen.), like
**cogo** (3), to compel
**efficio** (3), **-feci**, to produce, cause, create
**turba, -ae** (*f*), disturbance, commotion, scene
**item**, also, likewise
**filia, -ae** (*f*), daughter

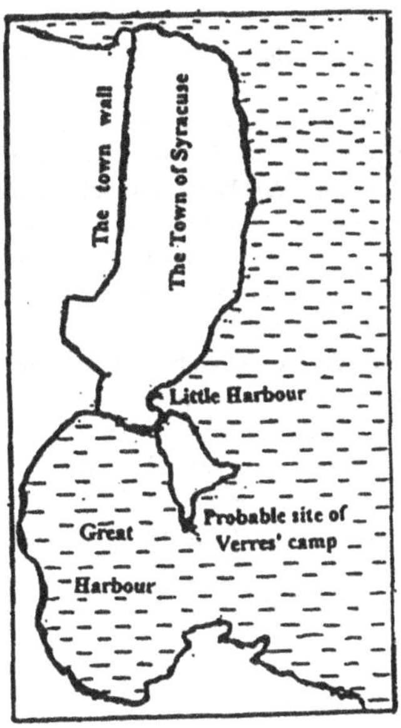


**The Harbours of Syracuse**

108 **deportaret**: *brought home.* This is the verb used to describe what a governor brought home from a province — often things that he had carried off as booty.

109 **cum pallio purpureo talarique tunica**: *wearing* (literally *with*) *a purple cloak and a tunic down to his ankles.* This was the sort of clothing worn by Greeks, and most Romans regarded it as somewhat effeminate. They were certainly not the sort of garments in which a Roman governor should be seen.

111 **moleste ferebant**: *were annoyed,* i.e. basically the same meaning as **offendebantur**. Note how Cicero again uses two similar expressions to emphasise the point he is making. (For Paired Words, see CAO on page 236.) Three Accusative and Infinitive clauses depend on these verbs.

111 **non ius dici, non iudicia fieri**: *that no legal decisions were being made, no trials taking place.* The magistrate had first to pass judgement on whether or not a trial should take place. (For Anaphora and Asyndeton, see CAO on page 238.)

112 **locum illum litoris percrepare**: *that that part of the shore resounded* — an Accusative and Infinitive clause depending on **non ferebant moleste** in line 113.

112 **cantu symphoniae**: *with the sound of music.* The noun **cantus** can refer to either vocal or instrumental music. Musical entertainment was common in fashionable circles.

113 **silentium esse summum causarum atque iuris**: *(while) there was absolutely no sound of (men) pleading cases or of (a judge) giving a verdict,* literally *that there was the utmost silence of cases and decision(s).* Just as he did in lines 111-12, Cicero omits the connective between the two Accusative and Infinitive clauses (lines 112-13), this time to draw a sharp contrast between them. In effect, he cleverly makes the same point three times in lines 111-14.

116 **hunc tu imperatorem esse defendis?**: *Is your defence that this man is a (real) general?* This sort of question depends very much on the intonation of the voice — probably with the emphasis on **hunc** and **imperatorem** to suggest incredulity. Note also the effects produced by the large number of words in the next few lines in which the '**c**' sound is prominent, and also how Cicero spits out his contempt through the frequent use of the letter '**s**'. (For **congeries verborum** in lines 116-17, see CAO on page 237.)

118 **hic scilicet est metuendum**: *at this point, no doubt, we must dread,* literally *here, of course, it must be feared.* (For the Gerundive used impersonally, see LL p. 62; for Fearing clauses, see LL p. 49.) Cicero is about to use more sarcasm.

119 **vetus illa Antoniana dicendi ratio atque auctoritas**: *that old lawyer's tactic originated by Antonius,* literally *that old method of speaking and invention of Antonius.* For the background to this statement, see lines 18-28.

120 **ne excitetur Verres**: *that Verres will be made to stand up* (literally *be roused*). This is another Fearing clause depending on **est metuendum**. (Compare **ne denudetur** and **ne cicatrices ...**) The repetition of **ne** is for dramatic effect. (For Anaphora, see CAO on page 238.)

120 **ne denudetur a pectore**: *that his chest will be laid bare,* literally *that he will be stripped from his chest.* (For Anaphora, see CAO on page 238.)

121 **ex mulierum morsu**: *left by* (literally *from*) *the love-bites of women.* The stinging sarcasm of this anti-climax is brilliantly done. The only battle-scars that Verres has to show are those he received while grappling with women in his bed.

certari, sic hanc Tertiam dilexit ut eam secum ex provincia deportaret.

ac per eos dies, cum iste cum pallio purpureo talarique tunica versaretur in conviviis muliebribus, non offendebantur homines neque moleste ferebant abesse a foro magistratum, non ius dici, non iudicia fieri. locum illum litoris percrepare totum mulierum vocibus cantuque symphoniae, in foro silentium esse summum causarum atque iuris, non ferebant homines moleste. non enim ius abesse videbatur a foro neque iudicia, sed vis et crudelitas et bonorum acerba et indigna direptio.

*Cicero challenges Hortensius to persist in his claim that Verres is a great general. If he does, there is much more that Cicero can reveal about Verres' shady military activities.*

hunc tu igitur imperatorem esse defendis, Hortensi? huius furta, rapinas, cupiditatem, crudelitatem, superbiam, scelus, audaciam, rerum gestarum magnitudine atque imperatoriis laudibus tegere conaris? hic scilicet est metuendum ne ad exitum defensionis tuae vetus illa Antoniana dicendi ratio atque auctoritas proferatur, ne excitetur Verres, ne denudetur a pectore, ne cicatrices populus Romanus aspiciat, ex mulierum morsu vestigia libidinis atque nequitiae.

**diligo** (3), **-lexi**, to love
**muliebris, -is, -e**, attended by women
**offendo** (3), to vex, irritate
**absum, -esse**, to be missing, absent
**fio, fieri**, to happen, take place
**bona, -orum** (*n.pl*), goods, property
**acerbus, -a, -um**, harsh, grievous, cruel
**indignus, -a, -um**, undeserved, unmerited, shameful
**direptio, -onis** (*f*), plundering, seizure
**furtum, -i** (*n*), theft
**rapina, -ae** (*f*), plundering, robbery
**cupiditas, -atis** (*f*), greed, avarice
**superbia, -ae** (*f*), arrogance
**scelus, -eris** (*n*), wickedness
**audacia, -ae** (*f*), boldness, audacity
**imperatorius, -a, -um**, due to a general
**tego** (3), to cover up, gloss over, whitewash
**exitus, -us** (*m*), end, climax
**profero, -ferre**, to bring forward, produce
**cicatrix, -icis** (*f*), scar
**vestigium, -i** (*n*), trace, (tell-tale) sign
**nequitia, -ae** (*f*), debauchery

At this point, Cicero proceeds to recount some of the despicable acts in which Verres indulged, including gambling, adultery and even prostitution. He then describes how meticulously and conscientiously he himself had carried out the duties he had undertaken for the state, and at the same time he contrasts this with the cavalier attitude adopted by Verres. It has to be remembered that this speech was never delivered, since Verres fled the city after the damning indictment of the **actio prima**. It therefore gave Cicero a good opportunity to sing his own praises unchallenged.

## Points for Discussion

1. Comment on the positioning of the following words and phrases: **servatam** (line 8), **servatus** (line 28), and **reservandus** (line 32); **adverso corpore acceptas** (line 24); **princeps** (line 31); **huc** (lines 94, 97, 98, 103) [why not **huc** instead of **in eum ipsum locum** (line 95)?]; **locum** and **totum** (line 112).
2. What, if anything, would be lost if one half of each of the following pairs was omitted?
   **furandi atque praedandi** (line 4), **dubiis formidolosisque** (line 7), **ratione consilioque** (line 43), **stupris et flagitiis** (line 52), **patientem atque impigrum** (line 56), **clamore atque convicio** (line 75), **ad pugnam atque ad manus** (line 76), **severus ac diligens** (line 77), **aditu atque ore** (line 91).
3. Sometimes Cicero uses lists of words without connectives, e.g. **furta, rapinas, cupiditatem, crudelitatem, superbiam, scelus, audaciam** (lines 116-17). What do you think is the purpose of such a list? What effect would it have on you if you were listening in court? How would the effect be altered if all the words were linked by **et, atque** or **-que**?
4. In lines 14-15, what do you think Cicero is implying in the clause **talem imperatorem populo Romano Siculorum testimoniis eripi**?
5. List the evidence produced by Cicero in this passage to disprove the claim that Verres was a good general. What accusations does he bring against Verres? How many of these do you think are relevant?
6. From what you have read in this passage, are you on the whole convinced by Cicero's arguments regarding Verres' ability as a general? Give reasons for your view.

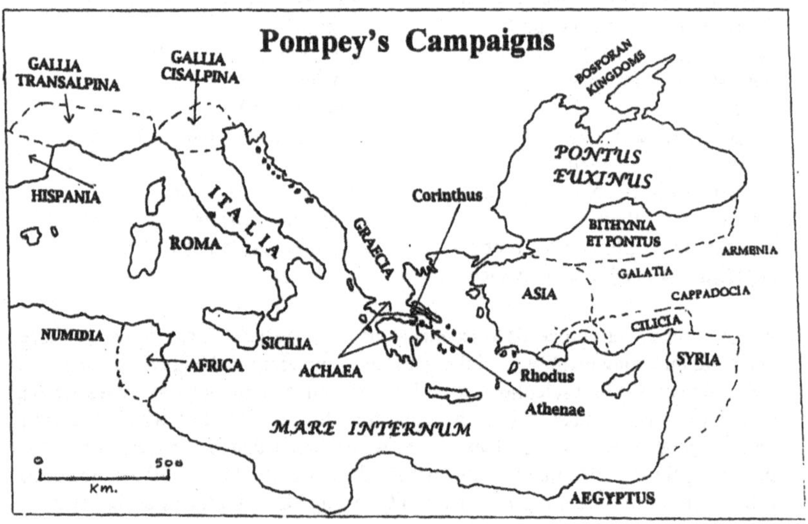

# Pompey and Mithridates

Since 92 BC, Mithridates VI of Pontus had been conducting a continuous campaign of harassment against the Romans. A succession of outstanding generals, including such great figures as Lucius Sulla and Lucius Lucullus, had been sent to deal with him. They had won notable victories over him; but Mithridates himself had always evaded capture and, after each defeat, he would lie low just long enough to repair his shattered fortunes before resuming his attack on Roman interests in the East. The inhabitants of the Roman provinces in Asia Minor, particularly the province of Asia, were happy to support him; for their wealth had made them vulnerable to the greed of the Roman governors and tax-collectors, and Mithridates offered them the opportunity to rid themselves of this tax burden.

Gnaeus Pompeius, born in the same year as Cicero (106 BC), had already gained the reputation of being an outstandingly successful general. The annihilation of the remnants of Marius' supporters in 81 BC, his victory in 77 BC over Marcus Aemilius Lepidus who tried to overthrow the constitution established by Sulla, and his claim to have ended the Slave War in 71 BC had made Pompey an obvious choice when the Romans decided in 67 BC to appoint a supreme commander to eliminate the menace of the pirates who had for many years hampered Roman trade and communications. So strong was the stranglehold which the pirates had over the entire Mediterranean that there was a danger that Rome's corn supply would be entirely cut off, and even Roman armies were at risk if they tried to cross the Mediterranean in summer-time. The pirates actually had the temerity to land on the coast of Italy near Rome itself, burn a fleet in Rome's harbour at Ostia, and kidnap two praetors and their retinues.

Pompey tackled this command with typical vigour and efficiency. Using the massive forces placed at his disposal, he systematically swept the Mediterranean clear of pirates within three months, until they were left with only a few hide-outs on the coast of Asia Minor, and Pompey was steadily driving them out of these as well.

It was at this point (66 BC) that Mithridates chose to launch a new offensive against the Romans in Asia Minor. As Pompey was already in the area and had formidable forces at his disposal, the tribune Manilius proposed a law which would hand over the command against Mithridates to Pompey, whose renown eclipsed that of any other living general.

Cicero had just become praetor, a position which entitled him to address the Assembly of the People. He eagerly grasped this opportunity and delivered a speech in support of Manilius' proposal (**Pro Lege Manilia**), partly to further his own career, but also because he was an ardent admirer of Pompey. This was his first speech from the speakers' platform (**rostra**) in the Forum.

The excerpts in this selection represent approximately a quarter of the speech. The whole speech — his first from the rostra — must have lasted about two hours.

The young Gnaeus Pompeius

1 **illud mihi laetandum esse video**: *I see that I have reason to rejoice over the fact*, literally *I see that that fact should be rejoiced over by me*. (For Dative of Agent with a Gerundive, see LL p. 62.) **illud** is explained in detail by the **quod** clause which follows: *the fact that...*

1 **in hac insolita mihi ratione dicendi**: *in this style of speaking which is unfamiliar to me*. Compare our expression "unaccustomed as I am to public speaking." (For Gerund, see LL p. 60.)

2 **ex hoc loco**: *from this place*. This was Cicero's first political speech from the speakers' platform (**rostra**) in the Forum.

2 **oratio deesse nemini possit**: *no one can fail to be eloquent*, literally *speech can be lacking to no one*. The previous achievements of Pompey provide ample subject-matter.

5 **mihi quaerendus est**: *I must try to find*, literally *must be sought by me*. (For Dative of Agent with a Gerundive, see LL p. 62.) Both **copia** and **modus** are subjects of **quaerendus est**, but the verb agrees with the nearer subject.

5 **non tam copia quam modus**: *not so much a good supply (of subject matter) as a limit (to what I say)*. (For Correlatives, see LL pp. 63-4.)

6 **causa quae sit**: *what the situation is*.

8 **de imperatore deligendo**: For this use of the Gerundive, see LL p. 61.

9 **genus est eius belli quod**: *it is the kind of war which*.

10 **ad persequendi studium**: *with a determination to pursue (it) vigorously*, literally *towards a keenness for pursuing (it)*. (For Gerund, see LL p. 60.)

10 **debeat**: *ought*. (For Generic Subjunctive, see LL p. 103.)

10 **in quo**: For Linking Relative, see LL p. 26.

10 **agitur**: *is at stake*.

11 **cum magna ... tum summa ...**: *not only great ... but supreme ...* The adjectives agree with **quae**. English might create another relative clause, e.g. *and which was*.

# 7. *The Brilliance of Pompey*

(Pro Lege Manilia 3, 6-9, 11-13, 27-9, 31-2, 35-6)

*Cicero congratulates himself on having such an excellent theme for his first speech before the Roman people.*

illud in primis mihi laetandum iure esse video, quod in hac insolita mihi ex hoc loco ratione dicendi causa talis oblata est, in qua oratio deesse nemini possit. dicendum est enim de Cn.Pompei singulari eximiaque virtute; huius autem orationis difficilius est exitum quam principium invenire. ita mihi non tam copia quam modus in dicendo quaerendus est.

The situation in the East is critical. Every day, letters are reaching Rome from businessmen who say that Mithridates and Tigranes, his son-in-law and king of Armenia, have overrun territory neighbouring on the Roman provinces of Asia and Bithynia, thus threatening Rome's tax revenues. They have also destroyed the towns and property of Rome's allies. Previous generals have failed to end this menace, and everyone now realises that there is only one man capable of dealing with it.

*Cicero identifies three main points that have to be considered. Firstly, he describes the nature of the war and lists four ways in which it is having a harmful effect.*

causa quae sit, videtis. nunc, quid agendum sit, considerate! primum mihi videtur de genere belli, deinde de magnitudine, tum de imperatore deligendo esse dicendum.

genus est eius belli quod maxime vestros animos excitare atque inflammare ad persequendi studium debeat: in quo agitur populi Romani gloria quae vobis a maioribus, cum magna in omnibus rebus tum summa

**in primis**, especially
**iure**, rightly
**insolitus, -a, -um**, unusual
**ratio, -onis** (*f*), method, style, type
**causa, -ae** (*f*), cause, case
**offero, offerre, obtuli, oblatum**, to present, offer
**singularis, -is, -e**, remarkable, unique
**eximius, -a, -um**, exceptional
**virtus, -utis** (*f*), ability, merit
**exitus, -us** (*m*), end, conclusion
**principium, -i** (*n*), beginning
**invenio** (4), to find
**ago** (3), **egi**, to do
**considero** (1), to consider, reflect
**genus, -eris** (*n*), nature, kind
**deligo** (3), to choose
**maxime**, most, especially
**animus, -i** (*m*), mind, heart, passion
**excito** (1), to rouse, spur on
**inflammo** (1), to kindle, inflame
**maiores, -um** (*m.pl*), ancestors

12 **sociorum atque amicorum**: *of our allies and friends*. This phrase denotes a relationship between Rome and another state, whereby Rome guaranteed protection to the state concerned, but the state remained autonomous. It was useful to Rome to have these friendly states as buffers between her provinces and the more hostile states beyond.

14 **quibus amissis**: *and if they are lost*, literally *which being lost*. (For Ablative Absolute, see LL p. 30.)

14 **pacis ornamenta**: *the trappings of peace*, i.e. all the things which may not be essential but bring extra comfort.

15 **quibus est a vobis consulendum**: *whose interests you ought to consult* (literally *must be consulted by you*). (For this impersonal use of the Gerundive, see LL p. 62.) When used with the accusative case, **consulere** means *to consult* (i.e. ask advice); when used with the dative case, it means *to consult the interests of.*

16 **et ipsorum causa**: *both for their own sake*, literally *both for the sake of themselves*. Note that **causa** also governs **rei publicae**.

18 **vobis**: *by you*. (For Dative of Agent with a Gerundive, see LL p. 62.)

20 **quod**: *(I refer to the fact) that*, explaining **macula**. The pronoun **is** refers to Mithridates.

21 **una significatione litterarum**: *by a single letter of instruction*, literally *by one notification of a letter*. The use of two nouns (**nuntio** and **significatione**) emphasises the devastating effect of a single written instruction.

22 **necandos trucidandosque denotavit**: *marked down to be murdered and butchered*. (For Gerundives, see LL p. 61.) In 88 BC, Mithridates had sent a messenger with a confidential letter to all the officials who governed the various districts of his vast kingdom. In this letter, he instructed them all to put to death on a specific day all Romans and Italians (men, women and children) and to leave their bodies lying without the rites of burial. He allowed the messenger thirty days in which to visit all the districts so that they could act in concert on the appointed day. Only two states in Asia Minor refused to take this action and, in all, about 80,000 were massacred.

23 **annum iam tertium et vicesimum regnat**: *has been reigning for twenty-two years*, literally *is now reigning for (his) twenty-third year*, i.e. from 88 BC to 66 BC. (For inclusive reckoning in time calculations, see LL p. 67.) The present tense is used in Latin when a situation which has existed in the past continues into the present (see LL p. 52).

24 **se** has to be taken with **occultare** in the next line: *to hide himself.* The places quoted are far inland, well away from the Roman provinces.

26 **vectigalibus**: This is not the noun **vectigal**, but the adjective **vectigalis**, agreeing with a noun (understood) such as **populus**, **ager** or **civitas**, meaning *a state which pays taxes*.

in re militari, tradita est; agitur salus sociorum atque amicorum, pro qua multa maiores vestri magna et gravia bella gesserunt; aguntur certissima populi Romani vectigalia et maxima, quibus amissis et pacis ornamenta et subsidia belli requiretis; aguntur bona multorum civium, quibus est a vobis et ipsorum et rei publicae causa consulendum.

*Rome's fine reputation is at stake since Mithridates, far from being punished for past atrocities, has dared to try to extend his kingdom at the expense of Rome's allies and even to violate Roman citizens. Sulla and Murena defeated him but did not finish him off.*

et quoniam semper appetentes gloriae praeter ceteras gentes atque avidi laudis fuistis, delenda vobis est illa macula Mithridatico bello superiore concepta, quae penitus iam insedit ac nimis inveteravit in populi Romani nomine: quod is, qui uno die tota in Asia, tot in civitatibus, uno nuntio atque una significatione litterarum cives Romanos necandos trucidandosque denotavit, non modo adhuc poenam nullam suo dignam scelere suscepit, sed ab illo tempore annum iam tertium et vicesimum regnat; et ita regnat ut se non Ponti neque Cappadociae latebris occultare velit, sed emergere ex patrio regno atque in vestris vectigalibus (hoc est in Asiae luce) versari.

**trado** (3), **-didi, -ditum**, to hand down
**salus, -utis** (*f*), safety, security, well-being
**pro** (+ abl.), in defence of
**gravis, -is, -e**, serious
**bellum gerere**, to wage war
**certus, -a, -um**, certain, reliable
**vectigal, -alis** (*n*), tax, revenue
**subsidia, -orum** (*n.pl*), resources
**requiro** (3), to lack, look in vain for
**bona, -orum** (*n.pl*), goods, property
**res publica, rei publicae** (*f*), state
**quoniam**, since
**appetens, -entis** (+ gen.), eager (for)
**praeter** (+ acc.), beyond, to a greater degree than
**ceteri, -ae, -a**, the rest, all other(s)
**gens, gentis** (*f*), nation
**avidus, -a, -um** (+ gen.), eager (for), desirous (of)
**laus, laudis** (*f*), praise, glory
**macula, -ae** (*f*), spot, stain
**superior, -oris**, previous, earlier
**concipio** (3), **-cepi, -ceptum**, to receive, incur
**penitus**, deeply
**insido** (3), **-sedi**, to become ingrained
**nimis**, too much
**inveterasco** (3), **-eravi**, to become established
**totus, -a, -um**, all, the whole of, entire
**tot**, so many
**nuntius, -i** (*m*), messenger, message
**adhuc**, up to this time, still
**poena, -ae** (*f*), punishment, penalty
**dignus, -a, -um** (+ abl.), worthy (of), in keeping (with)
**scelus, -eris** (*n*), crime
**suscipio** (3), **-cepi**, to receive, incur
**latebrae, -arum** (*f.pl*), hiding-place
**emergo** (3), to come forth, emerge
**patrius, -a, -um**, ancestral, of his fathers
**regnum, -i** (*n*), kingdom
**lux, lucis** (*f*), light, (broad) daylight
**versor** (1), to move about, strut about

28 **insignia victoriae**: *the trappings of victory*. Note the powerful effect of following this phrase immediately with **non victoriam**.

28 **triumphavit**: *celebrated a triumph*. Normally, generals had to disband their armies before they crossed the boundaries of Italy. After important victories, however, the Senate granted successful generals the right to lead their troops in procession through Rome, together with the prisoners and booty they had captured, and then to offer thanks to the gods. Lucius Sulla had celebrated a triumph over Mithridates in 83 BC; Lucius Murena triumphed in 81 BC.

30 **triumpharunt = triumphaverunt**. In verbs which have **-v-** in the perfect stem, the **-v-** and the vowel which follows it are sometimes dropped. (cf. **aedificasset** and **ornasset** in line 36, and **comparasset** in line 37.)

30 **pulsus superatusque**: *(though) routed and defeated*. (For Paired Words, see CAO on page 236.)

31 **laus est tribuenda quod egerunt**: *praise must be given for what they achieved*. This is balanced by **venia danda quod reliquerunt**, *pardon must be granted for what they left (undone)*. (For Balanced Phrases, see CAO on page 237.)

33 **Sullam**: Direct Object of **revocavit** (understood).

33 **res publica**: *the political situation (in Rome)*. Marius, Sulla's arch-rival, had gained political control in Rome during Sulla's absence (see page 1). Marius had died in 86 BC, but his supporters (the Marian faction, as they were called) continued to try to undo the constitutional reforms which Sulla had introduced. Sulla, therefore, after defeating Mithridates, made peace with him and returned to Italy to deal with his own opponents. He left behind his lieutenant, Lucius Licinius Murena, to hold Mithridates in check; but he soon had to recall Murena and his troops to bolster his own army.

34 **omne reliquum tempus**: *that whole interval*, literally *all the remaining time*, i.e. between the departure of Murena and the renewal of hostilities after the arrival of Lucullus.

34 **non ad oblivionem veteris belli**: *not (with a view) to forgetting the former war*. This phrase is balanced by **sed ad comparationem** (*preparation*) **novi (belli)**. (For Balanced Phrases, see CAO on page 237.)

35 **cum**: The clause introduced by **cum** extends as far as **simularet** in line 38. Note the change to the imperfect tense after several pluperfects.

37 **quibuscumque ex gentibus potuisset**: *from whatever tribes he could.*

39 **ad eos duces**: After their defeat by Sulla in Italy, the Marians continued their struggle abroad. One of them, Sertorius, fled to Spain and, having set up a rebel government there, for ten years (82-72 BC) successfully resisted all attempts by powerful Roman armies to overthrow him.

39 **ut** introduces a Purpose clause which explains Mithridates' motive in sending the envoys. (For Purpose, see LL p.44.)

40 **uno consilio**: *with concerted action*, literally *with one plan*.

41 **ancipiti contentione districti**: *torn by a struggle on two fronts*, literally *stretched by a double conflict*; i.e. the war in the East against Mithridates and the war in Spain against Sertorius.

etenim adhuc ita nostri cum illo rege contenderunt imperatores ut ab illo insignia victoriae, non victoriam reportarent. triumphavit L.Sulla, triumphavit L.Murena de Mithridate, duo fortissimi viri et summi imperatores; sed ita triumpharunt ut ille pulsus superatusque regnaret. verum tamen illis imperatoribus laus est tribuenda quod egerunt, venia danda quod reliquerunt, propterea quod ab eo bello Sullam in Italiam res publica, Murenam Sulla revocavit.

*Mithridates has been rebuilding his own forces and has sent overtures to our enemies in the West, in the hope that he will reduce the effectiveness of our armies by forcing them to fight on two widely-separated fronts. Pompey has brilliantly ended the threat in the West; Lucullus, despite his great achievements, has through bad luck been unable to end the war in the East.*

Mithridates autem omne reliquum tempus non ad oblivionem veteris belli sed ad comparationem novi contulit; qui postea, cum maximas aedificasset ornassetque classes, exercitusque permagnos quibuscumque ex gentibus potuisset comparasset, et se Bosporanis finitimis suis bellum inferre simularet, usque in Hispaniam legatos ac litteras misit ad eos duces quibuscum tum bellum gerebamus; ut, cum duobus in locis disiunctissimis maximeque diversis uno consilio a binis hostium copiis bellum terra marique gereretur, vos ancipiti contentione districti de imperio dimicaretis.

**etenim**, for in fact
**contendo** (3), **-tendi**, to fight
**reporto** (1), to bring back, carry off
**verum tamen**, but all the same, nonetheless
**propterea quod**, because of the fact that
**revoco** (1), to recall, call back
**confero, -ferre, -tuli**, to devote
**postea**, later, afterwards
**orno** (1), to equip, fit out
**classis, -is** (*f*), fleet
**exercitus, -us** (*m*), army
**permagnus, -a, -um**, very large
**comparo** (1), to collect
**Bosporani, -orum** (*m.pl*), inhabitants of the Crimean Bosporus
**finitimus, -i** (*m*), neighbour
**bellum inferre** (+ dat.), to wage war (upon)
**simulo** (1), to pretend
**usque in** (+ acc.), as far as, all the way to
**Hispania, -ae** (*f*), Spain
**legatus, -i** (*m*), ambassador, envoy
**litterae, -arum** (*f.pl*), letters, dispatches
**dux, ducis** (*m*), leader
**disiunctus, -a, -um**, separated, distinct, disconnected
**diversus, -a, -um**, different, remote, far apart
**bini, -ae, -a**, two, two at a time
**copiae, -arum** (*f.pl*), forces, armies
**terra marique**, by land and sea
**imperium, -i** (*n*), power, supremacy, empire
**dimico** (1), to fight, contend

43 **iniuriosius**: *somewhat unjustly*. **iniuriosius** is a comparative adverb. (cf. **superbius** in line 46.) This incident led to a campaign against the Illyrian pirates in 229 BC.

45 **quo tandem animo esse debetis?**: *what in the world ought your attitude to be?* This is a rhetorical question, i.e. a question to which the answer is obvious (see CAO on page 233); the use of **tandem** adds a note of sarcasm. (For Ablative of Description, see LL p. 15.) Note the sharp contrast drawn between **maiores** and **patres** on the one hand and **vos** and **vobis** on the other in lines 43-54.

45 **legati quod**: **legati** is the subject of the **quod** clause, but it is placed before the clause for emphasis. In actual fact, the ambassadors were subjected to physical as well as verbal abuse; but it suits Cicero's purpose to make the offence appear less serious.

46 **lumen exstinctum esse**: *the (shining) light to be snuffed out*. The destruction of Corinth in 146 BC was an example of the ruthless way in which Rome eliminated all rivals, real or imaginary, in order to achieve supremacy in the Mediterranean. Corinth had for centuries played a leading part in the political, economic and artistic life of Greece. Her destruction, according to Cicero, was like the sudden extinction of a very bright light. (For Metaphor, see CAO on page 235.)

48 **consularem**: *of consular rank*. Once a man had held the consulship, he ranked as **consularis**, a status of special privilege and precedence. Mithridates' offence was all the greater in that he had killed an ambassador of such importance.

48 **vinculis ac verberibus atque omni supplicio excruciatum**: *(after he had been) tortured by imprisonment* (literally *chains*), *scourging* (literally *blows and lashes*) *and every form of punishment*. After capturing Manius Aquilius, Mithridates led him about the countryside tied to an ass, scourged him in front of the mob until he said who and what he was, and eventually killed him by pouring molten gold down his throat as a sign that he despised the greed of the Romans.

49 **illi**: *they*, i.e. your ancestors. (cf. **illi** in line 51 and **illis** in line 52.)

49 **libertatem imminutam**: *the restriction of the freedom*, literally *reduced freedom*. Note how English uses a noun rather than a participle to translate the perfect participle passive in this type of phrase. (cf. **ereptam vitam** and **ius violatum** in lines 50-1, and **legatum interfectum** in lines 51-2.)

50 **ius legationis**: *the rights of envoys*, literally *the right of an embassy*.

51 **verbo violatum**: *infringed (only) verbally*, literally *violated by a (single) word*.

52 **relinquetis**: *will you do nothing about*, literally *will you leave alone (abandon)*.

52 **videte ne**: *take care in case*. In the rest of the sentence, Cicero contrasts the glorious achievements of their ancestors (introduced by **ut**, *just as*) with the possible disgrace which might follow (introduced by **sic**, *so*), if his audience fails to take the action recommended. The Overview technique (see pages xii-xiv of this book and LL pp. 121-31) makes the balance clear:

<table>
<tr><td>videte ne</td><td>ut illis pulcherrimum fuit</td><td>... tradere,</td></tr>
<tr><td></td><td>sic vobis turpissimum sit</td><td>... tueri et conservare non posse.</td></tr>
</table>

Mithridates VI of Pontus wearing animal head-dress

*Your ancestors went to war to avenge much less obvious affronts; are you going to permit the atrocities committed by Mithridates to go unpunished?*

maiores nostri saepe, mercatoribus aut naviculariis nostris iniuriosius tractatis, bella gesserunt; vos, tot milibus civium Romanorum uno nuntio atque uno tempore necatis, quo tandem animo esse debetis? legati quod erant appellati superbius, Corinthum patres vestri totius Graeciae lumen exstinctum esse voluerunt; vos eum regem inultum esse patiemini, qui legatum populi Romani consularem vinculis ac verberibus atque omni supplicio excruciatum necavit? illi libertatem imminutam civium Romanorum non tulerunt; vos ereptam vitam neglegetis? ius legationis verbo violatum illi persecuti sunt; vos legatum omni supplicio interfectum relinquetis? videte ne, ut illis pulcherrimum fuit tantam vobis imperii gloriam tradere, sic vobis turpissimum sit id quod accepistis tueri et conservare non posse.

**mercator, -oris** (*m*), merchant, trader
**navicularius, -i** (*m*), ship-owner
**tracto** (1), to treat
**mille**, (plur. **milia**), a thousand
**neco** (1), to kill, murder, slaughter
**appello** (1), to call, address
**superbe**, arrogantly, disrespectfully
**Corinthus, -i** (*f*), Corinth
**volo, velle, volui**, to wish, determine, resolve
**inultus, -a, -um**, unpunished
**patior** (3), to allow
**fero, ferre, tuli**, to bear, endure, tolerate
**eripio** (3), **eripui, ereptum**, to take away (violently), snatch away
**neglego** (3), to neglect, disregard, ignore
**persequor** (3), **-secutus sum**, to follow up, avenge
**interficio** (3), **-feci, -fectum**, to kill
**pulcher, -chra, -chrum**, fine, glorious, honourable
**turpis, -is, -e**, disgraceful, dishonourable
**tueor** (2), to defend, protect
**conservo** (1), to preserve

55 **quid?**: *then again.* Cicero is about to make a new point in support of his argument.

55 **quod**: *the fact that.* The whole **quod** clause is the object of **ferre** in line 56.

55 **summum in periculum ac discrimen**: *into critically serious danger*, literally *into the greatest danger and crisis.* (For Paired Words, see CAO on page 236.)

56 **Ariobarzanes**: The Romans had established him as king of Cappadocia in order to create a friendly buffer-state between Mithridates and their provinces. Mithridates, however, had conquered Cappadocia and driven Ariobarzanes from his throne.

57 **duo reges**: i.e. Mithridates and Tigranes, his son-in-law.

59 **cuncta Asia atque Graecia**: *in the whole of Asia and Greece.* The preposition **in** is regularly omitted in phrases containing **totus, cunctus, omnis** or **medius** and expressing Place Where (see LL p. 15).

60 **imperatorem certum deposcere**: *to demand (one) particular general*, namely Pompey. Rome had just sent Glabrio to succeed Lucullus. This phrase is governed by **neque audent**, but is placed first for emphasis. The idea is repeated in **neque se id facere posse arbitrantur**. According to Cicero, the states would not dare to make such a demand because they were in awe of Rome. There was also the danger that, by asking specifically for Pompey, they would offend any other general who might be sent to help them.

61 **alium** refers to Glabrio, whom the senate sent to succeed Lucullus.

63 **sentiunt hoc idem quod vos**: *they feel the same as you*, literally *they feel this same thing which you (feel).* **hoc idem** is explained in more detail in the two Accusative and Infinitive clauses which follow.

63 **in quo summa sint omnia**: *who possesses all the essential qualities*, literally *in whom there are all the highest things*, i.e. for the successful completion of this campaign. Note the emphatic position of **summa**.

64 **sint**: The subjunctive is used since this is part of what they thought. (For subordinate clauses in Indirect Speech, see LL p. 110.)

64 **quo etiam carent aegrius**: *as a result of which they miss him all the more keenly*, literally *from which they do without him even more unwillingly.*

65 **ad maritimum bellum**: Having cleared the whole of the Mediterranean of pirates, Pompey was now mopping up the remnants along the coasts of modern Turkey and Syria.

*Your allies are perplexed because they expect you to take decisive action to protect them. Everyone realises that there is only one general fit to tackle the task.*

quid? quod salus sociorum summum in periculum ac discrimen vocatur, quo tandem animo ferre debetis? regno est expulsus Ariobarzanes rex, socius populi Romani atque amicus; imminent duo reges toti Asiae non solum vobis inimicissimi sed etiam vestris sociis atque amicis; civitates autem omnes cuncta Asia atque Graecia vestrum auxilium exspectare propter periculi magnitudinem coguntur; imperatorem a vobis certum deposcere (cum praesertim vos alium miseritis) neque audent neque se id facere sine summo periculo posse arbitrantur.

vident et sentiunt hoc idem quod vos, unum virum esse in quo summa sint omnia, et eum propter esse, quo etiam carent aegrius; cuius adventu ipso atque nomine, tametsi ille ad maritimum bellum venerit, tamen impetus hostium repressos esse intellegunt ac retardatos.

**voco** (1), to call, bring
**expello** (3), **-puli, -pulsum**, to drive out, expel
**immineo** (2) (+ dat.), to threaten
**non solum ... sed etiam ...**, not only ... but also ...
**inimicus, -a, -um**, hostile
**civitas, -atis** (*f*), state, nation, country
**auxilium, -i** (*n*), help
**exspecto** (1), to look for, expect
**propter** (+ acc.), on account of
**cogo** (3), to compel
**deposco** (3), to demand
**cum praesertim**, especially when, especially since
**arbitror** (1), to think
**propter** (adverb), near at hand
**adventus, -us** (*m*), arrival
**nomen, -inis** (*n*), name, reputation
**tametsi**, although
**impetus, -us** (*m*), attack, offensive
**reprimo** (3), **-pressi, -pressum**, to check, curb
**intellego** (3), to realise
**retardo** (1), to slow down

Having listed several instances of how Rome in the past took military action to defend her own interests and those of her allies when the danger was much less threatening, Cicero then goes on to explain how the threat posed by Mithridates is not only affecting the business interests of people in the East but is also having financial repercussions in Rome itself, for so much depends on the revenues from the provinces. He points out that Asia is a particularly rich province, and the Romans must surely take action when so much is at stake.

Lucullus did a magnificent job in halting the aggression of Mithridates; but, despite winning several victories, he was not able to destroy him completely. In fact, Mithridates was able to escape because of the greed of Lucullus' troops who preferred to spend time in looting rather than in pursuing Mithridates. The troops then mutinied and refused to advance into Armenia where Mithridates was in hiding, protected by King Tigranes, his son-in-law. The danger is now greater than ever because Mithridates and Tigranes, besides mobilising huge forces of their own, have also stirred up several peoples whose territories border on Rome's provinces.

67 **quare**: *(to explain) why.*

67 **genere ipso necessarium**: *inevitable by its very nature.*

68 **restat ut dicendum esse videatur**: *it would seem that it (only) remains for me to speak*, literally *it remains that it seems to need speaking* — an awkward sentence, but the meaning is clear. The phrase **esse videatur** hardly seems necessary, but its sound seemed to appeal to Cicero, for he frequently used it at the end of sentences. (For Clausulae, see CAO on pages 238-9.)

68 **ad id bellum**: *for that war.* The preposition **ad** frequently expresses Purpose. The positioning of this phrase within **de imperatore deligendo** tells us to take the two phrases together. (For this use of the Gerundive, see LL p. 61.)

69 **ac tantis rebus praeficiendo**: *and appointing (him) to take charge of such important operations*, literally *and putting (him) in charge of such great matters.* **praeficiendo** (like **deligendo**) agrees with **imperatore**.

70 **innocentium**: *upright.* To be elected to high office in Rome, candidates regularly had to expend a great deal of money to win over the support of the electorate. At the end of their year in office, ex-magistrates normally spent another period governing a province or leading an army in a campaign. It was not uncommon for this further tour of duty to be used to recoup the fortunes spent on winning the election.

71 **quemnam potissimum praeficiendum (esse) putaretis**: *(namely) who especially you thought should be put in charge.* This Indirect Question explains **haec deliberatio** in more detail.

72 **nunc vero**: *but as things stand*, literally *but now.*

73 **sit unus**: *is the only one.*

73 **eorum hominum qui nunc sunt**: *of the present generation*, literally *of those people who now exist.* This personal phrase is balanced by the abstract noun **antiquitatis**, *of past generations.* The nouns **gloriam** (*the glorious exploits*) and **memoriam** (*the recorded achievements*) are the direct objects of **superarit**.

74 **virtute superarit**: *has eclipsed by his brilliance*, literally *has overcome by his natural ability.* **superarit** is a contracted form of **superaverit**.

75 **cuiusquam animum dubium facere possit**: *can raise doubts in anyone's mind*, literally *is able to make anyone's mind doubtful.*

76 **quattuor has res**: *these four qualities.* There is a wealth of meaning in the nouns which follow: **scientia** implies not only *knowledge* but also the ability to use it well; **virtus** includes *courage, nerve, talent, flair* and *all-round ability*; the person who has **auctoritas** commands the respect and devotion of those under him because they know they can rely on him, and this brings *prestige, influence* and *authority*; whereas modern society regards *good luck* as depending only on chance, to the Romans **felicitas** meant enjoying the goodwill of the gods.

78 **esse debuit**: *ought to have been.* In Cicero's opinion, Pompey was bound to be more knowledgeable because he began learning the craft of generalship when still very young.

78 **qui**: *for he.* (For Linking Relative, see LL p. 26.)

79 **bello maximo**: *during a very serious war* — an ablative expressing Time When (see LL p. 15). This refers to the Social War, i.e. the war Rome fought against its Italian allies (**socii**) when they revolted in 90 BC following the refusal of the Senate to grant them Roman citizenship. Pompey was 17 when he joined the army of his father, Gnaeus Pompeius Strabo, who is referred to as **summi imperatoris** (line 81).

*Whom should we choose to remove this danger once and for all? Surely the only possible choice is Pompey, for he is not only the most outstanding general of all time, but he also possesses the four essential qualities of a great general: military skill, all-round ability, personal prestige and consistent good fortune.*

satis mihi multa verba fecisse videor quare esset hoc bellum genere ipso necessarium, magnitudine periculosum. restat ut de imperatore ad id bellum deligendo ac tantis rebus praeficiendo dicendum esse videatur.

utinam, Quirites, virorum fortium atque innocentium copiam tantam haberetis ut haec vobis deliberatio difficilis esset, quemnam potissimum tantis rebus ac tanto bello praeficiendum putaretis! nunc vero, cum sit unus Cn.Pompeius qui non modo eorum hominum qui nunc sunt gloriam sed etiam antiquitatis memoriam virtute superarit, quae res est quae cuiusquam animum in hac causa dubium facere possit? ego enim sic existimo, in summo imperatore quattuor has res inesse oportere: scientiam rei militaris, virtutem, auctoritatem, felicitatem.

*Pompey's military skills have been acquired through first-hand experience in numerous campaigns, all of which he has brought to a successful conclusion.*

quis igitur hoc homine scientior umquam aut fuit aut esse debuit? qui e ludo atque e pueritiae disciplinis bello maximo atque acerrimis hostibus

**verbum, -i** (*n*), word
**periculosus, -a, -um**, dangerous
**deligo** (3), to choose
**praeficio** (3) (+ dat.), to put in charge (of)
**Quirites**, citizens of Rome
**utinam** (+ subjunctive), I wish that, would that
**copia, -ae** (*f*), supply
**deliberatio, -onis** (*f*), choice, decision
**quisnam?**, who, I ask you?
**antiquitas, -atis** (*f*), antiquity, former times
**quisquam**, anyone
**causa, -ae** (*f*), case, circumstance
**sic**, in this way, as follows
**insum, -esse**, to be in, be present, belong
**oportere** (2), to be necessary, ought
**felicitas, -atis** (*f*), luck, good fortune
**sciens, -ntis**, knowledgeable
**umquam**, ever
**ludus, -i** (*m*), school
**pueritia, -ae** (*f*), boyhood
**disciplina, -ae** (*f*), training, discipline, education
**acer, acris, acre**, fierce, bitter

81 **extrema pueritia**: *at the end of his boyhood* — another ablative expressing Time When (see LL p. 15). This was when the boy assumed the **toga virilis**.

81 **ineunte adulescentia**: *at the start of his youth*, literally *his youth beginning*. (For Ablative Absolute, see LL p. 30.) **adulescentia** was the period roughly between seventeen and thirty years of age.

82 **maximi ipse exercitus imperator**: At the age of 22, Pompey raised an army of his own to help the dictator Sulla. Greater emphasis is given to this phrase by placing **ipse** between **maximi** and **exercitus**.

82 **cum hoste ... cum inimico**: **hostis** is an enemy of the state, whereas **inimicus** is a personal enemy.

84 **provincias**: *commands*. The word applies not only to an area ruled by a governor but also to any official sphere of duty.

86 **suis imperiis**: *by holding command himself*, literally *by his own commands*.

87 **stipendiis**: *(the number of) campaigns (he fought)*. The word **stipendium** was originally used of the soldier's pay, but it later came to mean also a campaign.

87 **quod**: *what*, an adjective agreeing with **genus**.

89 **civile, Africanum**: These both agree with **bellum** (line 90) and refer to the Civil War in which Pompey supported Sulla against the Marians. After helping to drive the Marians out of Italy (82 BC), Pompey pursued them into Sicily and Africa where they had joined forces with the king of Numidia. He defeated them in 81 BC and, on his return to Rome, he was given a triumph and hailed as **Magnus** (*the Great*) by Sulla, after which he was known as Gnaeus Pompeius Magnus.

89 **Transalpinum, Hispaniense**: The latter adjective refers to the war in Spain against Sertorius (see line 39). After the failure of other generals to defeat Sertorius, the Senate ultimately decided to send Pompey (77 BC). While he was leading his army through Transalpine Gaul, he had to fight his way through Gallic tribes which Sertorius had incited to block his march into Spain.

89 **mixtum ex civibus atque ex bellicosissimis nationibus**: *(a war) in which citizens and the most warlike tribes combined against us*, literally *(a war) mixed up from citizens and very warlike tribes*.

90 **servile**: *the war against the slaves*. The Romans always feared slave revolts, but that which began in 73 BC posed a greater threat than usual, for the slaves were joined by gladiators and they were ably led by Spartacus. He defeated several Roman armies, and this encouraged more and more slaves to join his rebel army which grew to 90,000 and wreaked havoc all over Italy. Marcus Crassus eventually ended the war by defeating the rebels in a battle in which he slew 12,000, including Spartacus. Pompey arrived home from Spain with his army just in time to mop up the remnants, killing 5,000 of them. On the basis of this 'victory', Pompey claimed that it was he who ended the slave menace.

90 **navale**: This refers to the war against the pirates.

91 **varia et diversa genera**: Both adjectives mean *different*, the former probably referring to the type of fighting, the latter to the different type of locality. There is little doubt, however, that Cicero used two adjectives simply for emphasis and because he liked the sound they produced. (For Paired Words, see CAO on page 236.) The phrase sums up the list of wars with which the sentence began and itself becomes the composite subject of **declarant** (line 92).

91 **gesta** (*waged*) and **confecta** (*brought to an end*) are both participles.

92 **in usu positam militari**: *involving military experience*, literally *placed in military practice*. **positam** is a participle agreeing with **rem**.

ad patris exercitum atque in militiae disciplinam profectus est; qui extrema pueritia miles in exercitu summi fuit imperatoris, ineunte adulescentia maximi ipse exercitus imperator; qui saepius cum hoste conflixit quam quisquam cum inimico concertavit, plura bella gessit quam ceteri legerunt. plures provincias confecit quam alii concupiverunt; cuius adulescentia ad scientiam rei militaris non alienis praeceptis sed suis imperiis, non offensionibus belli sed victoriis, non stipendiis sed triumphis est erudita. quod denique genus esse belli potest in quo illum non exercuerit fortuna rei publicae? civile, Africanum, Transalpinum, Hispaniense mixtum ex civibus atque ex bellicosissimis nationibus, servile, navale bellum, varia et diversa genera et bellorum et hostium, non solum gesta ab hoc uno sed etiam confecta, nullam rem esse declarant in usu positam militari quae huius viri scientiam fugere possit.

**militia, -ae** (*f*), military service
**confligo** (3), **-flixi**, to fight, engage in combat with
**concerto** (1), to have a dispute
**lego** (3), **legi**, to read (about)
**conficio** (3), **-feci, -fectum**, to finish, complete, bring to an end
**concupisco** (3), **-cupivi**, to long for, aspire to, dream of
**alienus, -a, -um**, of another person, of someone else
**praeceptum, -i** (*n*), teaching, instruction, precept
**offensio, -onis** (*f*), reverse, disaster
**erudio** (4), to train, teach
**denique**, in short, to sum up
**exerceo** (2), to train, exercise, employ
**fortuna, -ae** (*f*), fortune, luck (good or bad)
**declaro** (1), to make clear, demonstrate
**fugio** (3), to escape, elude

94 **iam vero**: Cicero frequently uses these words to show that he is turning to a new point. Having discussed the magnitude of the war and Pompey's military skills, he now proposes to discuss his all-round ability (**virtus**). English would probably translate **iam vero virtuti** as *turning now to his all-round ability*. It is important to note, however, that the dative **virtuti** depends on **par**, *equal to his all-round ability*, i.e. adequate to describe it.

96 **solae virtutes imperatoriae**: *the only qualities required in a general.*

97 **labor in negotiis**: *hard work in (dealing with) problems.*

98 **consilia in providendo**: *good judgement in planning ahead*, literally *plans in foreseeing*. (For Gerund, see LL p. 60.)

99 **quae tanta sunt in hoc uno quanta ... non fuerunt**: Normally, correlatives (see LL p. 63) express the idea that one thing is *as great ... as* another, i.e. *equal* to it. Here, however, the negative **non** produces a comparative meaning. Translate *this one man possesses all of these qualities to a greater extent than ...*, literally *which are as great in this one man as they were not ...*

101 **quis**: *what*, an adjective agreeing with **locus**.

101 **toto mari**: *in the whole of the (Mediterranean) Sea.* (For the omission of the preposition in Place phrases involving **totus, cunctus**, etc., compare line 59).

102 **lateret**: *it remained out of sight (of the pirates)*, literally *it lay hidden.*

104 **hieme**: *in winter.* Roman sailors did not usually put to sea between November and March. (For ablative expressing Time When, see LL p. 15.) The phrase **referto praedonum mari**, *when the sea was swarming with* (literally *full of*) *pirates*, is also treated as a time expression.

104 **hoc tantum bellum** together with **confici posse** (line 107) forms an Accusative and Infinitive clause depending on **quis arbitraretur**, *who would have thought* (lines 105-6). (For Potential Subjunctive, see LL p. 108.)

105 **tam vetus**: *so prolonged.* The pirates had begun in a small way in Cilicia twenty-one years before this; but, supported by Mithridates and ignored by the Romans who were intent only on their own internal power struggles, their menace gradually spread until they controlled the whole Mediterranean with a fleet of 1,000 galleys, so that even Roman armies could not be transported safely. They captured 400 towns and harbours and turned them into strongly fortified arsenals. They captured at sea officials and distinguished citizens, including Julius Caesar, and even dared to sail into Ostia, destroy the Roman fleet berthed there, land on the coast of Italy near Rome, plunder villas along the Via Appia and kidnap two praetors and their entire retinues. The pirates sold their captives into slavery or released them for a ransom.

105 **tam late divisum atque dispersum**: *fought on such widely separated and scattered fronts*, literally *so widely separated and scattered.*

108 **hosce**: Cicero is fond of this more emphatic form of the demonstrative adjective **hic, haec, hoc**.

109 **cui praesidio fuistis?** For Predicative Dative, see LL p. 13.

110 **quam multas ...**: There are really three Accusative and Infinitive clauses in lines 110-11, all depending on **existimatis**:

| | | |
|---|---|---|
| **quam multas existimatis** | **insulas esse desertas,** | |
| **quam multas (existimatis)** | **aut metu relictas (esse)** | **(urbes sociorum)** |
| | **aut a praedonibus captasurbes esse sociorum** | |

Instead of repeating **quam multas** and **esse urbes sociorum**, Cicero has chosen to balance the second and third clauses by using **aut ... aut ...**

*These campaigns also bear witness to his all-round ability.*

iam vero virtuti Cn.Pompei quae potest oratio par inveniri? quid est quod quisquam aut illo dignum aut vobis novum aut cuiquam inauditum possit adferre? neque enim illae sunt solae virtutes imperatoriae, quae vulgo existimantur: labor in negotiis, fortitudo in periculis, industria in agendo, celeritas in conficiendo, consilia in providendo; quae tanta sunt in hoc uno quanta in omnibus reliquis imperatoribus, quos aut vidimus aut audivimus, non fuerunt.

*For many years now, the power of the pirates has been such that Rome has not been able to protect even itself and its citizens, let alone its allies.*

quis enim toto mari locus per hos annos aut tam firmum habuit praesidium ut tutus esset, aut tam fuit abditus ut lateret? quis navigavit qui non se aut mortis aut servitutis periculo committeret, cum aut hieme aut referto praedonum mari navigaret? hoc tantum bellum, tam turpe, tam vetus, tam late divisum atque dispersum quis umquam arbitraretur aut ab omnibus imperatoribus uno anno aut omnibus annis ab uno imperatore confici posse? quam provinciam tenuistis a praedonibus liberam per hosce annos? quod vectigal vobis tutum fuit? quem socium defendistis? cui praesidio classibus vestris fuistis? quam multas existimatis insulas esse desertas, quam multas aut metu relictas aut a praedonibus captas urbes esse sociorum?

**par, paris**, equal
**dignus, -a, -um** (+ abl.), worthy (of)
**novus, -a, -um**, new
**inauditus, -a, -um**, unheard of, unfamiliar, new
**adfero, -ferre**, to bring forward, assert
**vulgo**, commonly
**existimo** (1), to consider, think (of)
**fortitudo, -inis** (*f*), courage, bravery
**industria, -ae** (*f*), diligence, energy,
**ago** (3), to do, act, carry out
**celeritas, -atis** (*f*), speed
**reliquus, -a, -um**, remaining, the other, the rest of
**audio** (4), to hear, hear of
**firmus, -a, -um**, strong
**praesidium, -i** (*n*), garrison
**tutus, -a, -um**, safe
**abditus, -a, -um**, hidden, secluded
**servitus, -utis** (*f*), slavery
**committo** (3), to entrust, commit, expose
**turpis, -is, -e**, shameful, humiliating
**teneo** (2), to hold
**liber, -era, -erum**, free
**vectigal, -is** (*n*), tax, revenue from taxes
**praesidio esse** (+ dat.), to protect
**insula, -ae** (*f*), island
**relinquo** (3), **-liqui, -lictum**, to leave, abandon

112 **quo bello**: **bello** is repeated in the relative clause for emphasis. In English we would say *a war in which.*

114 **ineunte vere**: *at the beginning of spring*, literally *spring entering*. For Ablative Absolute, see LL p. 30.)

114 **est haec virtus imperatoris**: *such is his skill as a general*, literally *this is the skill (of him as) a general.*

## Points for Discussion

1. Read lines 1-5. What is the topic on which Cicero is going to speak, and why does it present him with a problem?
2. Read lines 9-16. What are the four things which Cicero says are at stake in this war? Which of these do you think Cicero considers most important? Give reasons for your answer.
3. By what stylistic means (e.g. anaphora, sentence structure) does Cicero in lines 9-16 achieve emotional intensity in order to highlight the gravity of the menace from Mithridates?
4. In lines 43-54, what effect do you think Cicero is trying to achieve through the following structure? Do you think he succeeds?

   **maiores nostri ... vos**     **patres vestri ... vos**
   **illi ... vos**     **illi ... vos**
   **illis ... vobis**
5. In your opinion, what effect is Cicero aiming at in his use of the comparative adverbs **iniuriosius** (line 43) and **superbius** (line 46) rather than their superlative or positive forms?
6. Read lines 70-2. Does Cicero think the Romans are faced with a difficult problem in choosing a general? Explain your answer.
7. In lines 94-100, Cicero makes careful use of many rhetorical devices (see CAO on pages 235-7). List examples of alliteration, rhyme, balanced phrases and **congeries verborum** which occur in these lines.
8. Read lines 101-111. Give examples of how the pirates hindered Rome's movements and damaged its influence in the Mediterranean. List any features of Cicero's account which strike you as exaggerated.

Cicero goes on to enumerate many more examples of how Rome had lost to the pirates its military grip on areas which it had previously controlled. He describes in detail how Pompey had systematically swept the whole of the Mediterranean clear of the pirates, and then he sums up that campaign with the following ringing endorsement of Pompey's achievements:

ita tantum bellum, tam diuturnum, tam longe lateque dispersum, quo bello omnes gentes ac nationes premebantur, Cn.Pompeius extrema hieme apparavit, ineunte vere suscepit, media aestate confecit. est haec divina atque incredibilis virtus imperatoris.

**diuturnus, -a, -um**, long-lasting
**longe**, far
**late**, wide(ly)
**natio, -onis** (*f*), people, tribe
**premo** (3), to burden, weigh down
**extremus, -a, -um,** the end of
**apparo** (1), to prepare for
**suscipio** (3), **-cepi**, to undertake
**aestas, -atis** (*f*), summer
**divinus, -a, -um**, god-like, superhuman, inspired

## Epilogue

Cicero's admiration of Pompey seemed boundless. In the remaining half of the speech, he spoke effusively of the other brilliant qualities which Pompey possessed, sweeping aside in the process objections raised by Pompey's opponents. In the end, the Manilian Law (**Lex Manilia**) was passed and Pompey, whose campaign against the pirates had taken him to Cilicia in Asia Minor, immediately took over the command against Mithridates and Tigranes. The speed and efficiency with which Pompey tackled the campaign thoroughly justified the claims that Cicero had made. Between 66 BC and 63 BC, he not only defeated the two kings but also greatly increased the size of the Roman empire by annexing as Roman provinces several kingdoms which had previously been only Roman protectorates. The settlement he made of the territories in the East paved the way for much greater stability on the eastern frontiers of the empire.

# Cicero's Letters

There were no multi-media communication systems in the Roman world — not even newspapers! For anyone who was away from Rome, whether in Italy or in the provinces, the main channel of information on events in the Capital was the letter; and likewise, those who were in Rome had to depend on letters from friends in order to learn what was happening elsewhere in the Roman world. Delivery, however, was irregular and unreliable. There was no public postal service, and only a few very rich individuals could afford to employ their own couriers (**tabellarii**). Occasionally, one might make use of the courier service organised by the companies of tax-gatherers (**publicani**); but, by and large, people had to depend on the goodwill of friends or even strangers who happened to be travelling to the place in question. Despite these uncertainties, however, Cicero living in his villa at Pompeii (more than 150 miles from Rome) could receive news from the city within three days; and two letters sent by Caesar from Britain took only 26 and 28 days respectively to reach him.

Cicero was a most prolific letter-writer. Over 900 letters have come down to us, more than 800 of which were written by Cicero himself and 99 by a variety of correspondents. There are two large collections, each comprising 16 'books' of letters. One of these collections consists of letters to Atticus (**Epistulae ad Atticum**, abbreviated to **Ad Att.**); the other contains correspondence with other friends and with his wife (**Epistulae ad Familiares**, abbreviated to **Ad Fam.**). There are also two smaller collections — one to Quintus Cicero (his younger brother), the other to Marcus Brutus (one of Caesar's assassins).

There is an immense variety of tone and subject-matter in these letters, ranging from the formality of dispatches to the Senate to the uninhibited expression of personal feelings — everything from high elation to utter despair. The fact that these letters, unlike his speeches, were not intended for publication constitutes their principal attraction, as they not only reveal their author's character (sometimes with damaging clarity) but also paint a vivid picture of the last two decades of Cicero's life (63-43 BC), when he was either a leading player in the drama of the closing years of the Roman Republic, or an agonised spectator of its disintegration.

It was mooted during Cicero's lifetime that a selection of his letters might be published. Fortunately that did not happen, as selection might have resulted in editorial interference, of which there is no sign in the corpus that we now possess. It is thought that the collections were put together by Tiro (Cicero's freedman and secretary) and by Atticus (*the Athenian*), a cognomen acquired by his friend Titus Pomponius because he spent most of his time in Athens to avoid the bitter controversies of Roman politics. This distaste may also have motivated Atticus to exclude utterly from the collection his own replies to Cicero's numerous letters!

It is not known exactly when the various collections of letters were published, but for centuries their existence was hardly known until AD 1345 when Petrarch, the Italian Renaissance poet, discovered a manuscript of the letters in Verona, probably in the Cathedral library. Cicero was by then hardly more than a name; indeed, in some parts of Tuscany, he had become a legendary figure, a warrior chief who had besieged

Fiesole and captured a local rebel hero called Catellina!

The uncertainties involved in sending letters are well illustrated in a letter which Cicero wrote to his friend Atticus on 25 January 61 BC. Cicero was in Rome and Atticus was in Greece:

*I have now had three letters from you: the first delivered by Marcus Cornelius which I suppose you gave him at Three Taverns, the second which your host at Canusium duly passed on, and the third which you say you sent from on board the boat just as you were ready to sail. These letters leave me in no doubt that you want a prompt reply, but I have been a little slow in doing that simply because I can't find a trustworthy letter-carrier. How rare it is to find someone who can convey a rather weighty letter without making it lighter by devouring the contents! Then there are the additional problems that I don't always know when people are leaving for Epirus, and I can't be sure when you are going off to visit Antonius or how much time you intend to spend in Epirus. So I don't dare to entrust to either Greeks or Epirotes letters in which I have expressed myself a little too frankly.*

*Since you left, plenty of things have happened that call for a letter from me; but they are not the sort of things I would want to expose to the risk of getting lost or opened or intercepted. But of these matters I will write to you in detail on another occasion, for I couldn't contemplate entrusting a letter on such important matters to any Tom, Dick or Harry.*

(Letters to Atticus I.13)

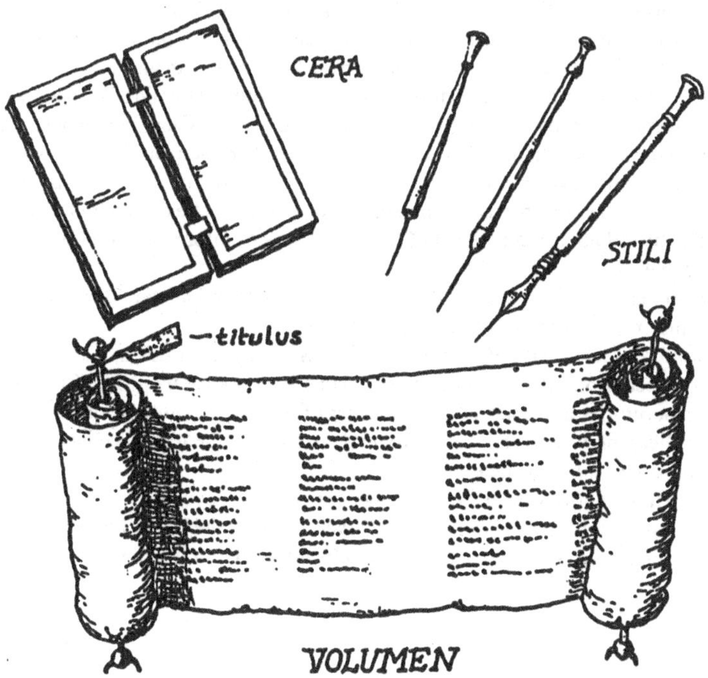

1 **ATTICO SAL.**: *(sends) greetings to Atticus*. The full formula was **salutem plurimam dicit** (or **dat**), abbreviated to **SPD, SD** or **SAL**. Atticus was a rich businessman (**eques**) who, since he preferred to stay neutral in political matters, left Rome and took up residence in Athens for some 20 years; hence his **cognomen** Atticus. Cicero and Atticus had studied together in Athens in 79 BC. When Cicero returned to Rome, the two remained good friends; and Cicero frequently wrote to him with details of his personal life and seeking his views on various political matters. In the latter half of 65 BC, Atticus was persuaded to leave Athens to support Cicero in his bid for the consulship of 63 BC.

2 **L.Iulio Caesare C.Marcio Figulo consulibus**: Normally, this type of Ablative Absolute means *in the consulship of*. Here, however, it means *on the day when Lucius Julius Caesar and Gaius Marcius Figulus were elected consuls*. They were therefore only **consules designati** (*consuls elect*). The exact date is unknown, but it was towards the end of July 65 BC.

2 **me auctum**: Supply **esse** — *my family has been enlarged*, literally *I have been enlarged*.

3 **salva Terentia**: *and Terentia is well*. (For this type of Ablative Absolute, see LL pp. 30-1.) Terentia was Cicero's wife.

4 **nihil litterarum**: For Partitive Genitive, see LL p. 9.

5 **Catilinam**: On returning to Rome from the province of Africa, which he had governed as propraetor in 67-66 BC, Lucius Sergius Catilina was accused of extortion by Publius Clodius. This prevented him from standing in 65 BC for the consulship of 64 BC. Although clearly guilty, he was able to secure his acquittal by bribing Clodius to mishandle the prosecution. There are two possible explanations of why Cicero considered defending him. His motive may have been political. Whereas Cicero was a **novus homo** (i.e. no one in his family had as yet been elected to the consulship), Catiline was **nobilis** (see line 10) and he had influential friends who might be persuaded to support Cicero in his attempt to become consul. On the other hand, it was perfectly reasonable for him, as an up-and-coming advocate, to defend clients who were patently guilty, just as present-day advocates and barristers sometimes do. We cannot be certain, but it is likely that he did not actually defend Catiline. (For more information on Catiline, see page 97.)

5 **nostrum**: *my*. Cicero frequently uses the plurals **nos** and **noster** when referring to himself. (Compare also lines 6, 7, 8, 9 and 10.)

6 **summa accusatoris voluntate**: As is the case today, each side in a trial was able to reject jurors who, they suspected, were biased against their side. Clodius, the prosecutor, was acting in collusion with Catiline (see note 5); and, far from challenging jurors who were favourable to Catiline, he may even have rejected some who were hostile to him.

7 **in ratione petitionis**: *in the planning of my election campaign*.

8 **sin aliter acciderit**: *but if it turns out otherwise*. (For the Future Perfect tense used in Conditions, see LL p. 54; compare **absolutus erit** in line 7.)

# *8. An Appeal for Support*

(ad Atticum I.2)

It is 65 BC and, although not permitted to *hold* the consulship until 63 BC, Cicero has already begun preparing his campaign for the elections which are to take place in 64 BC. In this letter, he writes to his friend Atticus in Athens, asking him to come to Rome to enlist support for him among the influential families of Rome.

CICERO ATTICO SAL.

L.Iulio Caesare C.Marcio Figulo consulibus, filiolo me auctum scito, salva Terentia.

abs te tam diu nihil litterarum! ego de meis ad te rationibus scripsi antea diligenter. hoc tempore Catilinam, competitorem nostrum, defendere cogitamus. iudices habemus quos voluimus, summa accusatoris voluntate. spero, si absolutus erit, coniunctiorem illum nobis fore in ratione petitionis; sin aliter acciderit, humaniter feremus.

**filiolus, -i** (*m*), little son (diminutive)
**scito!** (singular imperative), know! let me tell you
**litterae, -arum** (*f.pl*), letter, letters
**ratio, -onis** (*f*), tactic, plan
**scribo** (3), **scripsi**, to write
**antea**, before, previously
**diligenter**, conscientiously, faithfully
**competitor, -oris** (*m*), rival, fellow-candidate
**cogito** (1), to think, have in mind, plan
**iudices, -um** (*m.pl*), judges, jury
**voluntas, -atis** (*f*), willingness
**spero** (1), to hope
**absolvo** (3), **-solvi, -solutum**, to acquit
**coniunctus, -a, -um**, friendly, well-disposed
**fore = futurum esse**
**humaniter**, like a (reasonable) human being, with equanimity
**fero, ferre**, to bear, endure, accept

9 **maturo**: *(at an) early (date)*. Note the emphasis given to this adjective by separating it from **tuo adventu** and placing it at the end of the clause.

9 **summa hominum est opinio**: *the general feeling is*, literally *the most (common) opinion of people is*.

10 **nobiles**: This term refers to families whose ancestors had held high public office. In Rome, there was a recognised ladder of advancement which career politicians had to climb (see the **cursus honorum** on page 6). Most consuls came from the ranks of the **nobiles** because they could use their family contacts to secure great influence among the citizens. The somewhat derogatory use of **homines** (rather than **viri**) is interesting, in that it suggests that Cicero is sneering at the superior attitudes of these families who were prejudiced against the political aspirations of any **novus homo**.

10 **honori nostro**: *to my (election to) office*. Note again the use of **nostro** (*our*) to speak about himself.

11 **ad eorum voluntatem mihi conciliandam**: *in winning their support for me*, literally *for the purpose of winning their goodwill for me*. (For this use of the Gerundive, see LL p. 61.)

11 **maximo usui fore**: For Predicative Dative, see LL p. 13.

## Points for Discussion

1. In line 3, reference is made to the fact that Terentia came safely through the birth of young Marcus. In what ways would childbirth have been more dangerous in Roman times?
2. Comment on the use and position of **ego, meis** and **te** in line 4.
3. What do you think was the reaction of Cicero to the birth of his son (line 2)?
4. What are your views on lawyers defending people who are clearly guilty?
5. Do you think it is legitimate for politicians to ask influential people to 'pull strings' for them?

tuo adventu nobis opus est maturo; nam prorsus summa hominum est opinio tuos familiares, nobiles homines, adversarios honori nostro fore. ad eorum voluntatem mihi conciliandam maximo te mihi usui fore video. quare Ianuario mense, ut constituisti, cura ut Romae sis.

**adventus, -us** (*m*), arrival
**opus est** (+ abl.), there is need (of)
**prorsus**, certainly
**familiaris, -is** (*m*), friend
**adversarius, -a, -um**, opposed
**usui esse** (+ dat.), to be useful
**quare**, therefore
**mensis, -is** (*m*), month
**constituo** (3), **-ui**, to decide
**cura ut** (+ subjunctive), see that

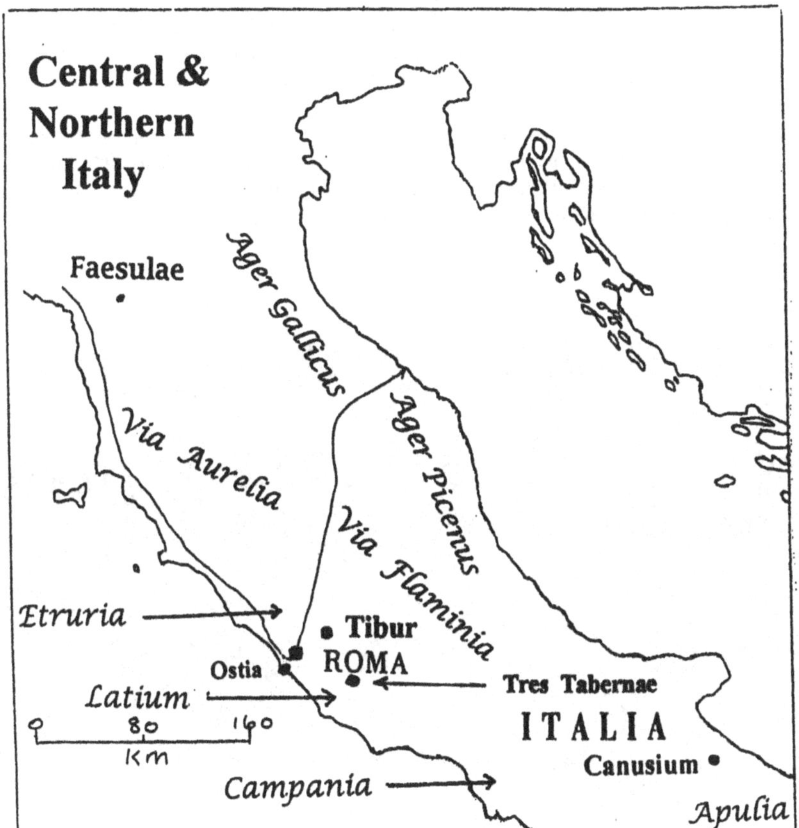

# The Catilinarian Conspiracy

L.Sergius Catilina, a political adventurer nearly contemporary with Cicero himself, is an enigmatic but fascinating figure in Roman history. He was a member of a patrician family which had sunk into poverty. The early part of his political career was marred by various forms of debauchery and crime, and he was deep in debt. However, he did rise to the rank of praetor in 68 BC; and in 67 BC he was governor of the province of Africa. On returning from there, he was impeached for maladministration of the province, which meant that he was not allowed to stand for the consulship while court proceedings were pending. In exasperation, he plotted to kill the incoming consuls on their first day in office and to seize power for himself, but the plan misfired. His trial continued beyond the elections held at the end of 65 BC; but, on his acquittal, he became eligible in 64 BC to stand for the consulship of the following year. However, the people elected C.Antonius and Cicero.

Catiline was becoming increasingly desperate and decided to seize power by force. During 63 BC, he began to organise a much more extensive conspiracy which was backed by some young nobles and by discontented elements among the populace, notably some former veteran soldiers of the dictator Sulla. Catiline's promise to cancel all existing debts, if his coup was successful, appeared like a lifeline to all those whose life-style had outstripped their means. The threat to the state was considerably increased by the fact that Pompey, the only man powerful enough to maintain order, had recently taken up a military command in the eastern Mediterranean.

Although he was standing for the consulship yet again, Catiline was not at all optimistic about his chances because both Cicero and Antonius were speaking out against him. The conspirators, therefore, gathered a body of troops at Faesulae (near modern Florence), intending to march on Rome, kill the consuls and stage a *coup d'état.* Catiline himself remained in Rome to direct operations there. Unfortunately for Catiline, some of his fellow-conspirators were not very reliable. Fulvia, the mistress of one of them, kept Cicero informed of their intentions, and Cicero was thus able to frustrate an attempt on his own life.

On 21 October 63 BC, Cicero, as consul, persuaded the Senate to pass an official decree (**senatus consultum ultimum**) investing the consuls with dictatorial powers and charging them 'to see that the state came to no harm' (**decrevit senatus ut consules viderent ne quid respublica detrimenti caperet**). The *coup* was expected on 28 October, but nothing happened. However, on 6 November, there were renewed reports of an attempt on Cicero's life. On 8 November, Cicero summoned another meeting of the Senate at which he delivered a blistering attack on Catiline (*First Speech Against Catiline*), confronting him with his plot to overthrow the government and urging him to quit Rome and take his degenerate supporters with him. Although Catiline had the effrontery to try to justify himself, he was howled down by the senators. After uttering some threatening words, he rushed from the Senate and left Rome that very night to take command of the army at Faesulae. He left several of his co-conspirators in Rome to continue preparations for the revolt. On the following day (9 November), Cicero assembled the people of Rome and, in what is called his *Second Speech Against Catiline*, he gave them details of the conspiracy and triumphantly summarised the previous day's denunciation of Catiline.

**quid quod adventu tuo ista subsellia vacuefacta sunt, quod omnes consulares, simulatque adsedisti, partem istam subselliorum nudam atque inanem reliquerunt?**

*What of the fact that on your arrival those seats beside you were emptied, that all the ex-consuls left that part of the benches bare and empty as soon as you sat down?*

First Speech against Catiline 16

1 **tandem aliquando**: Both words mean *at last*; by using them together, Cicero adds considerable emphasis to the opening of the speech — *now, at long last.*

1 **Quirites**: *citizens of Rome* — the term used by orators when addressing a public assembly. The word is of uncertain origin, but one theory is that it was derived from **Quirinus**, the title given to Romulus on his death; in which case, it would mean literally *descendants of Quirinus.*

1 **furentem audacia**: *lunatic in his effrontery*, literally *raving with brazenness.*

3 **ferro flammaque**: *with fire and sword* — a phrase designed to inflame his audience by conjuring up the image of the mass slaughter of citizens and the wholesale destruction of property.

3 **vel** is an old imperative of **velle**, meaning *make your own choice!* Here, it is used to link three verbs, each of which is milder than the one which precedes it: *we* (i.e. *I*) *have thrown (him) out* (**eiecimus**), *we have let (him) go* (**emisimus**), *we have helped him on his way*, literally *followed* (**prosecuti sumus**). Cicero leaves his audience to put their own interpretation on what happened. Any hint of weakness is quickly dispelled by the terseness of the four verbs of the next sentence which build up to a climax suggesting desperation on Catiline's part. (For Asyndeton, see CAO on page 238.) Note how Cicero regularly refers to himself as *we* or *us*, particularly when he is proud of something he has done.

4 **ipsum**: *of his own accord.*

4 **prosecuti sumus**: When someone was leaving Rome on an important mission, it was customary for friends to escort him as far as the gates of the city and to express their prayers and good wishes. The *words* (**verbis**) mentioned here by Cicero were jibes rather than good wishes.

5 **a monstro illo atque prodigio**: *by that unnatural monster.* Both nouns were originally religious words meaning *a portent which indicates impending disaster.* Their meaning was then extended to describe any unnatural monster. To emphasise a particular idea, Cicero frequently uses two words of similar meaning. (For Paired Words, see CAO on page 236.)

5 **moenibus ipsis intra moenia**: The city walls are virtually synonymous with the city of Rome. By repeating the word, Cicero emphasises how close the danger is to home.

6 **atque** is a much stronger word than **et**, meaning *and furthermore.*

7 **non iam inter latera nostra versabitur**: *will no longer be twisted in our ribs* (literally *sides*), i.e. there will no longer be an assassin (**sicarius**) in our midst.

8 **in campo**: *in the Campus Martius*, where the elections were held.

8 **denique**: *in short*, marking the last item in a list. Note how Cicero repeats **non** to build up to a climax, gradually narrowing the area in which the assassin might have scope to operate — from a wide open area, to the Forum, to the senate house, to his own home. (For Anaphora, see CAO on page 238.)

9 **loco**: *from his vantage-point*, literally *from his position* — a metaphor from the duelling of gladiators. (For Metaphor, see CAO on page 235.)

10 **cum hoste**: Catiline is no longer a political or personal enemy (**inimicus**), but an enemy of the state.

10 **bellum iustum**: *open* (literally *regular*) *warfare*, as opposed to the undercover treachery (**ex occultis insidiis**) mentioned in line 12.

# *9. Denunciation of Catiline*

(In Catilinam II, 1-2, 6-8, 12-13, 24-25, 27-29)

*The city has been saved from the wicked conspiracy which threatened murder and destruction. Now we can fight the enemy out in the open.*

tandem aliquando, Quirites, L.Catilinam furentem audacia, scelus anhelantem, pestem patriae nefarie molientem, vobis atque huic urbi ferro flammaque minitantem ex urbe vel eiecimus vel emisimus vel ipsum egredientem verbis prosecuti sumus. abiit, excessit, evasit, erupit. nulla iam pernicies a monstro illo atque prodigio moenibus ipsis intra moenia comparabitur. atque hunc quidem unum huius belli domestici ducem sine controversia vicimus. non enim iam inter latera nostra sica illa versabitur; non in campo, non in foro, non in curia, non denique intra domesticos parietes pertimescemus. loco ille motus est, cum est ex urbe depulsus. palam iam cum hoste, nullo impediente, bellum iustum geremus. sine dubio perdidimus hominem magnificeque vicimus, cum illum ex occultis insidiis in apertum latrocinium coniecimus.

**scelus, -eris** (*n*), crime, wickedness
**anhelo** (1), to breathe out
**pestis, -is** (*f*), ruin, destruction
**pat ria, -ae** (*f*), native land, homeland, country
**nefarie**, wickedly, impiously
**molior** (4), to plot
**minitor** (1) (+ dat.), to threaten
**egredior** (3), **egressus sum**, to go out, leave
**excedo** (3), **-cessi**, to go away, retire, withdraw
**evado** (3), **evasi**, to get away, escape
**erumpo** (3), **erupi**, to break out, burst out
**pernicies, -ei** (*f*), destruction
**comparo** (1), to plan, plot
**quidem**, certainly, in truth
**domesticus, -a, -um**, internal, civil
**sine** (+ abl.), without
**controversia, -ae** (*f*), doubt, dispute
**vinco** (3), **vici**, to conquer, defeat
**sica, -ae** (*f*), dagger
**curia, -ae** (*f*), senate house
**paries, -etis** (*m*), wall (of a house)
**pertimesco** (3), **-timui**, to be very afraid
**moveo** (2), **movi, motum**, to move, dislodge
**depello** (3), **-puli, -pulsum**, to drive away, expel
**palam**, openly
**impedio** (4), to hinder
**sine dubio**, without doubt, certainly
**perdo** (3), **-didi**, to destroy
**magnifice**, gloriously
**occultus, -a, -um**, hidden, secret
**insidiae, -arum** (*f.pl*), ambush
**apertus, -a, -um**, open
**latrocinium, -i** (*n*), banditry
**conicio** (3), **-ieci**, to hurl, drive, force

13 **quod ... quod ... quod ... quod ... quod**: Each of these means *as to the fact that.* Cicero lists five examples of how Catiline was thwarted in his attempted *coup* and then brings in the principal clause at the end of the sentence (**quanto ... putatis?**). This is one of his favourite oratorical techniques, used to create dramatic effect. (For Anaphora, see CAO on page 238.)

13 **vivis nobis**: *leaving me* (literally *us*) *alive*. (For this type of Ablative Absolute, see LL p. 31.)

15 **quanto tandem maerore**: *with what great sorrow, pray tell me*. Note this use of **tandem**, frequently inserted in questions to add emphasis.

16 **iacet ille nunc prostratus**: After the complexity of the previous sentence, the simplicity of these four words (beginning with the verb) is most effective. The metaphor (see CAO on page 235) in lines 16-18 is that of a wild beast which has been prevented from killing its prey and gazes back (**retorquet oculos**) at it as it slinks away.

19 **quae** refers to the city. (For Linking Relative, see LL p. 26.)

20 **evomuerit**: *has spewed out.* Cicero uses this medical metaphor (see CAO on page 235) to show that, just as the body is healthier when it gets rid of harmful substances through vomiting, so the body politic will be better without the harmful presence of Catiline. The subjunctives (**evomuerit** and **proiecerit**) indicate that Cicero is reporting the thoughts of the city. (For subordinate clauses in Reported Speech, see LL p. 111.)

21 **cui sit Apulia attributa**: *to whom Apulia has been assigned.* In this sentence, Cicero gives details of how the conspirators have organised themselves for the revolution. For the places mentioned, see the map on page 95.

21 **quis agrum Picenum**: Supply **habeat**. (cf. **quis Gallicum**, with which you should supply **agrum habeat**.) The narrow strip of land immediately to the north of Picenum was called **ager Gallicus** because a Gallic tribe called the Senones had settled there in the past.

23 **superioris noctis**: *of the previous night*, i.e. the night of 6-7 December, when the conspirators met in Laeca's house in Rome — three nights before this speech was delivered. (For inclusive reckoning in calculations, see LL p. 67.)

25 **hi** and **illi** both refer to those conspirators who still remain in Rome.

25 **ne** is an adverb, meaning *certainly.*

26 **futuram**: Supply **esse**.

quod vero non cruentum mucronem, ut voluit, extulit, quod vivis nobis egressus est, quod ei ferrum e manibus extorsimus, quod incolumes cives, quod stantem urbem reliquit, quanto tandem illum maerore esse adflictum et profligatum putatis? iacet ille nunc prostratus, Quirites, et se perculsum et abiectum esse sentit et retorquet oculos profecto saepe ad hanc urbem quam e suis faucibus ereptam esse luget: quae quidem mihi laetari videtur, quod tantam pestem evomuerit forasque proiecerit.

In an intervening section (here omitted), Cicero defends his action in letting Catiline escape and then describes some of Catiline's degenerate supporters.

*He reminds his audience that he knows every detail of the conspiracy and urges the conspirators to leave Rome while the going is good. There is still time for them to catch up with Catiline.*

video cui sit Apulia attributa, quis habeat Etruriam, quis agrum Picenum, quis Gallicum, quis sibi has urbanas insidias caedis atque incendiorum depoposcerit. omnia superioris noctis consilia ad me perlata esse sentiunt; patefeci in senatu hesterno die. Catilina ipse pertimuit, profugit. hi quid exspectant? ne illi vehementer errant, si illam meam pristinam lenitatem perpetuam sperant futuram.

**cruentus, -a, -um**, stained with blood
**mucro, -onis** (*m*), sword
**effero, -ferre, extuli**, to take away, carry off
**ferrum, -i** (*n*), sword, dagger
**extorqueo** (2), **-torsi** (+ dat.), to wrench (from)
**incolumis, -is, -e**, unharmed, safe and sound
**sto** (1), to stand
**relinquo** (3), **-liqui, -lictum**, to leave
**adfligo** (3), **-flixi, -flictum**, to lay low, cast down
**profligo** (1), to crush
**puto** (1), to think
**iaceo** (2), to lie
**prostratus, -a, -um**, laid low, felled
**percello** (3), **-culi, -culsum**, to strike down, ruin
**abicio** (3), **-ieci, -iectum**, to reject
**sentio** (4), to feel, realise
**profecto**, certainly, I am sure
**fauces, -ium** (*f.pl*), jaws
**eripio** (3), **eripui, ereptum**, to snatch
**lugeo** (2), to grieve, lament (the fact) that
**laetor** (1), to rejoice
**foras**, out of doors, out
**proicio** (3), **-ieci**, to cast out, eject
**ager, agri** (*m*), territory
**urbanus, -a, -um**, within the city
**insidiae, -arum** (*f.pl*), plot
**caedes, -is** (*f*), murder
**incendium, -i** (*n*), fire, arson
**deposco** (3), **-poposci**, to demand
**perfero, -ferre, -tuli, -latum**, to report
**patefacio** (3), **-feci**, to reveal
**hesterno die**, yesterday
**profugio** (3), **-fugi**, to flee
**vehementer**, entirely, very much
**erro** (1), to be wrong, be mistaken
**pristinus, -a, -um**, former
**lenitas, -atis** (*f*), leniency
**spero** (1), to hope

27 **quod exspectavi**: Supply **id** — *what* (literally *the thing which*) *I have been waiting for*.

27 **ut vos videretis**: *namely, that you should see*. This explains **quod exspectavi**.

28 **nisi si quis est**: *unless there is anyone*. Here, **si** reinforces **nisi** so that the two words together mean *unless*.

29 **qui putet**: For Generic Subjunctive, see LL p. 103.

29 **Catilinae similes**: *those who are like Catiline*. **Catilinae similes sentire** is an Accusative and Infinitive depending on **putet**.

31 **exeant**: For this type of Command or Exhortation, see LL p. 107.

31 **ne patiantur**: *let them not allow*. (For negative Commands and Exhortations, see LL p. 107.)

31 **desiderio sui tabescere**: *to pine away through longing for them*, i.e. because he is separated from them. **sui** is the genitive case of **se**, referring to the subject of the main verb — the conspirators who remain in Rome.

32 **Aurelia via** is ablative case. Catiline had fled north by the Via Aurelia which ran along the west coast of Italy.

34 **o fortunatam rem publicam**: For Accusative of Exclamation, see LL p. 6.

34 **hanc sentinam**: *this scum*, referring to Catiline. The basic meaning of **sentina** is *the bilge water* which gathered in the bottom of a ship. It is then used of any type of refuse or sewage which has to be got rid of. The metaphor (see CAO on page 235) is continued in the next sentence: firstly, the participle **exhausto** (meaning literally *drained off*) keeps up the image of bilge water being pumped out of a ship and sewage being disposed of down the drain; and, secondly, the verbs **levare** (*to relieve*) and **recreare** (*to refresh*) indicate that the ship is literally lightened and freshened when the bilge is removed.

36 **quid mali**: *what evil*. (For Partitive Genitive, see LL p. 9.)

36 **quod non ille conceperit**. For Generic Subjunctive, see LL p. 103.

37 **quis**: Note how Cicero repeats this word for rhetorical effect (cf. the use of **quod** in line 13). (For Anaphora, see CAO on page 238.)

37 **tota Italia**: Prepositions are regularly omitted in phrases containing the adjective **totus** (see LL p. 15).

39 **nepos**: *spendthrift*, literally *grandson*. The meaning *spendthrift* suggests that in Roman times, as today, grandparents often spoiled their grandchildren by over-indulgence.

41 **familiarissime**: *on the most intimate terms*.

41 **fateatur**: For Generic Subjunctive, see LL p. 103.

42 **per hosce annos**: *in these (past few) years*. Note how the addition of the **-ce** ending strengthens the demonstrative **hos** by its very sound.

42 **quod stuprum**: Supply **factum est**.

quod exspectavi iam sum adsecutus, ut vos omnes factam esse aperte coniurationem contra rem publicam videretis; nisi vero si quis est qui Catilinae similes cum Catilina sentire non putet. non est iam lenitati locus; severitatem res ipsa flagitat. unum etiam nunc concedam: exeant, proficiscantur, ne patiantur desiderio sui Catilinam miserum tabescere. demonstrabo iter: Aurelia via profectus est; si accelerare volent, ad vesperam consequentur.

*In driving out Catiline alone, the state has rid itself of the ringleader of every act of evil and corruption which has recently taken place. It is hardly surprising that he has been able to build up so quickly an army of scoundrels and profligates.*

o fortunatam rem publicam, si quidem hanc sentinam urbis eiecerit! uno mehercule Catilina exhausto, levata mihi et recreata res publica videtur. quid enim mali aut sceleris fingi aut cogitari potest quod non ille conceperit? quis tota Italia veneficus, quis gladiator, quis latro, quis sicarius, quis parricida, quis testamentorum subiector, quis circumscriptor, quis ganeo, quis nepos, quis adulter, quae mulier infamis, quis corruptor iuventutis, quis corruptus, quis perditus inveniri potest qui se cum Catilina non familiarissime vixisse fateatur? quae caedes per hosce annos sine illo facta est, quod nefarium stuprum non per illum?

**adsequor** (3), **-secutus sum**, to achieve
**aperte**, openly
**coniuratio, -onis** (*f*), conspiracy
**res publica, rei publicae** (*f*), the state
**sentire cum** (+ abl.), to agree with
**locus, -i** (*m*), place
**flagito** (1), to demand
**concedo** (3), to grant, make a concession
**proficiscor** (3), **-fectus sum**, to set out, leave
**demonstro** (1), to show
**accelero** (1), to hurry, make haste
**ad vesperam**, by the evening
**consequor** (3), to catch up, overtake
**eicio** (3), **eieci, eiectum**, to throw out
**unus, -a, -um**, alone
**mehercule**, by Hercules! heavens above!
**fingo** (3), to imagine, devise
**cogito** (1), to think, think up, plan
**concipio** (3), **-cepi**, to conceive, devise
**veneficus, -i** (*m*), poisoner
**latro, -onis** (*m*), bandit
**sicarius, -i** (*m*), cut-throat, assassin
**parricida, -ae** (*m*), parricide, parent-killer
**testamentum, -i** (*n*), will
**subiector, -oris** (*m*), forger
**circumscriptor, -oris** (*m*), cheat, fraud, swindler
**ganeo, -onis** (*m*), glutton
**mulier, -eris** (*f*), woman
**infamis, -is, -e**, notorious, of ill-repute
**iuventus, -utis** (*f*), youth
**corruptus, -i** (*m*), rogue, corrupt wretch
**perditus, -i** (*m*), scoundrel, waster
**invenio** (4), to find
**vivo** (3), **vixi**, to live
**fateor** (2), to confess, admit
**nefarius, -a, -um**, abominable
**stuprum, -i** (*n*), debauchery, lewdness

44 **iam vero**: *moreover* — a common way of introducing yet another example.

44 **tanta in ullo** is balanced by **quanta in illo**: *as great in anyone (else) as in him.* (For Correlatives, see LL p. 63.)

44 **iuventutis illecebra**: *talent for seducing young men*, literally *a lure for youth.*

45 **turpissime**: *in a most disgusting manner*. The verb **amabat** refers to Catiline's own homosexual advances, while **serviebat** tells us that he also *pandered to* (or *encouraged*) those who found him attractive.

47 **impellendo**: *by encouraging*. (For Gerund, see LL p. 60.)

47 **nunc vero**: *indeed, on this present occasion.* (cf. line 44.) Cicero gives a specific instance of how certain undesirable types of people were attracted to Catiline.

49 **nemo non modo Romae sed ne ullo quidem in angulo fuit**: The literal meaning is *There was no one not only in Rome but not even in any corner.* The negative force of **nemo** is not cancelled by **non modo** and **ne ... quidem**, but is strengthened by them. Translate: *Not only was there no one in Rome, but there was not even anyone in any corner (of Italy).*

50 **quem adsciverit**: For Generic Subjunctive, see LL p. 103.

51 **sceleris foedus**: *criminal alliance*, literally *a pact for crime.*

52 **etiam**: *still*, after all that has happened. The words **a me** imply that some people are suggesting that Cicero is carrying out a personal vendetta against Catiline.

52 **qui dicant**: For Generic Subjunctive, see LL p. 103.

53 **quod**: *that*, referring to the ejection of Catiline just mentioned. (For Linking Relative, see LL p. 26.)

53 **verbo**: *by word (alone)*, i.e. by telling Catiline to leave the city.

53 **istos**: *those men.* As usual, Cicero prefers the pronoun **iste** to **ille** when he is referring to his opponents.

53 **eicerem**: *I would be throwing out.* (For this tense and mood in Conditional sentences, see LL p. 54.)

54 **videlicet**: *of course*, used sarcastically, keeping up the derogatory use of **homo** (*fellow*). (For Sarcasm, see CAO on page 231.)

56 **quin**: *in fact.* (See also line 60.)

57 **Iovis Statoris**: Jupiter Stator was the protector of Rome. The title **Stator** was given to Jupiter as the god who would stand firm, like a rock, in times of trouble. The word is derived from the same root as the verb **stare**. The temple was selected as offering more security than the senate house.

58 **patres conscriptos**: *the Senate*, literally *the enrolled fathers.* This was the formal title given to those whose names were listed as being members of the Senate.

58 **quo**: *to that* (literally *which*) *place*. (For Linking Relative, see LL p. 26.)

59 **denique**: *in short* or *to sum up*. This word is commonly used to introduce the last example in a list — here, **quis, quis, quis**.

59 **ita aspexit ut**: *regarded (him) as.*

60 **quin etiam**: *in actual fact.* As in line 56, **quin** expands and/or corrects a statement which has just been made, and **etiam** adds emphasis.

60 **eius ordinis**: *of that body*, i.e. the Senate. **ordo** means *rank* or *class.*

iam vero quae tanta umquam in ullo iuventutis illecebra fuit, quanta in illo? qui alios ipse amabat turpissime, aliorum amori flagitiosissime serviebat, aliis fructum libidinum, aliis mortem parentum non modo impellendo verum etiam adiuvando pollicebatur. nunc vero quam subito non solum ex urbe verum etiam ex agris ingentem numerum perditorum hominum collegerat! nemo non modo Romae sed ne ullo quidem in angulo totius Italiae oppressus aere alieno fuit quem non ad hoc incredibile sceleris foedus adsciverit.

*Cicero rebuts the charge that he drove Catiline into exile and describes how, in his speech to the Senate, he confronted Catiline with the details of the plot, which clearly established Catiline's guilt. He claims that Catiline is not in exile; he has left to put himself at the head of a hostile army which he raised against the state.*

at etiam sunt qui dicant, Quirites, a me eiectum esse Catilinam. quod ego si verbo adsequi possem, istos ipsos eicerem qui haec loquuntur. homo enim videlicet timidus, aut etiam permodestus vocem consulis ferre non potuit; simulatque ire in exsilium iussus est, paruit. quin hesterno die, cum domi meae paene interfectus essem, senatum in aedem Iovis Statoris convocavi, rem omnem ad patres conscriptos detuli. quo cum Catilina venisset, quis eum senator appellavit, quis salutavit, quis denique ita aspexit ut perditum civem ac non potius ut importunissimum hostem? quin etiam principes eius ordinis partem illam subselliorum ad quam ille accesserat nudam atque inanem reliquerunt.

**umquam**, ever
**flagitiosissime**, most shamefully
**fructus, -us** (*m*), enjoyment
**libido, -inis** (*f*), lust
**verum**, but
**adiuvo** (1), to help, assist
**polliceor** (2), to promise
**agri, -orum** (*m.pl*), country districts
**ingens, -entis**, large, huge
**colligo** (3), **-legi**, to collect, gather
**opprimo** (3), **-pressi, -pressum**, to overwhelm, weigh down
**aes alienum, aeris alieni** (*n*), debt
**adscisco** (3), **-scivi**, to attach to
**at**, but
**loquor** (3), to speak
**permodestus, -a, -um**, over-sensitive
**fero, ferre**, to bear, endure, withstand
**simulatque**, as soon as
**exsilium, -i** (*n*), exile
**iubeo** (2), **iussi, iussum**, to order
**pareo** (2), to obey
**domi**, at home
**paene**, almost
**interficio** (3), **-feci, -fectum**, to kill
**aedes, -is** (*f*), temple
**convoco** (1), to call together, summon
**deferre ad** (+ acc.), to report to
**appello** (1), to speak to
**perditus, -a, -um**, corrupt, abandoned
**potius**, rather
**importunus, -a, -um**, dangerous
**princeps, -cipis** (*m*), leading man
**subsellium, -i** (*n*), bench, seat
**accedo** (3), **-cessi**, to approach
**inanis, -is, -e**, empty

63 **hic**: *then*, literally *at this point (of time)*.

63 **ego vehemens ille consul**: *I, that well-known bully of a* (literally *violent*) *consul*. Note that, when used in the sense *that well-known* or *that notorious*, **ille** usually comes second in the phrase. Cicero is, of course, making this remark tongue-in-cheek. (For Humour, see CAO on page 231.)

64 **quaesivi a Catilina** leads straight into an Indirect Question, without any introductory word for *whether*.

64 **ad M.Laecam**: *at Marcus Laeca's house*. In the first speech against Catiline, Cicero told the Senate that the conspirators had laid their final plans at this meeting: some conspirators were to start fires in Rome, others were to stir up revolts in different parts of Italy, and two men were detailed to murder the consul Cicero, while Catiline himself left Rome to take over command of the army that had been raised in Etruria.

65 **conscientia**: *by knowledge of his guilt*.

66 **in proximam**: Supply **noctem**, and translate *for the next night*.

67 **ei**: *by him*, to be taken with **esset descripta**. (For Dative of Agent, see LL p. 11.)

69 **iam pridem pararet**: *he had already for a long time been preparing (to set out)*. As usual, the imperfect tense with **iam pridem** shows that something had been, and still was, going on (see LL p. 52.)

70 **secures** (*axes*) and **fasces** (*fasces* or *rods*) were carried by lictors in front of consuls and praetors as symbols of their power. Having failed to win this power in the elections, Catiline intended to seize it by force.

70 **aquilam**: The general Gaius Marius had adopted the silver eagle as the standard of the legion, and it is said that the standard in question had actually been used in Marius' army.

72 **esse praemissam**: Each of the six nouns (**arma, secures, fasces, tubas, signa militaria** and **aquilam**) forms an Accusative and Infinitive clause with **esse praemissam** depending on **cum scirem**. As is often the case, the infinitive agrees with the nearest of these nouns. By repeating **cum** (*since*) in front of each of the nouns (lines 69-70), Cicero builds up to a magnificent climax. (For Climax, see CAO on page 232; for Anaphora, see CAO on page 238.)

72 **quem**: *(a man) whom*.

74 **hanc scortorum cohortem praetoriam**: *this élite corps of (male) prostitutes*. Every Roman general had a personal bodyguard of picked soldiers called the **cohors praetoria**.

The **fasces** were a bundle of rods carried by the attendants (**lictors**) of senior magistrates. They symbolised the magistrates' authority to punish by flogging. Outside the city, an axe was added to the rods since there, under military law, a magistrate could impose the death penalty.

hic ego vehemens ille consul, qui verbo cives in exsilium eicio, quaesivi a Catilina in nocturno conventu ad M.Laecam fuisset necne. cum ille homo audacissimus conscientia convictus primo reticuisset, patefeci cetera: quid ea nocte egisset, ubi fuisset, quid in proximam constituisset, quemadmodum esset ei ratio totius belli descripta edocui. cum haesitaret, cum teneretur, quaesivi quid dubitaret proficisci eo quo iam pridem pararet, cum arma, cum secures, cum fasces, cum tubas, cum signa militaria, cum aquilam illam argenteam, cui ille etiam sacrarium domi suae fecerat, scirem esse praemissam. in exsilium eiciebam quem iam ingressum esse in bellum videram?

In the middle section of the speech (not reproduced here), Cicero gives a perceptive and detailed account of the various groups in Rome to whom Catiline's proposed cancellation of all existing debts would be attractive — those who have incurred great debts but are wealthy in terms of property; men who are deeply in debt with no assets at all and who hope to have their debts cancelled; those who acquired a taste for a better life-style when Sulla settled them on land seized from his enemies but who have begun to live beyond their means; men who are natural losers through laziness and incompetence; men who have murdered people — even their own parents — in order to seize their possessions; and finally Catiline's own bosom friends — gamblers, adulterers, fops and perverts of various kinds.

*In the final section of the speech, Cicero calls for the support of all citizens who are on the side of patriotism and morality and opposed to the corrupt and evil régime which Catiline and his supporters would set up if their conspiracy succeeded. Good must surely triumph over evil.*

o bellum magnopere pertimescendum, cum hanc sit habiturus Catilina scortorum cohortem praetoriam! instruite nunc, Quirites, contra has

**quaero** (3), **quaesivi** (**a** + abl.), to ask
**conventus, -us** (*m*), meeting
**necne**, or not
**convinco** (3), **-vici, -victum**, to overpower, silence
**reticeo** (2), to remain silent
**ceteri, -ae, -a**, the rest
**ago** (3), **egi**, to do
**constituo** (3), **-ui**, to plan, decide
**quemadmodum**, how
**ratio, -onis** (*f*), plan
**describo** (3), **-scripsi, -scriptum**, to draw up, design
**edoceo** (2), to explain, disclose
**haesito** (1), to hesitate
**teneo** (2), to hold in check, trap
**quid**, why
**dubito** (1) (+ infinitive), to hesitate
**tuba, -ae** (*f*), trumpet
**signum, -i** (*n*), (military) standard
**argenteus, -a, -um**, silver
**sacrarium, -i** (*n*), shrine
**praemitto** (3), **-misi, -missum**, to send ahead
**ingredior** (3), **-gressus sum**, to enter, embark (upon)
**magnopere**, greatly
**instruo** (3), to draw up, make ready

76 **praeclaras**: *distinguished*, used sarcastically.

77 **gladiatori**: The word is used in a derogatory sense, implying that Catiline is little more than a professional killer.

77 **confecto et saucio**: *exhausted and crippled.* This possibly refers both to Catiline's previous life of profligacy and to the fact that Cicero has foiled the conspiracy. (For Paired Words, see CAO on page 236.)

79 **florem ac robur**: *the flower and strength*, a common way of describing top-class troops.

80 **urbes**: *the (walled) towns.* Some of these were **coloniae** (*colonies*) which were originally settlements of Roman citizens in Italy whose purpose was to keep local communities under control, others were **municipia** (self-governing allied *townships*) which had been granted full Roman citizenship roughly 25 years before this.

80 **respondebunt tumulis silvestribus**: *will be a match for* (literally *will answer*) *the wooded hillocks*, referring to the hideouts where Catiline's troops were lurking.

82 **inopia atque egestate**: *meagre resources*, literally *want and need.*

83 **eget ille**: These words balance **nos suppeditamur**, and should also be taken with **quibus**. Translate *and which he lacks.*

83 **equitibus**: The **equites** were the rich business class of Rome.

85 **si his rebus omissis**: Note how Cicero has repeated these words from lines 82-3, because it is likely that his audience will have lost the thread of the sentence after the expanded explanation in lines 83-5.

86 **ex eo ipso**: *from that very (comparison).*

86 **quam valde illi iaceant**: *how very low they lie*, i.e. how hopeless their situation is.

89 **omnium vestrum**: *of all of you.* **vestrum** is the genitive case of the pronoun **vos**.

90 **quia nati sunt cives**: One of the major considerations which made Cicero hesitate before taking drastic action against the conspirators was the fact that the rights of all Roman citizens were sacrosanct.

90 **monitos volo**: *I wish (them to be) warned.* **monitos** agrees with **illos** in line 88. Because he was reluctant to move against Roman citizens, Cicero preferred to give them repeated warnings.

91 **si cui solutior visa est**: *if anyone has felt it excessive*, literally *if it has seemed too lax to anyone.*

92 **ut id ... erumperet**: This clause amplifies **hoc**, explaining why Cicero had remained lenient for so long and giving his reason for waiting. Translate *namely, for that to break out (into the open).*

92 **quod reliquum est**: *as for the future*, literally *as to what is left*, contrasted with **adhuc** in line 91.

93 **horum** (line 93) and **his** (line 94) refer to the citizens whom he is addressing.

94 **mihi vivendum (esse)**: *I must live*, literally *it must be lived by me*. (For verbs used impersonally in the passive, see LL p. 57; for Dative of Agent, see LL pp. 11 and 62.)

94. **nullus est portis custos**:

95 **nullus insidiator viae**: *no one is waiting to ambush (them) on the way.*

95 **si qui**: *if any (of them).*

tam praeclaras Catilinae copias vestra praesidia vestrosque exercitus! et primum gladiatori illi confecto et saucio consules imperatoresque vestros opponite! deinde contra illam naufragorum eiectam ac debilitatam manum florem totius Italiae ac robur educite! iam vero urbes coloniarum ac municipiorum respondebunt Catilinae tumulis silvestribus. neque ego ceteras copias, ornamenta, praesidia vestra cum illius latronis inopia atque egestate conferre debeo. sed si, omissis his rebus quibus nos suppeditamur, eget ille — senatu, equitibus Romanis, urbe, aerario, vectigalibus, cuncta Italia, provinciis omnibus, exteris nationibus — si his rebus omissis causas ipsas quae inter se confligunt contendere velimus, ex eo ipso quam valde illi iaceant intellegere possumus.

*Catiline's co-conspirators may leave Rome if they wish; but, if they stay and move against the state, they will get a rude awakening.*

nunc illos qui in urbe remanserunt atque adeo qui contra urbis salutem omniumque vestrum in urbe a Catilina relicti sunt, quamquam sunt hostes, tamen, quia nati sunt cives, monitos etiam atque etiam volo. mea lenitas adhuc, si cui solutior visa est, hoc exspectavit ut id quod latebat erumperet. quod reliquum est, iam non possum oblivisci meam hanc esse patriam, me horum esse consulem, mihi aut cum his vivendum aut pro his esse moriendum. nullus est portis custos, nullus insidiator viae: si qui exire volunt, conivere possum.

**copiae, -arum** (*f.pl*), forces
**praesidium, -i** (*n*), defence
**exercitus, -us** (*m*), army
**oppono** (3) (+ dat.), to oppose, set against
**naufragus, -i** (*m*), castaway
**debilito** (1), to weaken, cripple
**manus, -us** (*f*), band
**vero**, in truth, certainly
**ornamenta, -orum** (*n.pl*), equipment
**confero, -ferre**, to compare
**omitto** (3), **-misi, -missum**, to omit, say nothing of
**suppeditor** (1), to be well supplied
**egeo** (2) (+ abl.), to lack, be without
**aerarium, -i** (*n*), treasury
**vectigal, -is** (*n*), tax, tax revenue
**cunctus, -a, -um**, all, whole
**exterus, -a, -um**, foreign, abroad
**natio, -onis** (*f*), people, tribe
**confligo** (3), to be in conflict
**contendo** (3), to compare, contrast
**intellego** (3), to understand, realise
**remaneo** (2), **-mansi**, to remain
**atque adeo**, or rather
**salus, -utis** (*f*), safety
**quia**, because
**nascor** (3), **natus sum**, to be born
**etiam atque etiam**, again and again
**lenitas, -atis** (*f*), leniency
**adhuc**, so far, up to now
**lateo** (2), to lie hidden
**obliviscor** (3), to forget
**pro** (+ abl.), on behalf of
**morior** (3), to die
**custos, -odis** (*m*), guard
**coniveo** (2), to connive, turn a blind eye

96 **qui vero se commoverit**: *but (anyone) who makes a move.*

96 **cuius ego factum deprehendero**: *(for) I will have detected his action*, literally *whose deed I will have detected.* Note the use of **ego** to emphasise Cicero's own involvement. The words bracketed in the text are uttered as an aside and in the nature of a warning.

99 **carcerem**: *prison.* This was not a custodial prison in the modern sense, but the place to which convicted criminals were taken prior to execution.

103 **post hominum memoriam**: *in living memory.*

103 **me uno togato duce et imperatore**: *under my sole leadership and command, but without any resort to arms*, literally *myself (being) the only leader and general dressed in a toga.* In times of war, the consuls normally put off their togas (worn in peacetime) and put on armour to lead the army.

104 **sedetur**: Although **sedetur** is present subjunctive since it is the verb of a Result clause, a future tense would probably be used in English. The literal meaning of **sedare** is *to settle*, but each of the three subjects (**res**, **pericula** and **bellum**) would probably require a different English verb.

104 **quod**: *all this.* (For Linking Relative, see LL p. 26.)

105 **ne improbus quidem quisquam**: *no one, however villainous*, literally *not even anyone wicked.*

106 **vis manifestae audaciae**: *the enormity of his blatant audacity.*

108 **illud quod vix optandum videtur**: *something which seems almost more than we can hope for*, literally *a thing which scarcely seems (something) to be hoped for.*

109 **ut neque bonus quisquam intereat**: *(namely) that no good man will perish.* (Compare line 105 for **quisquam** used with an adjective.) This clause and the next (**paucorumque ... possitis**) amplify **illud** in line 108. (cf. the use of **hoc** in line 91.)

110 **paucorum poena**: *if we punish a few*, literally *by the punishment of a few.*

111 **quae**: *this*, referring to all the assertions he has just made. (For Linking Relative, see LL p. 26.)

113 **significationibus**: *signs.* This is ablative case, depending on **fretus**.

113 **quibus ducibus**: *under whose guidance.* (For this type of Ablative Absolute, see LL pp. 30-1.)

114 **qui**: *they*, a Linking Relative referring back to **deorum immortalium**. (cf. the use of **quos** in line 116.)

115 **hic praesentes**: *here in person.* Most wars fought by Roman armies took place far from Rome, but the Romans nevertheless believed that the gods whom they worshipped would protect them wherever they were. The gods had usually lent their support from a distance (**procul**), since their temples were in Rome. This war, however, was in Rome itself and, as it were, on the gods' own doorstep.

qui vero se in urbe commoverit (cuius ego non modo factum vel inceptum ullum conatumve contra patriam deprehendero), sentiet in hac urbe esse consules vigilantes, esse egregios magistratus, esse fortem senatum, esse arma, esse carcerem quem vindicem nefariorum ac manifestorum scelerum maiores nostri esse voluerunt.

atque haec omnia sic agentur ut maximae res minimo motu, pericula summa nullo tumultu, bellum intestinum ac domesticum post hominum memoriam crudelissimum et maximum me uno togato duce et imperatore sedetur. quod ego sic administrabo, Quirites, ut, si ullo modo fieri poterit, ne improbus quidem quisquam in hac urbe poenam sui sceleris sufferat. sed si vis manifestae audaciae, si impendens patriae periculum me necessario de hac animi lenitate deduxerit, illud profecto perficiam quod in tanto et tam insidioso bello vix optandum videtur, ut neque bonus quisquam intereat paucorumque poena vos omnes salvi esse possitis.

quae quidem ego neque mea prudentia neque humanis consiliis fretus polliceor vobis, Quirites, sed multis et non dubiis deorum immortalium significationibus, quibus ego ducibus in hanc spem sententiamque sum ingressus: qui iam non procul, ut quondam solebant, ab externo hoste atque longinquo, sed hic praesentes suo numine atque auxilio sua templa atque urbis tecta defendunt. quos vos

**vel ... -ve ...**, or ... or ...
**inceptum, -i** (*n*), undertaking
**conatus, -us** (*m*), attempt, effort
**deprehendo** (3), **-hendi**, to detect, discover
**egregius, -a, -um**, outstanding
**fortis, -is, -e**, brave, resolute
**vindex, -icis** (*m*), avenger
**nefarius, -a, -um**, wicked, heinous
**manifestus, -a, -um**, clear, blatant
**scelus, -eris** (*n*), crime
**maiores, -um** (*m.pl*), ancestors
**motus, -us** (*m*), disturbance
**periculum, -i** (n), danger
**summus, -a, -um**, greatest
**tumultus, -us** (*m*), disturbance, upheaval
**intestinus, -a, -um**, internal, civil (war)
**crudelis, -is, -e**, cruel
**administro** (1), to manage, arrange
**ullo modo**, in any way, by any means
**fieri potest**, it is possible
**poena, -ae** (*f*), punishment
**impendens, -entis** (+ dat.), threatening
**necessario**, necessarily, of necessity
**deduco** (3), **-duxi**, to lead away from
**profecto**, certainly
**perficio** (3), to achieve
**insidiosus, -a, -um**, treacherous
**salvus, -a, -um**, safe
**quidem**, indeed
**prudentia, -ae** (*f*), wisdom, commonsense
**fretus, -a, -um** (+ abl.), relying (on)
**dubius, -a, -um**, uncertain, ambiguous
**spes, spei** (*f*), hope
**sententia, -ae** (*f*), opinion, policy
**quondam**, formerly
**soleo** (2), to be accustomed
**externus, -a, -um**, foreign, overseas
**longinquus, -a, -um**, distant
**numen, -inis** (*n*), divine power
**tectum, -i** (*n*), house, home

117 **quam urbem ... , hanc**: *this city which.* (For the antecedent incorporated into the relative clause, see LL pp. 26 and 98.) **hanc (urbem)** is the object of **defendant**.

120 **defendant**: This verb ends the Indirect Command which began at **ut** in line 117.

## Points for Discussion

1. In lines 1-10, Cicero employs a variety of techniques (see CAO on pages 235-7) to arrest the attention of his citizen audience. Collect examples of:
   (a) repeated words,
   (b) repeated sound patterns,
   (c) alliteration,
   (d) balanced phrases.
2. What emotions do you think Cicero is trying to arouse amongst his audience in the opening sentence of the speech (lines 1-4)? Why do you think he begins with such extravagant accusations?
3. What effect do you think Cicero is trying to produce by following the long, expansive opening sentence with the four simple verbs **abiit, excessit, evasit, erupit** in line 4?
4. Read lines 21-33. How confident do you think Cicero is at this point? Explain why you think this. Now read lines101-10. In what way do these lines strike a different tone?
5. In lines 34-43, Cicero depicts Catiline as the lowest of the low. Study the various terms of abuse that he hurls at Catiline and state how relevant you think each of them is to the allegation that Catiline plans to overthrow the government. To what emotions is he appealing? Character assassination is being used increasingly in present-day political campaigns. Do you think it is a legitimate tactic?

**o tempora! o mores!**
*What dreadful times we live in! What a low standard of morality!* (literally *What times! What habits!*) First Speech against Catiline 2

**vixere! (= vixerunt!)***They have lived!* Plutarch's Life of Cicero 22
Cicero's dramatic use of the perfect tense indicates that the conspirators have been executed. He avoids the ill-omened word *death.*

Quirites, precari, venerari, implorare debetis ut, quam urbem pulcherrimam, florentissimam potentissimamque esse voluerunt, hanc, omnibus hostium copiis terra marique superatis, a perditissimorum civium nefario scelere defendant.

**precor** (1), to pray to
**veneror** (1), to reverence, worship
**imploro** (1), to beseech
**florens, -entis**, flourishing
**potens, -entis**, powerful
**terra marique**, by land and sea
**supero** (1), to overcome

# Cicero Triumphs over Catiline

Although Cicero had persuaded the Senate and the people of the seriousness of the situation, he still did not have conclusive proof of the conspiracy. That came at the beginning of December when Gallic ambassadors were intercepted and found to be carrying letters from the conspirators urging the Gauls to join the revolt. On 3 December, the conspirators who had remained in Rome were arrested and brought before the Senate. Faced with the damning evidence that the letters were in their handwriting and bore their seals, they confessed and were handed over into the custody of certain senators. Cicero thereupon made a speech to the people (the Third Catiline Oration), in which he told them how the conspirators had been trapped, arrested and found guilty.

On 5 December, the Senate was convened to decide what was to be done with the prisoners. Silanus, the consul-elect, proposed that they should be executed, and the next speakers supported this. Julius Caesar, however, who at this time was beginning to manoeuvre himself into a position of power, said that it was the fundamental right of Roman citizens not to be executed without an appeal to the people. He therefore played safe by recommending that their property should be confiscated and that they be exiled from Rome and detained in different **municipia** for the rest of their lives. When Cicero saw that this speech had caused some senators to waver, he rose to deliver his fourth speech against Catiline, in which he claimed that the accused had forfeited their rights by conspiring against the state. The Senate voted overwhelmingly to execute them. As soon as the Senate broke up, Cicero ordered the prisoners to be taken to the state dungeons at the foot of the Capitol, where they were strangled.

As he left the Senate that night, the crowd outside cheered him and hailed him as **pater patriae**, indicating that they believed that he had saved the state. It was the proudest moment of Cicero's life. There were some, however, who continued to point out that he had executed Roman citizens without formal trial — an accusation which was later to be used against him.

In January 62 BC, Catiline's forces were decisively defeated and Catiline himself was killed.

1 The formality of the opening, using the fathers' names (**M.F. = Marci filius** and **Cn.F. = Gnaei filio**) as well as the greeting (**S.D. = salutem dicit**, *sends greetings*), suggests that Cicero and Pompey were not close friends. Contrast the casual opening used in letters to his close friend Atticus (e.g. page 93).

1 **Magno**: Pompey was hailed as 'The Great' by his troops after he defeated the Marians in Africa in 81 BC, when he was only 25 years old (see page 71). The title was later confirmed by the dictator Sulla.

2 **Imperatori**: *commander-in-chief (in the East)*. This noun is used in apposition to **Cn.Pompeio Magno**.

3 **S.T.E.Q.V.B.E.**: This abbreviation stands for **si tu exercitusque valetis, bene est**, *I hope that you and the army are in good heart*, literally *if you and your army are doing well, it is well.*

3 **publice misisti**: A reference to the official dispatches which Pompey sent to Rome to announce his victory over Mithridates and to report the political settlements he had made in the Middle East.

4 **tantam ... quantam ...**: *as much ... as*. (For Correlatives, see LL p. 64.)

5 **pollicebar**: *I repeatedly promised*, e.g. in the *Pro Lege Manilia* (see pages 72 to 89) and other speeches.

5 **hoc**: *this* is explained by the Accusative and Infinitive clause which follows.

6 **veteres hostes, novos amicos**: Politicians who had previously opposed Pompey, partly through jealousy and partly through fear of his becoming too powerful, now realised that it was expedient to become his supporters. Notable among these was Julius Caesar, who now sought to secure honours for Pompey. Caesar, Pompey and Crassus were soon to form an unofficial alliance known as the First Triumvirate.

7 **ex magna spe deturbatos iacere**: *are dejected, having been cheated of great expectations*, literally *are lying (prostrate), cast down from great hope.*

8 **litteras quas misisti**: This was Pompey's reply to the letter which Cicero sent describing how he 'had saved the state' by suppressing the Catilinarian conspiracy. Cicero's letter is no longer extant, but it is clear from other evidence that it adopted a rather superior tone; and it was probably this which evoked the cool response from Pompey.

10 **tam ... quam ...**: *as much ... as ...*: (For Correlatives, see LL p. 64.)

10 **meorum officiorum conscientia**: *in the knowledge that I have done my duty*, literally *in the knowledge of my duties*. **officium** is used to describe a service rendered to someone who has a right to claim it. In this case, Cicero refers to the services which, as a good citizen, he was obliged to give to the state.

11 **quibus si quando non mutue respondetur**: *if I sometimes do not receive full credit for what I have done*, literally *if sometimes there is no reciprocal response to them*. (For verbs used Impersonally, see LL p. 57.) The Linking Relative **quibus** (see LL p. 26) refers to the services which Cicero has rendered to the state.

11 **apud me plus offici residere facillime patior**: *I have no difficulty in accepting that I have done more than I needed to*, literally *I very easily allow that more service remains with me*. Cicero seems to be thinking of a kind of financial account in which his services to the state are listed on one side and the amount of grateful acknowledgement he has received from the state is listed on the other. Since the state's recognition of his achievements fell short of what he felt he deserved, he was left with, as it were, a 'credit balance' in his account.

# 10. A Letter to his Idol

(ad Familiares V.7)

As is very obvious from Cicero's speech in support of the Lex Manilia which proposed that Pompey be given the supreme command against King Mithridates (see pages 72-89), Cicero's admiration for Pompey was almost a form of hero-worship. It would seem that Pompey did not admire Cicero to the same extent. Cicero had written to Pompey giving him a very full and self-congratulatory account of how he had suppressed the Catilinarian conspiracy (see pages 97-113). In the following letter (written in Rome in April 62 BC to Pompey in Asia), Cicero shows his bitter disappointment that the 'great man' in his reply not only failed to lavish praise on Cicero for his magnificent achievement, but did not even make a polite reference to it.

M.TULLIUS M.F. CICERO S.D. CN.POMPEIO CN. F. MAGNO IMPERATORI

S.T.E.Q.V.B.E. ex litteris tuis, quas publice misisti, cepi una cum omnibus incredibilem voluptatem; tantam enim spem oti ostendisti quantam ego semper omnibus, te uno fretus, pollicebar. sed hoc scito, tuos veteres hostes, novos amicos, vehementer litteris perculsos atque ex magna spe deturbatos iacere.

ad me autem litteras quas misisti, quamquam exiguam significationem tuae erga me voluntatis habebant, tamen mihi scito iucundas fuisse; nulla enim re tam laetari soleo quam meorum officiorum conscientia. quibus si quando non mutue respondetur, apud me plus offici residere

**litterae, -arum** (*f.pl*), letter(s), dispatch(es)
**publice**, officially, by official courier
**capio** (3), **cepi**, to take, derive
**una cum** (+ abl.), along with
**voluptas, -atis** (*f*), pleasure
**spes, spei** (*f*), hope
**otium, -i** (*n*), peace
**ostendo** (3), **-tendi**, to show
**unus, -a, -um**, alone
**fretus, -a, -um** (+ abl.), relying (on)
**scito** (imperative) know, let me assure you
**vetus, -eris**, old
**vehementer**, greatly, severely
**percello** (3), **-culi, -culsum**, to strike (with consternation), shock
**autem**, however
**exiguus, -a, -um**, small, slight
**significatio, -onis** (*f*), indication, sign, expression
**erga** (+ acc.), towards
**voluntas, -atis** (*f*), goodwill
**iucundus, -a, -um**, pleasing, welcome
**laetor** (1) (+ abl.), to rejoice (in), take pleasure (in)
**soleo** (2), to be accustomed
**si quando**, if sometimes, if ever

12 **illud non dubito quin**: *on this point I have no doubt that.* (For this construction, see LL p. 105.) The pronoun **illud** adds emphasis.

12 **mea summa erga te studia**: *my supreme efforts on your behalf.* Cicero again alludes to the numerous occasions on which he spoke up publicly on Pompey's behalf (cf. line 5).

13 **res publica**: *the interests of the state.*

15 **ne ignores**: *so that you will be well aware*, literally *so that you may not be ignorant.*

15 **quid desiderarim** (= **desideraverim**): *what I found wanting*, i.e. what I was looking for but did not find.

16 **postulat**: In Latin, where there is more than one subject, the verb commonly agrees with the nearest one.

16 **res eas gessi quarum**: *my achievements were such that*, literally *I achieved those things for which.*

17 **et nostrae necessitudinis et rei p(ublicae) causa**: *in recognition of* (literally *for the sake of*) *both our own close ties and the interests of the state.* The noun **necessitudo** implies a much closer relationship than **amicitia**. Pompey clearly did not share Cicero's view of their relationship.

18 **quam**: A Linking Relative (see LL p. 26) referring to **gratulationem**.

19 **vererere = verereris**: *you were afraid.* The subjunctive is used to show that Cicero is assuming that this was Pompey's reason for not congratulating him. (For subjunctive expressing Alleged Reason, see LL p. 99.)

19 **ne cuius animum offenderes**: *that you would hurt anyone's feelings.* (For Fearing clauses, see LL p. 49.) Cicero is referring to people like Julius Caesar who criticised the execution of the Catilinarian conspirators (see page 113).

20 **nos**: Cicero frequently uses the more pompous plural *we* when referring to himself. Compare our 'royal we'.

21 **quae**: A Linking Relative referring to **ea** in line 20.

21 **cum veneris**: Supply **Romam**, *to Rome.*

21 **tanta animi magnitudine**: *with such magnanimity*, literally *with such greatness of spirit.*

22 **ut ... patiare**: *that you will readily allow me* (**ut me facile patiare**), *(who am) not much less great than Laelius* (**non multo minorem quam Laelium**), *to be joined* (**adiunctum esse**) *to yourself* (**tibi**), *(who are) much greater* (**multo maiori**) *than Africanus was* (**quam Africanus fuit**), *in public duties* (**in re publica**) *and in (personal) friendship* (**et in amicitia**). [**patiare** (line 24) = **patiaris**] The letter on the whole is rather critical of Pompey, and Cicero tries to atone for this by ending with an extravagant compliment which sounds artificial and contrived. Pompey is hailed as greater than Scipio Africanus who finally destroyed Carthage in the Third Punic War; and Cicero pictures himself as Pompey's mentor and friend in the same way as Laelius had been to Scipio.

## Points for Discussion

1. In lines 3 and 8 Cicero refers to two different letters sent by Pompey. To whom were these letters sent? Which gave Cicero greater pleasure, and why?
2. What aspects of Cicero's character are revealed in this letter?
3. What is the substance of Cicero's criticism of Pompey?

facillime patior. illud non dubito quin, si te mea summa erga te studia parum mihi adiunxerint, res publica nos inter nos conciliatura coniuncturaque sit.

ac ne ignores quid ego in tuis litteris desiderarim, scribam aperte, sicut et mea natura et nostra amicitia postulat. res eas gessi, quarum aliquam in tuis litteris et nostrae necessitudinis et rei p. causa gratulationem exspectavi; quam ego abs te praetermissam esse arbitror, quod vererere ne cuius animum offenderes. sed scito ea, quae nos pro salute patriae gessimus, orbis terrae iudicio ac testimonio comprobari; quae, cum veneris, tanto consilio tantaque animi magnitudine a me gesta esse cognosces ut tibi multo maiori quam Africanus fuit me non multo minorem quam Laelium facile et in re p. et in amicitia adiunctum esse patiare.

**parum**, too little, not enough
**adiungo** (3),**-iunxi, -iunctum**, to join, attach, ally
**concilio** (1), to bring together, reconcile
**coniungo** (3), **-iunxi, -iunctum**, to join together, unite
**aperte**, openly
**sicut**, just as
**amicitia, -ae** (*f*), friendship
**postulo** (1), to demand
**aliqui, -qua, -quod**, some
**gratulatio, -onis** (*f*), congratulation, thanks, gratitude
**abs = ab**
**praetermitto** (3), **-misi, -missum**, to neglect, overlook
**arbitror** (1), to think, suppose
**pro** (+ abl.), for the sake (of)
**salus, -utis** (*f*), safety, well-being
**orbis terrae** (*m*), the world
**iudicium, -i** (*n*), judgement, verdict
**testimonium, -i** (*n*), testimony, evidence
**comprobo** (1), to approve, acknowledge
**consilium, -i** (*n*), good judgement, wisdom
**cognosco** (3), to realise

# Patricians and Plebeians

Roman society was divided into patricians (**patricii**), a sort of aristocracy by birth, and plebeians (**plebs** or **plebeii**) consisting of the main populace of Rome. How and when these two classes were formed is unclear and much disputed. One view holds that the term *plebeian* originally encompassed the entire citizen body, but the patricians gradually acquired privileges through wealth and influence and became a class apart. In the early Republic, these privileges included the exclusive right to hold magistracies and the chief religious posts. These rights were protected in early times by forbidding marriage between patricians and plebeians.

Resentment over their treatment by the patricians grew among the plebeians and in 494 BC, following a kind of general strike by the plebeians, they were allowed to appoint two officers of their own, called **tribuni plebis** (*tribunes of the plebs*) to protect them against the patricians. Strictly speaking, the tribunes were never magistrates in the fullest sense and, as only plebeians could become tribunes, the office could never be part of the **cursus honorum** (see pages 6-7). Tribunes of the plebs did, however, have special powers. They exercised the **ius auxilii**, i.e. the right to help any plebeian who was being unjustly treated by a patrician magistrate. Even more significant was the right of veto (**intercessio**) by which each one of the tribunes could obstruct any business of the state or the action of a magistrate by simply uttering the word **intercedo** (*I oppose*). The number of the tribunes was soon increased from two to ten, and their persons were declared sacred and inviolate. Anyone who laid hands on them was declared an outlaw and forfeited his property.

Another significant power acquired by the **plebs** was the right to hold their own assemblies (**concilia plebis**) and there to pass resolutions (**plebiscita**) which eventually (from 287 BC) had the full force of laws, i.e. were binding on patricians and plebeians alike. Since the tribunes convened the plebeian assemblies, they were able to pass legislation without reference to the senate — a powerful weapon in the hands of unscrupulous politicians in that they could manipulate the tribunes for their own purposes. The tribunes, for their part, could both bypass the Senate as lawmakers and, by using the veto, frustrate the plans of the patricians and the senatorial class.

Gradually, over a period of about 200 years, and apparently without violence or bloodshed, the plebeians gained nearly all the rights and privileges of Roman citizens. Plebeians were allowed to marry patricians, and the children of a patrician father and a plebeian mother were regarded as patricians. The laws of Rome, originally known only to the patricians, were codified in 449 BC and inscribed on twelve bronze tablets which were displayed in the forum for all to see. All the highest offices of state were thrown open to the plebeians in 367 BC, and soon it was laid down that one of the two consuls must be a plebeian.

The distinction between patrician and plebeian was of less significance by Cicero's time, but ambitious politicians continued to use the tribunes for their own ends. This often disrupted the normal functioning of the state so much that, when the Republic came to an end, all the powers and privileges of the tribunes of the plebs were absorbed by Augustus Caesar himself, the first of the emperors.

# Cicero and Clodius

One of Cicero's dreams was that, following many years of political conflict, the Senate would regain supreme authority. He was sure that Pompey could make that dream come true. However, Pompey had his own ambitions and in 60 BC, along with Caesar and Crassus, he formed the First Triumvirate, which further decreased the power of the Senate. Caesar tried in vain to secure the support of Cicero, but the latter continued to speak out against the political pact.

As soon as his consulship ended, criticism began to be levelled at Cicero for the high-handed way in which he had dealt with the Catilinarian conspirators (see page 113). Matters reached a crisis in 58 BC when Publius Clodius Pulcher, a profligate aristocrat and bitter enemy of Cicero, was elected tribune.

In 62 BC, Clodius had been detected disguised as a slave girl in the house where the Mysteries of the Bona Dea were being celebrated — an outrage, since men were excluded from those Mysteries. He was brought to trial in 61 BC but secured his acquittal by bribing the judges. He claimed that he had been elsewhere at the time, but Cicero had produced evidence which proved that his alibi was false.

To take his revenge on Cicero, Clodius had himself adopted into a plebeian family, changing his patrician name (Claudius) to the plebeian spelling Clodius, so that he could be elected to the powerful position of tribune of the plebs. He immediately proposed a bill which would deny anyone who had executed a Roman citizen without trial the use of fire and water (the Roman formula for banishment). Cicero knew that he was the target of this bill; and, realising that the Senate and his idol Pompey would not defend him, he reluctantly left Rome around 20 March 58 BC. Immediately after this, Clodius' bill was passed, specifically naming Cicero and depriving him of the use of fire and water anywhere within a 400-mile radius of Rome. His house on the Palatine and his villa in Tusculum were ransacked by the mob. He decided to leave Italy altogether and go into exile in Greece.

Clodius, however, was not content with his success in banishing Cicero but went on to terrorise Rome with his gangster mob during the rest of his year as tribune (58 BC). The Triumvirs began to regret having unleashed Clodius and, by 57 BC, there emerged a set of tribunes more favourable to Cicero, including Milo and Sestius. When faced by Clodius' mobs, these two tribunes had to provide themselves with armed bodyguards. In one attack by Clodius, Cicero's brother Quintus was severely wounded and Sestius himself was lucky to escape alive. The Triumvirs and the Senate, as well as the tribunes, now began to favour Cicero's return and eventually, on 4 September 57 BC, Cicero was welcomed back to Rome.

Cicero later successfully defended Sestius against a charge of rioting during his tribunate. As for Milo and Clodius, their gang warfare continued sporadically until at last Milo killed Clodius in a clash between their rival gangs on the Via Appia in 52 BC. Milo was charged with murder, and Cicero failed to obtain an acquittal. Milo then went into exile at Massilia in Gallia Narbonensis.

But, at the time when Cicero was writing the letter to his wife and children as he was waiting to go on board ship at Brundisium on his way into exile in Greece (see Chapter 11), these events lay far in the future.

1 **S.D. = salutem dicit** (or **dat**): *sends greetings* — one of the regular openings in a Roman letter.

1 **suis**: The adjective is plural to include his wife, daughter and son.

2 **do**: *I send.*

2 **cum ... tum ...**: *not only ... but also ...*

4 **quod utinam fuissemus**: *I wish I had been,* literally *would that we had been.* Cicero often uses the plural (here **fuissemus**) when referring to himself. Compare our 'royal *we*'. **quod** is used here simply as a connective. No word is required in English, although the basic meaning is *but.* (Compare **quod** in line 6.) (For **utinam** used with the pluperfect subjunctive to express a Wish in the past, see LL p. 108.)

5 **nihil mali**: *no misfortune.* (For Partitive Genitive, see LL p. 9.)

6 **vidissemus**: *we would have seen.* This is the main clause of a conditional sentence in which the **si** clause has been omitted. (For Conditional sentences, see LL p. 54.)

6 **nos**: The plural is again used for the singular.

6 **ad aliquam alicuius commodi aliquando recuperandi spem**: *for some hope of some day regaining some form of happiness.* (For this use of the Gerundive, see LL p. 61.) The repetitive build-up of **aliquam ... alicuius ... aliquando** indicates how desperate and forlorn Cicero feels.

7 **minus est erratum a nobis**: *my mistake has been less serious,* literally *it has been less erred by us.* (For verbs used impersonally in the passive, see LL p. 107.)

8 **mea vita**: *my life* — a term of affection, just as we might say *my dearest one, my darling, my love,* etc.

13 **periculum fortunarum et capitis sui**: *the danger to his possessions and his own person.* Anyone who gave shelter to an exiled person within a prohibited area could have his own property confiscated and might even forfeit his life. The use of **sui** is emphatic and is contrasted with **mea** later in the line..

13 **prae mea salute**: *putting my safety first,* literally *for the sake of my safety.*

14 **legis improbissimae**: See the background notes on page 119.

14 **quominus praestaret**: *from fulfilling.* (For this construction, see LL p. 109.)

15 **ius officiumque**: *the conventional obligations,* literally *the obligation and duty.* In the Roman world, bonds of friendship between particular families were very strong; and it was customary for travellers to expect to be put up for the night in the homes of those with whom there were long-standing family ties, even though the individuals concerned might never actually have met.

16 **habebimus quidem semper**: Supply **gratiam**.

17 **a.d. ii K.Mai. = pridie Kalendas Maias**: *29 April.* Before Julius Caesar revised the calendar in 46 BC, there were only 355 days in the year. There were 31 days in March, May, July and October; 28 in February; and 29 in the remaining seven months. (For the calculation of Dates, see LL p. 67.) **a.d.II** (instead of **pridie**) is found on some inscriptions.

# *11. A Letter from Exile*

(ad Familiares XIV.4)

TULLIUS S. D. TERENTIAE ET TULLIAE ET CICERONI SUIS

ego minus saepe do ad vos litteras quam possum propterea quod cum omnia mihi tempora sunt misera, tum vero, cum aut scribo ad vos aut vestras lego, conficior lacrimis sic ut ferre non possim. quod utinam minus vitae cupidi fuissemus! certe nihil aut non multum in vita mali vidissemus. quod si nos ad aliquam alicuius commodi aliquando recuperandi spem fortuna reservavit, minus est erratum a nobis; sin haec mala fixa sunt, ego vero te quam primum, mea vita, cupio videre et in tuo complexu emori, quoniam neque di, quos tu castissime coluisti, neque homines, quibus ego semper servivi, nobis gratiam rettulerunt.

nos Brundisii apud M.Laenium Flaccum dies XIII fuimus, virum optimum, qui periculum fortunarum et capitis sui prae mea salute neglexit neque legis improbissimae poena deductus est quominus hospitii et amicitiae ius officiumque praestaret. huic utinam aliquando gratiam referre possimus! habebimus quidem semper. Brundisio profecti sumus a.d. ii Kal.Mai; per Macedoniam Cyzicum petebamus.

**minus**, less
**propterea quod**, because
**vero**, in truth, certainly
**lego** (3), to read
**conficio** (3), to overcome, weaken
**lacrima, -ae** (*f*), tear
**sic**, so
**fero, ferre, tuli**, to bear, endure
**vita, -ae** (*f*), life
**cupidus, -a, -um** (+ gen.), desirous
**certe**, certainly, surely
**commodum, -i** (*n*), advantage
**reservo** (1), to keep back, preserve
**sin**, but if
**fixus, -a, -um**, fixed, permanent
**quam primum**, as soon as possible
**cupio** (3), to desire, long for
**complexus, -us** (*m*), embrace
**emorior, emori** (3), to die
**quoniam**, since
**caste**, piously, virtuously
**colo** (3), **colui**, to cultivate, worship
**servio** (4) (+ dat.), to serve
**gratiam referre** (+ dat.), to return thanks (to), show gratitude (to)
**apud** (+ acc.), at the house of
**neglego** (3), **-lexi**, to ignore, disregard
**lex, legis** (*f*), law
**improbus, -a, -um**, wicked, shameful
**poena, -ae** (*f*), punishment, penalty
**deduco** (3), **-duxi, -ductum**, to deter
**hospitium, -i** (*n*), hospitality
**amicitia, -ae** (*f*), friendship
**proficiscor** (3), **-fectus sum**, to set out, leave
**peto** (3), to make for

18 **o me perditum!** and **o me adflictum**: For Accusative of Exclamation, see LL p. 6.
18 **rogem?**: *am I to ask?* (For Deliberative Questions, see LL p. 107; compare **rogem** in line 19 and **sim** in line 20.)
20 **opinor, sic agam**: *I shall make this plea, I think*, literally *I think I shall plead thus*. **agere** is the verb used of pleading a case in the law courts.
20 **eam confirmes et rem adiuves**: *please strengthen (that hope) and help my cause*, literally *may you strengthen it and help the matter*. (For Wishes and Commands, see LL p. 107.)
21 **transactum est**: *there is nothing that can be done*, literally *it has been brought to an end*. In other words, it is a fait accompli.
21 **quoquo modo**: *in whatever way*.
22 **fac venias**: *be sure to come*. (For the construction, see LL p. 109.)
24 **quid Tulliola mea fiet?**: *what will become of my dear little Tullia?* **Tulliola mea** is ablative. Cicero uses the diminutive ending **-ola** as a term of affection. Compare **misellae** (the diminutive of **miserae**) in line 25, and **filiola** in line 53.
24 **id videte!**: *see to that!*
24 **mihi deest consilium**: *I cannot offer advice*, literally *a plan is lacking to me*.
25 **se res habebit**: *the situation turns out*. (For this use of the future, see LL p. 52.)
26 **serviendum est**: *everything else must take second place (to)*, literally *(it) must be subservient (to)*. (For verbs used impersonally in the passive, see LL p. 57.) Tullia's dowry had not yet been settled in full.
27 **Cicero meus**: This refers to his son, also called Marcus, who was six years old.
27 **iste vero sit**: *in truth, I would wish him to be*. (For the present subjunctive expressing Wishes, see LL p. 107.)
29 **utrum aliquid teneas an**: *whether you are holding on to anything or*. Supply **nescio** before this Indirect Question. Cicero fears that all his property has been confiscated.
29 **quod metuo**: *as I fear*, literally *which I fear*.
30 **Pisonem**: Gaius Calpurnius Piso was Tullia's husband.
30 **fore semper nostrum**: *will always be true to us*, literally *will always be ours*, i.e. on our side. **fore** = **futurum esse** (cf. lines 49 and 50.)
30 **de familia liberata**: *concerning the freeing of our slaves*. Terentia had heard a rumour that Cicero had freed all his slaves, assuming that all his possessions might be confiscated. He tells her not to worry and explains exactly what he has arranged. (For this use of the perfect participle, see LL p. 29.)
31 **quod te moveat**: *to worry you*. (For Generic Subjunctive, see LL p. 102.)
31 **tuis ita promissum est**: *the following promise was made to your (slaves)*.
32 **ut**: *as*. (For the use of the subjunctive **esset**, see LL p. 111.)
32 **in officio**: *loyal*, literally *in duty*. Orpheus was one of Terentia's slaves and was accompanying Cicero.
33 **ceterorum servorum**: Having dealt with Terentia's own slaves (**tuis**, in line 31), he now turns to the arrangements for the rest of the slaves.
33 **ea causa est ut**: *the position is that*.
33 **si res a nobis abisset** (= **abiisset**): *if we should lose our property*, literally *if our property had departed from us*. (For Conditional sentences, see LL p. 54.) This past tense is used here and in the rest of the sentence to indicate that the arrangement had already been made, even though it had not yet been put into operation. He would appear to have set them free informally so that, if his property was not confiscated, he could revoke the manumission if he wished.

o me perditum! o me adflictum! quid nunc? rogem te ut venias, mulierem aegram et corpore et animo confectam? non rogem? sine te igitur sim? opinor, sic agam: si est spes nostri reditus, eam confirmes et rem adiuves; sin, ut ego metuo, transactum est, quoquo modo potes ad me fac venias! unum hoc scito; si te habebo, non mihi videbor plane perisse.

sed quid Tulliola mea fiet? iam id vos videte; mihi deest consilium. sed certe, quoquo modo se res habebit, illius misellae et matrimonio et famae serviendum est.

quid? Cicero meus quid aget? iste vero sit in sinu semper et complexu meo. non queo plura iam scribere; impedit maeror. tu quid egeris, nescio; utrum aliquid teneas an, quod metuo, plane sis spoliata. Pisonem, ut scribis, spero fore semper nostrum. de familia liberata nihil est quod te moveat. primum tuis ita promissum est te facturam esse ut quisque esset meritus. est autem in officio adhuc Orpheus, praeterea magno opere nemo. ceterorum servorum ea causa est ut, si res a nobis

**perditus, -a, -um**, destroyed, ruined
**adflictus, -a, -um**, utterly dejected
**mulier, -eris** (*f*), woman
**aeger, -gra, -grum**, sick, ill
**animus, -i** (*m*), mind
**confectus, -a, -um**, worn out, exhausted
**sine** (+ abl.), without
**spes, spei** (*f*), hope
**reditus, -us** (*m*), return
**ut** (+ indic.), as
**metuo** (3), to fear
**scito!** (singular imperative), know!, let me assure you
**plane**, completely, entirely
**perisse = periisse**
**pereo, -ire, -ii**, to perish, be lost
**matrimonium, -i** (*n*), marriage
**fama, -ae** (*f*), reputation, good name
**quid?** again (adding a further point)
**ago** (3), **egi**, to do, fare
**sinus, -us** (*m*), bosom, lap
**queo, quire**, to be able
**impedio** (4), to prevent, hinder
**maeror, -oris** (*m*), sorrow, grief
**nescio** (4), to be ignorant, not to know
**spolio** (1), to plunder, despoil, rob
**spero** (1), to hope
**quisque, quaeque, quidque**, each
**mereor** (2), **meritus sum**, to deserve
**adhuc**, still
**praeterea**, besides
**magno opere**, very much, to any great extent

34 **obtinere**: *to prove (their claim in court)*, literally *to lay hold of (it)*. The men confiscating his property might claim that the slaves were not his to set free.
35 **servirent**: *they would continue as slaves*.
36 **minora**: *minor matters*, literally *smaller things*.
36 **quod**: *as to the fact that*. The point is picked up again in **id** (line 37).
36 **animo sim magno**: *to keep my spirits up*, literally *to be with a big heart*. (For Ablative of Description, see LL p. 15.)
37 **id velim sit eius modi ut**: *I would wish that (prospect) to be such that*. (For Potential Subjunctive, see LL p. 108; for the omission of **ut** after **velim**, compare **fac venias** in line 22.)
39 **quas**: For Linking Relative, see LL p. 26.
39 **exspectassem = exspectavissem**: *I would have waited for*.
39 **si esset licitum per nautas**: *if the sailors had let (me)*, literally *if it had been allowed through the sailors*. (For Conditional sentences, see LL p. 54.)
41 **quod reliquum est**: *as for the rest*.
43 **nisi quod**: *but for the fact that*.
43 **una cum ornamentis**: *along with the good things in life*. For Cicero, this would include not only a comfortable life-style, but also the distinctions bestowed on him and the pleasure he derived from being an important statesman.
44 **gratius**: *more pleasing*. **gratius** is the neuter of the comparative adjective.
44 **nos vivere**: *that I should live*. This Accusative and Infinitive clause explains **hoc**.
47 **Clodium Philhetaerum**: Clodius Philhetaerus, Sallustius and Pescennius were all possibly freedmen of Cicero who had accompanied him into exile. Sicca was a friend, not a freedman.
47 **valetudine oculorum**: *by eye trouble*.
50 **mecum**: i.e. in exile in Greece.
51 **cura ut valeas**: *see that you take care of yourself*, literally *see that you keep well*.
51 **quod potes**: *as far as you can*.
51 **sic existimes**: *bear this in mind*, literally *think as follows*. **sic** is explained in detail in the Accusative and Infinitive clause which follows.
53 **valete!**: *goodbye*, literally *be well!*, a regular way of ending a Roman letter.
54 **Brundisio**: This makes it clear that Cicero wrote and handed over this letter before he sailed from Brundisium, despite what he said in lines 16-17. The past tenses (**profecti sumus ... petebamus**) are used since the events described in the letter will be in the past when Terentia receives the letter.

## Points for Discussion

1 Cicero's emphatic **ego** at the very outset of this letter seems to suggest that he is answering a question from Terentia. What do you think that question was?
2. From lines 2-11, quote and translate any Latin words and phrases which show how depressed Cicero is.
3. From lines 18-26, what do you judge Cicero's state of mind to be? How is this reflected in the style of his writing?
4. Summarise the 'mood-swings' which Cicero displays in lines 41-6
5. From lines 51-3, quote and translate the words which Cicero uses to describe (a) his wife, (b) his daughter and (c) his son. What do you think these lines tell us about his attitude to and relationship with each of them?

abisset, liberti nostri essent, si obtinere potuissent; sin ad nos pertinerent, servirent praeterquam oppido pauci.

sed haec minora sunt. tu quod me hortaris ut animo sim magno et spem habeam recuperandae salutis, id velim sit eius modi ut recte sperare possimus. nunc miser quando tuas iam litteras accipiam? quis ad me perferet? quas ego exspectassem Brundisii si esset licitum per nautas, qui tempestatem praetermittere noluerunt.

quod reliquum est, sustenta te, mea Terentia, ut potes. honestissime viximus, floruimus. non vitium nostrum sed virtus nostra nos adflixit. peccatum est nullum, nisi quod non una animam cum ornamentis amisimus. sed si hoc fuit liberis nostris gratius, nos vivere, cetera, quamquam ferenda non sunt, feramus. atque ego, qui te confirmo, ipse me non possum.

Clodium Philhetaerum, quod valetudine oculorum impediebatur, hominem fidelem, remisi. Sallustius officio vincit omnes. Pescennius est perbenevolus nobis, quem semper spero tui fore observantem. Sicca dixerat se mecum fore, sed Brundisio discessit.

cura, quod potes, ut valeas et sic existimes me vehementius tua miseria quam mea commoveri. mea Terentia, fidissima atque optima uxor, et mea carissima filiola et spes reliqua nostra, Cicero, valete! prid.Kal.Mai.Brundisio.

**libertus, -i** (*m*), freedman
**pertinere ad** (+ acc), to belong to
**praeterquam**, except, apart from
**oppido**, very
**hortor** (1), to urge, encourage
**recupero** (1), to recover
**salus, -utis** (*f*), freedom from danger
**eius modi**, of that kind, such
**recte**, rightly, with justification
**perfero, -ferre**, to bring
**tempestas, -atis** (*f*), (favourable) weather, a favourable wind
**praetermitto** (3), to let slip, lose
**sustento** (1), to support, sustain
**honeste**, honourably
**vivo** (3), **vixi**, to live
**floreo** (2), to flourish, be successful
**vitium, -i** (*n*), vice, fault, wrong-doing
**virtus, -utis** (*f*), virtue, goodness
**adfligo** (3), **-flixi**, to ruin, bring down
**peccatum, -i** (*n*), a wrong-doing, fault
**anima, -ae** (*f*), soul, life
**amitto** (3), **amisi**, to lose
**liberi, -orum** (*m.pl*), children
**ceteri, -ae, -a**, the rest
**ferendus, -a,-um**, bearable
**atque**, and yet
**confirmo** (1), to encourage, strengthen
**impedio** (4), to hinder, hamper
**fidelis, -is, -e**, loyal, faithful
**remitto** (3), **-misi**, to send back
**officium, -i** (*n*), loyalty
**vinco** (3), to surpass
**perbenevolus, -a, -um**, very kindly
**observans, -antis** (+ gen.), attentive (to), watchful (over)
**existimo** (1), to believe
**vehementer**, strongly, deeply
**miseria, -ae** (*f*), unhappiness
**commoveo** (2), to move, upset
**fidus, -a, -um**, faithful
**carus, -a, -um**, dear
**filiola, -ae** (*f*), little daughter
**reliquus, -a, -um**, remaining

1 **Tulliolae**: *my dear little Tullia*. The diminutive ending (a pet name) is used as a term of affection. Tullia was now about 20 years old and already married to Gaius Piso.

1 **S.D. = salutem dicit** (or **dat**): *sends greetings*, one of the traditional ways in which the Romans began a letter.

2 **perfertur ad me**: *news is reaching me*, literally *it is being reported to me.*

3 **te defatigari**: Cicero is referring to Terentia's delicate health and to her persistent lobbying of influential Romans to secure his return from exile.

4 **te incidisse**: *(to think that) you have fallen*. Here, the Accusative and Infinitive is used as an Accusative of Exclamation (see LL p. 6). Compare also **Tulliolam nostram percipere**.

4 **ista virtute**: *with (all) your courage*. (For Ablative of Description, see LL p. 15.)

5 **ex quo patre ... ex eo**: *from the father from whom*. As often in Latin, the relative clause appears before its antecedent for emphasis, and the antecedent (here **patre**) is placed in the relative clause instead of with **ex eo**. (See LL p. 26.)

6 **quid dicam?**: *what am I to say?* (For Deliberative Questions, see LL p. 107.)

7 **de Cicerone**: This refers to Cicero's only son, Marcus, who was then seven years old.

7 **qui**: For Linking **qui**, see LL p. 26.

7 **sapere coepit**: *was old enough to understand (anything)*, literally *began to be aware (of things)*.

9 **quae si fato facta (esse) putarem**: *if I thought that these (misfortunes) had been brought about by fate*. (For Unreal Conditions referring to present time, see LL p. 54.)

9 **paulo facilius**: *a little more easily*. (For the ablative used with a comparative adverb, see LL p. 16.)

10 **qui**: The antecedent is implied in **mea** (*my = of me*). English would most naturally begin a new sentence using the pronoun *I*. **qui** is the subject of both **putabam** and **sequebar**. Although there is no connective between the two clauses in Latin, English would probably use *but* or *and* to link them. (For Asyndeton, see CAO on page 238.)

10 **ab iis qui invidebant**: *by those who were jealous (of me)*. He is referring to the 'nobles' (or **optimates**) to whom he had looked in vain for support when he was threatened with exile. He felt that they had never really accepted him as one of themselves because he was a **novus homo** (i.e. someone who reached the highest office although not of patrician descent), and so they resented what he regarded as his glorious achievement in saving the state from the Catilinarian conspiracy (see page 97).

11 **eos qui petebant**: *those who sought (my support)*. He is referring to the Triumvirs, Caesar, Pompey and Crassus (see pages 119 and 140-1). Initially, Caesar in particular tried hard to secure Cicero's support; but Cicero rejected their offers because he believed that the Triumvirate threatened the freedoms enjoyed under the Senate.

11 **nostris consiliis**: *my own judgement*. Cicero often refers to himself in the plural. Compare **apud nos**, *with me*, i.e. in my mind.

12 **usi essemus ... viveremus**: The pluperfect subjunctive refers to events in the past, the imperfect refers to what would be true in the present. (For Unreal Conditions, see LL p. 54.)

# *12. Eight Months in Exile*

(ad Familiares XIV.1)

Cicero sailed from Brundisium on 29 April 58 BC and reached Thessalonica on 23 May. There he met with great kindness from Plancius, the quaestor of Macedonia, and remained as his guest for seven months. Most of the following letter was written there towards the end of November 58 BC. The final two lines were added as a postscript after he had moved to the Greek port of Dyrrachium, ready to sail back to Italy should the rumours prove true that his exile was soon to be ended.

TULLIUS TERENTIAE SUAE, TULLIOLAE SUAE, CICERONI SUO S.D.

et litteris multorum et sermone omnium perfertur ad me incredibilem tuam virtutem et fortitudinem esse teque nec animi neque corporis laboribus defatigari. me miserum! te ista virtute, fide, probitate, humanitate in tantas aerumnas propter me incidisse, Tulliolamque nostram, ex quo patre tantas voluptates capiebat, ex eo tantos percipere luctus! nam quid ego de Cicerone dicam? qui cum primum sapere coepit, acerbissimos dolores miseriasque percepit.

quae si, tu ut scribis, fato facta putarem, ferrem paulo facilius. sed omnia sunt mea culpa commissa, qui ab iis me amari putabam qui invidebant, eos non sequebar qui petebant. quod si nostris consiliis usi essemus neque apud nos tantum valuisset sermo aut stultorum amicorum aut improborum, beatissimi viveremus.

**sermo, -onis** (*m*), conversation, talk
**virtus, -tutis** (*f*), courage, virtue
**fortitudo, -inis** (*f*), bravery, courage
**animus, -i** (*m*), mind
**defatigo** (1), to weary, exhaust
**iste, ista, istud**, that of yours
**fides, -ei** (*f*), faithfulness, loyalty
**probitas, -atis** (*f*), goodness, uprightness
**humanitas, -atis** (*f*), kindness
**aerumna, -ae** (*f*), calamity, misfortune
**voluptas, -atis** (*f*), pleasure, joy
**capio** (3), to take derive
**percipio** (3), to experience, suffer
**luctus, -us** (*m*), grief, sorrow
**cum primum**, as soon as
**acerbus, -a, -um**, bitter, harsh, painful
**dolor, -oris** (*m*), grief, pain
**miseria, -ae** (*f*), misery, wretchedness
**fero, ferre**, to bear, endure
**culpa, -ae** (*f*), blame, fault
**committo** (3), **-misi, -missum**, to do, commit, bring about
**quod si**, but if
**utor** (3), **usus sum** (+ abl.), to use
**tantum valere**, to be so powerful *or* so influential
**stultus, -a, -um**, foolish
**improbus, -a, -um**, wicked, treacherous
**beatus, -a, -um**, happy , blessed
**vivo** (3), to live

15 **res quanta sit**: *what a difficult task it is*, i.e. to secure his return from exile.

15 **quanto fuerit facilius manere domi**: *how much easier it was to remain in Rome* (literally *at home*) — another Indirect Question depending on **intellego**. (For the ablative **quanto** used with a comparative, see LL p. 16.) With hindsight, Cicero now realises that he may have made a mistake in leaving Rome as soon as Clodius proposed the bill to exile him. Now that he is in exile, it is easy for his opponents to block efforts to secure his return. Change is always more difficult to achieve than maintaining the *status quo*.

17 **habemus**: *we have (on our side)*. Since the tribunes of the plebs were able to veto proposed legislation (see page 118), it was essential that none of them opposed the bill to permit Cicero's recall from exile.

17 **Lentulum**: Supply **habemus** here and also with **Pompeium** and **Caesarem**. Publius Lentulus Spinther was consul-designate, i.e. he would become consul in 57 BC. It was Lentulus who led the campaign to have Cicero recalled from exile. Caesar and Pompey agreed not to oppose the recall, on the understanding that Cicero did not attack their position as Triumvirs when he returned.

19 **de familia**: *concerning my slaves*. In Chapter 11 (line 30, page 123), Cicero had indicated that he intended to set his slaves free to avoid their being confiscated with the rest of his property.

19 **quo modo placuisse scribis amicis**: *as you say (in your letter) our friends have advised*, literally *in the way you write that it has pleased our friends*. There is no indication of what their advice was.

19 **de loco**: *concerning (this) place*, i.e. Thessalonica, where most of the letter had been written before he travelled to Dyrrachium. There had been a serious epidemic (cf. lines 14-15).

20 **nunc iam**: *only recently*.

21 **Plancius**: Gnaeus Plancius was at this time quaestor in Macedonia. He would be returning to Italy when his year of office expired, and he hoped to bring Cicero back with him. Cicero later successfully defended Plancius against a charge of political corruption (54 BC).

22 **loco magis deserto**: *in a more remote place*. (For the omission of the preposition **in** in phrases containing the word **locus**, see LL p. 15.) Cicero adds **in Epiro** to identify more precisely the place he has in mind.

22 **Piso**: This was Lucius Calpurnius Piso, who was to become governor of Macedonia at the end of his year as consul. He was no friend of Cicero, hence the latter's desire to be in some out-of-the-way place like Epirus.

24 **quem diem**: For Linking Relative, see LL p. 26.

24 **vestrum**: The plural is used since he is thinking of his children as well as his wife. (cf. **vos** in line 29.)

25 **recuperaro = recuperavero**: *I recover*. The future perfects (**videro**, **venero** and **recuperaro**) are used to indicate an action which has not happened yet but which will precede the action of the main verb (**videbor**).

26 **vestrae pietatis**: *for your dutiful devotion*. The noun **pietas** covers a much wider range of ideas than our word *piety*. The basic meaning is *dutifulness* or *loyalty*, in particular to the gods, the state, one's wife, one's husband, one's family and one's friends.

27 **Pisonis**: This refers, not to the consul (see line 22), but to Gaius Calpurnius Piso, Tullia's husband, who worked very hard to secure Cicero's recall from exile but died shortly before it took place.

nunc, quoniam sperare nos amici iubent, dabo operam ne mea valetudo tuo labori desit. res quanta sit intellego, quantoque fuerit facilius manere domi quam redire. sed tamen si omnes tribunos plebis habemus, si Lentulum tam studiosum quam videtur, si vero etiam Pompeium et Caesarem, non est desperandum.

de familia, quo modo placuisse scribis amicis, faciemus. de loco nunc quidem iam abiit pestilentia, sed quam diu fuit, me non attigit. Plancius, homo officiosissimus, me cupit esse secum et adhuc retinet. ego volebam loco magis deserto esse in Epiro, quo neque Piso veniret nec milites, sed adhuc Plancius me retinet; sperat posse fieri ut mecum in Italiam decedat. quem ego diem si videro et si in vestrum complexum venero ac si et vos et me ipsum recuperaro, satis magnum mihi fructum videbor percepisse et vestrae pietatis et meae.

Pisonis humanitas, virtus, amor in omnes nos tantus est ut nihil

**quoniam**, since
**spero** (1), to hope
**operam dare ne**, to make an effort (to see) that ... not
**valetudo, -inis** (*f*), health, state of health
**labor, -oris** (*m*), hard work, dedication
**desum, deesse** (+ dat.), to be lacking (to), fail, nullify
**intellego** (3), to understand, realise
**tam ... quam ...**, as ... as ...
**studiosus, -a ,-um**, friendly, sympathetic
**despero** (1), to despair
**quidem**, in fact, admittedly
**pestilentia, -ae** (*f*), plague, disease, epidemic
**quam diu**, as long as
**attingo** (3), **-tigi**, to touch, affect
**officiosus, -a, -um**, obliging, friendly
**cupio** (3), to desire, wish, want
**adhuc**, still
**retineo** (2), to keep back, detain
**quo**, (to) where, to which
**fieri potest ut** (+ subjunctive), it is possible that
**decedo** (3), to depart, leave a province
**complexus, -us** (*m*), embrace
**fructus, -us** (*m*), fruit, reward
**percipio** (3), **-cepi**, to receive, gain

28 **possit**: Supply **esse**.

28 **utinam ea res ei voluptati sit**: *I hope that that conduct is a source of pleasure to him*, literally *would that that thing may be a pleasure to him*. (For **utinam**, see LL p. 107; for Predicative Dative, see LL p. 13.)

29 **fore = futuram esse**: Supply **eam rem** from **ea res** in the previous sentence. **gloriae** is another Predicative Dative.

29 **de Quinto fratre**: There had been some sort of disagreement between Terentia and Quintus. Pomponia, Quintus' wife, and Terentia were never on the best of terms. We do not know what Cicero had said in a previous letter, but Terentia had taken it as a criticism of herself. Cicero says that all he meant was that in times of trouble members of a family should close ranks and give one another support. Note again the use of the plural **vos** (cf. line 24).

29 **vos**: Compare the note on **vestrum** (line 24).

30 **quam coniunctissimos**: *as united as possible*. (For **quam** + superlatives, see LL p. 145.)

31 **egi**: Supply **eis gratias**. (For the relative clause preceding its antecedent, see LL p. 26; compare line 5.)

32 **quod**: *as to the fact that.*

32 **vicum**: *a block of houses*, literally *a street*. Terentia proposed to sell the property to raise money, but Cicero fears that such a step might deprive his children of their inheritance.

32 **quid** is repeated in line 33, since the question has been interrupted by the two parenthetical phrases — **obsecro te** and **me miserum**.

33 **premet**: *(continues to) afflict*. (For Future Conditions, see LL p. 54.)

36 **erunt in officio**: *remain loyal (to us)*.

37 **efficere**: *to achieve (much)*. Terentia had a considerable fortune of her own.

37 **per fortunas miseras nostras**: *bearing in mind our own misfortunes*, i.e. let them be a warning to us.

37 **vide ne perdamus**: *see that we do not ruin (financially)*. Note the effective use of alliteration in **puerum perditum perdamus** (see CAO on page 235). Even in this personal letter, Cicero cannot lay aside the style of an orator!

38 **cui si aliquid erit ne egeat**: *so long as he has something to keep him from poverty*, literally *if he has something so that he is not in want*. (For Linking Relative, see LL p. 26; for the dative + **esse** expressing Possession, see LL p. 11.) The conjunction **ne** (*to prevent*) introduces a Purpose clause (see LL p. 44).

38 **mediocri virtute**: *(only) average ability*.

39 **cetera**: *the rest*, i.e. wealth and distinction. Cicero implies that the name 'Cicero' will stand his son in good stead.

40 **fac valeas**: *look after yourself*, literally *make sure that you are well*. (See LL p. 109.)

40 **tabellarios**: *couriers*. There was no regular postal system in the Roman world. Provincial governors could use official couriers, and really wealthy people might employ their own couriers; but, on the whole, most people simply gave their letters to a traveller who happened to be going to the same destination as the letter. Needless to say, some letters took a long time to reach their destination, and some never arrived.

40 **quid agatur et vos quid agatis**: *what is happening and how you are*.

41 **exspectatio**: *the waiting-time*. The question of his recall would soon be decided, one way or the other.

supra possit. utinam ea res ei voluptati sit! gloriae quidem video fore. de Quinto fratre nihil ego te accusavi; sed vos, cum praesertim tam pauci sitis, volui esse quam coniunctissimos. quibus me voluisti agere gratias, egi; et me a te certiorem factum esse scripsi.

quod ad me, mea Terentia, scribis te vicum venditturam, quid, obsecro te (me miserum!), quid futurum est? et si nos premet eadem fortuna, quid puero misero fiet? non queo reliqua scribere — tanta vis lacrimarum est — neque te in eundem fletum adducam. tantum scribo: si erunt in officio amici, pecunia non deerit; si non erunt, tu efficere tua pecunia non poteris. per fortunas miseras nostras, vide ne puerum perditum perdamus! cui si aliquid erit ne egeat, mediocri virtute opus est et mediocri fortuna ut cetera consequatur.

fac valeas et ad me tabellarios mittas, ut sciam quid agatur et vos quid agatis! mihi omnino iam brevis exspectatio est. Tulliolae et Ciceroni

**supra**, above, more impressive
**cum praesertim**, especially since
**pauci, -ae, -a**, few
**gratias agere** (+ dat.), to thank
**certiorem facere**, to inform
**vendo** (3), **-didi, -ditum**, to sell
**obsecro** (1), to beg, beseech
**quid fiet?** (+ abl.), what will become (of)?
**queo, quire**, to be able
**reliquus, -a, -um**, remaining, (the) rest
**vis** (*f*), force, flood
**lacrima, -ae** (*f*), tear
**fletus, -us** (*m*), weeping
**adduco** (3), to bring to
**tantum**, this much, only this
**officium, -i** (*n*), duty
**perditus, -a, -um**, ruined
**opus est** (+ abl.), there is need (of)
**consequor** (3), to attain, achieve
**omnino**, in any case, at all events
**brevis, -is, -e**, short

42 **salutem dic**: See line 1.

42 **d. = datae** (agreeing with **litterae** understood): *handed over*, i.e. to whoever was to carry it to Rome for him.

42 **a.d. VI Kal. Decembr**. The full form is **ante diem sextum Kalendas Decembres**, i.e. *25 November*. Prior to Julius Caesar's revision of the calendar in 46 BC, there were only 355 days in the year. There were 31 days in March, May, July and October; 28 in February; and 29 in the remaining seven months. (For the calculation of Dates, see LL p. 67.)

42 **Dyrrachii**: For Locative case, see LL p. 9.

43 The last three lines are a postscript.

43 **libera civitas**: *a free city*, i.e. it governed itself, was free from interference from the Roman governor, and paid lower taxes. Therefore, although Dyrrachium was within the 400 mile exclusion zone, Cicero was technically not breaching the terms of his exile. Since it was the nearest port for sailing from Greece to Italy, it would be crowded.

## Points for Discussion

1. How in this letter (lines 9-18) does Cicero now regard his decision to go into exile before he was actually forced to do so? What mistakes does he think he made at that time?
2. In lines 32-41, we find that Cicero's mood changes. What action apparently contemplated by Terentia brings about this change?
3. In lines 1-18, Cicero abandons the informal style which is common in his letters and, as a mark of his returning confidence, adopts a more oratorical style. What examples of his oratorical techniques can you identify in these lines? (See CAO on pages 231-9.)
4. How far do you think this letter helps us to understand Cicero's relationship with other people, including both friends and family?

salutem dic! valete! d. a.d.vi Kal.Decembr. Dyrrachii.

Dyrrachium veni, quod et libera civitas est et in me officiosa et proxima Italiae; sed si offendet me loci celebritas, alio me conferam. ad te scribam.

**officiosus, -a, -um**, friendly
**proximus, -a, -um**, very near, very close
**offendo** (3), to displease, annoy
**celebritas, -atis** (*f*), crowded nature, bustle
**alio**, to another place, elsewhere
**me confero**, I take myself off, go

1 **CICERO ATTICO SAL.**: *Cicero sends greetings to Atticus.* Because Atticus is a close friend, Cicero greets him in this informal way instead of using the more formal **S.P.D** greeting.

2 **fuit cui darem**: *there was (someone) to whom I could give.* (For Generic Subjunctive, see LL p. 103.) Although there is nothing of a confidential nature in this excerpt, other parts of the letter contained political views which might have brought Cicero into danger if it had fallen into the wrong hands.

3 **nihil prius faciendum mihi putavi quam ut tibi gratularer**: *I thought that the first thing I should do was to write and thank you,* literally *I thought that nothing should be done by me earlier than to thank you.* (For Dative of Agent with a Gerundive, see LL p. 62; for the splitting of **priusquam**, see LL p. 52.)

3 **tibi absenti**: Cicero would obviously have liked to thank him in person, but Atticus was in Athens.

4 **nostro**: Cicero often uses **nos** and **noster** when referring to himself and his activities.

5 **in nostro statu**: *as regards my (political) standing.*

5 **quod = id quod**: *what.* What he is thinking of is explained in lines 6-7 where he refers to **splendorem forensem** (*distinction in the law courts*), **auctoritatem** (*influence*) and **gratiam** (*esteem*).

7 **apud viros bonos**: He is thinking of the **Optimates** (i.e. those who supported the view that the Senate should govern the state). Their influence had been in decline for some time, as the **Populares** (those who used the support of the masses to further their own personal ambitions) gained the upper hand.

7 **magis quam optaramus (= optaveramus)**: *to a greater degree than we had wished.* If Cicero gained too much support, he might again attract both the hostility of the Triumvirs and the envy of some of the Optimates — two of the factors which had led to his exile in 58 BC.

8 **in re familiari**: *as far as my private property is concerned.* His house in Rome had been demolished, his country villas had been looted and the compensation which he later received was inadequate.

8 **quae quemadmodum fracta, dissipata, direpta sit non ignoras**: *you are well aware how it has been demolished, scattered and looted,* literally *which you are not ignorant how (it) has been demolished, scattered and looted.* The double negative (**non ignoras**) produces a strong positive statement. The three Indirect Questions (**quemadmodum ... direpta sit**) depend on **non ignoras**.

9 **valde laboramus**: *I am in serious difficulties.* Compare the slang expression 'I am toiling'.

10 **omnia scripta esse a tuis**: *that you have heard about it all in letters from your friends and associates,* literally *that everything has been written by your (people).* He is probably thinking about Atticus' business contacts.

12 **pr(idie) Nonas Sextiles**: *on 4th August,* literally *the day before the Nones (5th) of August.* In early times, March was the first month of the year. The sixth month was later called Augustus in honour of the emperor Augustus.

12 **Dyrrachio**: Crossings from Greece to Italy were normally made from Dyrrachium to Brundisium.

13 **lex est lata de nobis**: *the law about my recall* (literally *about us*) *was proposed.*

14 **Tulliola mea**: *my dear little Tullia.* By now, Tullia was in her early 20s; Cicero regularly uses the diminutive form to express the strong affection he has for his daughter.

# *13. Homecoming*

(ad Atticum IV.1, 3-5)

This is an excerpt from a letter which Cicero wrote to his friend Atticus to describe the enthusiastic reception he received on his return to Rome on 4 September 57 BC.

CICERO ATTICO SAL.

cum primum Romam veni fuitque cui recte ad te litteras darem, nihil prius faciendum mihi putavi quam ut tibi absenti de reditu nostro gratularer.

nos adhuc in nostro statu, quod difficillime recuperari posse arbitrati sumus, splendorem nostrum illum forensem et in senatu auctoritatem et apud viros bonos gratiam magis quam optaramus consecuti sumus; in re autem familiari (quae quemadmodum fracta, dissipata, direpta sit non ignoras) valde laboramus.

nunc etsi omnia aut scripta esse a tuis arbitror aut etiam nuntiis ac rumore perlata, tamen ea scribam brevi quae te puto potissimum ex meis litteris velle cognoscere. pr.Nonas Sextiles Dyrrachio sum profectus ipso illo die quo lex est lata de nobis. Brundisium veni Nonis Sextilibus. ibi mihi Tulliola mea fuit praesto, natali suo ipso die, qui

**cum primum**, as soon as
**recte**, rightly, properly, reliably
**litterae, -arum** (*f.pl*), a letter
**reditus, -us** (*m*), return
**gratulor** (1) (+ dat.), to thank
**adhuc**, so far, up till now
**difficillime**, with the greatest difficulty
**recupero** (1), to recover
**arbitror** (1), to think
**apud** (+ acc.), among
**consequor** (3), **-secutus sum**, to attain, gain, win
**autem**, however, but
**etsi**, although
**nuntius, -i** (*m*), report, message
**rumor, -oris** (*m*), rumour, hearsay
**perfero, -ferre, -tuli, -latum**, to bring (news), convey
**brevi**, briefly
**potissimum**, most, especially
**cognosco** (3), **-novi**, to learn
**praesto esse** (+ dat.), to be at hand, wait (for)
**natalis dies**, birthday

15 **idem**: *also*, literally *the same*.

15 **Brundisinae coloniae**: The anniversary of the founding of the colony at Brundisium in 244 BC was marked by a public holiday. The anniversary of the dedication of the temple of Salus (*the Welfare of the State*) on the Quirinal Hill in Rome (302 BC) also fell on the same day. Cicero prides himself on the fact that the people of Brundisium noticed that these important events happened on the same day as his return from exile. Atticus had recently inherited a house near the temple; hence the use of **vicinae** (*neighbouring*).

17 **ante diem VI Idus Sextiles**: *on 8th August*. (For the calculation of Dates, see LL p. 67.) The messenger sent by Quintus, Cicero's brother, must have made exceptionally good time to travel the 360 miles from Rome to Brundisium in four days.

19 **comitiis centuriatis**: *in the Assembly of the Centuries*. In the **comitia centuriata**, the Roman people (i.e. all citizens including those from outside Rome) met in 'classes' or 'centuries' which were based on property qualifications in such a way that the richest class had as many centuries as all the other centuries put together. Since each century had only one vote, the majority in each group determining which way the century would vote, the rich could always outvote the rest. The **comitia centuriata** was used mainly to elect the consuls, praetors and censors and, although it did have legislative powers, it had to have permission from the Senate to use these powers. The fact that Cicero's supporters used this Assembly to pass the law recalling Cicero, instead of the **comitia tributa** where the plebeian influence was greater, may suggest that the influence of Clodius, who was originally responsible for Cicero's being sent into exile (see page 119), was still strong.

19 **esse perlatam**: *was passed*. Note the difference between **legem ferre** (*to propose a law*, as in line 13) and **legem perferre** (*to pass a law*, i.e. see it through all the stages until it becomes law).

21 **honestissime ornatus**: *having had the highest honours conferred upon me*, literally *having been honoured in a most distinguished way*.

22 **urbem**: *the city*, i.e. Rome.

22 **nemo homo nomenclatori notus**: *no person known to my nomenclator*. The **nomenclator** was a slave who whispered in his master's ear the names of the people he met in the street. Anyone not known by a nomenclator would have been a really insignificant person. The nomenclator's services were particularly useful at election times when candidates wished to flatter potential supporters by addressing each one of them by name.

24 **quibus non liceret**: *who found it impossible*, literally *to whom it was not permitted*.

24 **id ipsum**: *that very fact*. This is the object of **dissimulare** and **negare**, and it is explained in the Accusative and Infinitive clause (**se inimicos esse**).

25 **ad portam Capenam**: The Porta Capena was the gate through which the Via Appia (the road from Brundisium) entered the city.

26 **ab infima plebe**: *by the lowest classes*. Cicero is emphasising the point that he was welcomed by the poor as well as the rich.

26 **a qua** refers to **plebe**. (For Linking Relative, see LL p. 26.)

28 **Capitolium**: On the Capitoline Hill was the Capitol, i.e. the Temple of Jupiter, the most important temple in Rome. On his return, Cicero visited the legal, religious and political centres of Rome's life.

casu idem natalis erat et Brundisinae coloniae et tuae vicinae Salutis; quae res animadversa a multitudine summa Brundisinorum gratulatione celebrata est. ante diem VI Idus Sextiles cognovi, cum Brundisi essem, litteris Quinti mirifico studio omnium aetatum atque ordinum, incredibili concursu Italiae legem comitiis centuriatis esse perlatam.

inde a Brundisinis honestissime ornatus, iter ita feci ut undique ad me cum gratulatione legati convenerint. ad urbem ita veni ut nemo ullius ordinis homo nomenclatori notus fuerit qui mihi obviam non venerit, praeter eos inimicos quibus id ipsum, se inimicos esse, non liceret aut dissimulare aut negare. cum venissem ad portam Capenam, gradus templorum ab infima plebe completi erant. a qua plausu maximo cum esset mihi gratulatio significata, similis et frequentia et plausus me usque ad Capitolium celebravit, in foroque et in ipso Capitolio miranda multitudo fuit. postridie in senatu, qui fuit dies Nonarum Septembr., senatui gratias egimus.

**casu**, by chance, as it so happened
**animadverto** (3), **-verti, -versum**, to notice
**summus, -a, -um**, the greatest, immense
**gratulatio, -onis** (*f*), rejoicing, congratulation(s)
**celebro** (1), to celebrate, hail
**mirificus, -a, -um**, wonderful, amazing, extraordinary
**studium -i** (*n*), enthusiasm
**aetas, -atis** (*f*), age, age-group
**ordo, -inis** (*m*), rank, class
**incredibilis, -is, -e**, incredible, extraordinary
**concursus, -us** (*m*), gathering, flocking together
**inde**, from there
**ita ... ut ...**, in such a way that
**undique**, from all sides, on all sides
**legatus, -i** (*m*), envoy, member of a deputation
**nemo**, no, no one
**obviam venire** (+ dat.), to come to meet
**praeter** (+ acc.), except, apart from
**inimicus, -i** (*m*), (personal) enemy
**dissimulo** (1), to conceal, disguise
**nego** (1), to deny
**gradus, -us** (*m*), step
**compleo** (2), **-evi, -etum**, to fill, cram full
**plausus, -us** (*m*), applause
**significo** (1), to show, display, express
**similis, -is, -e**, similar
**frequentia, -ae** (*f*), crowd, great number(s), throng
**usque ad** (+ acc.), right up to
**mirandus, -a, -um**, wonderful, spectacular
**postridie**, on the following day
**gratias agere** (+ dat.), to thank, express gratitude

32 **quaedam domestica**: *certain family matters*. This probably refers to disagreements he was having with his wife, Terentia.
33 **insigni pietate praeditum**: *for* (literally *endowed with*) *his remarkable devotion (to his brother)*.
34 **eo animo**: *with the intention*.
35 **alterius vitae quoddam initium ordimur**: *I am, as it were, beginning a new life*, literally *we are starting a certain beginning of a second life*. Exile had seemed like virtual death to him; he feels as if he has been brought back to life.
36 **praesentibus**: Supply **nobis**.

## Points for Discussion

1. Cicero was clearly delighted with the reception he received on his return from exile. His description of his return sounds almost like a triumphal procession. List, in order, the various groups of people who welcomed him, and quote and translate the Latin words describing the form each welcome took.
2. Despite his joy at the reception he received, there were four things which seemed to concern him. What were these things, and how do you think the presence of his friend Atticus might have helped him to handle each of them?
3. In lines 35-7, what do you think Cicero is hinting at, to whom do you think he is referring, and what might have been responsible for their change of attitude?
4. Even though this is an informal letter written to a close friend, Cicero still cannot resist the temptation to write as if he was delivering a speech. From lines 5-12, quote examples of oratorical techniques discussed in Cicero and Oratory on pages 231-9.

in re familiari valde sumus, ut scis, perturbati. praeterea sunt quaedam domestica, quae litteris non committo. Quintum fratrem insigni pietate, virtute, fide praeditum sic amo ut debeo. te exspecto et oro ut matures venire eoque animo venias ut me tuo consilio egere non sinas. alterius vitae quoddam initium ordimur. iam quidam, qui nos absentes defenderunt, incipiunt praesentibus occulte irasci, aperte invidere. vehementer te requirimus.

**perturbo** (1), to distress, embarrass
**praeterea**, besides
**committo** (3), to commit, entrust
**virtus, -utis** (*f*), courage
**fides, -ei** (*f*), loyalty
**exspecto** (1), to wait for, hope to see
**oro** (1), to beg
**maturo** (1), to hurry, make haste
**consilium, -i** (*n*), advice
**egeo** (2) (+ abl.), to be without
**sino** (3), to allow
**incipio** (3), to begin
**praesens, -entis**, present
**occulte**, secretly, inwardly
**irascor** (3) (+ dat.), to be angry (with)
**aperte**, openly
**invideo** (2) (+ dat.), to envy, show resentment (towards)
**requiro** (3), to miss, need

Some personal feelings expressed by Cicero while he was in the political wilderness:

(a) Out of politics (59 BC) and living at his villa on the coast, Cicero is bored and has no inclination for creative writing:

**aut libris me delecto aut fluctus numero … a scribendo abhorret animus.**
*Either I amuse myself with reading or I count the waves ... My whole mind shrinks from writing.*
Ad Atticum II, 6

(b) Out of politics again (54 BC) but enjoying what he does best — defending his clients in the law-courts:

**dicendi laborem delectatione oratoria consolor.**
*I lighten the effort involved in pleading (a case) by the pleasure I get from oratory.*
Ad Atticum IV,18

# The First Triumvirate

When Pompey returned from his successes in the Eastern Mediterranean (see page 89), the Senate failed to ratify his arrangements for ruling the states there. It also refused to reward his troops with plots of land in Italy. Crassus, a wealthy financier, was also annoyed with the Senate. A syndicate with which he was associated had offered too much for the right to collect taxes in Asia, and the Senate was refusing to give it a rebate. In 60 BC, therefore, when Caesar was standing for the consulship, Pompey and Crassus agreed to support him on condition that he secured these favours for them. This unofficial agreement is usually referred to as the First Triumvirate. As consul in 59 BC, Caesar passed the necessary legislation and also secured for himself the governorship of Gaul for five years.

On his return from exile in September 57 BC, Cicero hope to resume his political activities where he had left off. His successful defence of Sestius, who had been accused of violence in opposing the terrorist activities of Clodius, encouraged him to believe that the citizens could be rallied to defend the Republic. He also had reason to hope that the Triumvirate was breaking up. Pompey envied Caesar's successes in Gaul and also suspected that Crassus was plotting against him. Hoping for Pompey's support, therefore, Cicero early in 56 BC attempted to repeal the Land Act which Caesar, as consul, had enacted in 59 BC to give land to Pompey's soldiers. Caesar realised that a repeal of this Act would prevent him from rewarding his own troops with grants of land when they left his army; and so he took immediate steps to renew his coalition with Pompey and Crassus. At a conference at Luca in northern Italy in April 56 BC, the three Triumvirs came to a new agreement: Caesar's command in Gaul would be extended for another five years, and he was promised the consulship in 48 BC; Pompey and Crassus would become consuls in 55 BC and, at the end of their term of office, they would be given important provinces with armies, also for five years.

The renewal of the Triumvirate was a dreadful blow to Cicero. He was forced to withdraw his proposed repeal of the Land Act and to apologise to Caesar. He was even persuaded to deliver, in May or June 56 BC, a speech in the Senate (**Oratio de Provinciis Consularibus**) in support of granting the provinces of Spain and Syria to Pompey and Crassus respectively and of continuing Caesar's command in Gaul. He then withdrew from politics, although he was still very active in the law courts.

Three events influenced the break-up of the Triumvirate. In 54 BC, the death in childbirth of Caesar's daughter Julia, who had been the wife of Pompey since 59 BC, broke the family tie which had kept Caesar and Pompey on reasonably good terms for five years. Then, in June of 53 BC, Crassus' attempt to win riches and glory in the wilds of Parthia ended with his defeat at Carrhae and his subsequent murder by the Parthians. Finally, in the closing months of 53 BC, there was growing disorder in Rome with constant clashes between the rival gangs of Milo, who was standing for the consulship, and Clodius, who was aiming at the praetorship. On 17 January 52 BC, Clodius, the man who had caused Cicero to be sent into exile (see page 119), was killed in a fight between the gangs on the Appian Way; and there was such widespread rioting during Clodius' funeral in Rome that the Senate proclaimed martial law. A

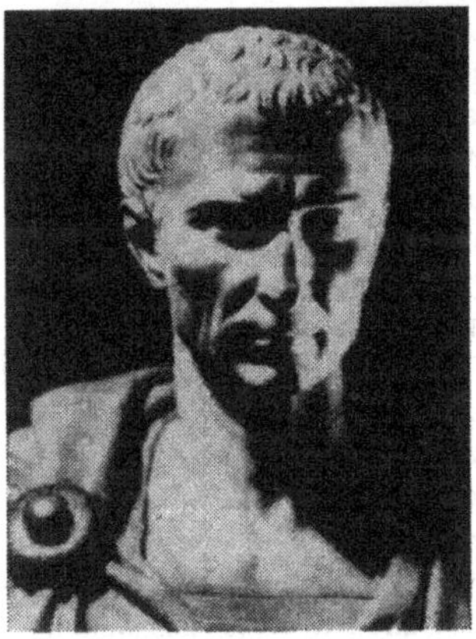

Gaius Julius Caesar
(*Rex Features/Mansell Collection*)

Gnaeus Pompeius Magnus

few weeks later, Pompey was appointed sole consul (i.e. virtual dictator in Rome), while still being allowed to retain his command in Spain. He was, therefore, in a very powerful position and became the likely champion of the Senate if there was ever a confrontation with Caesar.

In April 52 BC, Milo was brought to trial for the murder of Clodius. Cicero spoke in his defence, but he was so unnerved by the fact that armed guards occupied the Forum to keep the noisy crowd under control that he delivered a poor speech; and Milo was condemned and forced into exile at Massilia (modern Marseilles). [When Cicero later sent Milo the splendid defence speech which he had prepared, Milo retorted that he was glad the speech had not been delivered, since he might never have discovered how tasty the mullets in Marseilles were!]

One of the many laws passed by Pompey in 52 BC during his sole consulship was to the effect that an interval of five years had to elapse between holding office in Rome and taking command of a province. To fill this five-year gap, the Senate decreed that all ex-magistrates who had not yet governed a province should now do so. Much to Cicero's disgust, it was decided that he should take over the governorship of Cilicia, together with Pisidia, Pamphylia, Lycaonia, Isauria and Cyprus, in the following year. Although he left Rome at the beginning of May 51 BC, he took as long as he could on the journey and did not enter his province until the last day of July. He found the people demoralised and the country in a state of economic ruin as a result of the corrupt and oppressive administration of the previous governor, Appius Claudius, the brother of Clodius. He also faced the threat of a Parthian invasion.

1 **salutem**: Supply **dicit** — *sends greetings.*

2 **discedebant**: *are leaving.* In using the past tense (Epistolary Imperfect), Cicero puts himself in the position of the person reading the letter at a date later than the events mentioned in it. (cf. **eramus.**)

2 **publicanorum tabellarii:** *the tax-gatherers' couriers.* Companies of businessmen (**publicani**) bought the right to collect taxes in the provinces and then extracted as much as they could from the provincials. The provincial governor was supposed to ensure that the taxes were not exorbitant, but most did not interfere and it was easy for companies to make huge profits. Note what Cicero says later in the letter about the tax burdens endured by the Cilicians. As communication was not easy in the Roman world (see pages 90-1), the tax-gatherers employed their own couriers to provide a speedy and reliable postal service.

3 **in cursu**: *on the move,* literally *in the journey.*

3 **surripiendum aliquid spatii**: Supply **esse** to complete this Accusative and Infinitive — *that I should snatch a moment,* literally *that some time should be snatched.* (For Gerundives, see LL p. 61; for Partitive Genitive, see LL p. 9.)

4 **mandati tui**: *of your instruction.* Atticus had asked him to write whenever he could.

4 **dum perscriberem**: *long enough to write down,* literally *until I could write down.* The subjunctive indicates Purpose (see LL p. 91).

6 **maxima exspectatione**: *amidst the greatest expectation.* The provincials had high hopes that Cicero would treat them fairly.

7 **prid(ie) Kal(endas) Sext(iles)**: *on 31st July,* literally *on the day before the Kalends of the sixth month.* The Roman year originally began in March; so, **mensis Sextilis,** *the sixth month,* was August. The month names **Quintilis** and **Sextilis** were changed to **Iulius** (in honour of Julius Caesar's reform of the calendar) and **Augustus** (to mark his own reforms). (For the calculation of Roman Dates, see LL pp. 66-7.)

7 **moratos**: Supply **esse**. Note that no conjunction joins this infinitive to **venisse.** (For Asyndeton, see CAO on page 238.)

8 **Laodiceae**: Laodicea, Apamea and Synnada were the chief towns of three districts in Phrygia which had been temporarily transferred from the province of Asia to Cilicia. Cicero would have held assizes in the three towns during his stay.

9 **nihil aliud nisi non posse**: *only* (literally *no other thing except*) *that (people) cannot.*

9 **imperata ἐπικεφαλια**: *the poll-tax (which has been) demanded.* This was a *per capita* tax (i.e. all paid the same irrespective of their income). It could be especially burdensome if, for example, the crops failed. Just as people today often use foreign words and phrases (particularly Latin and French) in conversation and writing, so educated Romans often used Greek expressions. There was a strong Greek influence in this part of the Middle East after the conquests of Alexander the Great (4th century BC). ἐπικεφαλια (pronounced 'epikephalia') means *associated with the head* (cf. *per capita*).

10 **monstra quaedam**: *the sort of monstrous deeds.* As often in Latin, **quidam, quaedam, quoddam** is used to tone down a particularly strong expression.

10 **ferae nescio cuius immanis**: *of some kind of horrible wild beast.*

11 **quid quaeris?**: *to cut a long story short,* literally *what (more) do you ask?* (cf. **quid plura?** and **quid multa?** which have similar meanings.)

11 **taedet eos**: *they are tired.* (For Impersonal Verbs, see LL p. 58.)

# *14. Arrival in Cilicia*

(Ad Atticum V.16)

*Although I am still on the road, I am snatching a moment or two to write a short note about what I have found here. Everywhere it is the same story — ruin brought about by an inhumane tax burden.*

CICERO ATTICO SALUTEM

etsi in ipso itinere et via discedebant publicanorum tabellarii et eramus in cursu, tamen surripiendum aliquid putavi spatii ne me immemorem mandati tui putares. itaque subsedi in ipsa via dum haec, quae longiorem desiderant orationem, summatim tibi perscriberem.

maxima exspectatione in perditam et plane eversam in perpetuum provinciam nos venisse scito prid. Kal. Sext., moratos triduum Laodiceae, triduum Apameae, totidem dies Synnadae. audivimus nihil aliud nisi imperata ἐπικεφαλια solvere non posse, civitatum gemitus, ploratus, monstra quaedam non hominis sed ferae nescio cuius immanis. quid quaeris? taedet omnino eos vitae.

**etsi**, although
**iter, itineris** (*n*), journey, march
**via, -ae** (*f*), road
**puto** (1), to think
**immemor, -oris**, unmindful, forgetful
**subsido** (3), **-sedi**, to sit down
**desidero** (1), to desire, need, require, deserve
**oratio, -onis** (*f*), description, account
**summatim**, in summary, briefly
**perditus, -a, -um**, ruined
**plane**, clearly, completely, entirely
**everto** (3), **everti, eversum**, to overthrow, devastate
**in perpetuum**, for ever, irretrievably
**scito!** (singular imperative), know!, let me tell you
**moror** (1), to delay, stay, remain
**triduum, -i** (*n*), (a period of) three days
**totidem**, just as many, the same number
**Synnada, -ae** (*f*), Synnada
**solvo** (3), to pay
**civitas, -atis** (*f*), community
**gemitus, -us** (*m*), groan, groaning
**ploratus, -us** (*m*), wailing, lamentation, moaning
**omnino**, altogether, utterly
**vita, -ae** (*f*), life

12 **nullus fit sumptus in nos**: *there is no expenditure on me* (literally *us*). Cicero often uses the first person plural when he wishes to draw attention to his own importance. In lines 7 and 14, the use of *we*, *us* and *our* could refer to Cicero himself or to Cicero and his entourage. In lines 12, 19 and 21, however, there seems little doubt that the plurals refer only to Cicero himself.

13 **quaestorem**: The quaestor was responsible to the governor for the financial administration of the province.

14 **quod = id quod.**

14 **e lege Iulia**: *under the terms of the Julian law*. The **Lex Iulia de Repetundis** (i.e. about the restoration of money and goods that had been illegally extorted by the governors of provinces) was passed by Julius Caesar during his consulship in 59 BC. It laid down the things which the governor could requisition, including the amounts of corn, hay, wood and salt. The law also required the governor to deposit copies of his accounts in the two main towns in his province.

15 **nec quemquam accipere quicquam**: *and no one accepts anything* — another Accusative and Infinitive clause depending on **scito** (see LL p. 35).

16 **multis locis**: The preposition **in** is usually omitted in phrases containing the noun **locus** in the ablative case (see LL p.15).

18 **incredibilem in modum**: *incredibly*, literally *in an incredible way.*

18 **concursus fiunt**: *people are thronging*, literally *runnings together are made.*

19 **etiam adventu nostro**: *merely* (literally *even*) *at my approach.*

20 **iustitia**: *thanks to the justice*. (For Causal Ablative, see LL p. 141.)

20 **tui Ciceronis**: *of your (friend) Cicero.*

*However, it is a great consolation to them that I am not a financial burden to them, not even in the case of things to which I am legally entitled. It is hardly surprising that they flock to greet me. Compared with my predecessor, I treat them so well.*

levantur tamen miserae civitates quod nullus fit sumptus in nos neque in legatos neque in quaestorem neque in quemquam. scito non modo nos faenum aut quod e lege Iulia dari solet non accipere sed ne ligna quidem, nec praeter quattuor lectos et tectum quemquam accipere quicquam, multis locis ne tectum quidem et in tabernaculo manere plerumque.

itaque incredibilem in modum concursus fiunt ex agris, ex vicis, ex domibus omnibus; et omnes mehercule etiam adventu nostro reviviscunt iustitia, abstinentia, clementia tui Ciceronis; itaque

**levo** (1), to lighten, relieve
**miser, -era, -erum**, wretched, poor
**legatus, -i** (*m*), senior officer, deputy
**quisquam, quicquam** anyone/thing
**faenum, -i** (*n*), hay, fodder
**soleo** (2), to be accustomed
**lignum, -i** (*n*), log, firewood
**praeter** (+ acc.), except for
**lectus, -i** (*m*), bed
**tectum, -i** (*n*), roof (over one's head)
**tabernaculum, -i** (*n*), tent
**maneo** (2), to remain, stay
**plerumque**, mostly, as often as not
**vicus, -i** (*m*), village
**domus, -us** (*f*), house, home
**mehercule**, by Hercules!
**revivisco** (3), to come to life again
**abstinentia, -ae** (*f*), self-restraint
**clementia, -ae** (*f*), mercy, compassion

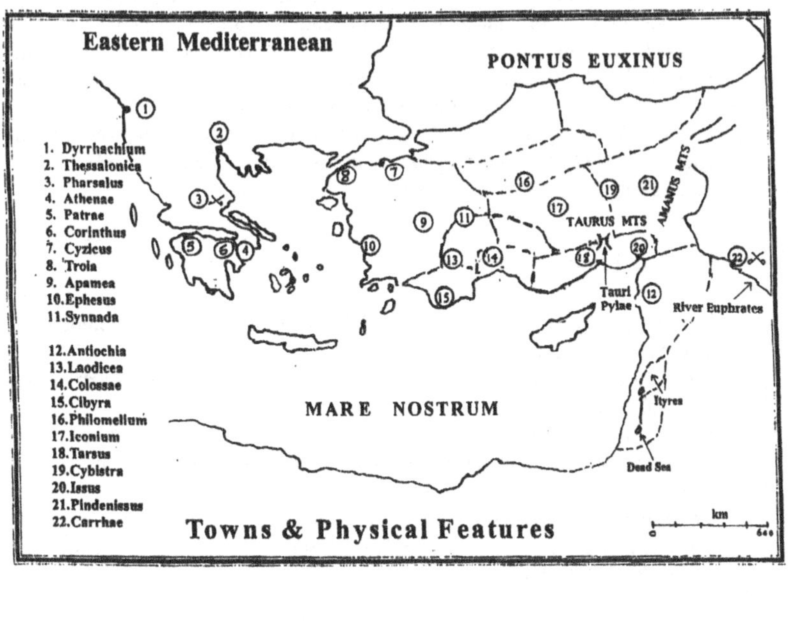

21 **superavit**: Supply **Cicero tuus** as the subject.

21 **Appius**: Appius Claudius Pulcher was Cicero's predecessor as governor.

21 **in ultimam provinciam, Tarsum usque**: *to the farthest (corner of) the province, as far as Tarsus.* It was quite improper for Claudius to remain in the province after Cicero's arrival, let alone hold an assize (**forum agere**).

23 **de Partho**: The singular here is used for the plural. There was a persistent rumour that the Parthians were going to invade the province, and it is not surprising that Cicero was concerned, as he had only two under-manned legions at his disposal.

23 **concisos**: Supply **esse** — *have been cut to pieces.*

24 **ii qui veniebant**: *people coming (from that direction)*, literally *those who come.* As in line 2, the tense of **nuntiabant** and **veniebant** is epistolary. (cf. **cogitabat** in line 24, **dicebant, vellet, properabamus** and **aberant** in lines 26-7. Translate them all as present tenses in English.) The imperfect tense suggests that there were repeated reports of the impending invasion. The invasion did not, in fact, take place since Gaius Cassius, who had been Crassus' quaestor in Syria, had had a very successful year's campaign against the Parthians after they defeated and killed Crassus in 53 BC.

24 **Bibulus** had been consul along with Caesar in 59 BC but had as yet not governed a province. Like Cicero, he was now required by Pompey's law (see page 141) to take over a province, in his case, Syria.

25 **id autem facere**: Supply **eum** to complete the Accusative and Infinitive clause depending on **dicebant.** The person copying the manuscript may, in fact, have inadvertently omitted **eum** after **autem**.

26 **quod**: This clause explains **ob eam causam,** *for that reason.*

26 **tardius**: *at a later date.* According to Pompey's law, a governor had to leave his province a year after he entered it. Cicero appears to be hinting that Bibulus, who disliked Caesar, wanted still to be governor of Syria when the next allocation of provinces was made and so force the Senate to look elsewhere for suitable proconsular provinces. This would increase the likelihood that the Senate would allocate the Gallic provinces to someone other than Caesar when the latter's command there ended in 50 BC.

26 **decedere**: This was the technical term for a governor leaving his province. The subjunctive **vellet** gives the alleged reason for his delay (see LL p. 99).

27 **bidui**: Supply **iter** — *two days' journey.*

## Points for Discussion

1. In line 12, why do you think Cicero did not simply use **nos** to include his staff as well as himself?
2. What do lines 13-17 tell us about how well many governors supervised their subordinates?
3. Identify in the letter three instances in which you feel that Cicero is exaggerating for dramatic effect in what he says and how he says it. Quote and translate the Latin as appropriate.
4. Comment on the Roman system of collecting taxes. Consider your answer from three points of view — the Roman state, the tax-gatherers and the people in the provinces.

opiniones omnium superavit. Appius, ut audivit nos venire, in ultimam provinciam se coniecit Tarsum usque. ibi forum agit.

de Partho silentium est, sed tamen concisos equites nostros a barbaris nuntiabant ii qui veniebant. Bibulus ne cogitabat quidem etiam nunc in provinciam suam accedere; id autem facere ob eam causam dicebant, quod tardius vellet decedere. nos in castra properabamus quae aberant bidui.

**opinio, -onis** (*f*), hope, expectation
**supero** (1), to surpass
**ut**, when
**se conicere**, to rush off, flee
**equites, -um** (*m.pl*), cavalry
**nuntio** (1), to report
**cogito** (1), to think, contemplate
**accedo** (3), to approach, go to
**castra, -orum** (*n.pl*), camp
**propero** (1), to hasten, hurry
**absum, -esse**, to be distant

For the background to this letter, see page 141.

1 **salutem**: *(sends) greetings.* Supply **dicit**.

2 **Saturnalibus mane**: *on the morning of (the start of) the Saturnalia.* The Saturnalia began on 17 December and lasted several days. It was a time of great feasting, drinking and merry-making. Friends gave presents to one another, all animosity ceased, schools were closed, war was never declared, no criminals were executed, and slaves were given considerable freedom, even to the extent of being allowed to ridicule their masters.

2 **Pindenissitae**: *the people of Pindenissus.*

3 **qui, malum!**: *who the devil,* literally *who, evil thing!* — a phrase common in Roman comedy.

4 **quid ego faciam?**: *what do you expect me to do about that?*, literally *what am I to do?* In other words, it is not **my** fault that they are out-of-the-way places which are unknown to you. Aetolia and Macedonia would have been well known to Atticus since he had a country house in northern Greece. (For Deliberative Questions, see LL p. 107.)

5 **Ciliciam Aetoliam reddere**: *change* (literally *render*) *Cilicia into Aetolia.*

6 **hoc iam sic habeto**: *you must realise,* literally *know this now as follows.* **habeto** is the most common form of the imperative of **habere**.

6 **nec hoc exercitu nec hic tanta negotia geri potuisse**: *that such big operations could not be undertaken with this army* (i.e. the one I have) *or in this area.* He is trying to forestall possible criticism by stating that his army is too small and that the terrain in Cilicia is too difficult for major campaigns.

7 **quae cognosce ἐν ἐπιτομῃ**: *here is a summary of what happened,* literally *learn about these things* (i.e. the military operations) *in outline.* (For Linking Relative, see LL p. 26.) For the use of Greek words, see note 9 on page 142. 'Epitome' has become an English word meaning 'a résumé' or 'something which embodies the characteristics of a whole class.'

7 **sic concedis**: *you agreed to that,* literally *you give permission for this.* Cicero uses the present tense because the letter from Atticus (though written in the past) is in front of him, as if Atticus were speaking to him at that moment.

9 **qui**: *for you,* literally *who.*

9 **illius diei celebritatem**: *that so many turned out on that day,* literally *the large gathering of that day.* Large numbers of people came to get a look at the new governor as he came ashore.

10 **qua**: *than which.* (For Ablative of Comparison, see LL p. 16.)

11 **accepti ... venimus:** Cicero frequently uses the first person plural when referring to himself, especially when he is describing something grand or something of which he is very proud.

11 **Sextiles**: The month of August was called **Sextilis**, *the sixth month*, since the Roman calendar originally began in March. (For Dates, see LL p. 67.)

13 **revellimus**: *I removed,* literally *we tore away.* The metaphor (see CAO on page 235) is of pulling out a thorn. Cicero's attitude towards the provincials was so different from what they had experienced under Appius Claudius, the previous governor, that they almost forgot what they had suffered in the past.

13 **quod idem fecimus**: *I achieved the same result.*

13 **Colossis, Apameae, Synnadis, Philomeli** and **Iconi** are all locatives (see LL p. 20). [Here Cicero uses the neuter plural form **Synnada** instead of the feminine singular form which was used in Chapter 14.]

# 15. *Cicero the General*

(ad Atticum V.20)

CICERO ATTICO SALUTEM

Saturnalibus mane se mihi Pindenissitae dediderunt septimo et quinquagesimo die, postquam oppugnare eos coepimus. 'qui, malum! isti Pindenissitae qui sunt?' inquies; 'nomen audivi numquam.' quid ego faciam? num potui Ciliciam Aetoliam aut Macedoniam reddere? hoc iam sic habeto, nec hoc exercitu nec hic tanta negotia geri potuisse. quae cognosce ἐν ἐπιτομῃ; sic enim concedis mihi proximis litteris.

Ephesum ut venerim nosti, qui etiam mihi gratulatus es illius diei celebritatem, qua nihil me umquam delectavit magis. inde oppidis iis, quae erant in via, mirabiliter accepti Laodiceam pridie Kal. Sextiles venimus. ibi morati biduum, perillustres fuimus honorificisque verbis omnes iniurias revellimus superiores; quod idem Colossis, dein Apameae quinque dies morati et Synnadis triduum, Philomeli quinque dies, Iconi

**se dedere**, to hand oneself over, surrender
**quinquagesimus, -a, -um**, fiftieth
**oppugno** (1), to attack
**coepi**, I began
**inquies**, you will say
**num?**, surely ... not?
**proximus, -a, -um**, last, most recent
**litterae, -arum** (*f.pl*), letter, note
**ut**, how
**nosti = novisti**, you know
**gratulor** (1) (+ dat.), to congratulate
**umquam**, ever
**delecto** (1), to delight, please
**inde**, from there, after that
**oppidum, -i** (*n*), town, township
**mirabiliter**, marvellously, wonderfully
**accipio** (3), **-cepi, -ceptum**, to receive, welcome
**pridie**, on the day before
**moror** (1), to stay, remain
**biduum, -i** (*n*), (a period of) two days
**perillustris, -is, -e**, greatly honoured
**honorificus, -a, -um**, complimentary, courteous
**verbum, -i** (*n*), word
**iniuria, -ae** (*f*), injustice, wrong, grievance
**superior, -oris**, previous, earlier
**triduum, -i** (*n*), (a period of) three days

15 **nihil aequabilius**: *nothing (could have been) fairer.* Where the meaning is obvious, the verb in Latin is often omitted.

17 **a.d. VII Kal. Septembres**: For the calculation of Roman dates, see LL p. 67. With **a.d. III**, supply **Kalendas Septembres.**

18 **de Parthis**: For the background to the fears of a Parthian invasion, see pages 140, 146 and 156.

18 **venirent**: Note the use of the imperfect tense. The reports *kept coming in.*

20 **eo consilio ut putarent**: *with the intention of making ... think*, literally *with that plan so that ... might think.* The use of **eo consilio** makes the Purpose clause much stronger.

20 **Artavasdes** was the son of Tigranes, the king of Greater Armenia, who had supported Mithridates against the Romans (see p.81) but had retained his kingdom by making peace with Pompey. Artavasdes, who succeeded his father around 55 BC, was ostensibly an ally of Rome, but he contributed to Crassus' defeat by the Parthians at Carrhae in 53 BC by arriving too late to help him. He then joined forces with the Parthians and had his sister married to the son of the Parthian king.

21 **Cappadociae**: *in* (literally *of*) *Cappadocia.*

24 **per Tauri pylas**: *through the Gates of Taurus.* This was a narrow gorge leading into the Taurus Mountains.

26 **in aquarum divortio**: *at its watershed*, literally *at the separation-point of the waters.*

26 **qui mons**: *this mountain-range*, i.e. Amanus. (For Linking Relative, see LL p. 26.)

28 **Pomptini**: Pomptinus was one of Cicero's officers.

29 **nostro matutino**: Supply **adventu**.

29 **imperatores appellati sumus**: *I was hailed as 'General'.* After winning a battle, it was customary for the soldiers on the battlefield to hail their commanding-officer as **imperator**. This act had no official standing, unlike a triumph accorded by the Senate to a successful general on his return to Rome, but it was an honour which, by use and wont, the general could mark by putting the letters **IMP** after his name in any correspondence he sent. Note again how Cicero tends to use the first person plural (*we*) when he is discussing something of which he is particularly proud. (cf. **venimus** in line 12, **nostri** in line 33, and **nostrum** in line 37.)

30 **ea ipsa**: *(on) the very (site)*, literally *that very (camp).*

30 **Darium**: Darius was king of the vast Persian empire until he was totally defeated by Alexander the Great at the Battle of Issus in 333 BC.

31 **haud paulo melior quam**: *much superior to*, literally *not a little better than.*

33 **et ... et ...**: *both ... and ...*

33 **Cassio animus accessit**: *Cassius took heart*, literally *spirit was added to Cassius.* This was the same Cassius who later helped to assassinate Caesar. Although Cicero somewhat plays down Cassius' achievements, there is no doubt that he was an excellent general and that this victory virtually eliminated the Parthian menace.

33 **qui Antiochia tenebatur**: *who was pinned down in Antioch.*

decem fecimus. nihil ea iurisdictione aequabilius, nihil lenius, nihil gravius.

inde in castra veni a.d. VII Kal. Septembres. a.d. III exercitum lustravi apud Iconium. ex his castris, cum graves de Parthis nuntii venirent, perrexi in Ciliciam per Cappadociae partem eam quae Ciliciam attingit, eo consilio ut Armenius Artavasdes et ipsi Parthi Cappadocia se excludi putarent. cum dies quinque ad Cybistra Cappadociae castra habuissem, certior sum factus Parthos ab illo aditu Cappadociae longe abesse, Ciliciae magis imminere. itaque confestim iter in Ciliciam feci per Tauri pylas.

Tarsum veni a.d. III Nonas Octobres. inde ad Amanum contendi, qui Syriam a Cilicia in aquarum divortio dividit; qui mons erat hostium plenus sempiternorum. hic a.d. III Idus Octobr. magnum numerum hostium occidimus. castella munitissima nocturno Pomptini adventu, nostro matutino cepimus, incendimus. imperatores appellati sumus.

castra paucos dies habuimus ea ipsa quae contra Darium habuerat apud Issum Alexander, imperator haud paulo melior quam aut tu aut ego. ibi dies quinque morati, direpto et vastato Amano, inde discessimus. interim rumore adventus nostri et Cassio, qui Antiochia tenebatur, animus accessit et Parthis timor iniectus est. itaque eos cedentes ab oppido Cassius insecutus rem bene gessit. qua in fuga,

**iurisdictio, -onis** (*f*), administration of law
**lenis, -is, -e**, moderate, lenient
**gravis, -is, -e**, serious, authoritative
**castra, -orum** (*n.pl*), camp
**exercitus, -us** (*m*), army
**lustro** (1), to review, inspect
**nuntius, -i** (*m*), news, message, report
**pergo** (3), **perrexi**, to go on, march
**attingo** (3), to touch, border on
**excludo** (3), to shut out (from), cut off
**castra habere**, to stay in camp
**certior fio**, to be informed
**aditus, -us** (*m*), approach
**longe**, far
**absum, -esse**, to be distant
**immineo** (2) (+ dat.), to threaten
**confestim**, immediately
**contendo** (3), **-tendi**, to hasten, hurry
**divido** (3), to separate
**plenus, -a, -um**, full
**sempiternus, -a, -um**, long-standing
**occido** (3), **-cidi**, to kill, slaughter
**castellum, -i** (*n*), fortified post
**munitus, -a, -um**, fortified
**nocturnus, -a, -um**, by night, at night
**adventus, -us** (*m*), arrival
**matutinus, -a, -um**, in the early morning
**incendo** (3), **-cendi**, to burn
**diripio** (3), **-ripui, -reptum**, to plunder
**vasto** (1), to lay waste
**discedo** (3), **-cessi**, to leave, move on
**interim**, meanwhile
**rumor, -oris** (*m*), rumour
**accedo** (3), **-cessi**, to be added to
**timor, -oris** (*m*), fear
**inicio** (3), **-ieci, -iectum**, to put into, inject, inspire
**cedo** (3), to withdraw, retreat
**insequor** (3), **-secutus sum**, to pursue
**rem bene gerere**, to be successful
**fuga, -ae** (*f*), flight

36 **magna auctoritate**: *(a man) of great authority.* (For Ablative of Description, see LL p. 15.)

36 **eoque interiit**: *died from it.*

38 **Bibulus**: Marcus Bibulus was the new governor of Syria.

38 **appellatione hac inani**: *in the matter of this meaningless* (literally *empty*) *title*, i.e. by winning the title of **imperator** for an unimportant victory.

39 **loreolam in mustaceo quaerere**: *to search for a small piece of laurel leaf in a wedding cake.* Wedding cakes contained strips of laurel and were baked on laurel leaves, some small pieces of which would, no doubt, stick to the bottom when it was served up. It would be very easy therefore to find them. A victor's crown was made of laurel (**laurus**), and **loreola** is a diminutive form. By combining the two ideas of wedding cake and small laurel, Cicero ridicules Bibulus' attempt to win glory by starting a campaign which would be easy to win. Even then, however, he bungled it.

40 **centurionem primi pili**: *his most senior centurion.* The centurions were the backbone of the Roman army, not unlike sergeant-majors in modern armies. Promotion for them was up through the cohorts, from the tenth to the first. The centurions of the First Cohort, therefore, were the most experienced, and the most senior of them all was the **centurio primi pili**.

41 **reliquos**: Supply **centuriones.**

42 **tribunum militum**: The commander of a legion was the **legatus**, and under him there were six *tribunes of the soldiers*. These were usually young men who were serving in the army to gain administrative experience before returning to civilian life.

42 **cum re tum tempore**: *both in what happened* (**re**) *and because of the time (at which it happened).*

44 **ad Pindenissum**: Supply a verb such as **contendimus** or **iter fecimus**.

44 **Eleutherocilicum**: *of the Eleutherocilices* (which means *the free Cilicians*). These were possibly the original inhabitants of the area, who now lived in the mountains.

45 **omnium memoria**: *as far back as people can remember*, literally *within the memory of all.*

45 **omnibus rebus**: *in every way*, literally *in all things.*

48 **incolumi exercitu**: *without loss of life*, literally *with the army intact.*

50 **militibus quoque**: *for the soldiers also*, i.e. as well as for me.

50 **exceptis captivis**: *apart from the prisoners*, literally *the prisoners having been taken out.* It was customary for successful generals to reward their men with captured booty. Prisoners were sometimes handed over to the soldiers as booty, though most often they were auctioned, as here. The money raised from an auction belonged to the state, but corrupt governors would easily find ways of syphoning off some of the money for their own use

51 **Saturnalibus tertiis**: *on the third day of the Saturnalia*, i.e. 19th December.

magna auctoritate Osaces dux Parthorum vulnus accepit eoque interiit paucis post diebus. erat in Syria nostrum nomen in gratia.

venit interim Bibulus. credo, voluit appellatione hac inani nobis esse par. in eodem Amano coepit loreolam in mustaceo quaerere. at ille cohortem primam totam perdidit centurionemque primi pili Asinium Dentonem et reliquos cohortis eiusdem et Sex.Lucilium, tribunum militum. sane plagam odiosam acceperat cum re tum tempore.

nos ad Pindenissum, quod oppidum munitissimum Eleutherocilicum omnium memoria in armis fuit. feri homines et acres et omnibus rebus ad defendendum parati. cinximus vallo et fossa, aggere maximo, vineis, turre altissima, magna tormentorum copia, multis sagittariis: magno labore, apparatu, multis sauciis nostris, incolumi exercitu, negotium confecimus.

hilara sane Saturnalia, militibus quoque quibus (exceptis captivis) reliquam praedam concessimus. mancipia venibant Saturnalibus tertiis.

**vulnus, -eris** (*n*), wound
**gratia, -ae** (*f*), favour, popularity
**credo** (3), to believe, suppose
**par, paris**, equal, even, on a par
**at**, but
**perdo** (3), **-didi**, to lose
**sane**, certainly, really
**plaga, -ae** (*f*), blow, misfortune
**odiosus, -a, -um**, annoying, nasty
**ferus, -a, -um**, wild
**acer, acris, acre**, fierce
**cingo** (3), **cinxi**, to surround
**vallum, -i** (*n*), rampart
**fossa, -ae** (*f*), ditch, moat
**agger, -eris** (*m*), mound (of earth)
**vinea, -ae** (*f*), penthouse
**turris, -is** (*f*), tower
**tormentum, -i** (*n*), catapult, siege-artillery
**copia, -ae** (*f*), supply
**sagittarius, -i** (*m*), archer
**apparatus, -us** (*m*), preparation, equipment
**saucius, -a, -um**, wounded
**negotium, -i** (*n*), business, job
**conficio** (3), **-feci**, to finish, complete
**hilarus, -a, -um**, happy, merry
**reliquus, -a, -um**, remaining
**praeda, -ae** (*f*), booty, plunder
**concedo** (3), **-cessi**, to give, hand over
**mancipium, -i** (*n*), prisoner of war
**veneo, -ire**, to be sold

52 **scribebam**: By using the epistolary imperfect tense, Cicero puts himself in the position of the reader who receives the letter some time later.

52 **in tribunali res**: *the sum realised from the auction*, literally *the amount on the platform.* The **tribunal** was the platform from which the general normally addressed his troops. Here it is being used as a stand by the auctioneer.

52 **ad HS $\overline{CXX}$**: *around 120,000 sesterces.* The derivation of **HS** is || **S(emis)**, i.e. 2½ asses, which was the original value of a sesterce. (The **as** was the smallest Roman coin.) The Roman method of expressing numerals was lengthy even for small numbers. For large numbers, therefore, they used a kind of shorthand, e.g. **xx** = 20; $\overline{XX}$ = 20,000 [i.e. 1,000 x 20]; $|\overline{xx}|$ = 2,000,000 [i.e. 100 x 1,000 x 20].

With such a system, it is not surprising that numbers could be corrupted in the process of copying manuscripts. In this passage, some editors read **HS $\overline{cxx}$** (i.e. 120,000 sesterces), others read **HS $|\overline{cxx}|$** (i.e. 12,000,000 sesterces). We have no way of knowing which is correct, nor what the equivalent sum would be today. The important point here is that Cicero thought that even a very wealthy man such as Atticus would be impressed by the sum he had raised from the auction.

53 **in hiberna agri male pacati deducendum**: *to take (them) into winter-quarters in an area that is far from settled*, literally *to be taken into winter-quarters in territory (that is) not well pacified.* (For this use of the Gerundive, see LL p. 61.)

53 **dabam**: *I am giving* (Epistolary Tense — see line 52). (cf. **recipiebam** in line 54.)

## Points for Discussion

1. In lines 5-6, explain what you think Cicero means when he asks the question: **num potui Ciliciam Aetoliam aut Macedoniam reddere?**
2. In lines 6-7, Cicero says that Cilicia is not the sort of area in which big campaigns can be fought. Contrast this with what he says in lines 44-9, and comment on both statements.
3. In lines 13-14, Cicero mentions several place names in an area which was probably unfamiliar to Atticus. Why do you think he does this?
4. Is there any evidence in the passage to suggest that the reference to Alexander the Great (lines 30-2) is made in jest?
5. Quote examples of how Cicero boasts about his military achievements as he proceeds through the province.
6. Find examples in the text of how Cicero regards himself as a successful military commander. Do you think his claims are convincing?

cum haec scribebam, in tribunali res erat ad HS $\overline{\text{CXX}}$. hinc exercitum in hiberna agri male pacati deducendum Quinto fratri dabam; ipse me Laodiceam recipiebam.

**hinc**, from here

**se recipere**, to return

# Break-up of the Triumvirate

The political coalition of Pompey, Caesar and Crassus (known as the First Triumvirate) was renewed at Luca in 56 BC, but in the next few years several things combined to break it up and drive a wedge between Caesar and Pompey, which ultimately led to civil war.

Julia, Caesar's daughter, who had married Pompey in 59 BC, died in childbirth in 54 BC; Crassus was defeated by the Parthians and subsequently murdered in 53 BC; a small group of hard-liners in the Senate, alarmed at Caesar's growing popularity after his successful campaigns in Gaul, began to cultivate the support of Pompey, who was jealous of Caesar's growing stature; in 52 BC, they succeeded in having Pompey elected as sole consul to restore order in the city following gang riots which culminated in Clodius' murder (see pages 140-1) and the burning down of the senate-house; in 52 BC also, Pompey's command in Spain was extended by five years, although he still remained in Rome; in 51 BC, the Senate rejected a request by Caesar that his command in Gaul be extended to the end of 49 BC, and one of the consuls actually proposed that Caesar be deprived of his command on the grounds that the war in Gaul was over — a move which was vetoed by one of the tribunes of the plebs; a similar attempt was made in March 50 BC, but it also was vetoed; soon afterwards, the Senate demanded that Caesar and Pompey each hand over one legion for use against the growing threat to Syria by the Parthians; Caesar complied, but Pompey 'gave up' a legion which he had lent to Caesar three years earlier, and the legions remained in Italy. From Caesar's point of view, Pompey's increased influence with the Senate was a particular concern.

Towards the end of 50 BC, when his governorship of Gaul had only a short time to run, Caesar asked the Senate's permission to stand *in absentia* for the consulship of 48 BC, which he had been promised under the Triumvirs' agreement at Luca. He realised that he would be at the mercy of his enemies if he disbanded his army and returned to Rome as a private citizen. The Senate refused this request. On 1 December 50 BC, Caesar (through a tribune) proposed that both he and Pompey should resign their commands and disband their armies. This proposal was carried in the Senate by 370 votes to 22, but the 22 hard-liners had the decision vetoed. On the following day, after a false rumour reached Rome that Caesar's army had crossed the Alps, the consul Marcellus, one of the hard-liners, asked Pompey to take over command of all the forces in Italy. This was quite unconstitutional, but Pompey agreed.

Caesar continued to offer to disband if Pompey would do the same. He even agreed to accept a compromise proposal, probably engineered by Cicero who was working hard to prevent war, that he retain only Illyricum and one legion. The new consuls, however, were both hostile to him and his offers were refused. Almost unanimously, the Senate passed a motion that Caesar disband his forces or be declared an enemy of the state. Two tribunes who were favourable to Caesar immediately vetoed the decision. On 7 January 49 BC, the consul Lentulus announced his intention to propose the **senatus consultum ultimum**, the equivalent of martial law, and advised the two tribunes to withdraw if they valued their lives. They fled to Caesar.

The violation of the sacred rights of the tribunes gave Caesar an excuse to use force to get what he wanted, on the pretext of defending the constitution. On 11 January 49 BC, he crossed the River Rubicon, the boundary of his province, making the famous comment **iacta alea est** (*the die is cast*), for he knew that by leading his army on to Italian soil without permission he was guilty of high treason; he then immediately marched into Italy with the single legion which he had available. Pompey and the senatorial forces were taken completely by surprise and withdrew to the south of Italy. Caesar did not pause to capture Rome but marched on south and set up garrisons in key towns.

Cicero also left Rome, but he went only as far as his villa at Formiae. His son Marcus went with him; Terentia and Tullia, his wife and daughter, remained in Rome. Although Caesar made repeated attempts to win Cicero's support, at no time did Cicero contemplate joining Caesar, as he regarded him as a danger to the constitution of the Republic. Despite Pompey's coolness towards him and his own growing doubts about Pompey's competence, he still regarded Pompey as the only man who could save the Republic. [What is surprising is that Cicero seemed oblivious to the fact that almost all the commands held by Pompey throughout his career had been obtained unconstitutionally.]

Cicero was, in fact, torn between openly throwing in his lot with Pompey and remaining neutral in order to act as a mediator between Caesar and Pompey. On 22 January, he left Formiae to join Pompey's forces near Minturnae. From there, at Pompey's request, he went on to Capua where many of the senators had gathered. As he says in the following letter written to his secretary Tiro on 27 January, he still hoped that Caesar could be persuaded to pull back from the awful consequences of civil war. His own analysis of the situation was that Caesar might face serious problems if he sought a military solution.

1 **S.D. = salutem dicit**: *sends greetings.*

1 **Tironi**: Marcus Tullius Tiro was Cicero's secretary. Originally a slave, Tiro took his master's name after Cicero gave him his freedom in 54 or 53 BC. He was intelligent and well educated and is said to have invented a form of shorthand. He was not simply a secretary but, according to the Roman writer Aulus Gellius, was used by Cicero as an assistant, almost a partner, in his literary work. It was Tiro who collected Cicero's letters and preserved them for posterity. He also wrote at least four books about his former master. Cicero was very fond of Tiro as a person, treated him as a close friend and constantly expressed concern about his health. Despite his earlier ill health, Tiro lived to the age of ninety-nine. At the time of this letter, he was in Patrae (on the Gulf of Corinth) recuperating from an illness which had struck him down when Cicero and he were returning from Cilicia, where Cicero had been governor (51-50 BC).

2 **quo in discrimine versetur salus**: An Indirect Question depending on **scire potes.**

2 **salus mea et bonorum omnium**: *my own safety and (that) of all loyal (citizens).*

3 **ex eo quod**: *from the fact that.* The **quod** clause explains the phrase **ex eo.**

4 **diripiendam**: *to be plundered.* (For the Gerundive, see LL p. 61.)

4 **in eum locum res deducta est**: *things have reached such a state*, literally *the matter has been led to that place.*

5 **qui deus**: *some god (or other).*

7 **ad urbem**: *to Rome.*

8 **quae ad concordiam pertinerent**: *which might promote (the cause of) peace*, literally *which might relate to harmony.* (For Generic Subjunctive, see LL p. 103.)

10 **me clamante**: *in spite of my cries*, literally *me shouting.* (For this type of Ablative Absolute, see LL p. 31.)

10 **bello civili**: For Ablative of Comparison, see LL p. 16.

11 **nominis**: *his reputation*, literally *his (good) name.*

12 **occupavisset**: The subjunctive depends on **cum**. Note the change of tense from the imperfect (**raperetur**) which describes his state of mind at the time when he captured these towns. See the map on page 157 for the location of the towns.

13 **reliquimus**: *I left.* Cicero frequently uses the plural when referring to himself.

13 **quam sapienter**: *how wise a decision this was*, literally *how wisely (I acted).*

13 **nihil attinet disputari**: *there is no point in discussing*, literally *it is of no concern at all that it be discussed.* (For Impersonal Verbs, see LL p. 57.)

# *16. Civil War Imminent*

(ad Familiares XVI.12)

TULLIUS S. D. TIRONI SUO

quo in discrimine versetur salus mea et bonorum omnium atque universae rei publicae, ex eo scire potes quod domos nostras et patriam ipsam vel diripiendam vel inflammandam reliquimus. in eum locum res deducta est ut, nisi qui deus vel casus aliquis subvenerit, salvi esse nequeamus.

equidem ut veni ad urbem, non destiti omnia et sentire et dicere et facere quae ad concordiam pertinerent: sed mirus invaserat furor non solum improbis sed etiam iis qui boni habentur, ut pugnare cuperent, me clamante nihil esse bello civili miserius. itaque, cum Caesar amentia quadam raperetur et, oblitus nominis atque honorum suorum, Ariminum, Pisaurum, Anconam, Arretium occupavisset, urbem reliquimus; quam sapienter aut quam fortiter nihil attinet disputari.

**discrimen, -inis** (*n*), danger, critical situation
**versor** (1), to be
**universus, -a, -um**, entire, as a whole
**res publica, rei publicae** (*f*), state
**scio** (4), to know
**domus, -us** (*f*), home
**vel ... vel ...**, either ... or ...
**inflammo** (1), to burn, set on fire
**relinquo** (3), **-liqui**, to leave, abandon
**casus, -us** (*m*), chance, change of fortune
**aliquis, -quis, -quid**, some
**subvenio** (4), **-veni**, to come to one's aid
**salvus, -a, -um**, safe
**nequeo, -ire**, to be unable
**equidem**, certainly, for my own part
**ut**, from the time when, ever since
**desisto** (3), **destiti** (+ infinitive), to stop (doing), cease (from doing)
**sentio** (4), to think
**mirus, -a, -um**, strange, extraordinary
**invado** (3), **-vasi** (+ dat.), to take hold of, possess, grip
**furor, -oris** (*m*), madness
**non solum ... sed etiam**, not only ... but also
**improbus, -a, -um**, disloyal, unprincipled
**habeo** (2), to regard, consider
**pugno** (1), to fight
**cupio** (3), to desire, be keen to
**miser, -era, -erum**, miserable, wretched
**amentia, -ae** (*f*), madness
**rapio** (3), to seize
**obliviscor** (3), **oblitus sum** (+ gen.), to forget
**honos, honoris** (*m*), honour, public office
**occupo** (1), to occupy, seize
**fortiter**, bravely, courageously

14 **ab illo** refers to Caesar.

15 **ut Pompeius eat**: This Indirect Command contains the first of the terms laid down by Caesar. **eat** is present subjunctive of **ire**.

16 **dimittantur**: *must be disbanded.* Another Indirect Command containing the second condition laid down by Caesar. The indirect speech continues with four Accusative and Infinitive clauses (lines 16-19) which state what Caesar has promised to do. Unlike English, Latin has no need of a verb of speaking to introduce each of these clauses.

16 **ulteriorem Galliam**: *Transalpine* (literally *farther*) *Gaul.* **citeriorem (Galliam)** is normally called Cisalpine Gaul. These provinces had been assigned (**obtigerunt**, literally *fell to their lot*) to L.Domitius Ahenobarbus and M.Considius Nonianus about three weeks before this letter was written.

18 **se venturum (esse)**: Supply **Romam**. That is, he agreed to give up his claim to stand for the consulship *in absentia* (**absente se**).

18 **rationem haberi suam**: *to stand as a candidate*, literally *a count (of votes) for himself to be held.* The phrase **rationem habere** is used of magistrates recording the votes cast in favour of a candidate.

19 **trinum nundinum**: *for twenty-four days*, literally *three nundina*, a **nundinum** being the period of eight days between two market-days (called **nundinae**). This was the minimum period required by law for a candidate's **professio** (i.e. his public declaration that he was a candidate and what he stood for).

25 **possit**: For the Generic Subjunctive, see LL p. 103. Earlier in the letter, Cicero's mood was almost one of despair since he realised that Pompey and the Senate were so ill-prepared. Why the more hopeful tone at this point? He may be trying to spare the sick Tiro further worry, or he may have received an optimistic dispatch from Pompey while writing this letter (for it is possible that he did not write it at one sitting), or he may simply be assuming that Caesar would probably lose popular support if he reneged (**fugerit**) on the terms he himself had set.

26 **tantum modo ut**: *provided only that.*

27 **sperabamus**: *we are hoping.* The imperfect is used here, later in the line (**habebamus**) and in the next line (**putabamus**) because, by the time Tiro is reading the letter, all of this will be in the past. This use of the imperfect, common in letters, is called the Epistolary Imperfect.

28 **Gallias** refers to both Cisalpine Gaul and Transalpine Gaul (see note 16).

29 **quas ambas habet inimicissimas**: *both of which are utterly hostile (to him)*, literally *which both he has very hostile.*

29 **praeter Transpadanos**: *apart from Transpadane Gaul* (i.e. the part of Cisalpine Gaul north of the River Po). The Transpadani were on Caesar's side because he had previously supported their claim to citizenship. He granted them citizenship later, when he came to Rome in April 49 BC.

30 **magna auxilia**: *a large number of auxiliary troops*. The legions contained the highly trained Roman foot-soldiers; the auxiliary troops (light-armed soldiers, bowmen, slingers, cavalry and artillery) were recruited mainly from Rome's allies.

30 **Afranio et Petreio ducibus**: For this type of Ablative Absolute, see LL p. 30.

31 **a tergo**: *threatening his rear*, literally *from his back.*

31 **modo ut urbe salva**: Supply **opprimatur** — *provided that (he can be crushed) without any harm to the city.* (For **modo ut**, compare line 26; for the Ablative Absolute **urbe salva**, see LL pp. 30-1.)

34 **idem** is neuter singular.

quo quidem in casu simus vides. feruntur omnino condiciones ab illo, ut Pompeius eat in Hispaniam; dilectus, qui sunt habiti, et praesidia nostra dimittantur; se ulteriorem Galliam Domitio, citeriorem Considio Noniano (his enim obtigerunt) traditurum; ad consulatus petitionem se venturum; neque se iam velle, absente se, rationem haberi suam; se praesentem trinum nundinum petiturum. accepimus condiciones, sed ita ut removeat praesidia ex iis locis quae occupavit, ut sine metu de his ipsis condicionibus Romae senatus haberi possit.

id ille si fecerit, spes est pacis, non honestae (leges enim imponuntur), sed quidvis est melius quam sic esse ut sumus. sin autem ille suis condicionibus stare noluerit, bellum paratum est, eius modi tamen quod sustinere ille non possit, praesertim cum a suis condicionibus ipse fugerit; tantum modo ut eum intercludamus ne ad urbem possit accedere, quod sperabamus fieri posse. dilectus enim magnos habebamus putabamusque illum metuere, si ad urbem ire coepisset, ne Gallias amitteret, quas ambas habet inimicissimas praeter Transpadanos; ex Hispaniaque sex legiones et magna auxilia, Afranio et Petreio ducibus, habet a tergo. videtur, si insaniet, posse opprimi, modo ut urbe salva. maximam autem plagam accepit quod is qui summam auctoritatem in illius exercitu habebat, T.Labienus, socius sceleris esse noluit; reliquit illum et nobiscum est; multique idem facturi esse dicuntur.

**casus, -us** (*m*), critical situation
**fero, ferre**, to lay down, impose
**omnino**, entirely
**condiciones, -um** (*f.pl*), conditions
**Hispania, -ae** (*f*), Spain
**dilectus, -us** (*m*), levy (of troops), recruiting campaign
**praesidium, -i** (*n*), garrison
**trado** (3), **-didi, -ditum**, to hand over
**consulatus, -us** (*m*), consulship
**petitio, -onis** (*f*), candidacy
**praesens, -entis**, present, in person
**peto** (3), **-ivi, -itum**, to seek election
**ita ut**, on condition that
**removeo** (2), to remove, withdraw
**metus, -us** (*m*), fear
**habeo** (2), to hold, convene
**spes, spei** (*f*), hope
**pax, pacis** (*f*), peace
**honestus, -a, -um**, honourable
**lex, legis** (*f*), condition
**impono** (3), to impose
**quidvis**, anything at all
**sin**, but if
**autem**, however, moreover
**sto** (1) (+ abl.), to stand (by), adhere (to)
**eius modi**, of such a kind
**sustineo** (2), to sustain, keep going
**praesertim**, especially
**intercludo** (3), to cut off
**accedo** (3), to come to, approach
**puto** (1), to think
**metuo** (3), to fear
**coepi, -isse**, to have begun
**amitto** (3), to lose
**inimicus, -a, -um**, hostile
**insanio** (4), to act like a madman
**opprimo** (3), to overwhelm, crush
**plaga, -ae** (*f*), blow
**auctoritas, -atis** (*f*), authority, status, influence
**socius, -i** (*m*), ally, accomplice, partner
**scelus, -eris** (*n*), crime, criminal act

35 **a Formiis**: *from (my base at) Formiae*. Cicero had been asked by Pompey to supervise the recruiting of troops on the west coast of Italy in the area north of Capua.

36 **quo plus valerent**: *so that ... might carry more weight*. (For Purpose clauses introduced by **quo**, see LL p. 45.)

36 **apud illum** refers to Caesar.

39 **Dolabella noster**: Dolabella was the third husband of Cicero's daughter Tullia. One of the evils of civil war is the fact that friends and even members of the same family often find themselves fighting on opposite sides.

40 **quae cave ne te perturbent**: *don't let them worry you*, literally *take care that these things do not disturb you*. (For Linking Relative, see LL p. 26.) **cave** followed by the subjunctive (with or without **ne**) is a polite way of telling someone not to do something.

41 **A.Varroni**: Aulus Terentius Varro was a supporter of Pompey. It would appear that he was travelling to Patrae (on the Gulf of Corinth), where Tiro was recovering from illness, and that he would be there for some time.

41 **mei** is the genitive of **ego**, and **tui** (line 42) is the genitive of **tu**.

43 **ut rationem haberet**: *(asking him) to give thought*, literally *to take account*. This Indirect Command is implied in **commendavi**.

43 **navigationis**: *to your voyage (home)*. In other words, Varro is asked to assess whether Tiro is fit to travel. This genitive, like **valetudinis**, depends on **rationem**.

43 **totum te susciperet**: *to take you completely into his care*, literally *to undertake the whole of you*.

44 **quem facturum**: Supply **esse** to complete the Accusative and Infinitive clause. (For Linking Relative, see LL p. 26.)

44 **recepit**: *he said that he would*, literally *he accepted*.

46 **eo tempore quo**: *at the time when*.

47 **operam et fidelitatem tuam**: *your faithful services*, literally *your effort and faithfulness*. (For Hendiadys, see CAO on page 234.)

47 **cave festines**: *see that you don't hurry*, i.e. don't attempt the voyage until you are completely fit. For **cave** (+ the subjunctive) used in polite negative commands, compare line 40.

48 **hieme**: *in stormy weather*.

49 **videram**: *I have seen*. As in lines 27-8, Cicero uses the tense which fits the time when Tiro would be reading the letter rather than the time when Cicero was writing it.

49 **postea ... quam = posteaquam**. Latin writers frequently split this conjunction (see LL p. 52). Supply **te vidisset** after **Volusius**.

50 **quod non mirabar**: Cicero was not surprised, because foreign correspondence was often delayed in bad weather.

51 **tanta hieme**: *in such stormy weather*. Compare line 48.

52 **cum recte navigari poterit**: *when conditions are right for sailing*, literally *when sailing can be done rightly*. (For verbs used impersonally in the passive, see LL p. 57.)

53 **Cicero meus**: *my (son Marcus) Cicero*. Note again the use of Epistolary Imperfect (**erat**) and compare lines 27-8 and 49.

53 **in Formiano**: *at my villa near Formiae*.

54 IIII: Note that the number 4 was by no means universally written as IV. (For the calculation of Dates, see LL p. 66.)

54 **Capua**: *(sent) from Capua*.

ego adhuc orae maritimae praesum a Formiis. nullum maius negotium suscipere volui, quo plus apud illum meae litterae cohortationesque ad pacem valerent. sin autem erit bellum, video me castris et certis legionibus praefuturum. habeo etiam illam molestiam, quod Dolabella noster apud Caesarem est.

haec tibi nota esse volui; quae cave ne te perturbent et impediant valetudinem tuam. ego A.Varroni, quem cum amantissimum mei cognovi tum etiam valde tui studiosum, diligentissime te commendavi, ut et valetudinis tuae rationem haberet et navigationis et totum te susciperet ac tueretur. quem omnia facturum confido; recepit enim et mecum locutus est suavissime.

tu quoniam eo tempore mecum esse non potuisti quo ego maxime operam et fidelitatem desideravi tuam, cave festines aut committas ut aut aeger aut hieme naviges. numquam sero te venisse putabo si salvus veneris. adhuc neminem videram qui te postea vidisset quam M.Volusius, a quo tuas litteras accepi. quod non mirabar; neque enim meas puto ad te litteras tanta hieme perferri. sed da operam ut valeas et, si valebis, cum recte navigari poterit, tum naviges. Cicero meus in Formiano erat, Terentia et Tullia Romae. cura ut valeas. IIII Kal. Febr. Capua.

**adhuc**, still
**ora maritima** (*f*), sea-coast
**praesum, -esse, -fui** (+ dat.), to be in command (of), in charge (of)
**negotium, -i** (*n*), task, responsibility
**suscipio** (3), to undertake
**apud** (+ acc.), with, on the side of
**litterae, -arum** (*f.pl*), letter(s)
**cohortatio, -onis** (*f*), exhortation
**castra, -orum** (*n.pl*), camp
**certus, -a, -um**, certain, specific, regular
**molestia, -ae** (*f*), annoyance, worry
**notus, -a, -um**, known
**impedio** (4), to hinder, affect adversely
**valetudo, -inis** (*f*), health
**cum ... tum ...**, both ... and ...
**amans, -antis** (+ gen.), friendly (towards), fond (of), devoted (to)
**cognosco** (3), **-novi**, to discover, find (out)
**valde**, very
**studiosus, -a, -um** (+ gen.), devoted (to)
**diligenter**, diligently, earnestly
**commendo** (1), to commend, entrust
**tueor** (2), to protect, look after
**confido** (3), to be confident, be sure
**suaviter**, charmingly, agreeably
**quoniam**, since
**desidero** (1), to long for, need, miss
**committere ut** (+ subjunctive), to make the mistake of
**aeger, -gra, -grum**, ill, unwell
**navigo** (1), to sail
**sero**, late
**miror** (1), to wonder at, be surprised at
**perfero, -ferre**, to convey; (passive + **ad**) to reach
**operam dare** (**ut** + subjunctive), to do one's best (to)
**valeo** (2), to be well

## Points for Discussion

1. In lines 2-6, Cicero suggests that the situation is desperate. What points does he make to back up this assertion? Quote from the Latin to support your answer.
2. In lines 7-13, how does Cicero make clear, by his choice of words, his own personal views about the 'leading players' in this crisis? Quote from the Latin, and translate, where appropriate.
3. The style of this letter is more literary than his notes to Atticus. From lines 2-13, gather as many examples of balanced constructions as you can find. (See CAO on pages 236-7.)
4. List the conditions for peace detailed in lines 14-21. What do you think is Cicero's attitude to these conditions?
5. What is the significance of the use and repetition of **suis** in lines 23 and 25?
6. Read lines 26-34. In lines 26-7, Cicero shows that he is anxious to prevent Caesar from marching on Rome. What considerations does Cicero think will discourage Caesar from doing so?
7. What was the criminal act (**sceleris**) to which Cicero refers in line 33?
8. Which statements in this letter show that Cicero sees himself as a peacemaker between Caesar and Pompey?
9. Quote statements made by Cicero in this letter which indicate the relationship of trust and friendship between himself and Tiro.

# Caesar Defeats Pompey

Pompey's hope that most of the towns of Italy would close their gates to Caesar and that others, like Caesar's lieutenant Labienus, would desert him proved ill-founded. By using clemency wherever he went, Caesar won over more and more of Italy and his forces grew rapidly. In March, Pompey was forced to flee from Italy to Greece where he hoped to regroup his forces. Caesar reached Brundisium just too late to prevent his sailing.

Having failed in his bid to intercept Pompey, Caesar went to Rome to take up the reins of power. On the way, he met Cicero and tried to win him over. Cicero's support would have meant a lot to him in dealing with the rump of the Senate that remained. Cicero could not but be impressed by the courtesy shown to him by Caesar, but he still did not trust him. In June, he slipped out of Italy and joined Pompey in Greece.

Pompey was defeated by Caesar at Pharsalus in Greece in August 48 BC and, having fled to Egypt, he was assassinated by the soldiers of King Ptolemy as he tried to land. Cicero decided that further resistance to Caesar was useless and returned to Italy in October 48 BC. However, since he did not know whether Caesar would take revenge on him for having supported Pompey, he did not return to Rome but remained in Brundisium until September 47 BC, when Caesar granted him an unconditional pardon.

# Cicero's Personal Problems

The letters which Cicero sent to his wife and family during his eighteen months of exile (March 58 BC to August 57 BC) were written in very endearing terms (see Chapters 11 and 12 starting on pages 120 and 126 respectively). The structure of the sentences would suggest that he must also have taken a great deal of time and care over their composition. By contrast, those that he sent home while he was with Pompey's army during the Civil War (June 49 BC to August 48 BC) and those which he wrote on his return to Italy were decidedly scrappy and offhand, as can be seen from the selection which follows.

The explanation is to be found, not in the fact that he was 'on active service' (for he still found time to write long, thoughtful letters to Atticus and other friends), but rather in his growing coolness towards Terentia whom he suspected of defrauding him of some of his property. In hindsight, his letters from exile may be seen to show not so much true love as the formal expression of affection from a dutiful husband.

He was also very concerned about how Caesar would treat him for having supported Pompey. Caesar had certainly permitted him to return to Italy, but Cicero felt it would be unsafe to return to Rome until Caesar himself returned from the East, where he was mopping up the remnants of Pompey's defeated army. This uncertainty, rather than his coolness towards Terentia, might explain why Cicero lingered for eleven months in Brundisium after returning from Greece, instead of going home to Terentia.

His estrangement from Terentia was not Cicero's only domestic worry at this time. His son Marcus was not living up to his father's hopes and expectations, preferring to devote himself to high living rather than to his education and career. Cicero's greatest concern, however, was over his daughter Tullia, the darling of his life, who was now in poor health and suffering from the extravagance and infidelity of her third husband, Publius Cornelius Dolabella.

In the end, Cicero divorced Terentia in 46 BC. He then married Publilia, a wealthy young woman who had been his ward. This marriage was far from successful, however; and, unable to forgive her for showing insufficient sorrow over the death of Tullia in 45 BC, Cicero divorced her too and refused to see her again.

(a)

1 **S.D.**: This is an abbreviated way of saying **salutem dicit** (*sends greetings*).
2 **quod**: *as to the fact that.*
2 **nos**: *I.* Note the mixture of 1st person singular and 1st person plural which Cicero uses to refer to himself.
2 **perpetuo gaudeas velim**: *I would wish you always to be glad.* (For the Potential use of **velim**, see LL p. 108. It may be followed either by an infinitive or by a subjunctive, as here, usually without **ut**.)
3 **id consili**: *a course of action.* (For Partitive Genitive, see LL p. 9.)
4 **quantum potes**: *to the best of your ability*, literally *(as much) as you are able (to help)*. (For the Correlatives **tantum ... quantum**, see LL pp. 63-4.)
5 **quid possis**: Supply **facere**.
5 **mihi in mentem non venit**: *I have no idea*, literally *it has not come into the mind to me.*
5 **in viam quod te des nihil est**: *there is no reason for your making the journey*, literally *there is nothing which (justifies) your giving yourself onto the road.* Interestingly enough, Plutarch in his 'Life of Cicero' says that one of the grievances which Cicero had against Terentia at the time of their divorce was her failure to travel to Brundisium to meet him.
7 **d.**: *handed over*, i.e. to the person who was to convey the letter to its destination. An abbreviation either for **data** (agreeing with **epistola** understood) or, more likely, for the neuter form **datum**, which occurs consistently at the end of medieval charters. The English word 'date' is derived from **datum**.
7 **prid. Non. Nov.**: For the calculation of Dates, see LL p. 67.

(b)

3 **nihil est quod plura scribam**: *there is nothing more I can write*, literally *there is nothing which I may write more.* (For Generic Subjunctive, see LL p. 103.)
4 **curae esse**: *(that) it is a concern.* (For Predicative Dative, see LL p. 13.)
4 **quod**: Compare line 2 of letter (a).
4 **ita esse faciendum**: *that this is what I must do*, literally *that it must be done thus.* (For the Gerundive used impersonally, see LL p. 62.)
5 **fecissem**: *I would have done (this).* (For this type of Conditional clause, see LL p. 54.) Caesar's attitude towards Cicero was still unknown.

# *17. Coolness Towards Terentia*

(a) Written at Brundisium on 4 November 48 BC on his way home from war

(ad Familiares XIV.12)

TULLIUS TERENTIAE SUAE S. D.

quod nos in Italiam salvos venisse gaudes, perpetuo gaudeas velim. sed perturbati dolore animi magnisque iniuriis metuo ne id consili ceperimus quod non facile explicare possimus. quare, quantum potes, adiuva. quid autem possis, mihi in mentem non venit. in viam quod te des hoc tempore nihil est. et longum est iter, et non tutum; et non video quid prodesse possis, si veneris. vale! d. prid. Non. Nov. Brundisio.

**salvus, -a, -um**, safe
**perturbo** (1), to confuse, disturb
**dolor, -oris** (*m*), grief, agony, anxiety
**iniuria, -ae** (*f*), injustice, wrong
**metuo** (3), to fear
**capio** (3), **cepi**, to take, adopt
**explico** (1), to undo, reverse
**quare**, therefore
**adiuvo** (1), to help
**autem**, however, but
**et ... et ...**, both ... and ...
**tutus, -a, -um**, safe
**prosum, prodesse**, to be useful, do good, benefit
**vale! valete!**, goodbye! farewell!

(b) Written at Brundisium on 27 November 48 BC

(ad Familiares XIV.19)

TULLIUS TERENTIAE SUAE S. D.

in maximis meis doloribus excruciat me valetudo Tulliae nostrae. de qua nihil est quod ad te plura scribam: tibi enim aeque magnae curae esse certo scio. quod me propius vultis accedere, video ita esse faciendum. et iam ante fecissem, sed me multa impediverunt quae

**excrucio** (1), to torture, torment
**valetudo, -inis** (*f*), health
**aeque**, equally
**certo**, certainly, for sure
**scio** (4), to know
**propius**, nearer
**accedo** (3), to come to, approach
**impedio** (4), to hinder, prevent

6 **a Pomponio**: This was Titus Pomponius Atticus, the friend to whom Cicero wrote numerous letters containing his innermost thoughts.

7 **quas ad me perferendas cures velim**: *and I'd like you to arrange for them to be brought to me.* (For the Gerundive used with **curare**, see LL p. 61; for this use of **velim**, compare line 2 of letter (a).)

(c)

2 **S.V.B.E.V.**: A shorthand way of writing **si vales, benest** (= **bene est**); **ego valeo.**

2 **si quid haberem, facerem**: For Conditional sentences, see LL p. 54.

2 **quod ad te scriberem**: Compare line 3 of letter (b).

3 **nunc**: *as things are.*

4 **quomodo sim adfectus**: *my state of mind*, literally *how I am affected.*

4 **ex Lepta et Trebatio**: Quintus Paconius Lepta had been Cicero's **praefectus fabrum** (*chief engineer*) when he was governor of Cilicia (51-50 BC). Gaius Trebatius Testa was a friend whom Cicero had recommended to Caesar in 54 BC and who had supported Caesar in the Civil War. Both men had visited Cicero in Brundisium and had now left for Rome.

5 **fac ut cures**: Compare **da operam ut valeas** in lines 7-8 of letter (b).

(d)

2 **velim cures**: Compare line 2 in letter (a) and line 7 in letter (b).

3 **febrim**: An alternative form of the accusative singular.

4 **de Caesaris litteris**: This was possibly a letter written by Caesar to Mark Antony. Cicero was anxious about Caesar's likely attitude towards him and would be grateful for any information which might shed light on this.

5 **si quid opus erit**: *if anything is needed.*

5 **si quid acciderit novi**: *if there is any new development*, literally *if anything new shall have happened.* (For Partitive Genitive, see LL p. 9.)

6 **facies ut**: *you will make (sure) that.* The future tense is particularly curt. It suggests a command rather than a request.

6 **d.**: See line 7 of letter (a).

6 **IIII Non. Iun**: A shorthand way of writing **a.d. IIII Nonas Iunias**. (For Roman Dates, see LL p. 66.) Note that the number four may be written as IIII or IV.

ne nunc quidem expedita sunt. sed a Pomponio exspecto litteras, quas ad me quam primum perferendas cures velim. da operam ut valeas.

**ne ... quidem**, not even
**expedio** (4), to resolve, put right
**litterae, -arum** (*f.pl*), a letter
**quam primum**, as soon as possible
**operam dare ut**, to give attention to, take care to
**valeo** (2), to be well

## (c) Written at Brundisium in late December 48 BC

(ad Familiares XIV.17)

TULLIUS TERENTIAE SUAE S. D.

S.V.B.E.V. si quid haberem quod ad te scriberem, facerem id et pluribus verbis et saepius. nunc, quae sint negotia vides. ego autem quomodo sim adfectus ex Lepta et Trebatio poteris cognoscere. tu fac ut tuam et Tulliae valetudinem cures. vale!

**si quid**, if anything
**verbum, -i** (*n*), word
**negotium, -i** (*n*), problem, trouble
**cognosco** (3), to learn, find out
**fac ut** (+ subjunctive), see to it that
**curo** (1), to look after, see to, attend to

## (d) Written at Brundisium on 2 June 47 BC

(ad Familiares XIV.8)

TULLIUS TERENTIAE SUAE S.

si vales, bene est. ego valeo. valetudinem tuam velim cures diligentissime. nam mihi et scriptum et nuntiatum est te in febrim subito incidisse. quod celeriter me fecisti de Caesaris litteris certiorem, fecisti mihi gratum. item posthac, si quid opus erit, si quid acciderit novi, facies ut sciam. cura ut valeas. vale! d. IIII Non. Iun.

**diligenter**, carefully
**febris, -is** (*f*), fever
**incido** (3), **-cidi**, to fall into
**certiorem facere**, to inform
**gratus, -a, -um**, pleasing, agreeable
**item**, likewise
**posthac**, after this, in future

(e)

2 **quod**: For the omission of the antecedent **id**, see LL p. 26.
3 **provideas**: *consider*. (For this use of the present subjunctive to express a Command, see LL p. 107.) Compare **administres** and **mittas**.

(f)

3 **litterae**: Caesar had written from Egypt, where he was warring against the Pompeians, to assure Cicero that he would be treated with respect, despite the fact that he had supported Pompey.
3 **opinione celerius**: *sooner than people believe*, literally *more quickly than belief*. (For Ablative of Comparison, see LL p. 16.)
4 **cui**: *him*. (For Linking Relative, see LL p. 26.)
5 **velim**: Compare line 2 of (a), line 7 of (b) and line 2 of (d).
6 **d. prid. Id. Sext(iles)**: *handed over (to the courier) on 12th August*. The old Roman year began in March. The sixth month was later renamed **Augustus** in honour of the emperor Augustus.

Caesar's emphasis on leniency towards those who had opposed him in the Civil War was marked by the building of a temple dedicated
**CLEMENTIAE CAESARIS**
This coin was probably minted after his death.

## (e) Written at Brundisium in June 47 BC

(ad Familiares XIV.21)

TULLIUS TERENTIAE SUAE S. D.

si vales, bene est; valeo. da operam ut convalescas. quod opus erit, ut res tempusque postulat, provideas atque administres, et ad me de omnibus rebus quam saepissime litteras mittas. vale!

**convalesco** (3), to get well, recover one's health
**postulo** (1), to demand
**administro** (1), to administer, arrange, carry out
**quam** (+ superlative), as ... as possible

## (f) Written at Brundisium on 12 August 47 BC

(ad Familiares XIV.23)

TULLIUS TERENTIAE SUAE S. D.

si vales, bene est; valeo. redditae mihi tandem sunt a Caesare litterae satis liberales, et ipse opinione celerius venturus esse dicitur. cui utrum obviam procedam an hic eum exspectem, cum constituero, faciam te certiorem. tabellarios mihi velim quam primum remittas. valetudinem tuam cura diligenter. vale! d. prid. Id. Sext.

**reddo** (3), **-didi, -ditum**, to deliver, hand over
**satis**, quite, fairly
**liberalis, -is, -e**, gracious, courteous
**utrum ... an ...**, whether ... or ...
**obviam procedere** (+ dat.), to go to meet
**constituo** (3), **-ui**, to decide
**tabellarius, -i** (*m*), letter-carrier, courier

(g)

2 **in Tusculanum**: *to my villa at Tusculum* (see map on page 229). Tusculum was a town in Latium, only about 12 miles from Rome. After defeating the Pompeians in the East, Caesar returned to Italy in late September 47 BC. He landed at Tarentum, and Cicero travelled from Brundisium to meet him. Caesar assured Cicero that he had nothing to fear and could live anywhere he liked in Italy. Cicero lost little time in starting his journey along the Via Appia to Rome. Venusia is about a third of the way from Brundisium to Rome, some four days' journey. For the plural **nos**, compare line 2 of letter (a).

2 **ibi ut sint omnia parata**: Supply **cura** or **fac** — *(see to it) that everything is ready there*. (For the construction, compare line 5 of letter (c) and line 6 of letter (d).)

4 **labrum**: As can be seen from the illustration, this was a basin (raised about a metre above the floor) round which bathers stood while they splashed cold water over their bodies and used a **strigil** to remove the perspiration after being in the 'sweat-bath'. They would then immerse themselves in the **piscina**, a bath sunk in the floor. The **balineum** here refers to that room of a private villa which was set aside for bathing.

4 **ut sit**: Again supply **cura** or **fac** — *get one (installed)*, literally *(see) that there is (one)*. The curtness illustrates the worsening relationship. Cicero divorced Terentia soon after this, in January 46 BC.

6 **de Venusino**: Supply **agro** — *(dispatched from) the district around Venusia.*

## Points for Discussion

1. The opening sentence in the first letter is very formal and not what one would expect of a husband writing to a wife. What do you think Cicero is implying when he says **perpetuo gaudeas velim** in line 2 of letter (a)?
2. In lines 6-7 of letter (a), he gives several reasons why Terentia should not come to meet him. Do you think he is showing concern for her, or is there some other reason?
3. How do you think you would have felt if you had been Terentia receiving the fourth letter? Give reasons for your answer.
4. From the seven letters, pick out phrases and words which illustrate Cicero's coolness towards Terentia.
5. Why do you think Cicero uses the 2nd person plural (**vultis**) in line 4 of letter (b), whereas he uses 2nd person singular in the rest of the letter?

## (g) Cicero's last letter to Terentia, written at Venusia on 1 October 47 BC

(ad Fam. XIV.20)

TULLIUS S. D. TERENTIAE SUAE

in Tusculanum nos venturos putamus aut Nonis aut postridie. ibi ut sint omnia parata. plures enim fortasse nobiscum erunt et, ut arbitror, diutius ibi commorabimur. labrum si in balineo non est, ut sit; item cetera quae sunt ad victum et ad valetudinem necessaria. vale! Kal. Oct. de Venusino.

**postridie**, on the following day
**plures**, several
**fortasse**, perhaps
**arbitror** (1), to think
**diutius**, for quite some time
**commoror** (1), to linger, remain
**ceteri, -ae, -a**, the rest
**victus, -us** (*m*), sustenance, subsistence

**Labrum**
(drawing taken from a vase painting,
"Roman and Greek Antiquities" by Anthony Rich)

# Cicero the Philosopher

After his return from exile in September 57 BC, Cicero had hoped to renew his campaign to defend the Republic and restore the authority of the Senate. However, the renewal of the First Triumvirate at Luca in April 56 BC ended such hopes and, in the next few years, only rarely did he play an active part in Roman politics.

Nowadays, many of our politicians turn to writing their memoirs when they retire from public office. In his disillusionment after Luca, Cicero turned to writing about a subject in which he was an expert. In the three books of the De Oratore (55 BC), he drew on his vast experience as a statesman and advocate to produce a detailed description of how an orator was trained.

After the break-up of the Triumvirate (see pages 156-7), Cicero was tempted back into politics and eventually threw in his lot with Pompey in the Civil War; but Pompey was defeated. When Cicero returned to Italy, Caesar gave him an unconditional pardon for having supported Pompey and treated him with great respect; but, since Caesar ruled Rome as a dictator and all decisions of the courts and of the Senate were effectively in his hands, Cicero's career as an advocate and statesman was essentially over. Early in 46 BC, therefore, at the age of 60, he retired from public life and began to devote himself to writing on philosophical subjects, which up to that time had been largely ignored by Roman writers.

One of the earliest fruits of this enforced retirement was the *Brutus* (46-45 BC), an extract from which appears in Chapter 3 (see pages 12-17), and this was followed soon after by the *Orator*. These two and the earlier *De Oratore* all dealt with a subject which featured prominently in Roman education, namely, the theory and practice of oratory. Whereas nowadays we train people for a vast range of careers, there were for an ambitious Roman only three career possibilities — law, politics and the army — all closely interlinked and all requiring skill in public speaking. Hence the importance of training in rhetoric, i.e. the art of oratory.

Cicero's writings, however, were not confined to oratory. Indeed, there was a vast range of subjects on which he wrote. Utterly devastated by the death of his beloved daughter Tullia in February 45 BC, he threw himself into his writings with a new intensity in order to take his mind off his grief. Over the years 45-44 BC, he produced an amazing number of treatises, on such topics as old age (*De Senectute*), friendship (*De Amicitia*), theories about the existence and nature of the gods (*De Natura Deorum*), divination (*De Divinatione*), various doctrines regarding good and evil (*De Finibus Bonorum et Malorum*), moral issues (*De Officiis*), and death, pain, grief and happiness (*Tusculan Disputations*). Other works of this period which were famous in antiquity, notably that on self-consolation (*De Consolatione*) which he wrote after the death of his daughter, have not survived.

In these writings, Cicero drew heavily on earlier Greek philosophers, particularly the Academics, Stoics and Epicureans.

The Academy was founded by the philosopher Plato in the 4th century BC in order to train young men who would serve the state according to the doctrine he expounded in *The Republic*. Initially, most of the teaching consisted of science and philosophy, but later mathematics and astronomy were also introduced.

The Stoics believed that virtue is based on knowledge founded on logic and reason. They accepted that they should live in harmony with nature, which they understood as a divine 'reason' or controlling power that pre-destined everything. Pleasure and pain, even death itself, were unimportant and should not affect one's happiness. The Stoics lived an austere life and 'stoically' accepted whatever fate brought.

The Epicureans also pursued happiness, but in a different way. Pleasure for them was the avoidance of pain, and this could best be achieved by contemplation, particularly through the study of philosophy. Thinking about a physical pleasure was better than the pleasure itself since the latter could bring pain if not adequately satisfied. In other words, absence of pain rather than actual pleasure was regarded as the goal of the wise man. They believed that there was no controlling divine power, and no such thing as fate. Epicurus believed that gods did exist, but that they took no interest in human affairs and lived a life of enviable happiness. The soul was made up of atoms and died with the body. Epicureanism was frequently misrepresented, even in antiquity, as simply the pursuit of pleasure — 'Let us eat and drink, for tomorrow we shall die.'

People in the Graeco-Roman world of the first century BC were increasingly attracted to philosophies that offered them tranquillity of mind and a guide to life in times of uncertainty or political unrest. Indeed, Epicurus had advised his followers to reject ambition and public life, as peace of mind was impossible in such circumstances.

Cicero did not simply translate the Greek works. Rather, he interpreted them and added his own views. Each of the works is written in the form of a dialogue in which distinguished Romans (sometimes of Cicero's own day, but more often of the past) are used as mouthpieces to express various views on the matter under discussion. Interspersed within these philosophical dialogues are to be found stories, told in a straightforward narrative form, which Cicero uses to illustrate a particular point that he is making.

Book III of the *De Officiis* deals specifically with the question of whether honesty and expediency (i.e. the sacrifice of principle for personal gain or advantage) can ever be reconciled; and Chapter 18 poses the question, 'When something is being sold, is it less dishonest to keep quiet about its defects than to make false claims about it?'

**nihil tam absurde dici potest quod non dicatur ab aliquo philosophorum.**
*No statement is so absurd as not to be said by some philosopher.*
De Divinatione II.58
This is Cicero's sharp comment on the assertion made by Plato and Pythagoras that we can have really prophetic dreams if we don't eat beans!

**errare malo cum Platone quam cum istis vera sentire.**
*I would prefer to go wrong with Plato than to think straight with those (who disagree with him).* Tusculan Disputations I. 17. 39
Philosophy father-figures have often been treated with exaggerated respect — with harmful results!

1 **nec infacetus**: *a man of considerable wit*, literally *not without wit*. The double negative produces a stronger statement than the adjective **facetus** on its own would. 'Wit' refers not so much to a sense of humour as to sharpness of mind and brightness of personality. In other words, he was far from dull and stupid. (For Litotes, see CAO on page 235.)

2 **otiandi**: Supply **causa** from the end of the line — *(in order) to be at leisure*, literally *(for the sake) of being at leisure*. (For the use of **causa** with a Gerund to express Purpose, see LL p. 45.) The opposite of **otiari** is **negotiari**, *to be engaged in business*.

3 **hortulos aliquos**: *a small country estate*, literally *some small gardens*. The diminutive form ending in **-ulus** is intended to suggest a false sense of modesty. Although he says he does not want anything too ostentatious, he wants everyone to be aware that he could afford something really grand.

4 **quod**: *this (information)*. (For Linking Relative, see LL p. 26.)

5 **qui argentariam faceret**: *being a banker*, i.e. someone who would be expected to handle financial transactions such as the sale of property. Canius would be likely to trust such a professional. (For Causal **qui**, see LL p. 103.)

6 **venales quidem se hortos non habere**: Supply **dixit** with this Accusative and Infinitive clause. There is an ellipsis here. Cicero has condensed two statements into one: **se hortos habere** and **se venales hortos non habere**.

6 **licere uti Canio, ut suis**: *(that) Canius was at liberty to use (them) as (if they were) his own*. **suis** is ablative, agreeing with **hortis** (understood) and depending on **uti**. (For **ut**, see LL p. 93.)

7 **in posterum diem**: *on the following day*. The accusative case is used to indicate that, when he issued the invitation, he was looking forward *into the next day*.

8 **cum ille promisisset**: *when he* (i.e. Canius) *accepted the invitation*, literally *when he promised (that he would come)*.

8 **qui esset**: *since he was*. (For Causal **qui**, see LL p. 103, and compare line 5.)

8 **ut argentarius**: *as (might be expected of) a banker*. (For this use of **ut**, see LL p. 93.)

11 **adparatum**: Supply **erat** — *had been prepared*.

12 **pro se quisque quod ceperat adferebat**: *each (fisherman) in turn brought all (the fish) that he had caught*, literally *each man for himself brought what he had caught*. The imperfect tense indicates a constant procession of fishermen.

# 18. A Case of Fraud

(De Officiis III, 58-60)

*The businessman Canius lets it be known that he is looking for a house with grounds where he can escape from the pressures of business. The banker Pythius lays a trap which appeals to Canius' instinctive greed.*

C.Canius, eques Romanus nec infacetus et satis litteratus, cum se Syracusas otiandi, ut ipse dicere solebat, non negotiandi causa contulisset, dictitabat se hortulos aliquos emere velle, quo invitare amicos et ubi se oblectare sine interpellatoribus posset. quod cum percrebruisset, Pythius ei quidam, qui argentariam faceret Syracusis, venales quidem se hortos non habere sed licere uti Canio, si vellet, ut suis; et simul ad cenam hominem in hortos invitavit in posterum diem.

cum ille promisisset, tum Pythius, qui esset ut argentarius apud omnes ordines gratiosus, piscatores ad se convocavit et ab eis petivit ut ante suos hortulos postridie piscarentur, dixitque quid eos facere vellet. ad cenam tempori venit Canius: opipare a Pythio adparatum convivium; cumbarum ante oculos multitudo; pro se quisque quod ceperat adferebat; ante pedes Pythii pisces abiciebantur.

**eques, -itis** (*m*), knight, businessman
**satis**, quite, fairly
**litteratus, -a, -um**, well-read, cultured
**se conferre**, to go to, make for
**Syracusae, -arum** (*f.pl*), Syracuse
**ut**, as
**soleo** (2), to be accustomed
**dictito** (1), to say repeatedly, assert
**emo** (3), **emi**, to buy
**quo**, to which, (to) where
**oblecto** (1), to entertain, amuse, enjoy
**interpellator, -oris** (*m*), intruder
**percrebresco** (3), **-brui**, to spread abroad, become widely known
**quidam, quaedam, quoddam**, a certain
**argentaria, -ae** (*f*), banking
**venalis, -is, -e**, for sale
**quidem**, in fact, actually
**licet** (2) (+ dat.), to be allowed
**utor** (3) (+ abl.), to use
**simul**, at the same time
**cena, -ae** (*f*), dinner
**apud** (+ acc.), among
**ordo, -inis** (*m*), rank, social class
**gratiosus, -a, -um**, accepted, in favour, popular
**piscator, -oris** (*m*), fisherman
**convoco** (1), to summon
**peto** (3), **petivi** (**a** + abl.), to ask
**ante** (+ acc.), in front of
**postridie**, on the following day
**piscor** (1), to fish
**tempori**, on time, punctually
**opipare**, splendidly, sumptuously
**convivium, -i** (*n*), banquet, meal
**cumba, -ae** (*f*), fishing-boat
**multitudo, -inis** (*f*), great number
**pes, pedis** (*m*), foot
**abicio** (3), to throw down

14 **quaeso**: *please tell me*, literally *I ask.*

14 **tantumne piscium**: *All these fish?*, literally *so much (of) fish?* (For Partitive Genitive, see LL p. 9.)

15 **hoc loco**: *in this place*. In phrases containing the ablative of **locus**, the preposition is regularly omitted (see LL p. 15).

16 **quidquid est piscium**: *all the fish*, literally *whatever there is of fish.* (For Partitive Genitive, see LL p. 9.)

16 **hic aquatio**: *(it's) good water here.*

16 **isti**: *those fellows* (i.e. the fishermen).

18 **gravate**: Supply a verb such as **agit**, *acted.*

18 **emit tanti quanti**: *he paid as much as*, literally *he bought (it) at as high a price as.* (For Genitive of Price, see LL p. 8; for Correlatives, see LL pp. 63-4.)

19 **instructos**: Supply **hortos**. Translate *the estate and all that went with it*, literally *equipped.*

19 **nomina facit**: *he entered the names (of buyer and seller) in the ledger* — a technical phrase used in accounting. This action freed Pythius from answering any later charge of misrepresentation regarding the sale of the property; once the contract had been completed, there was no 'come-back'.

22 **scalmum nullum**: *not (even) a single rowlock (let alone a fishing-boat)*, literally *no rowlock.* The **scalmus** was a *peg* to which the oar was strapped.

23 **quod sciam**: *as far as I know.*

26 **stomachari**: *was furious.* The Historic Infinitive (see LL pp. 32-3) is used to add vividness and to indicate how quickly he became furious.

26 **quid faceret?**: *what was he to do?* (For Deliberative Subjunctive, see LL p. 108.)

27 **collega**: C.Aquilius and Cicero had been praetors in the same year (66 BC).

27 **de dolo malo formulas**: *his rules of procedure (in a court case) about criminal fraud.* When a case came to court, the praetor appointed a **iudex** to make the final judgement. Before handing the case over to the **iudex**, however, the praetor listened to the arguments put forward by the plaintiff and by the defendant and then gave the **iudex** some guidance by preparing a formula for him, i.e. an analysis (**definitio**) of the issues on which the **iudex** had to adjudicate. These formulae were often named after the praetor who formulated them (e.g. that on criminal fraud was called the **formula Aquiliana**), and they were used in future judgements, just as precedent is cited in case-law in modern times.

27 **in quibus ipsis**: *with regard to these very rules.* (For Linking Relative, see LL p. 26.)

28 **cum ex eo quaereretur**: *when he* (Aquilius) *was asked.* (For intransitive verbs used impersonally in the passive, see LL p. 57.)

29 **cum esset aliud simulatum, aliud actum**: *pretending one thing and doing another*, literally *when one thing had been pretended and another thing had been done.*

29 **hoc quidem sane luculente**: Supply **respondebat** — *this was in fact a quite brilliant answer*, literally *(he answered) this indeed very brilliantly.*

30 **ut ab homine perito definiendi**: *as (one might expect) from a man skilled in defining (things).* (For this use of **ut**, see LL p. 93; for **peritus** + genitive, see LL p. 8; and for Gerund, see LL p. 60.)

31 **perfidi, improbi, malitiosi**: Supply **sunt**.

*Canius falls into the trap and persuades Pythius to sell. His keenness to show off his business acumen to his friends compounds his embarrassment when he discovers too late that he has been hoodwinked.*

tum Canius: 'quaeso' inquit 'quid est hoc, Pythi? tantumne piscium? tantumne cumbarum?' et ille 'quid mirum?' inquit. 'hoc loco est Syracusis quidquid est piscium, hic aquatio, hac villa isti carere non possunt.' incensus Canius cupiditate contendit a Pythio ut venderet. gravate ille primo. quid multa? impetrat. emit homo cupidus et locuples tanti quanti Pythius voluit, et emit instructos. nomina facit, negotium conficit.

invitat Canius postridie familiares suos, venit ipse mature, scalmum nullum videt. quaerit ex proximo vicino num feriae quaedam piscatorum essent, quod eos nullos videret. 'nullae, quod sciam' inquit. 'sed hic piscari nulli solent: itaque heri mirabar quid accidisset.'

stomachari Canius: sed quid faceret? nondum enim C. Aquilius collega et familiaris meus protulerat de dolo malo formulas: in quibus ipsis, cum ex eo quaereretur quid esset dolus malus, respondebat, cum esset aliud simulatum, aliud actum. hoc quidem sane luculente, ut ab homine perito definiendi. ergo et Pythius et omnes aliud agentes, aliud simulantes perfidi, improbi, malitiosi. nullum igitur eorum factum potest utile esse, cum sit tot vitiis inquinatum.

**mirus, -a, -um**, strange, surprising
**careo** (2) (+ abl.), to do without
**incensus, -a, -um**, inflamed
**cupiditas, -atis** (*f*), passionate desire, covetous desire, greed
**contendo** (3), **-tendi** (**a** + abl.), to press, urge
**vendo** (3), to sell
**gravate**, reluctantly, unwillingly
**primo**, at first
**quid multa?** to cut a long story short
**impetro** (1), to get what one asks for
**cupidus, -a, -um**, eager, greedy
**locuples, -etis**, rich
**negotium, -i** (*n*), business
**conficio** (3), to finish, conclude
**familiaris, -is** (*m*), friend
**mature**, early
**quaero** (3) (**ex** + abl.), to ask
**proximus, -a, -um**, nearest, next-door
**vicinus, -i** (*m*), neighbour
**num**, whether, if
**feriae, -arum** (*f.pl*), holiday
**miror** (1), to wonder, be surprised, be puzzled
**accidit** (3), **accidit**, to happen
**nondum**, not yet
**profero, -ferre, -tuli**, to bring forward, introduce
**ergo**, therefore
**perfidus, -a, -um**, treacherous, deceitful
**improbus, -a, -um**, dishonest
**malitiosus,-a, -um**, malicious, wicked
**factum, -i** (*n*), act, action
**utilis, -is, -e**, useful, advantageous
**vitium, -i** (*n*), vice, crime
**inquino** (1), to stain, contaminate

34 **simulatio dissimulatioque**: *pretence and concealment*. **simulatio** means *pretending that something is what it is not*; **dissimulatio** means *concealing what something actually is*.
35 **ita**: *if that is the case*, literally *thus*.
35 **ut emat melius**: *to strike a better bargain*, literally *so that he may buy better*. (For Purpose clauses, see LL p. 44.) Supply **melius** with **ut vendat**.

## Points for Discussion

1. Translate the clause **qui esset ut argentarius apud omnes ordines gratiosus** (lines 8-9), and explain in your own words what you think it means.
2. Write short character sketches of Pythius and Canius.
3. In your opinion, did Pythius cheat Canius, or did Canius cheat himself? Give reasons for your answer.
4. In the hypothetical court case of Canius v. Pythius, whom would you prefer to defend and why? What arguments would you put forward to help your client?
5. Read lines 26-33. Do you think that the formula introduced by Aquilius would have altered the course of events if it had been in place at the time of this incident? Give reasons for your answer.

quodsi Aquiliana definitio vera est, ex omni vita simulatio dissimulatioque tollenda est. ita, nec ut emat melius nec ut vendat, quicquam simulabit aut dissimulabit vir bonus.

**quodsi**, but if
**verus, -a, -um**, true, correct
**vita, -ae** (*f*), life
**tollo** (3), to remove, banish
**quicquam**, anything

**cui bono?** *Who benefits?* (literally *for whom is it a source of advantage?*)
Pro Milone 12
A pithy legal maxim — in any criminal investigation, always consider who stands to gain by the crime.

# Predicting the Future

The ancient Greeks and Romans believed that the future could be predicted by interpreting signs or omens sent by the gods. The ability to do this is called 'divination', and the practical means by which it is done is called 'augury.' It was believed that the gods communicated with human beings in various ways, directly through visions and dreams and prophetic utterances, and indirectly through natural phenomena, such as the flight of birds (where significance was attached to the number and type of birds seen and to the direction of their flight), the feeding habits and calls of animals, and the appearance and condition of the entrails of animals which had been sacrificed. There was also a wide belief in astrology.

Taking the auspices, i.e. studying the omens, played a very important part in both public and private life. No important enterprise was ever undertaken nor any meeting held without studying the omens; and, if they were unfavourable, the enterprise or meeting was abandoned, at least for the time being. The task of interpreting the omens was in the hands of 'soothsayers', experts to whom various titles were given:

**augur**, *soothsayer*. Originally used of a priest who interpreted the activities of birds, this word came to be the general word covering all those engaged in prophecy.

**hariolus** and **haruspex**, *entrail-examiner*. Alternative words for those who foretold the future by studying the entrails of animals which had been sacrificed.

**auspex**, *bird-watcher*. One who watched the flight and movement of birds to predict the future.

**coniector**, *interpreter of dreams and omens*.

**vates** and **divinus**, *seer* or *prophet*. Alternative words for one 'inspired' by the gods.

There was a college or society of augurs, and it was regarded as a very great honour to be elected to it. It was politically and socially important to recognise publicly the significance of augury, but accepting election to the college did not necessarily imply that one believed in the practice. Cicero himself was a member of this college, but this did not prevent him from being sceptical about augury. In one passage where he is questioning the reliability of divination, he applauds a comment attributed to Cato the Elder (2nd century BC), who was a devout upholder of Roman tradition and belief, that it was a wonder that one **haruspex** was able to keep his face straight when he saw another **haruspex**!

In the *De Divinatione*, Cicero imagines that he is having a discussion with his brother Quintus, who opens the debate by stating that he is not satisfied with the arguments put forward in Cicero's *De Natura Deorum*. Cicero invites him to state his views on the subject. This he does at great length, using the techniques for delivering persuasive speeches which sons of the upper classes were taught in the schools of rhetoric in preparation for a career in the law-courts, the army and politics. Cicero listens to Quintus, makes notes on what he says, and then argues in turn (also at great length) against each of the points he has made.

The gist of Quintus' argument is that, if the gods do exist (and he believes that they do), it is inconceivable that they do not send messages to human beings indicating how they should act. The gods cannot communicate these messages in person, and so they send signs through dreams, the flight of birds, the entrails of sacrificed animals, and so on. The correct interpretation of these signs requires the training and skill of soothsayers, just as every other human skill needs experts such as doctors, lawyers, politicians, generals and ship-captains. To support his contention, Quintus quotes countless examples from history which show that people have been saved from disasters by acting upon the omens or destroyed by ignoring them. He claims that this theory is not disproved by the rare examples of events not turning out as the soothsayers predicted; such examples only show that divination is a human art, and people can make mistakes, just as a brilliant general can miscalculate and lose a battle, or an experienced sea-captain can lose his ship. Nor must the existence of crooks and impostors discredit the genuine soothsayer, any more than the dealings of quack doctors or crooked lawyers should discredit the true professionals in medicine and law.

The following three passages, which are excerpts from the Second Book of the *De Divinatione*, illustrate the ways in which ancient philosophers used to try to 'prove' or 'disprove' statements, definitions or theories — often called Socratic argument after the Greek philosopher Socrates, who was probably the most famous exponent of this technique. Every statement was examined in great detail to see whether it could stand up to the test of sheer logic. If it led to a ludicrous conclusion, it was rejected as false. Such was the faith which the Greeks and Romans had in the supremacy of the intellect.

2 **quae vita fuisset Priamo**: *what would Priam's life have been (like)?*, literally *what life would there have been for Priam?* (For Unreal Past Conditions, see LL p. 54.) Priam, king of Troy, lived to see most of his many sons killed and his prosperous city captured and destroyed by the Greeks. The full story is told in Homer's Iliad and in Virgil's Aeneid Book II.

3 **quos eventus senectutis esset habiturus**: *what was going to happen to him in his old age*, literally *what outcomes of old age he was going to have.*

3 **abeamus a fabulis**: *let us leave mythology aside*, literally *let us depart from myths*. (For the present subjunctive used in Commands and Exhortations, see LL p. 107.)

3 **propiora**: *events (that are) nearer (in time and place)*, literally *nearer things*.

5 **Consolatione**: After the death of his daughter Tullia in 46 BC, Cicero tried to find comfort and consolation by gathering in a book entitled *De Consolatione* the stories of how certain great men had met their ends. This work is no longer extant.

5 **quid igitur?**: *for example.*

5 **ut omittamus superiores**: *to say nothing of men of earlier times*, literally *to omit previous men*. The violent deaths of all three Triumvirs provided Cicero with recent examples of the dangers of ignoring the omens.

6 **Marco Crasso**: Marcus Crassus was an extremely wealthy financier and businessman. He was a member of the First Triumvirate with Caesar and Pompey and, following his consulship in 55 BC, he became governor of Syria. From there, he launched an ill-fated expedition against the Parthians. In 53 BC, this culminated in the death of his son and a humiliating defeat at Carrhae, in which his army was almost wiped out and suffered the dreadful disgrace of having its standards captured by the enemy. Crassus himself was later murdered by the Parthians.

6 **fuisse**: *it would have been.*

6 **tum cum**: *at the time when.*

7 **sibi**: Take this dative with **esse pereundum** in line 8 — *he was destined to perish*, literally *he would have to perish*. (For Dative of Agent with a gerundive, see LL p. 62.)

8 **trans Euphratem**: Crassus had to cross the River Euphrates to invade the land of the Parthians, a warlike people whom the Romans had never succeeded in subduing. They were expert horsemen and archers who had devised the devastating tactic of firing a hail of arrows backwards at their pursuers while retreating at full speed.

9 **Cn.Pompeium**: From the early age of 25, Gnaeus Pompeius enjoyed a series of brilliant military successes which earned him the cognomen **Magnus**, two official triumphs and great popularity in Rome. He was a member of the First Triumvirate along with Caesar and Crassus and was consul three times. He and Caesar eventually quarrelled and, in the civil war which followed, Pompey was decisively defeated by Caesar and fled to Egypt where he was murdered on the orders of the young King Ptolemy as he stepped ashore. His head was cut off and sent to Caesar, much to the latter's disgust; and his naked body was left lying for some time on the beach until his freedman and one of his former soldiers cremated it and buried the ashes under a small mound in drifting sand. For a fuller account of his life and career, see page 71.

# *19. Is Prediction Useful?*

(De Divinatione II.22-24)

*Priam, Crassus, Pompey and Caesar all came to violent ends. Would they have led different lives if they had known their fates in advance?*

atque ego ne utilem quidem arbitror esse nobis futurarum rerum scientiam. quae enim vita fuisset Priamo, si ab adulescentia scisset quos eventus senectutis esset habiturus? abeamus a fabulis, propiora videamus. clarissimorum hominum nostrae civitatis gravissimos exitus in *Consolatione* collegimus. quid igitur? ut omittamus superiores, Marcone Crasso putas utile fuisse, tum cum maximis opibus fortunisque florebat, scire sibi interfecto Publio filio exercituque deleto trans Euphratem cum ignominia et dedecore esse pereundum? an Cn.Pompeium censes tribus suis consulatibus, tribus triumphis,

**ne ... quidem**, not even
**utilis, -is, -e**, useful, helpful, advantageous
**arbitror** (1), to think
**scientia, -ae** (*f*), knowledge
**adulescentia, -ae** (*f*), youth
**scio** (4), to know
**scisset = scivisset**
**clarus, -a, -um**, famous
**civitas, -atis** (*f*), state, city
**gravis, -is, -e**, serious, grievous
**exitus, -us** (*m*), death
**colligo** (3), **-legi**, to collect, gather together
**opes, opum** (*f.pl*), wealth, power
**floreo** (2), to flourish, prosper
**interficio** (3), **-feci, -fectum**, to kill
**deleo** (2), **-evi, -etum**, to destroy
**ignominia, -ae** (*f*), disgrace
**dedecus, -oris** (*n*), dishonour, shame
**an**, or
**censeo** (2), to think
**consulatus, -us** (*m*), consulship

10 **laetaturum fuisse**: *would have rejoiced (in).*

10 **se trucidatum iri**: *that he would be butchered.* The supine plus **iri** (present infinitive passive of **eo**) supplies the future infinitive passive of Latin verbs.

10 **in solitudine Aegyptiorum**: *in the lonely wastes of Egypt* (literally *of the Egyptians*).

11 **ea consecutura**: Supply **esse** to form another Accusative and Infinitive clause depending on **sciret** — *that those events* (literally *things*) *would follow* — a reference to the treatment his dead body received.

13 **quid vero Caesarem putamus**: Grammatically, the accusative (**Caesarem**) is picked up later by the infinitive (**acturum fuisse**) in line 18; but so much information is given in the intervening lines that Cicero changes from a question beginning with **quid** to one beginning **quo cruciatu**. (See also note on line 18.) Possibly the neatest way to handle this in English is to translate this part as *And what about Caesar?* — leaving the translation of **putamus** until the question in line 18.

13 **Caesarem**: Caesar was assassinated on the Ides of March 44 BC after ruling for five years as supreme dictator. Among the assassins were some of his former supporters and men whom he had appointed (**cooptasset**) to the Senate. On this occasion, as the senate-house had been burned down in the riots of 52 BC (see pages 140 and 156), the Senate was meeting in the hall next to the magnificent stone theatre which Pompey had built in 55 BC to glorify his achievements. It is interesting to note that this is the first extant account of Caesar's death.

13 **fore ut**: *that it would come about that.*

14 **maiore ex parte**: *for the most part.*

16 **partim etiam a se omnibus rebus ornatis**: *some of whom had even had all (sorts of) honours bestowed on them by him*, literally *some* (**partim**) *even decorated with all things by him.* **a se** refers to Caesar. After defeating Pompey, Caesar had treated his former enemies very graciously and had even promoted some of them to high office.

16 **trucidatus ita iaceret ut**: *after being hacked to death he would lie in such a state that*, literally *having been butchered he would lie in such a way that.* The subjunctive **iaceret** depends on **fore ut** in line 13.

16 **ita ... ut non modo amicorum sed ne servorum quidem quisquam accederet**: *in such a state that not only would none* (literally *not any*) *of his friends come near but not even any of his slaves.* We might have expected **non modo non, sed ne ... quidem**; but, where the two negative clauses have the same verb (here **accederet**), Latin regularly omits the second **non** of **non modo non**.

18 **quo cruciatu animi**: *with what agony of mind.* It is at this point that **Caesarem putamus** is to be brought in (see note on line 13) to link up with **acturum fuisse**. For the translation of this infinitive, compare **laetaturum fuisse** in line 10.

20 **illud quidem dici nullo modo potest**: *certainly, in no way can the following statement be made* (literally *can that be said*). As so often in Latin, **illud** refers to a more detailed explanation which follows.

20 **praesertim a Stoicis**: *especially by the Stoics.* The Stoics believed that there was a divine power which rationally controlled everything that happened. Everyone's fate was predetermined, and so people should 'stoically' (i.e. without emotion or complaint) accept whatever lay in store for them.

20 **isset, transisset, suscepisset**: For Unfulfilled Conditions, see LL p. 54. With each of these verbs a clause such as 'if he had had knowledge (**scientia**) of what his fate would be' must be understood.

maximarum rerum gloria laetaturum fuisse, si sciret se in solitudine Aegyptiorum trucidatum iri amisso exercitu, post mortem vero ea consecutura quae sine lacrimis non possumus dicere?

quid vero Caesarem putamus, si divinasset fore ut in eo senatu, quem maiore ex parte ipse cooptasset, in curia Pompeia ante ipsius Pompei simulacrum, tot centurionibus suis inspectantibus, a nobilissimis civibus, partim etiam a se omnibus rebus ornatis, trucidatus ita iaceret ut ad eius corpus non modo amicorum sed ne servorum quidem quisquam accederet, quo cruciatu animi vitam acturum fuisse?

*The Stoics cannot have it both ways. If everything is controlled by fate, as they claim, knowing their eventual fate would not help people to change it; and foreknowledge of their fates would have deprived people such as Pompey, Crassus and Caesar of the pleasure which their earlier achievements had given them.*

certe igitur ignoratio futurorum malorum utilior est quam scientia. nam illud quidem dici, praesertim a Stoicis, nullo modo potest: non isset ad

**gloria, -ae** (*f*), fame
**amitto** (3), **-misi, -missum**, to lose
**exercitus, -us** (*m*), army
**vero**, and in fact
**lacrima, -ae** (*f*), tear
**divinasset = divinavisset**, he had foreseen
**cooptasset = cooptavisset**
**curia, -ae** (*f*), senate-house
**simulacrum, -i** (*n*), statue
**inspecto** (1), to look on, watch
**quisquam**, anyone
**vitam agere**, to spend one's life
**ignoratio, -onis** (*f*), ignorance
**malum, -i** (*n*), evil, misfortune
**modus, -i** (*m*), way
**isset = ivisset**

22 **fatales exitus**: *deaths which were determined by fate.*
23 **vultis autem**: *but you (Stoics) want.* Cicero is alternately presenting and dismissing the arguments of the Stoics.
23 **nihil illis profuisset divinare**: *(being able) to foretell the future would not have helped them in any way*, literally *divining would have benefited them nothing*. (For Unfulfilled Conditions, see LL p. 54.) If everything that happens to people has already been determined, knowing what is going to happen will not enable them to change it. Conversely, if it is possible for them to avoid a particular happening by knowing about it beforehand, everything cannot be predetermined.
25 **quid posset eis esse laetum**: *what pleasure could there have been for them*, literally *what could have been pleasing to them*. (For Unfulfilled Conditions, see LL p. 54. The participle **cogitantibus**, which agrees with **eis**, has the force of a **si** clause.)

## Points for Discussion

1. Many English words are derived from the practice of augury. Consult a dictionary to find out the derivation and meaning of the following: *abominable, ominous, inaugurate, inaugural, auspices, (in)auspicious, prodigy.*
2. Refer to the note on line 8 and (using a dictionary, if necessary) explain the meaning and origin of the English expression 'a Parthian shot'.
3. Using the information supplied in this passage and your wider knowledge of the relationship between Cicero and Pompey, do you think that Cicero is sincere when he says **sine lacrimis non possumus dicere** (line 12) in relation to Pompey's death?
4. 'The circumstances of Caesar's death are both tragic and ironic.' From lines 13-18 of the passage, quote any points which support this statement.
5. The deaths of Pompey and Caesar are described in lines 9-12 and 13-18. Which account do you find more moving, and why?
6. Read lines 23-5. Do you think that your own future has already been pre-determined, or that a person's future is largely determined by decisions he/she makes at different times, i.e. that life is a series of options like a computer program? Give reasons for your answer.
7. Would you like to know what your future holds? What do you think would be the advantages and disadvantages of this? Do you think that knowledge of your fate would influence the way you live?
8. Do you think that either Pompey or Caesar would have made any changes in their lives if they had known what was ultimately going to happen to them? Give reasons for your answer.

arma Pompeius, non transisset Crassus Euphratem, non suscepisset bellum civile Caesar. non igitur fatales exitus habuerunt.

vultis autem evenire omnia fato; nihil ergo illis profuisset divinare; atque etiam omnem fructum vitae superioris perdidissent. quid enim posset eis esse laetum exitus suos cogitantibus?

**suscipio** (3), **-cepi**, to undertake
**evenio** (4), to happen, turn out
**fatum, -i** (*n*), fate, destiny
**ergo**, therefore, so
**fructus, -us** (*m*), enjoyment
**superior, -oris**, earlier
**perdo** (3), **-didi**, to lose, forfeit
**cogito** (1), to think about

1 **dicendum est mihi ad**: *I must reply to*. (For Dative of Agent with a Gerundive, see LL p. 62.)

1 **a te** refers to his brother Quintus, with whom he is conducting this imaginary dialogue (see pages 182-3).

1 **ita nihil ut affirmem**: *without being dogmatic about anything*, literally *in such a way that I affirm nothing*. In other words, like a true philosopher, he hopes to examine the issue with an open mind. Emphasis is added to **nihil** by placing it outside the **ut** clause. (For Chiasmus, see CAO on page 237.)

3 **si aliquid certi haberem quod dicerem**: *if I claimed any certainty for what I was saying*, literally *if I had something certain to say*. (For Partitive Genitive, see LL p. 9; for Unreal Conditions, see LL p. 54; for **qui** in Generic clauses, see LL p. 103.)

3 **divinarem**: *I would be indulging in divination.*

3 **qui nego**: *(I) who deny*. The antecedent of **qui** is **ego**.

5 **illud quod**: *the (question) which.*

5 **Carneades** was a Greek philosopher of the second century BC. He opposed those philosophical theories which claimed to have found definitive answers about reality. He argued that, since the evidence of both the senses and the intellect is unreliable, we can make decisions only on what appears most reasonable. In particular, he challenged the existence of the gods and the ability of man to use omens to foretell the future.

6 **quarumnam rerum divinatio esset**: *what, in fact, were the things to which divination applied*, literally *of what things was divination*. The addition of **-nam** (*in fact*) to **quarum** indicates incredulity. Carneades wants to be given specific examples.

6 **earumne**: Supply **rerum** — *(was it) those things ... ?* This is an extension of the question posed in the previous sentence (**quarumnam ... esset**).

6 **quae perciperentur**: For Generic Subjunctive, see LL p. 103.

8 **num quid est?**: *is there anything?* He implies that there is not.

8 **permotione mentis**: *by using our intelligence*, literally *by the movement of the mind.*

9 **natura ipsa**: *with (the aid of) nature itself*, i.e. naturally, through the senses.

9 **num nescio qui ille divinus possit**: *Would some soothsayer or other be able?* Again he implies that he would not. (For Unfulfilled Conditions, see LL p. 54.)

10 **Tiresias** was a celebrated seer in Greek mythology. Though blind, he is reputed to have been infallible in his prophecies of the future.

12 **noscere**: Supply **possit**.

# 20. *The Case against Divination*

(De Divinatione II.8-13)

*In my reply, I must be careful not to claim that I am infallible if I am to avoid falling into the same trap as those I criticise.*

dicendum est mihi igitur ad ea quae sunt a te dicta; sed ita nihil ut affirmem, quaeram omnia, dubitans plerumque et mihi ipse diffidens. si enim aliquid certi haberem quod dicerem, ego ipse divinarem qui esse divinationem nego.

*Has divination any place in matters where the senses are involved?*

etenim me movet illud quod in primis Carneades quaerere solebat, quarumnam rerum divinatio esset: earumne quae sensibus perciperentur? at eas quidem cernimus, audimus, gustamus, olfacimus, tangimus. num quid ergo in his rebus est quod provisione aut permotione mentis magis quam natura ipsa sentiamus? aut num nescio qui ille divinus, si oculis captus sit (ut Tiresias fuit), possit quae alba sint, quae nigra, dicere? aut, si surdus sit, varietates vocum aut modos noscere? ad nullam igitur earum rerum, quae sensu accipiuntur, divinatio adhibetur.

**quaero** (3), to ask, question, investigate,
**dubito** (1), to doubt, question
**plerumque**, generally, on the whole
**diffido** (3) (+ dat.), to distrust, doubt
**etenim**, for indeed, for in fact
**in primis**, especially, in particular
**soleo** (2), to be accustomed
**sensus, -us** (*m*), sense
**percipio** (3), to perceive
**at**, but
**quidem**, actually
**cerno** (3), to see
**gusto** (1), to taste
**olfacio** (3), to smell
**tango** (3), to touch
**ergo**, therefore
**provisio, -onis** (*f*), foresight, seeing into the future
**sentio** (4), to perceive
**oculis captus, -a, -um**, blind
**albus, -a, -um**, white
**niger, -gra, -grum**, black
**surdus, -a, -um**, deaf
**varietas, -atis** (*f*), variety, difference
**vox, vocis** (*f*), voice
**modus, -i** (*m*), tone, inflection
**nosco** (3), to get to know, recognise
**adhibeor** (2), to apply, be applicable

14 **quae arte tractantur**: *which are treated by (professional) skill.*
16 **qui**: *those who.*
17 **in litteris**: *in literature.*
18 **quarum est disciplina**: *in which instruction can be given*, literally *of which there is instruction.*
19 **sol maiorne sit**: *whether* (**-ne**) *the sun is bigger* — an Indirect Question depending on **respondere**. The noun **sol** is placed at the beginning of the double Indirect Question to indicate that it is the subject of both parts.
20 **luna ... utatur**: Another double Indirect Question depending on **respondere** (understood from line 19).
20 **solis**: Supply **lumine**.
21 **quem motum habeat**: *the movement (of)*, literally *what movement (it) has* — another Indirect Question depending on **respondere**. Both **sol** and **luna** are subjects of **habeat**.
21 **quem quinque stellae**: Supply **motum habeant**. This refers to the five planets known to the ancient world (Mercury, Venus, Mars, Jupiter and Saturn). More have been discovered since then. The belief was that the earth was stationary and that these five, along with the sun and the moon, revolved round the earth.
22 **haec** is the object of **esse dicturos**.
22 **qui**: *those who.* (Compare **qui** in line 16.)
22 **nec**: This balances **nec** at the beginning of the line — *neither ... nor.*
23 **eorum quae**: *of the things which.*
23 **quae vera (sint), quae falsa sint**: Indirect Questions depending on **profitentur se esse dicturos** (understood).
24 **mathematicorum**: *(the business) of mathematicians.* (For this genitive denoting Sphere of Activity or Characteristic, see LL p. 8.)
25 **num quid est?**: *Is there anything?*, again implying that there is nothing. Compare lines 8 and 9.
26 **quid bonum sit**: *(on the question of) what is good.*
27 **propria**: *the province (of)*, literally *belonging (to).*
28 **quid?**: *again* (giving another example). Cicero regularly uses this idiom to introduce a fresh point or argument — a particularly effective technique in public speaking.
28 **sit**: This is to be taken with **vivendum** — *(how) one ought to live.* (For the Gerundive used impersonally, see LL p. 62.)
30 **utendum**: Supply **sit** — *(how) one ought to use.* (For the Gerundive used impersonally, see LL p. 62.)

*What about the learned professions?*

atqui ne in eis quidem rebus, quae arte tractantur, divinatione opus est. etenim ad aegros non vates aut hariolos, sed medicos solemus adducere; nec vero qui fidibus aut tibiis uti volunt, ab haruspicibus accipiunt earum tractationem, sed a musicis. eadem in litteris ratio est reliquisque rebus, quarum est disciplina. num censes eos qui divinare dicuntur posse respondere, sol maiorne quam terra sit an tantus quantus videatur? luna suo lumine an solis utatur? sol, luna quem motum habeat? quem quinque stellae quae errare dicuntur? nec haec, qui divini habentur, profitentur se esse dicturos; nec eorum quae in geometria describuntur, quae vera, quae falsa sint. sunt enim ea mathematicorum, non hariolorum.

*What about philosophy and physics and good government? Does divination help in any of these?*

de illis vero rebus, quae in philosophia versantur, num quid est quod quisquam divinorum respondere soleat, quid bonum sit, quid malum, quid neutrum? sunt enim haec propria philosophorum. quid? de officio num quis haruspicem consulit, quemadmodum sit cum parentibus, cum fratribus, cum amicis vivendum? quemadmodum utendum pecunia, quemadmodum honore, quemadmodum imperio? ad sapientes haec, non ad divinos referri solent.

**atqui**, and yet
**opus est** (+ abl.), there is need (of)
**aegri, -orum** (*m.pl*), the sick
**vates, -is** (*m*), prophet, seer
**hariolus, -i** (*m*), soothsayer
**medicus, -i** (*m*), doctor, physician
**vero**, truly, indeed
**fides, -ium** (*f.pl*), lyre, lute
**tibiae, -arum** (*f.pl*), flute, pipes
**utor** (3) (+ abl.), to use, play
**haruspex, -spicis** (*m*), soothsayer
**tractatio, -onis** (*f*), instruction
**ratio, -onis** (*f*), rule, principle
**censeo** (2), to think, believe
**tantus ... quantus ...**, as big as
**videor** (2), to seem
**luna, -ae** (*f*), moon
**lumen, -inis** (*n*), light
**erro** (1), to wander, move about
**divinus, -i** (*m*), soothsayer
**habeo** (2), to consider
**profiteor** (2), to profess, claim
**describo** (3), to define, deal with
**verus, -a, -um**, true
**versor** (1), to be, exist, be involved
**quisquam**, anyone
**respondeo** (2), to reply, respond
**malus, -a, -um**, (morally) bad, evil
**neuter, -tra, -trum**, neither (of two)
**officium, -i** (*n*), duty, obligation(s)
**num quis?**, surely no one?
**consulo** (3), to consult
**quemadmodum**, how
**pecunia, -ae** (*f*), money
**honos, -oris** (*m*), public office
**imperium, -i** (*n*), (supreme) power
**sapiens, -entis** (*m*), wise man, sage
**refero, -ferre**, to refer, bring

32 **quae**: The antecedent is **eorum**. (For the relative pronoun preceding its antecedent, see LL p. 26.)

33 **unusne mundus sit an plures** and **quae sint initia rerum**: These are both Indirect Questions depending on **divinari potest** (understood).

35 **quaeritur**: *the question is*, literally *it is being asked*. (For verbs used impersonally in the passive, see LL p. 57.)

35 **quae leges, qui mores**: Supply **sint** — another Indirect Question depending on **quaeritur**.

36 **ex Etruria**: The art of divination was said to have originated in Etruria (see the maps on pages 7 and 95).

39 **nec earum rerum ulla divinatio est**: *there is no (place for) divination in those things*.

40 **artibus continentur**: *are dependent on* (literally *are included in*) *skills*.

42 **quarum rerum sit nihil prorsus intellego**: *I have absolutely no idea to what category it* (i.e. divination) *belongs*, literally *I understand absolutely nothing of what things it is*. **quarum rerum sit** is an Indirect Question depending on **intellego**.

42 **aut omnium debet esse**: *either it ought to have a place* (literally *be*) *in all of them*.

43 **aut aliqua ei materia danda est**: *or it ought to be given a subject area*. (For Gerundive of Obligation, see LL p. 61.)

44 **ut ratio docuit**: *as reasoned argument has shown*.

45 **possimus**: For Generic Subjunctive, see LL p. 103.

45 **vide igitur ne nulla sit divinatio**: *therefore I am inclined to think there is no such thing as divination*, literally *therefore suppose that there may be no divination*. The phrase **vide ne nulla** is used as a polite way of saying **dubito an ulla** (literally *I doubt whether ... any*).

46 **in hanc sententiam**: *expressing* (literally *towards*) *the following thought*. The sentiment expressed in the line quoted appears in one of the plays of Euripides, the Greek playwright, and may have been incorporated into one of the popular plays of the day in Rome, so that it became a catch-phrase.

48 **qui**: The antecedent of **qui** is **hunc**. Latin writers frequently place the relative clause in front of its antecedent (see LL p. 26).

48 **vatem**: The poet uses the word here in the wider sense of anyone who predicts what is going to happen. The best 'soothsayer', he says, is not the person who is supposed to be divinely inspired, but the person who uses his experience and knowledge to make an intelligent guess regarding what is likely to happen in a particular situation. In line 49, on the other hand, **vates** is used only of the person involved in augury.

48 **optumum**: An archaic spelling of **optimum**.

quid? quae a dialecticis aut a physicis tractantur, num quid eorum divinari potest? unusne mundus sit an plures, quae sint initia rerum, ex quibus nascuntur omnia? physicorum est ista prudentia.

quid? cum quaeritur qui sit optimus rei publicae status, quae leges, qui mores aut utiles aut inutiles, haruspicesne ex Etruria arcessentur, an principes statuent et delecti viri periti rerum civilium?

*The fact that divination is useless in all of these situations makes me feel it has no validity. Is it any more useful in the practical situations of daily life?*

quodsi nec earum rerum, quae subiectae sensibus sunt, ulla divinatio est, nec earum quae artibus continentur, nec earum quae in philosophia disseruntur, nec earum quae in re publica versantur, quarum rerum sit nihil prorsus intellego. nam aut omnium debet esse, aut aliqua ei materia danda est in qua versari possit. sed nec omnium divinatio est, ut ratio docuit, nec locus nec materia invenitur cui divinationem praeficere possimus. vide igitur ne nulla sit divinatio. est quidam Graecus vulgaris in hanc sententiam versus:

'bene qui coniciet, vatem hunc perhibebo optumum.'

**dialecticus, -i** (*m*), logician, a person skilled in logic
**physicus, -i** (*m*), physicist, natural philosopher
**tracto** (1), to deal with, handle
**divino** (1), to foretell, predict
**mundus, -i** (*m*), world, universe
**plures, -a**, more (than one), several
**initium, -i** (*n*), beginning, origin
**nascor** (3), to be born, originate
**iste, ista, istud**, that
**prudentia, -ae** (*f*), knowledge, skill
**res publica**, state, government
**status, -us** (*m*), form, constitution
**lex, legis** (*f*), law
**mos, moris** (*m*), custom
**utilis, -is, -e**, useful, beneficial
**arcesso** (3), to summon, send for
**princeps, -ipis** (*m*), leader, leading statesman
**statuo** (3), to decide, settle (a dispute or question)
**deligo** (3), **-legi, -lectum**, to choose, pick, select
**peritus, -a, -um** (+ gen.), skilled (in)
**civilis, -is, -e**, concerned with public or political life
**quodsi**, but if
**subicio** (3), **-ieci, -iectum** (+ dat.), to place under the control (of)
**contineo** (2), to hold, contain
**dissero** (3), to discuss
**prorsus**, absolutely
**locus, -i** (*m*), topic, field (of study)
**invenio** (4), to find
**praeficio** (3) (+ dat.), to put in control (of)
**vulgaris, -is, -e**, popular, common, everyday
**versus, -us** (*m*), line
**conicio** (3), **-ieci**, to guess, predict
**vates, -is** (*m*), soothsayer, prophet
**perhibeo** (2), to consider, call

51 **coniectura** is ablative case.
52 **adsequetur**: *will he* (i.e. the soothsayer) *understand?*
52 **Quinte**: See line 1 and *Predicting the Future* on pages 182-3.
52 **te** along with **abducere** and **definire** (line 54) forms an Accusative and Infinitive clause depending on **animadverti** (*I have noticed*).
53 **quae haberent artem atque prudentiam**: *which involved skill and judgement,* literally *which had skill and wisdom.*
56 **primum eodem revolveris**: *in the first place you are repeating what you said before* literally *first, you are rolling back to the same place.* In other words, this definition does not add anything new.
57 **est rerum fortuitarum**: *applies in* (literally *is of*) *chance situations.*
58 **quis**: *any.* This adjective is to be taken with **haruspex**, **augur**, **vates** and **somnians** (see *Predicting the Future* on page 182). These four nouns are linked by the first four uses of **aut**. The next three uses of **aut** (in line 59) link three Accusative and Infinitive clauses which depend on **melius coniecerit**, — *will (any of them) make a better prediction*, literally *will have guessed better.*

## Points for Discussion

1. In line 28, Cicero mentions **officium**. Refer to lines 28-30 and write down the range of relationships and situations to which Cicero says the word **officium** applies.
2. Refer to lines 55-61. Who does Cicero think will give the best advice in chance situations (**res fortuitae**)? What are his reasons for thinking so?
3. Do you think that there is any difference between the Romans' reliance on reading the auspices and the modern practice of reading one's horoscope? Give reasons for your answer.

*The methods used by soothsayers to predict what is going to happen are quite different from those used by professionals like helmsmen and doctors.*

num igitur aut, quae tempestas impendeat, vates melius coniciet quam gubernator? aut morbi naturam acutius quam medicus aut belli administrationem prudentius quam imperator coniectura adsequetur? sed animadverti, Quinte, te caute et ab eis coniecturis quae haberent artem atque prudentiam, et ab eis quae sensibus aut artificiis perciperentur, abducere divinationem eamque ita definire: 'divinationem esse earum rerum praedictionem et praesensionem, quae essent fortuitae.' primum eodem revolveris: nam et medici et gubernatoris et imperatoris praesensio est rerum fortuitarum. num igitur aut haruspex aut augur aut vates quis aut somnians melius coniecerit aut e morbo evasurum aegrotum aut e periculo navem aut ex insidiis exercitum quam medicus, quam gubernator, quam imperator?

**tempestas, -atis** (*f*), weather
**impendeo** (2), to threaten
**gubernator, -oris** (*m*), helmsman, navigator, pilot
**morbus, -i** (*m*), disease, illness
**acute**, sharply, accurately
**administratio, -onis** (*f*), management, direction
**prudenter**, wisely, skilfully
**coniectura, -ae** (*f*), conjecture, guess, guesswork
**caute**, carefully
**artificium, -i** (*n*), skill
**percipio** (3), to perceive, grasp
**abduco** (3), to withdraw, remove
**definio** (4), to define
**praedictio, -onis** (*f*), prediction, foretelling
**praesensio, -onis** (*f*), foreknowledge, insight
**fortuitus, -a, -um**, happening by chance, accidental
**somnians, -antis** (*m*), dreamer
**evado** (3), **evasi, evasum**, to escape from, come safely out of
**aegrotus, -i** (*m*), invalid
**insidiae, -arum** (*f.pl*), ambush

# Antony and Octavian

Although Cicero was not involved in the conspiracy to assassinate Caesar on 15 March 44 BC, he was overjoyed that the tyrant had been removed and the constitutional Republic restored. His joy was short-lived, however. The Liberators, as Cicero called the conspirators, had made no definite plans to fill the power vacuum, and neither the Senate nor the people showed much enthusiasm for what had been done. The Liberators' lack of resolution enabled Marcus Antonius to seize the initiative from them.

At the time of the assassination, Antony was Caesar's fellow-consul. This put him in a strong position as legitimate authority automatically passed to him. Immediately after the murder, he had remained in hiding, but he still had the presence of mind to seize the treasure which Caesar had deposited in the Temple of Ops (Goddess of Plenty) and to persuade Caesar's widow to hand over Caesar's private papers to him.

To begin with, Antony pretended to be reconciled with the conspirators and treated them and Cicero politely. But he soon cast aside his pretence of moderation and gradually turned public opinion against them by bribing certain influential Romans and by publishing the contents of Caesar's papers which contained proposals that were likely to win the support of various individuals and groups. He insisted that there be a public funeral for Caesar and in the funeral oration, by reading out the contents of Caesar's will which made generous gifts to the citizens and the veteran soldiers, he stirred up anger against the assassins. There was rioting in the city and, although Cicero had persuaded the Senate two days after the assassination to declare a general amnesty, the conspirators, fearing for their safety, had all fled from Rome by the middle of April.

Antony continued to use the Senate and the people's Assembly very cleverly to consolidate his position. The Senate granted him a personal bodyguard in Rome; and in June he persuaded the Assembly to pass a law changing his proconsular province from Macedonia to the provinces of Cisalpine and Transalpine Gaul, which were strategically more important to him. Not only that: he was to be allowed to keep these provinces for five years and to transfer to his new command the four legions which were in Macedonia.

Antony did not have things all his own way, however. At the time of the assassination, 18-year-old Gaius Octavius, Caesar's great-nephew, was on military service in Greece. Having been named Caesar's heir in his will, he immediately crossed into Italy to claim his inheritance. Antony rejected Octavius' claim to the bequests which Caesar had made to him; but Octavius was able to sell property he had inherited from Caesar and, using these funds and trading on the prestige of his adopted name — Gaius Julius Caesar Octavianus — he at once began, without any legal warrant at first, to hire an army of his own, appealing especially to veterans who had served under Caesar.

Despite his youth, Octavian displayed considerable shrewdness. He courted popularity with the people by carrying out some of the promises Caesar had made to them. He also realised that, because he was so young and did not hold any public office, he needed the support of influential politicians.

The political manoeuvrings continued over the summer, each man trying to gain the upper hand, but neither feeling strong enough to denounce the other openly. Antony, however, began to feel that the tide was turning in Octavian's favour.

By September 44 BC, the Liberators felt so insecure in Italy that they withdrew to Greece, hoping to rebuild their forces there before returning triumphantly to Italy to restore constitutional government.

Already worried by the growing popularity of Octavian and concerned that he might lose the initiative if he waited until the end of his consular year before proceeding to his proconsular province, Antony left Rome on 9 October to take command of the four legions, which had just landed from Macedonia, in preparation for taking over his provinces. However, he found the legions disgruntled and mutinous, and even the promise of increased pay and the summary execution of those he claimed to be the ringleaders failed to retain their complete allegiance.

While Antony was absent from Rome, Octavian marched on the city with a force of veterans whom he had recruited in Campania and, on 10 November, he occupied the Forum; but the coup collapsed when his political backers failed to support him; and many of his troops deserted when they heard that Antony was returning to Rome with his army. Antony convened the Senate on 28 November, but during the debate came the news that two of the Macedonian legions (the Martian and the Fourth) had deserted him and gone over to Octavian on the promise of higher pay. Antony immediately cut short the proceedings, donned military garb and, instead of waiting to denounce Octavian as a public enemy (for he was undoubtedly guilty of treason), left Rome with only his crack Fifth Legion and his veteran levies at his back. He headed north to take up his command in Cisalpine Gaul a month early, as he was entitled to do. Decimus Brutus, whom Caesar had made governor of that province, refused to give it up, and so Antony besieged him in Mutina.

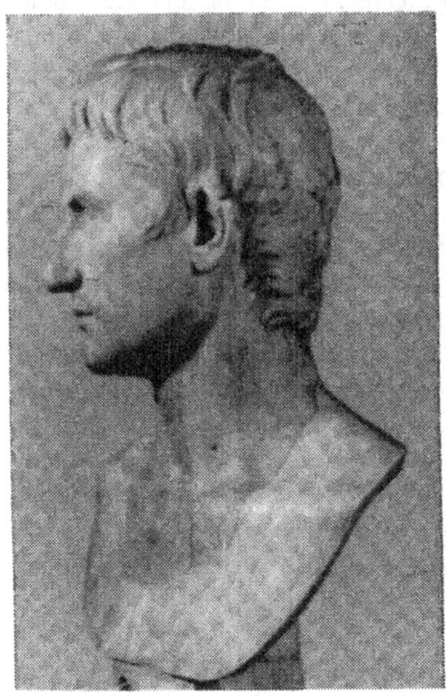

The young Octavian
(from a bust in the British Museum)

# The Philippics

Cicero realised soon after Caesar's murder that there was little likelihood of restoring the Republic, at least until the new consuls assumed office on 1 January 43 BC. He neither trusted nor liked Antony, and he despaired of the indecisiveness of the Liberators. He therefore decided in mid-July 44 BC to go to Greece on the pretext of seeing how his son's education in Athens was progressing. Bad weather interrupted his voyage and, when he heard in mid-August that there was a chance of reconciliation between Antony and the republican party, he returned to Rome on 31 August.

Antony had called a meeting of the Senate for 1 September to propose that special honours be paid to the deified Caesar. Cicero did not attend this meeting, using the excuse that he was tired after the journey. The real reason for his absence was probably political expediency. At the time, there were several political groupings, all of which were manoeuvring for power. One of these groups consisted of past supporters of Caesar who were not at all happy with the actions of Antony. The support of this group could prove crucial in any conflict between Antony and the Liberators. Cicero disapproved of the honours proposed for Caesar, but he could not openly oppose these without alienating this group.

At the meeting on 1 September, Antony fiercely attacked Cicero for his absence and threatened to have his house burned down. Antony then left the city and went to a friend's villa at Tibur (modern Tivoli), which lay a few miles east of Rome.

In Antony's absence, Cicero delivered his reply in the Senate on 2 September in the first of fourteen speeches in which he attacked Antony. Cicero, half-jokingly, entitled these speeches Philippics because he thought that their personal denunciation of Antony was reminiscent of the speeches delivered by the Athenian orator Demosthenes against King Philip of Macedon who overthrew the Athenian democracy in the early 4th century BC.

In the First Philippic, Cicero simply explained the reasons for his absence on the previous day and then went on to remonstrate with Antony for his changed attitude. He contrasted the moderate and conciliatory line adopted by Antony immediately after Caesar's murder with his high-handed and menacing treatment of the Senate and the people's Assemblies since 1 June. He appealed to Antony to aim at true glory rather than domination over his fellow-citizens.

Although the speech was generally moderate, there was an undertone of criticism which irritated Antony. He summoned the Senate to meet on 19 September and ordered Cicero to be present. At that meeting, Antony uttered a furious tirade against Cicero, accusing him of the murder of the Catilinarians (see page 113) and of instigating the death of Clodius (see page 140), creating the conflict between Caesar and Pompey (see pages 156-7) and generally fomenting discord in the state; he even went so far as to suggest that Cicero was the real leader of the conspiracy to murder Caesar.

Cicero did not attend the meeting. He withdrew to the countryside in October and, between then and the end of November, he composed his famous Second Philippic in which he not only replied to Antony's accusations but delivered a scathing attack on Antony's tyrannical abuse of power and profligate life-style, including drunkenness and sexual perversion. The speech, one of the most powerful which Cicero ever wrote, was never delivered but was circulated as a political pamphlet among his friends. In it, Cicero defiantly threw down the gauntlet to Antony in the hope that it would encourage patriots to rally round and preserve the republican constitution against a tyranny which he regarded as worse than that of Caesar.

Cicero sent the draft of the Second Philippic to his friend Atticus for appraisal and, having polished it up in the light of the criticisms received, he published it shortly after Antony left for Cisalpine Gaul at the end of November.

Mark Antony
This gold aureus was struck in 40 BC to commemorate his marriage to Octavia, the sister of Octavian. He later deserted her for the Egyptian queen Cleopatra.

The following are two statements made by Cicero in letters written in April 44 BC, only a few weeks after Caesar's assassination. In the first, he gives Atticus his initial impressions of Octavius (shortly to be known by his adopted name Octavianus). The second comes from a letter he wrote to Antony. [It is included in the Atticus collection because Cicero sent Atticus a copy.] It is hard to reconcile these remarks with what eventually happened. Did Cicero really mean what he says here, or was he saying what he thought was politically expedient at the time?

**nobiscum hic perhonorifice et peramice Octavius.**
*Octavius is with me here — very respectful, very friendly.*

Ad Atticum XIV.12

Yes, but in 43 BC, Octavius yielded to Antony's insistence that Cicero be killed.

**nam cum te semper amavi ... tum his temporibus respublica te mihi ita commendavit ut cariorem habeam neminem.**
*For not only have I always had an affection for you, but your recent public acts have so endeared you to me that there is now no one whom I hold more dear.*

Ad Atticum XIV.13 (b)

1 **rem unam pulcherrimam**: *(his) single most admirable act.* Note the emphatic effect produced by using **unam** (contrasted with **multis**) along with the superlative.

2 **Lupercalia**: This ancient fertility festival, celebrated annually on 15 February, began with the sacrifice of two goats. Their skins were cut into strips and youths, dressed only in goat-skin aprons, used these to whip everyone they met as they ran through the streets of Rome. Women in particular were keen to be struck in this way since the leather strips (**februa**, from which *February* may be derived) were thought to purify them and help them conceive children.

2 **veniamus**: *let us come.* (For Commands and Exhortations, see LL p. 107; compare **nauseet** and **faciat** in line 4.)

2 **patres conscripti**: *senators*, literally *enrolled fathers.* This was the formal way of addressing the Senate. The verb **conscribere** means *to enrol on a special list*, and **patres** is used in the sense of *elders* or *elder statesmen.*

3 **esse commotum**: Supply **eum**.

3 **modo ne nauseet**: *provided he does not vomit*, literally *only let him not vomit.* (For **dummodo**, the more common form of **modo**, see LL p. 91.) The reference is to an occasion when Antony, as Caesar's second-in-command, was conducting an Assembly of the People and was violently sick because he had drunk so much during a meal on the previous evening.

4 **in porticu Minucia**: *in the Portico of Minucius*, where the Assembly was held.

6 **collega tuus**: *your fellow-consul*, i.e. Julius Caesar. Note how Cicero switches from speaking about Antony in the third person (*he*) to addressing him directly in the second person (*you*).

6 **purpurea**: The normal toga worn by magistrates was white with a purple border. It appears that Julius Caesar wore a toga which was completely purple, a colour favoured by kings and, in later times, by the Roman emperors.

7 **coronatus**: *wearing a (laurel) garland.* He was entitled to wear this since he had been given a triumph to celebrate a famous victory. The Roman historian Suetonius says that Caesar greatly valued this privilege, as the garland helped to conceal his balding temples.

7 **ita eras Lupercus ut**: *although you were a Lupercus*, literally *you were a Lupercus in such a way that.* The Luperci were the leaders of the bands of youths.

8 **meminisse deberes**: *you ought to have remembered*, literally *you were under an obligation to remember.*

8 **toto foro**: *in the whole Forum.* The preposition **in** is normally omitted from phrases containing the adjective **totus**. Note how the shock felt by the onlookers is highlighted by the fact that there is no verb.

9 **abiectum** agrees with **diadema** (understood).

10 **meditatum et cogitatum scelus**: *a premeditated and carefully planned crime.* The phrase is in apposition to the clause **(diadema) attuleras domo**.

10 **imponebas**: The imperfect is used here and in **reiciebat** to indicate repeated action. To offer the crown once was bad enough; to persist was much worse.

10 **cum plangore**: *to the accompaniment of wailing.* Note the effect produced by the carefully balanced clauses.

11 **tu unus inventus es qui idem temptares**: *you were shown to be* (literally *were found*) *the only man who also tried to find out* (literally *test*). (For Generic Subjunctive, see LL p. 103.) **idem** is masculine reinforcing **tu**, *you also*, literally *you the same man.*

# *21. A Crown for the Taking*

(Philippics II.84-87)

*Antony disgraced the office of consul by acting like an irresponsible youth at the Lupercalia. He offered Caesar a crown to see what the reaction of the people would be. To the crowd's relief, Caesar rejected it.*

sed ne forte ex multis rebus gestis M.Antoni rem unam pulcherrimam transiliat oratio, ad Lupercalia veniamus. non dissimulat, patres conscripti; apparet esse commotum; sudat, pallet. quidlibet, modo ne nauseet, faciat, quod in porticu Minucia fecit. quae potest esse turpitudinis tantae defensio?

sedebat in rostris collega tuus, amictus toga purpurea, in sella aurea, coronatus. escendis, accedis ad sellam (ita eras Lupercus, ut te consulem esse meminisse deberes), diadema ostendis. gemitus toto foro. unde diadema? non enim abiectum sustuleras, sed attuleras domo, meditatum et cogitatum scelus. tu diadema imponebas cum plangore populi; ille cum plausu reiciebat. tu ergo unus, scelerate, inventus es qui,

**forte**, by chance, accidentally
**res gestae**, achievements, exploits
**transilio** (4), to leap over, skip over, omit
**oratio, -onis** (*f*), speech
**dissimulo** (1), to disguise, hide feelings
**apparet**, it is evident
**commotus, -a, -um**, disturbed, agitated
**sudo** (1), to sweat
**palleo** (2), to look pale, be pale
**quidlibet**, anything at all
**turpitudo, -inis** (*f*), outrageous behaviour, shamelessness
**defensio, -onis** (*f*), excuse, justification
**rostra, -orum** (*n.pl*), Rostra, speakers' platform
**amictus, -a, -um** (+ abl.), dressed (in), wearing
**sella, -ae** (*f*), chair
**aureus, -a, -um**, golden
**escendo** (3), to climb up, mount
**accedo** (3), to go forward, approach
**diadema, -atis** (*n*), royal headband, diadem
**ostendo** (3), to show, display, hold out
**gemitus, -us** (*m*), groan
**abicio** (3), **-ieci, -iectum**, to throw away, cast aside
**tollo** (3), **sustuli**, to pick up
**affero, -ferre, attuli**, to bring
**plausus, -us** (*m*), applause
**reicio** (3), to reject, refuse
**ergo**, therefore
**sceleratus, -i** (*m*), scoundrel, villain

12 **cum auctor regni esses**: *when you were urging him to become king*, literally *when you were the instigator of kingship.*

12 **dominum habere**: *to have as your master.* The two consuls were intended to be equal in power and status; the use of **dominus** implies that Antony was willing to be Caesar's servant, if not his slave.

13 **idem temptares**: See the note on line 11.

15 **supplex**: *as a suppliant.* When pleading for mercy from someone, suppliants would throw themselves at his feet to show their total submission.

16 **tibi uni peteres**: *you would have been seeking (it) for yourself alone.* Understand a clause such as *if it was slavery you were seeking.* (For Conditional sentences, see LL p. 54.) The antecedent of **qui** is **tibi.**

16 **ut omnia paterere, ut facile servires**: *that you endured any indignity* (literally *everything) and readily played (the part of) a slave.* (For Result clauses, see LL p. 47.) **paterere** is another form of **patereris** (imperfect subjunctive of **patior**). Cicero is alluding to the time (mentioned earlier in the speech) when Antony, bankrupt because of his reckless and extravagant way of life, entered into a homosexual relationship with Curio.

19 **nudus**: *naked*, i.e. wearing only goat-skin aprons. (See the note on **Lupercalia** — line 2.)

19 **quid hoc turpius?**: W*hat (could be) more disgraceful than this?* (For Ablative of Comparison, see LL p. 16.)

20 **suppliciis omnibus**: *all (kinds of) punishment.*

20 **dum te stimulis fodiamus**: *for us to prod you with goads*, literally *until we prod you with goads.* (For **dum** used with the subjunctive to indicate Purpose, see LL p. 91.) Ox-goads were commonly used to punish recalcitrant slaves.

21 **haec ... haec**: Both of these adjectives are to be taken with **oratio**, *this speech (of mine).* (For Anaphora, see CAO on page 238.)

21 **ullam partem sensus**: *a scrap of feeling*, literally *any part of feeling.*

22 **summorum virorum**: *of very eminent men.* Cicero is referring to Brutus, Cassius and the other Liberators, as he called those who assassinated the tyrant, Caesar.

23 **quid indignius quam vivere eum**: *what (could be) more scandalous than that he (should) live.* The Accusative and Infinitive (**vivere eum**) refers to Antony.

24 **interfectum esse**: Supply **eum**, referring to Caesar.

26 **adscribi iussit in fastis ad Lupercalia**: *he gave instructions that an additional entry should be made in the public records under the heading Lupercalia (that),* literally *he ordered to be added in writing to the Lupercalia in the records*, i.e. opposite that date in the records. The two Accusative and Infinitive clauses depending on **adscribi iussit** (i.e. **M. Antonium detulisse** and **Caesarem noluisse**) contain the wording of the entry in the records.

26 **dictatori perpetuo**: *dictator for life*, literally *perpetual dictator.* Under the Roman constitution, when the state faced a really serious crisis, a dictator could be appointed for a maximum period of six months, during which time his powers superseded those of the consuls. By making himself *dictator in perpetuity* in 45 BC, Caesar placed himself above everyone else in the state for the rest of his life and so acted unconstitutionally.

cum auctor regni esses eumque quem collegam habebas dominum habere velles, idem temptares quid populus Romanus ferre et pati posset.

at etiam misericordiam captabas: supplex te ad pedes abiciebas. quid petens? ut servires? tibi uni peteres, qui ita a puero vixeras ut omnia paterere, ut facile servires; a nobis populoque Romano mandatum id certe non habebas. o praeclaram illam eloquentiam tuam, cum es nudus contionatus! quid hoc turpius, quid foedius, quid suppliciis omnibus dignius? num exspectas dum te stimulis fodiamus? haec te, si ullam partem habes sensus, lacerat, haec cruentat oratio. vereor ne imminuam summorum virorum gloriam; dicam tamen dolore commotus. quid indignius quam vivere eum qui imposuerit diadema, cum omnes fateantur iure interfectum esse qui abiecerit?

at etiam adscribi iussit in fastis ad Lupercalia C.Caesari dictatori perpetuo M.Antonium consulem populi iussu regnum detulisse, Caesarem

**fero, ferre**, to bear, endure, tolerate
**patior** (3), to suffer, endure
**at**, moreover
**misericordia, -ae** (*f*), pity, compassion
**capto** (1), to strive after, try to win
**pes, pedis** (*m*), foot
**abicio** (3), to throw down, humble
**servio** (4), to be a slave
**a puero**, from boyhood
**vivo**, (3), **vixi**, to live
**mandatum, -i** (*n*), instruction, mandate
**certe**, certainly, definitely
**praeclarus, -a, -um**, famous, splendid
**eloquentia, -ae** (*f*), eloquence
**contionor** (1), to deliver a speech, address the assembly
**foedus, -a, -um**, loathsome, detestable
**dignus, -a, -um** (+ abl.), worthy (of), deserving (of)
**num?**, surely not?
**exspecto** (1), to wait
**lacero** (1), to tear, tear apart
**cruento** (1), to make to bleed, wound
**vereor** (2), to fear
**imminuo** (3), to lessen, diminish, detract from
**dico** (3), to speak
**dolor, -oris** (*m*), grief, indignation
**commotus, -a, -um**, moved
**fateor** (2), to acknowledge, admit, agree
**iure**, rightly
**interficio** (3), **-feci, -fectum**, to kill
**iussu** (+ gen.), by the command (of), by order (of)
**regnum, -i**, (*n*), kingship, kingly power
**defero, -ferre, -tuli**, to offer

28 **L. Tarquinius (Superbus)**, the seventh and last king of Rome, was expelled in 509 BC and the Republic was established.

28 **exactus**: Supply **est**.

28 **Sp. Cassius**: Having defeated the Hernici, a tribe in Latium, during his third consulship in 486 BC, Spurius Cassius proposed a law to distribute public land among Roman citizens. The existing land-owners were annoyed, and he was put to death on the grounds that he was using this proposal to win favour and make himself sole ruler of Rome. Similarly, the nobles arranged the assassination in 439 BC of Spurius Maelius, a rich plebeian, who during a period of famine used his own wealth to distribute corn to the poor people at very low prices. He too was accused of aiming to become king.

29 **Marcus Manlius** was the hero who was awakened by the sacred geese and saved the citadel of Rome when the Gauls attempted to capture it in 390 BC. He later incurred the anger of the patricians by championing the cause of citizens who had fallen into debt during war service and by accusing the senate of embezzling money captured from the Gauls which, he said, should have been used to help those in debt. He was tried and executed on suspicion of aiming at kingly power.

29 **quod fas non est**: *an act of sacrilege*, literally *(a thing) which is not right (in the eyes of the gods)*. This clause is in apposition to the content of the **ut** clause.

## Points for Discussion

1. In lines 6-11, Cicero presents a vivid picture of Antony offering the crown to Caesar. What techniques of language and style does Cicero employ to produce this effect? (See CAO on pages 231-9.)
2. In line 19, why do you think Cicero placed the adjectives **nudus** and **contionatus** side by side?
3. In lines 15-25, Cicero employs a number of rhetorical techniques. Identify as many of these as you can. What effect is he trying to achieve through these, and do you think he succeeds?
4. Summarise the charges Cicero makes against Antony in this passage.
5. List from the passage some of the words and phrases Cicero uses to blacken Antony's character.

uti noluisse. ideone L.Tarquinius exactus, Sp.Cassius, Sp.Maelius, M.Manlius necati ut multis post saeculis a M.Antonio, quod fas non est, rex Romae constitueretur?

**utor** (3) (+ abl.), to use, accept
**nolo, nolle, nolui**, to refuse, decline
**ideo**, for that reason
**exigo** (3), **-egi, -actum**, to drive out, banish
**neco** (1), to murder, execute, put to death
**saeculum, -i** (*n*), century, generation
**constituo** (3), to establish, set up

Coin of Lucius Aemilius Buca (44 BC) dedicated to Caesar as
**DIC[tatori] PERPETUO**

1 **omittamus**: For this use of the subjunctive, see LL p. 107.

1 **hunc unum diem defende**: *defend (your actions on) this single day*. Cicero is speaking directly to Antony.

1 **hodiernum diem**: *today*, literally *today's day*. Note how Cicero repeats **unum** and uses three different expressions for *today* to create dramatic effect.

4 **valvae Concordiae**: *the doors of (the Temple of) Concord*. The Senate had met in the Temple of Concord on 19 September, the occasion on which Antony had strongly criticised Cicero's past conduct (see page 200). The double-doors had been closed, presumably to intimidate the Senate. Cicero pretends that the Second Philippic was delivered in the Senate on 19 September in response to Antony's attack. It was actually written over several weeks and never delivered, but only issued as a political pamphlet.

5 **maxime barbaros**: *most uncivilised* — a highly racist remark designed to prejudice his audience against Antony.

5 **Ityraeos**: The inhabitants of Ityraea, a district to the south of Syria, were renowned for their skill in archery. Antony had been in Pompey's army when he defeated the Ityraeans in 63 BC and may have brought some of them to Rome as part of his personal retinue.

6 **praesidi sui causa**: *for his own protection*. (For this use of **causa**, see LL p. 45.)

8 **nullum est istuc praesidium**: *that protection of yours is no protection*. In other words, it is a delusion. **istuc** is another form of **istud**. Cicero frequently used the adjective **iste** to convey contempt for his opponent. (cf. lines 10, 11 and 12.)

10 **ista**: *those (weapons)*.

10 **utinam salvis nobis**: *(and) may we live (to see that day)*, literally *may it (happen), us surviving*. (For this type of Ablative Absolute, see LL pp. 30-1; for **utinam**, see LL p. 107.)

11 **quoquo modo**: *in whatever way*.

12 **ista tua minime avara coniunx**: *that most generous wife of yours*, literally *that by no means greedy wife of yours*. Although Cicero says that he is not being disrespectful (**sine contumelia**, *without insult*) to Antony's wife Fulvia, the biting sarcasm is obvious when he speaks of the *third instalment* (**tertiam pensionem**) which she should pay. **pensio** was the technical word for the payment of debts by instalments at regular intervals, particularly the repayment of a dowry, which the husband had to make by three annual payments to his wife if he divorced her. Publius Clodius and Gaius Curio, the previous husbands of Fulvia, had both died violent deaths. According to Cicero, the welfare of the state now demands that Fulvia should as soon as possible pay the third instalment of a sort of 'alimony in reverse' by disposing of her third husband, Antony.

13 **debet**: *has owed* (and still owes). The present tense is used in Latin with words like **diu** when a situation which developed in the past still continues in the present (see LL p. 52).

14 **ad quos**: *(men) to whom*. As often in Latin, the antecedent of the relative clause is omitted. Cicero is probably thinking of Brutus, Cassius and the other conspirators.

# 22. Attack on a New Tyrant

(Philippics II.112-119)

*Let us not dwell on what is past: explain your present actions. Why this display of armed force? That won't really give you protection. Your power will not last: possibly your wife will help get rid of you; certainly there are patriots who will defend the state against tyranny. But the price of peace must not be slavery.*

sed praeterita omittamus. hunc unum diem, unum, inquam, hodiernum diem, hoc punctum temporis quo loquor, defende, si potes. cur armatorum corona senatus saeptus est? cur me tui satellites cum gladiis audiunt? cur valvae Concordiae non patent? cur homines omnium gentium maxime barbaros, Ityraeos, cum sagittis deducis in forum? praesidi sui causa se facere dicit. non igitur miliens perire est melius quam in sua civitate sine armatorum praesidio non posse vivere? sed nullum est istuc, mihi crede, praesidium. caritate te et benevolentia civium saeptum oportet esse, non armis.

eripiet et extorquebit tibi ista populus Romanus, utinam salvis nobis! sed quoquo modo nobiscum egeris, dum istis consiliis uteris, non potes, mihi crede, esse diuturnus. etenim ista tua minime avara coniunx, quam ego sine contumelia describo, nimium diu debet populo Romano tertiam pensionem. habet populus Romanus ad quos

**praeterita, -orum** (*n.pl*), past events
**omitto** (3), to disregard, leave aside
**inquam**, I say
**punctum, -i** (*n*), point, moment
**loquor** (3), to speak
**armati, -orum** (*m.pl*), armed men
**corona, -ae** (*f*), ring, cordon
**saepio** (4), **saepsi, saeptum**, to fence in, surround
**satelles, -itis** (*m*), attendant, henchman
**gladius, -i** (*m*), sword
**pateo** (2), to lie open
**gens, gentis** (*f*), tribe, race
**sagitta, -ae** (*f*), arrow
**deduco** (3), to bring, lead down
**miliens**, a thousand times
**pereo, -ire**, to perish, die
**civitas, -atis** (*f*), the state
**credo** (3) (+ dat.), to believe, trust
**caritas, -atis** (*f*), affection, love
**benevolentia, -ae** (*f*), goodwill
**te oportet**, you ought
**eripio** (3) (+ dat.), to snatch (from)
**extorqueo** (2) (+ dat.), to wrench (from), wrest (from)
**ago** (3), **egi**, to deal
**consilium, -i** (*n*), plan, scheme
**utor** (3) (+ abl.), to use, adopt
**diuturnus, -a, -um**, long-lasting
**etenim**, for indeed
**describo** (3), to describe, portray
**nimium**, too much, too

15 **gubernacula**: *government.* The noun **gubernaculum** means literally *ship's rudder*, and the plural form **gubernacula** is frequently used metaphorically (see CAO on page 235) of steering (i.e. directing) the affairs of state. The English word *government* is derived from **gubernare**.

15 **deferat**: For Generic Subjunctive, see LL p. 103.

15 **ubicumque terrarum**: *no matter where they are*, literally *wherever on earth.* (For Partitive Genitive, see LL p. 9.) Note the emphatic position of **ibi** (*that is where*). Cicero asserts that the withdrawal of Brutus and Cassius to Greece should not be interpreted as an act of desertion. In fact, they represented the Republic's main hope of survival.

17 **se ulta est**: *has avenged itself*, i.e. by removing Caesar. However, the state had merely exchanged the tyranny of Caesar for that of Antony. Note the effect produced by not having any word linking the two parts of the relative clause (**ulta est** and **nondum recuperavit**). (For Asyndeton, see CAO on page 238.)

18 **paratos defensores**: *ready champions*, i.e. Brutus and Cassius, whom Cicero called the Liberators for having killed the tyrant Caesar. Although they were both over 40, they are described as **adulescentes** because Romans were still liable for military service until approximately the age of 46.

18 **quam volent illi cedant**: *however much they keep in the background*, literally *let them withdraw as much as they will wish.* (For the present subjunctive used in Commands and Exhortations, see LL p. 107.)

19 **otio consulentes**: *in their desire to avoid civil war*, literally *consulting the interests of peace.* **otium** is often used to mean *the absence of war.*

20 **ipsa**: *(peace) itself.*

21 **plurimum interest**: *there is a world of difference*, literally *it differs very much.*

23 **repellendum**: *to be repelled.* Both this gerundive **repellendum** (see LL p. 61) and **postremum** (line 22) agree with **malum** (understood).

25 **quod**: *what*, literally *(something) which.* As often, the antecedent **id** is omitted (see LL p. 26).

26 **Tarquinium**: Tarquinius Superbus, the last king of Rome, was driven out by Lucius Junius Brutus and others, and the Republic was established in 509 BC. As one of the two consuls elected to replace the king, Brutus led the army which prevented the Etruscans from restoring Tarquinius to the throne.

27 **Spurius Cassius, Spurius Maelius** and **Marcus Manlius** were all put to death after being accused of aiming at kingly power (**regni appetendi**) by currying favour with the people. For fuller details, see Notes 28-9 on page 206.

28 **hi** refers to the Liberators (line 24) who, Cicero says, provided the first example, since the expulsion of the kings, of citizens assassinating someone who had actually made himself sole ruler.

29 **in regnum appetentem**: *on someone aiming at kingly power.* Compare **in regnantem**. (For this use of the present participle, see LL p. 28.)

30 **quod factum**: *that deed.* (For Linking Relative, see LL p. 26.)

30 **cum ... tum ...**: *both ... and ...* Do not confuse this with **tum ... cum ...** in line 26.

31 **expositum ad imitandum**: *displayed (for us) to emulate*, literally *laid out for imitation*, i.e. the murder of Antony would be regarded as a patriotic act. (For **ad** + Gerund used to express Purpose, see LL p. 61.)

31 **illi** refers to the Liberators.

gubernacula rei publicae deferat: qui ubicumque terrarum sunt, ibi omne est rei publicae praesidium vel potius ipsa res publica, quae se adhuc tantum modo ulta est, nondum recuperavit. habet quidem certe res publica adulescentes nobilissimos, paratos defensores. quam volent illi cedant otio consulentes, tamen a re publica revocabuntur.

et nomen pacis dulce est et ipsa res salutaris. sed inter pacem et servitutem plurimum interest. pax est tranquilla libertas, servitus postremum malorum omnium, non modo bello sed morte etiam repellendum.

*There are examples in our past history of would-be tyrants being assassinated, but Brutus and Cassius are the first since the expulsion of the kings to remove someone who had actually made himself sole ruler. They have set us a glorious example to follow.*

quodsi se ipsos illi nostri liberatores e conspectu nostro abstulerunt, at exemplum facti reliquerunt. illi, quod nemo fecerat, fecerunt. Tarquinium Brutus bello est persecutus, qui tum rex fuit cum esse Romae regem licebat. Sp.Cassius, Sp.Maelius, M.Manlius propter suspicionem regni appetendi sunt necati. hi primum cum gladiis non in regnum appetentem, sed in regnantem impetum fecerunt. quod cum ipsum factum per se praeclarum est atque divinum, tum expositum ad imitandum est, praesertim cum illi eam gloriam

**res publica, rei publicae** (*f*), the state, Republic
**defero, -ferre**, to hand over, entrust
**vel**, or
**potius**, rather
**adhuc**, as yet, so far
**tantum modo**, only just
**ulciscor** (3), **ultus sum**, to avenge
**nondum**, not yet
**se recuperare**, to recover, re-establish oneself
**revoco** (1), to recall
**pax, pacis** (*f*), peace
**dulcis, -is, -e**, sweet
**salutaris, -is, -e**, beneficial
**servitus, -utis** (*f*), slavery
**tranquillus, -a, -um**, tranquil, undisturbed
**libertas, -atis** (*f*), freedom, liberty
**postremus, -a, -um**, last, most extreme, worst
**malum, -i** (*n*), evil
**bellum, -i** (*n*), war
**quodsi**, but if
**conspectus, -us** (*m*), sight, view
**aufero, -ferre, abstuli**, to remove, withdraw
**at**, nevertheless, yet
**factum, -i** (*n*), deed, action
**relinquo** (3), **-liqui**, to leave behind
**persequor** (3), **-secutus sum**, to pursue
**tum ... cum ...**, at a time when
**licet**, it is allowed, it is permitted
**primum**, for the first time
**regno** (1), to reign, rule as king
**impetus, -us** (*m*), attack
**per se**, in itself
**praeclarus, -a, -um**, illustrious, glorious
**divinus, -a, -um**, god-like, inspired
**praesertim cum**, especially since

32 **quae vix caelo capi posse videatur**: *which (the vast expanse of) heaven, it seems, can scarcely hold within its bounds*, literally *which seems scarcely able to be contained by the sky*.

32 **satis fructus**: *sufficient reward*. (For Partitive Genitive, see LL p. 9.)

32 **in ipsa conscientia pulcherrimi facti**: *in the actual knowledge of (having done) a very noble deed*.

33 **mortali**: *by a mortal*. (For Dative of Agent with a gerundive, see LL p. 62.)

35 **recordare**: *recall!* (imperative).

35 **dictaturam sustulisti**: *you abolished the dictatorship*. In the early Republic, the dictatorship was used sparingly, only to meet a serious crisis and for a limited period of no more than six months. Its use lapsed after 202 BC until Sulla seized supreme power and appointed himself dictator in 82 BC. Julius Caesar was the next to use it. During the five years in which he held supreme power in Rome, he was appointed dictator four times and then finally assumed the title of **dictator perpetuus**, with trappings not unlike those of a king. The nature of the dictatorship had changed markedly and it had become highly unpopular among the ruling class. Its abolition, therefore, was among the measures which Antony proposed shortly after Caesar's funeral in order to win popularity for himself and to strengthen his own position.

36 **confer**: Supply **eum diem**.

37 **nundinatione tua tuorumque**: *trafficking carried out by you and your friends*, literally *your and your friends' trafficking*. The reference is to the various ways used to win power and popularity, such as the granting of exemption from taxes and the sale of honours. [**nundinatio** is derived from **nundinae** (*f.pl*), *the market held every ninth day*.]

37 **quantum intersit**: *how much difference there is*.

38 **lucrum et laudem**: Note the Alliteration (see CAO on page 235). Compare **sensus stupore suavitatem cibi non sentiunt** in line 39.

38 **morbo aliquo et sensus stupore**: *because of some illness or deadening of the sense (of taste)*. (For Causal Ablative, see LL p. 15.)

42 **si propter innocentiam**: Supply **iudicia non metuis** here and with **sin propter vim**.

43 **non intellegis**: *do you not understand?* On this depends the Indirect Question **ei quid timendum sit**, *what that man must fear* (line 44). (For Dative of Agent with a gerundive, see LL p. 62.) Cicero implies that the man who relies on armed guards must fear something else, namely, his own assassination. Note the very emphatic position of **ei**, coming after its relative clause and at the beginning of the clause to which it belongs (see LL p. 26).

43 **isto modo**: *like you*, literally *in that way of yours*.

45 **viros fortes egregiosque cives**: For Chiasmus, see CAO on page 237.

46 **tui**: *your own cronies*. Note the juxtaposition of **tui te**.

47 **timere a suis**: *to go in fear of one's own people*, literally *to fear (danger) from one's own people*.

consecuti sint quae vix caelo capi posse videatur. etsi enim satis in ipsa conscientia pulcherrimi facti fructus erat, tamen mortali immortalitatem non arbitror esse contemnendam.

*Remember how glad people were when you abolished the dictatorship, and contrast their attitude towards your present conduct. Can nothing deter you? If you do not fear patriots, perhaps you should fear your friends. Remember what happened to Caesar.*

recordare igitur illum, M.Antoni, diem quo dictaturam sustulisti. pone ante oculos laetitiam senatus populique Romani. confer cum hac immani nundinatione tua tuorumque. tum intelleges quantum inter lucrum et laudem intersit. sed nimirum, ut quidam morbo aliquo et sensus stupore suavitatem cibi non sentiunt, sic libidinosi, avari, facinorosi verae laudis gustatum non habent. sed si te laus allicere ad recte faciendum non potest, ne metus quidem a foedissimis factis potest avocare? iudicia non metuis. si propter innocentiam, laudo. sin propter vim, non intellegis, qui isto modo iudicia non timeat, ei quid timendum sit?

quodsi non metuis viros fortes egregiosque cives quod a corpore tuo prohibentur armis, tui te, mihi crede, diutius non ferent. quae est autem vita dies et noctes timere a suis? nisi vero aut maioribus habes

**consequor** (3), **-secutus sum**, to win
**capio** (3), to keep, contain
**etsi**, even if, although
**arbitror** (1), to think, consider
**contemno** (3), **-tempsi**, to despise
**tollo** (3), **sustuli**, to remove, abolish
**oculus, -i** (*m*), eye
**laetitia, -ae** (*f*), joy, gladness
**confero, -ferre**, to compare
**immanis, -is, -e**, monstrous, infamous
**lucrum, -i** (*n*), profit, gain
**laus, laudis** (*f*), glory, honour
**nimirum**, doubtless, no doubt
**ut**, just as
**suavitas, -atis** (*f*), sweetness, flavour
**cibus, -i** (*m*), food
**sentio** (4), to feel, be aware of
**libidinosus, -a, -um**, lustful
**avarus, -a, -um**, greedy, grasping
**facinorosus, -a, -um**, criminal
**verus, -a, -um**, true
**gustatus, -us** (*m*), taste
**allicio** (3), to attract, entice
**recte**, rightly, in an upright manner
**ne ... quidem**, not even
**metus, -us** (*m*), fear
**foedus, -a, -um**, foul, loathsome
**avoco** (1), to call away, divert
**iudicia, -orum** (*n.pl*), law-courts
**metuo** (3), to fear
**sin**, but if
**egregius, -a, -um**, distinguished
**prohibeo** (2), to keep away
**diutius**, (any) longer
**fero, ferre, tuli**, to tolerate
**autem**, moreover
**vero**, indeed, actually
**maior, maioris**, greater

48 **obligatos**: *men bound (to you).*

48 **quam ille quosdam habuit (obligatos) ex eis**: *than (the favours by which) he kept (bound to him) some of those.* **ille** refers to Caesar, and **quosdam ex eis** refers to two groups among the conspirators — those like Casca, Cimber and Trebonius (to whom Caesar had given favours for directly supporting him in the past) and others like Brutus and Cassius, whose lives Caesar had spared even though they had supported Pompey in the Civil War.

49 **aut tu es ulla re**: *or you are not in any respect.* Note that this clause also is influenced by the negative force of **nisi** (*if ... not*), hence **ulla** where **nulla** might have been expected. Cicero here suggests that Antony may be thinking that there is nothing to worry about because *he* can trust his friends, or because *he* is quite different from Caesar and presents no threat to the state.

50 **litterae**: *literary ability*, i.e. he was a man of culture. Besides writing the histories of the Gallic War and the Civil War, Caesar was a fine orator and wrote treatises on grammar, astronomy and augury.

51 **quamvis calamitosas**: *(which) though disastrous.* Both **calamitosas** and **magnas** agree with **res**.

53 **(id) quod cogitarat**: *what he had intended.* [**cogitarat = cogitaverat**.]

53 **muneribus**: *by staging* (literally *with*) *gladiatorial games.* Like most ambitious politicians, Caesar had courted popularity through lavish games (**munera**), erecting impressive public buildings (**monumenta**), giving money and land to his veterans (**congiaria**, *largesse*), providing free or cheap corn and even a feast (**epulae**) for the whole population at one sitting, using 20,000 dining couches.

54 **suos**: *his own followers.*

55 **clementiae specie**: *by a show of clemency.* The word **species** might suggest that this was only a pretence; but Caesar genuinely wished to reconcile the warring factions, and many of his opponents in the Civil War, including Cicero, readily agreed that he was remarkably generous and forgiving towards them.

56 **consuetudinem serviendi**: *acceptance of slavery*, literally *the habit of being a slave.* (For Gerund, see LL p. 60; compare **dominandi cupiditate** in line 57.)

57 **cum illo** refers to Caesar; **te** refers to Antony.

58 **comparandus es**: Note the repetition of these words from line 49.

59 **hoc boni est**: *this much good has emerged*, literally *there is this (amount) of good.* (For Partitive Genitive, see LL p. 9.) **hoc** is explained in the **quod** clause which follows.

60 **quantum cuique crederet**: *how much to trust each man* — the first of three Deliberative Indirect Questions depending on **didicit**. (For Deliberative Questions, see LL p.108.)

62 **quam sit re pulchrum**: *what a noble act it is*, literally *how noble in the act it is.* This is an Indirect Question depending on **didicisse**, as are **(quam sit) beneficio gratum** (*what a welcome benefit it is*, literally *how welcome in the benefit it is*) and **(quam sit) fama gloriosum** (*what a proud boast it is*, literally *how glorious in the reputation it is*).

64 **ad hoc opus curretur**: *men will rush to (carry out) this task*, i.e. of assassinating you, Antony. (For verbs used impersonally, see LL p. 57.)

64 **neque occasionis tarditas exspectabitur**: *and they will not wait for an opportunity which may take a long time to come*, literally *and the slowness of an opportunity will not be waited for.* In other words, having seen how it feels to have removed one tyrant, they will not delay in getting rid of another.

beneficiis obligatos quam ille quosdam habuit ex eis a quibus est interfectus, aut tu es ulla re cum eo comparandus.

*Your position is quite different from Caesar's because he was a much more talented person than you could ever be. But there is one respect in which you do resemble him, and that is your lust for power. That will be your undoing because you must realise that the Roman people will not easily give up the freedom which it has just regained.*

fuit in illo ingenium, ratio, memoria, litterae, cura, cogitatio, diligentia; res bello gesserat quamvis rei publicae calamitosas, at tamen magnas; multos annos regnare meditatus, magno labore multis periculis quod cogitarat effecerat; muneribus, monumentis, congiariis, epulis multitudinem imperitam delenierat; suos praemiis, adversarios clementiae specie devinxerat. quid multa? attulerat iam liberae civitati partim metu, partim patientia consuetudinem serviendi.

cum illo ego te dominandi cupiditate conferre possum, ceteris vero rebus nullo modo comparandus es. sed ex plurimis malis quae ab illo rei publicae sunt inusta hoc tamen boni est, quod didicit iam populus Romanus quantum cuique crederet, quibus se committeret, a quibus caveret. haec non cogitas? neque intellegis satis esse viris fortibus didicisse quam sit re pulchrum, beneficio gratum, fama gloriosum tyrannum occidere? an, cum illum homines non tulerint, te ferent? certatim posthac, mihi crede, ad hoc opus curretur neque occasionis tarditas exspectabitur.

**beneficium, -i** (*n*), favour
**comparandus, -a, -um**, comparable
**ingenium, -i** (*n*), genius, flair
**ratio, -onis** (*f*), intellect
**cura, -ae** (*f*), thoroughness
**cogitatio, -onis** (*f*), powers of thought
**gero** (3), **gessi**, to do, achieve
**at tamen**, nevertheless, yet
**meditor** (1), to contemplate, aim at
**efficio** (3), **-feci**, to achieve
**multitudo, -inis** (*f*), crowd, mob
**imperitus, -a, -um**, ignorant, illiterate
**delenio** (4), to charm, win over
**praemium, -i** (*n*), reward
**adversarius, -i** (*m*), opponent
**devincio** (4), **-vinxi**, to bind to oneself
**quid multa?**, to cut a long story short
**affero, -ferre, attuli**, to bring to
**liber, -era, -erum**, free
**partim**, partly
**patientia, -ae** (*f*), acquiescence
**dominor** (1), to have absolute power
**cupiditas, -atis** (*f*), longing, lust
**vero**, but
**nullo modo**, in no way, not at all
**plurimi, -ae, -a**, very many
**inuro** (3), **-ussi, -ustum** (+ dat.), to brand, inflict (upon)
**disco** (3), **didici**, to learn
**committo** (3), **-misi, -missum** (+ dat.), to entrust (to), rely (upon)
**caveo** (2) (**a** + abl.), to beware (of)
**cogito** (1), to think about, consider
**occido** (3), to kill
**certatim**, in rivalry, eagerly
**posthac**, after this

66 **quibus ortus sis**: *(the men) from whom you have sprung*. Cicero urges Antony to model his actions on what his esteemed ancestors would have done rather than on the behaviour of the dissolute characters with whom he now associates.

67 **mecum**: Supply **redi in gratiam**, *make your peace with me*, literally *return into friendship with me*.

68 **de te tu videris**: *come to your own decision about yourself* (i.e. about whether or not you are going to mend your ways), literally *see about yourself*. The future perfect (**videris**) is used here as an imperative.

70 **Catilinae**: For details of the Catilinarian conspiracy, see pages 96-7.

71 **obtulerim**: *I would offer*. (For Potential Subjunctive, see LL p. 108.)

72 **pariat quod iam diu parturit**: *may give birth to something* (i.e. freedom) *which it has been carrying within it for a long time*. The metaphor (see CAO on page 235) is of a woman in the labour of child-birth. She carries the baby for a long time in her womb and then, after the pain of giving birth, there is the joy of seeing the new-born child. (For the present indicative with **iam diu**, see LL p. 52.)

73 **hoc ipso in templo**: i.e. the Temple of Concord (see note on line 4).

73 **negavi**: Cicero refers to what he said in his Fourth Speech Against Catiline in 63 BC, namely, that death could not be described as untimely if one died defending the state after attaining the noble rank of consul.

74 **quanto verius**: *with how much greater truth*, literally *how much more truly*. (For the ablative used with a comparative to express Measure of Difference, see LL p. 16.)

75 **seni**: Supply **posse mortem immaturam esse**.

75 **mihi**: Compare line 33 for Dative of Agent with a gerundive.

75 **patres conscripti**: *senators*, literally *enrolled fathers* (or *elders*) — the traditional way of addressing members of the Senate. (See also Note 2 on page 202.)

76 **perfuncto rebus eis quas adeptus sum quasque gessi**: *after all the honours I have won and the deeds I have carried out*, literally *having completed those things which I have attained and which I have done*. **perfuncto** is dative, agreeing with **mihi** in line 75.

78 **hoc**: *than this*. (For Ablative of Comparison, see LL p. 16.)

78 **ut ita cuique eveniat ut de re publica quisque mereatur**: *that things* (literally *it*) *may turn out for each man as he* (literally *each man*) *deserves of the state*, i.e. in proportion to the services he has given to the state. The first **ut** introduces an Indirect Command depending on **opto** (line 77); the second is a correlative following on **ita**.

*Show some consideration for the state instead of for your dissolute companions. I for my part was not deterred by danger when I was young: why should it deter me now that I am old? I wish only that Rome should be free and that every man should get his just deserts.*

respice, quaeso, aliquando rem publicam, M.Antoni! quibus ortus sis, non quibuscum vivas, considera! mecum, uti voles: redi cum re publica in gratiam! sed de te tu videris: ego de me ipse profitebor. defendi rem publicam adulescens, non deseram senex; contempsi Catilinae gladios, non pertimescam tuos. quin etiam corpus libenter obtulerim, si repraesentari morte mea libertas civitatis potest, ut aliquando dolor populi Romani pariat quod iam diu parturit!

etenim si abhinc annos prope viginti hoc ipso in templo negavi posse mortem immaturam esse consulari, quanto verius nunc negabo seni! mihi vero, patres conscripti, iam etiam optanda mors est, perfuncto rebus eis quas adeptus sum quasque gessi. duo modo haec opto: unum, ut moriens populum Romanum liberum relinquam (hoc mihi maius ab dis immortalibus dari nihil potest); alterum, ut ita cuique eveniat ut de re publica quisque mereatur.

**respicio** (3), to have a care for, respect
**quaeso**, I beg (you), please
**aliquando**, now at last, even at this late hour
**considero** (1), to consider, think about
**uti** = **ut**, as
**profiteor** (2), to declare publicly, make a statement
**desero** (3), to desert
**senex, senis** (*m*), old man
**pertimesco** (3), to fear greatly
**quin etiam**, moreover
**libenter**, gladly, willingly
**offero, -ferre, obtuli**, to offer, expose
**repraesento** (1), to bring back
**dolor, -oris** (*m*), grief, pain, suffering
**abhinc** (+ acc.), ago
**prope**, almost
**nego** (1), to deny, say that ... not
**immaturus, -a, -um**, untimely, premature
**consularis, -is, -e**, of consular rank
**opto** (1), to desire, wish for
**perfungor** (3), **-functus sum** (+ abl.), to perform, complete
**adipiscor** (3), **adeptus sum**, to attain, achieve
**modo**, only
**morior** (3), to die
**di, deorum** (*m.pl*), gods
**alter, -era, -erum**, the other, the second
**mereor** (2) **(de** + abl.), to deserve (of)

## Points for Discussion

1. Read lines 1-9. What act of Antony particularly annoys Cicero here? How does he show this annoyance (a) by the words he uses, and (b) by the style of his address?
2. In lines 6-10, some words are in unusual positions in their phrases and sentences. Identify these words and indicate what effects you think Cicero is trying to achieve in these instances.
3. Read lines 20-3. Explain in your own words the point Cicero is making in what he says about **pax** and **servitus**.
4. Read lines 24-34.
   (a) In what ways were the positions of Tarquin and Caesar comparable? What, in Cicero's view, was the real difference between them?
   (b) In what way did Maelius and Manlius present less of a threat to Rome than either Tarquin or Caesar?
   (c) Why does Cicero say of Brutus and Cassius (the Liberators) — **illi, quod nemo fecerat, fecerunt**?
   (d) Do you think that Cicero's claims in lines 30-4 are excessive? Why do you suppose he uses such powerful language here?
5. In lines 50-1, Cicero lists Caesar's outstanding qualities. In lines 51-6, which aspects of Caesar's achievements do you think Cicero admires, and which features does he deplore?
6. In lines 58-9, Cicero declares that Caesar's acts have been harmful to the Republic, but in lines 59-65 he lists some positive lessons that have been learnt from these events and from the assassination of Caesar which stemmed from them. What were these lessons? And do you think that, overall, Cicero's assessment was correct? Give reasons for your answer.
7. Read lines 66-79. What features of style and language (see CAO on pages 231-9) does Cicero employ here to make the greatest impact? Do you think he succeeds or not? Give reasons for your answer.

This coin was issued by the Liberators in 43/42 BC to mark the assassination of Julius Caesar. The letters **EID.MART** (*Ides of March*) give the date of the assassination (15 March). Between the two daggers is a **pileus** (a sort of felt cap worn by freed slaves) used here as a symbol of freedom restored.

# Cicero Backs Octavian

During the summer of 44 BC, Cicero resisted efforts by Octavian to win him over by flattery but, towards the end of the year, he began to promote him as a possible guardian of the Republic, although privately he admitted that he was just using 'the young lad' to get rid of Antony, after which he could be discarded and the Republic restored. To reinforce his oratorical campaign, he sent letters to provincial governors urging them to back the Senate against Antony. His first success was with Decimus Brutus who refused to hand over Cisalpine Gaul to Antony. On 20 December, Cicero in his Third Philippic persuaded the Senate to order all governors to stay in post, thus backing Decimus Brutus' refusal to hand over Cisalpine Gaul. On the same day, he addressed the people in the Fourth Philippic, praising the patriotism of Decimus Brutus and Octavian.

On 1 January 43 BC, during a debate in the Senate on whether to send an embassy to warn Antony, Cicero delivered a rousing call to arms (Fifth Philippic). On 3 January, he persuaded the Senate to make Octavian a senator and give him formal authority (**imperium**) as a praetor to recruit troops and support the consuls in military action against Antony. On 4 January, however, the Senate decided to give Antony one last chance by sending three envoys to demand his withdrawal from Cisalpine Gaul. On 5 January, Cicero denounced this weak action in a speech to the people (Sixth Philippic), claiming that Antony would ignore the order; and in the Seventh Philippic he told the Senate that, even if peace was possible (which he doubted), it would be dishonourable and dangerous.

In the past, Cicero had tended to be an advocate for peace. When a rift between Caesar and Pompey seemed likely, he had remained neutral, hoping to arrange a reconciliation between them. Immediately after Caesar's assassination, he had hoped that Antony and the Liberators could avoid conflict and join in restoring the Republic. Now, convinced that Antony wished to establish himself as dictator, he called upon the Senate to declare war on him. When the embassy returned with counter-proposals from Antony, the Senate rejected them and, on 2 February, proclaimed a state of war. Cicero criticised its use of the term **tumultus** (*disturbance*), instead of **bellum**, to describe Antony's attack on Decimus Brutus (Eighth Philippic). Antony's friends in Rome were unable to win support for him, thanks largely to further speeches by Cicero (Philippics 9-13).

The consuls and Octavian moved against Antony and defeated him near the end of April 43 BC. Forced to abandon the siege of Decimus Brutus at Mutina, he retreated into Transalpine Gaul where in May he joined up with Lepidus, the governor of that province. There was great rejoicing when news of Antony's defeat reached Rome on 20 April, and a 50-day thanksgiving was proposed. In the Fourteenth Philippic Cicero said that this was wrong unless Antony was declared a public enemy, the successful generals hailed as victors, a monument erected to the fallen, and the kindred of the dead given the same rewards as the surviving soldiers. The Senate declared Antony a public enemy on 26 April, and on 30 June passed a similar decree against Lepidus.

Cicero began to see himself as saviour of the state again, as he had been in putting down the Catilinarian Conspiracy in 63 BC. The numerous letters he wrote at this time reveal how confident he was of his position, including the following one written in Rome around 2 February 43 BC to Trebonius, who had been one of Caesar's assassins.

1 **Trebonio S**: *sends greetings to Trebonius.* **S** stands for **salutem (dicit** or **dat)**, which is the regular greeting at the start of a Roman letter. On the Ides of March 44 BC, Trebonius had been given the task of keeping Antony engaged in conversation, away from the place where Caesar was to be murdered (see line 5). Following the murder, he became governor of the province of Asia in June 44 BC. This letter was probably written on 2 February 43 BC, but Trebonius never received it because, towards the end of January, he was murdered at Smyrna by Dolabella whom Antony had sent to seize the governorship of Syria.

2 **quam vellem invitasses**: *how I would have wished you had invited.* (For the Potential use of **vellem**, see LL p. 108.) Note the abbreviated form **invitasses = invitavisses.**

2 **epulas**: *banquet.* Cicero is gloating over the murder of Caesar. The tone of this letter is unpleasant, even virulent; but, of course, it reveals Cicero's inner feelings and was not intended for publication.

3 **reliquiarum nihil haberemus**: *we would (now) have no left-overs.* The scraps left over at the end of a meal were usually unimportant, but Cicero implies that, on this occasion, the left-overs were important and that the conspirators had made a serious mistake in not murdering Antony at the same time as Caesar. (For Partitive Genitive, see LL p. 9; for Unreal Conditions in present time, see LL p. 54.)

3 **cum iis**: Supply **reliquiis.**

3 **tantum negoti**: For Partitive Genitive, see LL p. 9. (cf. **negoti plus** in line 7.)

4 **vestrum**: *your.* This is plural because it refers to all the conspirators, not only to Trebonius.

4 **in rem p(ublicam)**: *to the state*; to be taken closely with **beneficium.**

4 **nonnullam habeat querelam**: *gives some cause for complaint*, literally *has some complaint.*

5 **tuo beneficio**: *thanks to you*, literally *by your kindness.*

6 **haec pestis**: *this noxious creature*, literally *this pestilence.* Cicero is referring to Antony, hence the masculine form of the verb (**seductus est**) although the subject of the verb (**pestis**) is feminine.

6 **quod mihi vix fas est**: *though I am scarcely entitled to do so*, literally *(a thing) which is scarcely right for me.*

7 **mihi ... uni**: Note how emphatic **uni** (*alone*) becomes through being separated from **mihi.**

7 **praeter me omnibus**: *to all the rest put together*, literally *to all except me.*

8 **foedissimum discessum**: *utterly shameful departure.* On hearing that the Martian and Fourth Legions had been persuaded by Octavian's agents to defect from him, Antony hurriedly left Rome in the early hours of 29 November 44 BC and marched north to claim the province of Cisalpine Gaul from Decimus Brutus. Two ideas are probably contained in the adjective **foedissimum** — by leaving Rome without taking the auspices, Antony offended against the religious rites of the state; Cicero also implies that he had made a cowardly escape under cover of darkness.

10 **cum civi acerrimo**: *and (that) zealous patriot*, literally *along with (that) very spirited citizen.* **civi** is commonly used as an alternative form of the ablative singular.

10 **in ore et amore habuisti**: *you praised and prized*, literally *held in your mouth* (i.e. talked about) *and in your affection.*

# 23. I'm Doing All I Can

(ad Familiares X.28)

CICERO TREBONIO S.

quam vellem ad illas pulcherrimas epulas me Idibus Martiis invitasses! reliquiarum nihil haberemus. at nunc cum iis tantum negoti est ut vestrum illud divinum in rem p. beneficium nonnullam habeat querelam. quod vero a te, viro optimo, seductus est tuoque beneficio adhuc vivit haec pestis, interdum (quod mihi vix fas est) tibi subirascor; mihi enim negoti plus reliquisti uni quam praeter me omnibus.

ut enim primum post Antoni foedissimum discessum senatus haberi libere potuit, ad illum animum meum reverti pristinum, quem tu cum civi acerrimo, patre tuo, in ore et amore semper habuisti. nam

**at**, but
**nunc**, as things stand
**negotium, -i** (*n*), trouble
**divinus, -a, -um**, divinely-inspired
**beneficium, -i** (*n*), favour, kindness, service
**vero**, actually
**seduco** (3), **-duxi, -ductum**, to take aside, lure away
**adhuc**, still
**interdum**, sometimes, occasionally
**subirascor** (3) (+ dat.), to be slightly annoyed (with)
**ut primum**, as soon as
**habeo** (2), to hold, convene
**libere**, freely, without constraint
**animus, -i** (*m*), spirit, courage, vigour
**reverto** (3), **-verti**, to return
**pristinus, -a, -um**, former

11 **a.d. XIII K. Ian.**: This refers to the meeting of the Senate on 20 December 44 BC when Cicero delivered the Third Philippic, after which he went to the Forum and, in the Fifth Philippic, told the people what had happened. (For the Roman calendar, see LL pp. 66-7.)

11 **tr(ibuni) pl(ebis)**: There were ten Tribunes of the Plebs (see page 118). In the absence of the consuls, they had the right to convene the Senate. On this occasion (1 January) they put forward a motion to guarantee the safety of the Senate and of the new consuls. Cicero went beyond the strict terms of the motion and spoke on the general crisis facing the state (**totam rem publicam sum complexus** in line 12). He persuaded the Senate to annul the edicts which Antony had forced the Senate to pass, by which provinces were reassigned to himself and his friends. He also persuaded the Senate to confirm Decimus Brutus as governor of Cisalpine Gaul and to pass votes of thanks to Octavian and the defecting legions (see page 199 and note on line 26) for resisting Antony.

13 **virtutem consuetudinemque**: *traditional courage*, literally *courage and custom.* (For Hendiadys, see CAO on page 234.)

14 **magis animi quam ingeni viribus**: *more by dint of passion than skilful argument*, literally *more by strength of spirit than of intellect.*

15 **libertatis recuperandae**: For this use of the Gerundive, see LL p. 61.

16 **tempus cogitandi ... agendi**: For Gerund, see LL p. 60.

18 **quod ipse perscriberem**: *I would personally be giving you a full account of this*, literally *which thing I myself would be writing at length.* (For Linking Relative, see LL p. 26; for Conditionals, see LL p. 54.)

18 **res urbanas actaque omnia**: *the news from the city and (reports of) all (official) proceedings.* There may be a reference here to the **acta diurna**, a daily gazette instituted by Caesar which contained a short account of the business of the Senate and other public news.

19 **eram impeditus**: *I am hindered.* In using this past (Epistolary) tense, Cicero puts himself in the position of the person reading the letter long after the event.

21 **male sentientes**: *disloyal*, literally *thinking evilly.* He is referring to Antony's supporters. (cf. **optime sentit** in lines 22-3.) The ex-consuls were expected to lead Senate opinion. At this time, there were only fourteen ex-consuls in Rome.

22 **in Servio**: *in (the case of) Servius.* Servius Sulpicius had been one of the three ambassadors sent by the Senate on 4 January 43 BC to tell Antony that he must obey the Senate and give up his claim to Cisalpine Gaul. Servius, a staunch friend and supporter of Cicero, had died in the course of this mission.

22 **Lucius Caesar** was Antony's uncle and, although by no means a traitor to the state, he had not wanted any extreme measures to be taken against his nephew.

23 **consules**: A reference to Aulus Hirtius and Gaius Vibius Pansa, who had taken up office on 1 January 43 BC.

24 **Decimus Brutus**: Though favoured by Caesar, he had been one of the assassins. As governor of Cisalpine Gaul, he was now being besieged in Mutina by Antony.

24 **egregius puer**: *a fine young fellow.* Although Cicero condescends to call Octavian by his adopted name **(Caesar)** now that he seems to be supporting the republican cause, the use of the word **puer** is more than a little patronising.

24 **de quo spero equidem reliqua**: *of whom I certainly have high hopes for the future*, literally *concerning whom I certainly hope for the remaining things.* Others were not so confident that the welfare of the state was Octavian's main concern.

cum senatum a.d. XIII K.Ian. tr. pl. vocavissent deque alia re referrent, totam rem p. sum complexus egique acerrime senatumque iam languentem et defessum ad pristinam virtutem consuetudinemque revocavi magis animi quam ingeni viribus. hic dies meaque contentio atque actio spem primum populo R. attulit libertatis recuperandae; neque vero ipse postea tempus ullum intermisi de re p. non cogitandi solum sed etiam agendi.

quod, nisi res urbanas actaque omnia ad te perferri arbitrarer, ipse perscriberem quamquam eram maximis occupationibus impeditus. sed illa cognosces ex aliis; a me pauca, et ea summatim.

habemus fortem senatum, consulares partim timidos partim male sentientes; magnum damnum factum est in Servio; L.Caesar optime sentit sed, quod avunculus est, non acerrimas dicit sententias; consules egregii, praeclarus D.Brutus, egregius puer Caesar, de quo spero

**refero, -ferre** (**de** + abl.), to put forward a motion (on)
**complector** (3), **-plexus sum**, to embrace, cover
**ago** (3), **egi**, to debate, speak, act
**languens, -entis**, feeble, inactive, faint-hearted
**defessus, -a, -um**, weary
**contentio, -onis** (*f*), effort, vigour
**actio, -onis** (*f*), pleading, appeal
**adfero, adferre, attuli**, to bring to
**recupero** (1), to recover, regain
**tempus, -oris** (*n*), time, opportunity
**intermitto** (3), **-misi**, to let slip, allow to elapse
**cogito** (1), to think, reflect, plan
**solum**, only
**perfero, -ferre**, to carry, deliver, reach
**arbitror** (1), to think, suppose
**occupatio, -onis** (*f*), public duty, matter of state
**cognosco** (3), to learn, find out
**summatim**, in summary, briefly
**fortis, -is, -e**, strong, resolute
**consularis, -is** (*m*), ex-consul
**partim ... partim**, some ... others
**timidus, -a, -um**, weak-kneed, cowardly
**damnum, -i** (*n*), loss
**avunculus, -i** (*m*), uncle
**acer, acris, acre**, vigorous, strong, critical
**sententia, -ae** (*f*), opinion, view
**egregius, -a, -um**, excellent, distinguished
**praeclarus, -a, -um**, splendid, outstanding

25 **hoc certum habeto**: *be sure of this*, literally *hold this (as) definite*. **habeto** is the most common form of the imperative of **habere**.
25 **ille** refers to Octavian, as does **eius** in line 26.
26 **legiones duae**: This refers to the Martian and Fourth Legions, which had defected from Antony to Octavian early in November 44 BC. (See also the note on line 8.)
27 **atque is oppositus esset terror Antonio**: *and (if) that had (not) given Antony cause for alarm*, literally *and (if) that terror had (not) been put in Antony's way*.
28 **nihil sceleris**: *no crime*. (For Partitive Genitive, see LL p. 9.)
28 **Antonium praeteriturum fuisse**: *Antony would have omitted*, (i.e. *failed to commit*). This Accusative and Infinitive clause depends on **hoc certum habeto**.
29 **arbitrabar**: Again, a past (epistolary imperfect) tense is used (cf. line 19). **haec** is to be taken with both **audita esse** and **notiora esse**.
30 **si habuero**: For the future perfect used in Conditional sentences, see LL p. 54.
30 **plus oti**: Another example of Partitive Genitive. (cf. **nihil sceleris** in line 28.)

## Points for Discussion

1. Read lines 2-7. Do you think Cicero means to be taken seriously in these lines? Quote from the passage to support your answer.
2. Cicero complains about the part Trebonius played in the conspiracy. In lines 5-7, what expressions does he use to tone down his complaint?
3. Read lines 8-17. What words and expressions does Cicero use here to show the significant role he played after Antony left Rome? If you had been a member of the Senate, what would your comments have been on Cicero's activities?
4. Read lines 21-8. Do you think Cicero's mood is optimistic? Quote from the passage to support your answer.
5. Can you think of any reasons why the Liberators did not include Cicero in their plans?

equidem reliqua; hoc vero certum habeto, nisi ille veteranos celeriter conscripsisset legionesque duae de exercitu Antoni ad eius se auctoritatem contulissent atque is oppositus esset terror Antonio, nihil Antonium sceleris, nihil crudelitatis praeteriturum fuisse.

haec tibi, etsi audita esse arbitrabar, volui tamen notiora esse. plura scribam, si plus oti habuero.

**veteranus, -i** (*m*), veteran (soldier)
**conscribo** (3), **-scripsi**, to recruit
**se conferre**, to transfer, come over
**auctoritas, -atis** (*f*), authority, allegiance
**crudelitas, -atis** (*f*), cruelty
**praetereo, -ire, -ii, -itum**, to pass by, pass over, omit
**etsi**, even if, although
**notus, -a, -um**, known
**otium, -i** (*n*), leisure

**salus populi suprema lex esto!** *Let the supreme law be the welfare of the people!*
De Legibus III. 3. 8

**silent leges inter arma.** *Laws are silent in the midst of armed conflict.*
Pro Milone 4

**cedant arma togae, concedat laurea laudi!** *Let arms give way to the toga, let the laurel wreath (of the victorious general) yield to (civic) praise.*
De Officiis I. 22

Cicero's fond hope — that he could achieve by his eloquence what others achieved by military success.

# The Second Triumvirate

The consuls Hirtius and Pansa had died in the fighting to save Cisalpine Gaul. Octavian therefore demanded the consulship and with it expected to secure the sole command of the armies. The Senate, however, was so confident that it had removed the threat of Antony and Lepidus by declaring them public enemies that it rejected Octavian's demand and, instead, appointed Decimus Brutus to the military command. But Octavian's troops refused to join Brutus, and Octavian did nothing to help him pursue and eliminate Antony. The Senate further annoyed Octavian by voting a triumph to Decimus Brutus, but awarding him only an ovation, thus implying that his was an easy, bloodless victory. Octavian resented these snubs and also the efforts of the Senate to create discontent among his troops by setting up a commission to review the distribution of land promised to the veterans as a reward for their campaigns.

Such moves only strengthened the support which the legions were prepared to give to Octavian, and in July they sent a deputation to Rome demanding that Octavian be appointed consul. The Senate refused on the grounds that he was too young to hold office, even though in January they had seen no such difficulty in giving him **imperium** to lead an army against Antony. When the deputation returned empty-handed, Octavian's legions called on him to lead them to Rome. Having inspired the demand in the first instance, Octavian readily obliged. The Senate had no option but to accede to his demands; and on 19 August 43 BC, five weeks before his twentieth birthday, Octavian was appointed consul. One of his first acts was to set up a court to try anyone who had been involved directly or indirectly in the murder of Caesar.

Decimus Brutus made little headway against Antony and Lepidus; and when, in the autumn of 43 BC, the governors of Further Spain and Northern Gaul threw in their lot with Antony and Lepidus, Brutus was forced to retreat. During the withdrawal, his troops mutinied and he was treacherously murdered. Antony and Lepidus marched into Italy with a force of seventeen legions. Octavian marched north with his legions to meet their challenge. Instead of fighting, however, the three leaders held a conference on an island in a tributary of the River Po near Bononia.

The outcome of this conference was a coalition, known as the Second Triumvirate. In November, the Triumvirs 'persuaded' the Assembly to appoint them *commissioners for the reorganisation of the state* for a period of five years. The three leaders also agreed to share the western provinces among themselves, to wage all-out war against the conspirators Marcus Brutus and Gaius Cassius (who had in the meantime established a power-base for themselves in the eastern Mediterranean), and to proscribe their political opponents, removing them by execution or expulsion and confiscating their wealth and property for distribution among their own soldiers as a reward for loyalty. 300 senators and 2,000 **equites** were proscribed. Cicero's name was one of those on the lists. The Greek historian and biographer Plutarch gives the following account of Cicero's death on 7 December 43 BC.

# 24. *Death of Cicero*

(Plutarch *Life of Cicero* 46)

It was at this point in particular that Cicero was manipulated and deceived, an old man by a young man. By supporting Octavian in his bid for the consulship and by winning senatorial support for him, Cicero incurred the immediate criticism of his friends and fairly soon realised that he had ruined himself and surrendered the liberty of the people. For, when the young man had become powerful and had been elected consul, he had no further use for Cicero: he befriended Antony and Lepidus, joined his forces to theirs and divided the government with them as if it were a piece of property.

A list was now prepared of more than two hundred people who were to be put to death. The most contentious issue that faced them, however, was the proscription of Cicero: Antony refused to accept any of the terms of agreement unless Cicero was the first man to be killed; Lepidus supported him; Octavian held out against both of them.

They met secretly on their own for three days near the town of Bononia, at a place some distance from their camps and encircled by a river. It is said that, during the first two days, Octavian made every effort to save Cicero but that on the third day he gave in and abandoned him to his fate. The concessions they made to one another were as follows: Octavian was to abandon Cicero, Lepidus was to give up his brother Paulus, Antony was to surrender his maternal uncle Lucius Caesar. They were overcome by furious anger to such an extent that they lost all touch with rational behaviour; or rather, they demonstrated that no wild beast is more savage than man when he gets the chance to give way to his baser instincts.

While this was going on, Cicero was at his private villa near Tusculum. His brother Quintus was there too. When they learned of the proscriptions, they decided to move to Astura, where Cicero had a house on the coast, and to sail from there to join Brutus in Macedonia. For, according to reports, Brutus already had a power-base there. They were carried along in litters, quite exhausted with grief; and, as they went along, they kept halting, putting their litters side by side and commiserating with each other. Quintus was the more depressed and kept thinking of his lack of preparation for the journey. He therefore suggested that it would be better for Cicero to continue with his escape, while he himself collected some supplies from home before hurrying after him. This was agreed and, having embraced each other, they parted, sobbing bitterly.

Not many days later, Quintus was betrayed by his servants to those who were searching for him; and he and his son were both put to death. Cicero reached Astura where he found a boat. He went on board at once and, benefiting from a following wind, sailed as far as Circaeum. The pilots were for putting out to sea from there straight away; but Cicero, either because he was afraid of the sea or because he had not yet lost all faith in Octavian, went ashore and travelled about twelve miles overland in the direction of Rome. Yet again he gave way to doubts, changed his mind and went back down to the sea at Astura. There he spent the night, a prey to wild thoughts and desperate schemes. He even contemplated entering Octavian's house secretly and killing himself there at the altar of the household gods so as to bring down divine vengeance on Octavian. But fear of arrest and torture drove him from this plan also. So, still turning over in his mind confused and contradictory courses of action, he put himself in the hands of his servants to take him by sea to Caieta where he had an estate which provided an agreeable retreat in summer when northern winds bring pleasant relief.

The place also has a temple of Apollo situated a little above the sea. From there ravens rose in crowds and flew noisily towards Cicero's boat as it was being rowed towards the land; and, alighting on either end of the yard-arm, some cawed, others pecked at the ends of the ropes. Everyone thought that this was a bad omen. Nevertheless, Cicero landed, went into the house and lay down to rest. Then most of the ravens perched at the window, cawing loudly; but one of them alighted on the couch where Cicero lay with his head covered, and little by little it pulled the covering from his face with its beak. Seeing this, his servants reproached themselves for standing idly by, just to become witnesses of their master's murder. Wild creatures were helping him and taking care of him in his undeserved plight, while they themselves were not lifting a finger to protect him. So, partly by entreaty, partly by force, they got him into his litter and carried him towards the sea.

Meanwhile, the assassins had arrived on the scene, a centurion Herennius and a tribune Popillius (whom Cicero had once defended when he was on trial for the murder of his father) at the head of a gang of men. When they found the doors shut, they broke them down; but Cicero was nowhere to be found, and the staff in the house said that they did not know where he was. It is said, however, that a young man called Philologus, who had been educated by Cicero in literature and philosophy and who was a freedman of Cicero's brother Quintus, told the tribune that the litter was being carried along thickly shaded paths through the woods to the sea.

The tribune accordingly took a few men with him and ran round to the point of exit from the woods. Herennius, however, ran along the paths and, when Cicero heard him coming, he ordered the bearers to set the litter down there and then. Then, resting his chin on his left hand, as he often did, he looked unflinchingly at his murderers, his hair dusty and dishevelled, his face pinched with anxiety — so pitiful a sight that most of those present covered their faces while Herennius was killing him. He was killed as he stretched out his neck from the litter. He was in his 64th year. On Antony's instructions, Herennius cut off his head and his hands, the hands with which he had written the Philippics. (It was Cicero himself who called these speeches against Antony 'Philippics', a title they have retained up to the present day.)

When Cicero's head and hands were brought to Rome, Antony happened to be conducting an election of magistrates. When he heard they had arrived and saw them with his own eyes, he cried out, 'Now let there be an end to the proscriptions!' He gave orders that the head and hands were to be fixed on top of the ships' beaks on the Rostra — a sight that made the Romans shudder, not because they thought they were looking at Cicero's face but rather because they felt they were seeing the image of Antony's soul.

I understand that, long after this, Augustus Caesar (see Note below) was visiting one of his daughter's sons. The boy had a book of Cicero's in his hand and, afraid of his grandfather, tried to hide it under his toga. Augustus saw this and took the book from him. Then he stood and read a long passage from it, finally giving it back to the boy with the words, 'An eloquent man, my boy, eloquent and a true patriot.'

Moreover, as soon as he had defeated Antony and was himself consul, he chose

Cicero's son as his fellow-consul; and it was in his consulship that the Senate pulled down the statues of Antony and cancelled the other honours that had been given to him, decreeing in addition that no one belonging to the family of the Antonii should bear the name Marcus. So divine justice entrusted to the family of Cicero the final acts of retribution upon Antony.

**Note**: In 42 BC, Antony and Octavian defeated the Liberators at Philippi in Greece, but not long afterwards the Second Triumvirate broke up. Lepidus was never really an equal partner in the Triumvirate, and a struggle soon developed between Octavian and Antony, in which Octavian eventually defeated Antony in a naval battle at Actium in 31 BC. Although he was now the unchallenged master of Rome, he did not make the same mistake as Julius Caesar. He simply called himself **princeps** (*first citizen*). In gratitude for his restoration of peace and stability, the Senate conferred on him the honorary title of Augustus. He is now generally regarded as the first emperor of Rome.

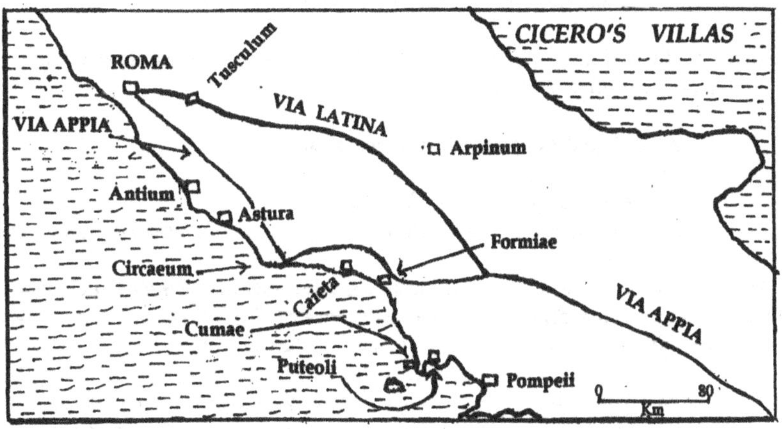


**ocellos Italiae, villulas meas,** *the jewels* (literally *little eyes*) *of Italy, my little country houses*

Ad Atticum XVI. 6

As Cicero became wealthier, he developed a mania for acquiring country houses. Eventually, he had nine!

**noli putare amabiliora fieri posse villa, litore, prospectu maris, tumulis, his rebus omnibus.**

*Don't imagine that anything* (literally *things*) *could be more enchanting than the house, the beach, the sea-view, the little hills, this whole scene.*

Ad Atticum XII. 9

Cicero speaks here of his newly-acquired villa at Astura — the place where he was later assassinated.

# Epilogue

## The Legacy of Cicero

Cicero's versatility of mind led him to explore every aspect of literary activity. Following the fashion of the time, he also turned his hand to the writing of poetry, but the fact that very little of his poetry survives would suggest that his efforts in that direction were less successful, although it has to be remembered that, at that time, poets were still experimenting with adapting the Greek hexameter to Latin.

Writing more than a century later, the Roman satirist Juvenal quotes the following line from Cicero's epic poem *De Consulatu.*

> **o fortunatam natam, me consule, Romam!**
> *o fortunate Roman state, born in the year of my consulate!*

After this, Juvenal goes on to mock the 'jingle' of the words **fortunatam natam** by adding the interesting comment:

> **Antoni gladios potuit contemnere, si sic**
> **omnia dixisset.**
> *If he had written everything like that,*
> *He could have scorned the swords of Antony.* (Juvenal, Satires X.123-4)

These lines echo words from one of Cicero's greatest speeches: **contempsi Catilinae gladios, non pertimescam tuos** (see p. 217, lines 69-70), in which Cicero throws down a challenge to Antony. In effect, therefore, although Juvenal is poking fun at Cicero's poetic efforts, he is actually acknowledging the power of Cicero's oratory by admitting that it was his eloquence which effectively condemned him to death.

Cicero's reputation as a stylist fluctuated in the centuries after his death; but, following the Renaissance, which began in Italy in the 14th century, his prose style emerged as the model for the writing of Latin (the *lingua franca* of Europe until the 19th century), and his thinking on oratorical style and presentation has greatly influenced the structure of the English language as used by writers and public speakers up to the present day.

In politics and in the law-courts, Cicero successfully pursued such timeless issues as the abuse of power, corruption in high places and conspiracy against the state. In his philosophical works (most of which he translated or adapted from Greek originals), he has preserved much Greek thought, incorporating his own views, where appropriate, on moral, religious and social issues which still concern us today.

Cicero's patriotism was not in doubt when the Republic was under threat, and he displayed remarkable courage in confronting rogues, revolutionaries and would-be tyrants. At the same time, he had less appealing characteristics, for he could be vain, boastful, naive and indecisive. But it is this mixture of strengths and weaknesses which makes him a fully-rounded human being and marks him off as one of the most fascinating personalities of Roman times.

## Appendix 1

# Cicero and Oratory

The theory and practice of oratory or public speaking is called rhetoric, which was defined in Classical times as 'the art of persuasion'. The word *oratory* is derived from the Latin verb **orare**, *to plead; rhetoric* is derived from the Greek word ῥητωρ ('rhetor'), *a public speaker.*

Cicero, one of the greatest orators of Roman times, uses many rhetorical and linguistic techniques to 'persuade' or influence his audience, whether he is addressing the Senate, a jury or an assembly of fellow-citizens. Some of these techniques, such as humour, sarcasm, irony, exaggeration and invective, would win the attention of his audience in an obvious and direct way. He also plays on the emotions of his listeners in an attempt to gain their sympathy or support; and sometimes he even appeals to the gods, implying that they would be on his side! His basic aim is to win the argument, but at the same time he hopes to belittle his opponents and to enhance his own standing.

More subtle in Cicero's oratory are linguistic and stylistic devices, which depend for their effect on sound and rhythm and on their appeal to the ear. These include deliberate repetition of key words and phrases, balanced phrases, paired words of similar meaning, sound effects (e.g. assonance, alliteration and rhythmic patterns) and **congeries verborum** (i.e. the 'piling up' of a series of nouns or verbs).

The actual delivery of a speech requires a further range of skills: Cicero was well aware of the importance of posture, tone of voice, facial expression and appropriate gestures.

## A. COMMON RHETORICAL TECHNIQUES

### 1. Humour

Cicero often aims to amuse his audience with humour — sometimes at his own expense, but more often designed to mock the target of his attack (e.g. Verres, Catiline, Antony). This involves puns and amusing anecdotes, as well as personal abuse and sarcasm.

For example, he amusingly describes his own less than triumphant return from Sicily (pages 9 and 11, lines 11-19), mocks Verres with a pun on the words **tectum** and **lectum** (p. 59, lines 50-1), gives a hilarious account of Verres' riotous banquets (pages 63 and 65, lines 79-83), and describes himself as **vehemens ille consul** (*that well-known violent consul*) when denying that he drove Catiline into exile (p. 107, line 63).

### 2. Sarcasm and Irony

Sarcasm is used to ridicule or sneer at someone in a rather cruel or bitter way, often by saying the opposite of what one really means. Cicero often uses sarcasm against Verres, e.g. **praeclari imperatoris egregia ac singularis diligentia**, *the outstanding and exceptional diligence of our distinguished general* (p. 63, lines 67-8), and **iste novo quodam genere imperator**, *that newfangled sort of general of yours* (p. 65, lines 89-90).

Irony may also involve using words which suggest the very opposite of their literal meaning, but it is generally more subtle or less personal than sarcasm. The aim is simply to mock or criticise. With heavy irony, Cicero exclaims that war with Catiline must inspire dread:

**o bellum magnopere pertimescendum, cum hanc sit habiturus Catilina scortorum cohortem praetoriam!** (p. 107, lines 74-5)
*O war greatly to be feared, as Catiline is going to have this elite corps of rent-boys!*

## 3. Invective

Cicero regularly indulges in slander and personal abuse, some of which would not be acceptable in a modern British court or even in a political context. This type of 'character assassination' may be viewed as a poor substitute for reasoned argument, but it appealed to the Romans and was no doubt effective in influencing the attitude of an audience towards the individual under attack.

Cicero states, for example, that **consuetudo ac disciplina** (*association and upbringing*) forced Verres' teenage son to be as debauched as his father (p. 67, line 101). He also lists the many kinds of disreputable characters who, he claims, associated with Catiline (p. 103, lines 37-41); and he suggests that Antony was willing to suffer any indignity to serve Caesar like a slave (p. 205, lines 15-17).

## 4. Exaggeration

This technique is often used by Cicero for dramatic effect to make a point more forcefully or, sometimes, to conceal the weakness of his own case. For example, in praising Pompey, Cicero doubts whether any speech would do justice to the man's ability:

**iam vero virtuti Cn. Pompei quae potest oratio par inveniri?** (p. 87, line 94)
*Regarding Pompey's all-round ability, what speech can be devised adequate to describe it?*

**ad urbem ita veni ut nemo ullius ordinis homo nomenclatori notus fuerit qui mihi obviam non venerit.** (p. 137, lines 22-4)
*My arrival in Rome created such a stir that there was no one known to my nomenclator from any social class who did not come up to greet me.*

## 5. Climax and Anti-Climax

Sometimes, Cicero makes his points in ascending order of importance, building up to a *climax* to keep his audience in suspense or to heighten the tension. For example, when he is challenging Catiline to leave Rome, he develops a damning picture of his subversive preparations (p. 107, lines 69-72); and, when describing Verres' banquets in graphic detail as ending up like battlefields, he cleverly builds up to his witty conclusion that a casual observer would have thought he was witnessing **Cannensem pugnam nequitiae,** *a Cannae battle of debauchery* (p. 65, lines 82-3).

Conversely, he can produce a humorous effect by a deliberate *anti-climax,* where the conclusion is feeble or not at all what was expected. For example, he expresses the 'fear' that the old court-room tactic of appealing dramatically to the military record of the accused may be used by Verres' defenders. Then comes the brilliant *anti*-climax: once Verres has been made to stand up and bare his chest, the jury will indeed see scars — not battle scars, but **ex mulierum morsu vestigia libidinis atque nequitiae**, *tell-tale signs of lust and debauchery left by the love-bites of women* (p. 69, lines 121-2).

## 6. Appealing to Emotions

Cicero continually plays on the emotions of his audience, trying to stir up feelings favourable to his case, such as indignation, disgust, pride or fear. Sometimes, his method is to make the listeners feel important by seeming to share confidential information with them; sometimes, he appeals to their patriotism by suggesting that wider issues and even the national interest may be involved, or by implying that, as right-thinking citizens, they are bound to share his view. For example, Cicero assumes that the people are on his side against Antony:

**eripiet et extorquebit tibi ista populus Romanus, utinam salvis nobis!** (p. 209, lines 10-11)
*The Roman people will snatch and wrest those weapons from you, and may we survive long enough to see it!*

Often, he appeals to the emotions through the dramatic effect of an exclamation, e.g.

**respice, quaeso, aliquando rem publicam, M. Antoni !** (p. 217, line 66)
*Have some respect for the Republic at long last, I beg you, Mark Antony!*

## 7. Rhetorical Questions

A *rhetorical question* is one where an answer is not actually expected or required, but is usually obvious or supplied by the speaker himself. Cicero often uses this technique to capture the attention of his listeners by involving them more intimately in the proceedings, or to mock or embarrass particular individuals, e.g.

**hunc tu igitur imperatorem esse defendis, Hortensi?** (p. 69, line 116)
*Do you plead in his defence, then, Hortensius, that this man is a real general?*

**quid hoc turpius, quid foedius, quid suppliciis omnibus dignius? num exspectas dum te stimulis fodiamus?** (p. 205, lines 19-21)
*What could be more disgraceful than this, what more loathsome, what more deserving of all kinds of punishment? Surely you are not waiting for us to prod you with goads?*

## 8. Digression

Cicero sometimes departs or digresses from the main issue to matters which are not always strictly relevant, but designed to hold the interest of his audience or show off his own wider knowledge. For example, before going on to describe the theft by Verres of the statue of Diana from Segesta, he traces the earlier history of the town (p. 39, lines 1-8) and relates how Scipio restored the statue of Diana to Segesta after the defeat of Carthage (p. 41, lines 15-19).

## 9. Praeteritio (Omission)

This is a device by which a speaker or writer claims that he is going to omit some fact or incident potentially damaging or embarrassing to his opponent(s), but then proceeds to mention it. Cicero is not averse to such tactics in his speeches. For example, when alleging that Verres turned a blind eye to the corrupt practices of Apronius, a tax-collector, he first of all gave several examples of Apronius' wrong-doing and then said:

**audistis haec, iudices; quae nunc ego omnia praetereo et relinquo. nihil de luxuria Apronii loquor, nihil de insolentia, nihil de permissa ab isto licentia, nihil de singulari nequitia ac turpitudine.** (Speech against Verres II.iii.106)
*You have heard all these things, members of the jury; I pass them all by unmentioned. I say nothing about Apronius' extravagant lifestyle, nothing about his insolence, nothing about the licence given to him by Verres, nothing about his unparalleled villainy and depravity.*

## 10. Dubitatio (Doubt)

This is a technique by which a speaker, with mock modesty, pretends to be less knowledgeable, experienced or confident than he actually is, i.e. he pretends to hesitate or be in doubt. In the following example, Cicero feigns doubt by means of three rhetorical questions:

**quid agam, iudices? quo accusationis meae rationem conferam? quo me vertam?** (pages 53 and 55, lines 9-10)
*What am I to do, members of the jury? Where am I to direct my line of prosecution? Where am I to turn?*

## 11. Hendiadys

Hendiadys (literally *one through two*) is the use of *two* linked words or phrases to express what is really *one* idea, e.g.

**flagrare cupiditate atque amentia coepit.** (p. 41, line 26)
*He began to burn with a mad desire*, literally *with desire and madness.*

**dabat se labori atque itineribus.** (p. 61, line 55)
*He devoted himself to the hardship of travel,* literally *to hardship and travels.*

## 12. Alliteration

Alliteration occurs when two or more words beginning with the same sound or letter (usually a consonant) appear in close succession, e.g.

**multis malis magnoque metu victi** (p. 43, line 44)
**vide ne puerum perditum perdamus!** (p. 131, lines 37-8)

## 13. Assonance

This term is used to describe sound effects produced by the deliberate repetition of words which have the same or similar vowel sounds, e.g.

**dicenda, demonstranda, explicanda sunt omnia.** (p. 29, line 60)

**L.Catilinam furentem audacia, scelus anhelantem, pestem patriae nefarie molientem, vobis atque huic urbi ferro flammaque minitantem ex urbe vel eiecimus vel emisimus vel ipsum egredientem verbis prosecuti sumus.** (p. 99, lines 1-4)

## 14. Simile

In a simile, a person or thing is said to be *like* another in one or more respects, e.g.

**ad omnes enim meos impetus quasi murus quidam boni nomen imperatoris opponitur.**
*For his reputation as a good general is put up like a kind of wall as a defence against my attacks.* (p. 55, lines 10-11)

## 15. Metaphor

A metaphor is a figure of speech used to make a vivid comparison. A person or object is stated *to be* something else which he, she or it resembles in only one respect, e.g.

**cur ego tuas partes suscipio?** (p. 49, lines 87-8)
*Why do I undertake your rôle?* (i.e. as if I were an actor on the stage).

**habet populus Romanus ad quos gubernacula rei publicae deferat.** (p. 209, lines 14-15)
*The Roman people has those to whom it may entrust the helm (government) of the state* (i.e. as if the state was a ship).

## 16. Litotes

Litotes involves an apparent *understatement.* A strong affirmative statement is produced by combining a negative and the opposite of that statement, e.g.

**ex aliqua familia non ignobili delecta mulier esset** (p. 63, lines 70-1)
*a woman had been chosen from some highly respectable* (literally *not low born*) *family.*

**C.Canius, eques Romanus nec infacetus et satis litteratus** (p. 177, line 1)
*Caius Canius, a Roman knight and a man of sharp wit* (literally *and not without wit*) *and quite cultured.*

## B. LINGUISTIC AND STYLISTIC DEVICES

The aim of orators like Cicero is to use language in such a way as to make the maximum impact on their audience and thus ensure that their message is clearly received and understood. Cicero was aware that his listeners might miss a point if it was not emphasised by repetition or other linguistic techniques. For this purpose, as well as for reasons of style, he makes frequent use of the following devices:

### 1. The Grouping of Words

#### (a) Paired Words

Cicero frequently uses two words of the same or similar meaning, the combined effect being stronger than the single word, e.g.

**qui illi inimici infensique sunt** (p. 31, line 80)
*(those) who are unfriendly and hostile to him*

**praetor populi Romani turpissimus atque impurissimus** (p. 45, lines 59-60)
*an utterly foul and vile praetor of the Roman people*

#### (b) Tricolon

This is a grouping of three phrases, e.g.

**belli pericula, tempora rei publicae, imperatorum penuriam commemorabit.** (p.55, lines 12-13)
*He will mention the dangers of war, the critical times of the state, the shortage of generals.*

**ita tantum bellum, tam diuturnum, tam longe lateque dispersum Cn.Pompeius extrema hieme apparavit, ineunte vere suscepit, media aestate confecit.** (p.89, lines 112-14)
*Thus Gnaeus Pompey, at the end of winter prepared for a war that was so great, so long-lasting, and so far and widely spread, undertook (it) at the beginning of spring, finished (it) in the middle of summer.*

## (c) Congeries Verborum

This term means a 'piling up' of words, a dramatic series of nouns or verbs in rapid succession, e.g.

**abiit, excessit, evasit, erupit.** (p. 99, line 4)
*He went off, he withdrew, he got away, he cleared out.*

**fuit in illo ingenium, ratio, memoria, litterae, cura, cogitatio, diligentia.**
*He had flair, a logical mind, a good memory, literary ability, concern for detail, aptitude for deep thought, a capacity for hard work.* (p. 215, lines 50-1)

## (d) Balanced Phrases

Cicero frequently uses two or more phrases which correspond or contrast with one another, e.g.

**negotiatoribus comis, mercatoribus iustus, mancipibus liberalis, sociis abstinens** (p. 9, lines 6-7)
*courteous to bankers, fair to merchants, generous to tax-gatherers, not exploiting our allies*

**luxuries in flagitiis, crudelitas in suppliciis, avaritia in rapinis, superbia in contumeliis** (p. 23, lines 14-15)
*over-indulgence in immoral acts, cruelty in (inflicting) punishments, greed in his robberies, arrogance in his insults*

Often the balance is pointed up by 'markers' which provide helpful clues, e.g.

**non modo ... sed etiam** and **cum ... tum,** *not only ... but also*

**ego A.Varroni, quem cum amantissimum mei cognovi tum etiam valde tui studiosum diligentissime te commendavi.** (p. 163, lines 41-2)
*I have commended you most earnestly to Aulus Varro, whom I have found to be not only very fond of me but also devoted to you.*

## (e) Chiasmus

When the order of words in the second phrase is deliberately reversed (e.g. noun-adjective, adjective-noun), this is called **chiasmus** after the Greek letter ***chi*** (χ), e.g.

**non metuis viros fortes**

**egregiosque cives**

*You do not fear brave men and distinguished citizens.* (p. 213, line 45)

## 2. Emphatic Position

To make an impact on an audience, a word is often placed in an unusual position in a sentence. In the following sentence, for example, note the emphatic separation of **nullum** and **praesidium** and also the intrusion of **te** between **caritate** and **et benevolentia:**

**nullum est istuc, mihi crede, praesidium. caritate te et benevolentia civium saeptum oportet esse, non armis.** (p. 209, lines 8-9)
*That protection of yours, believe me, is no protection at all. You of all people ought to be shielded by the affection and goodwill of your fellow-citizens, not by weapons.*

## 3. Anaphora

Cicero often repeats the same word or phrase several times for rhetorical effect or to drive home a point, e.g.

**tu horum nihil metuis, nihil cogitas, nihil laboras.** (p. 31, lines 81-2)
*You fear none of these things, do not think about them, are not at all troubled by them.*

**sit fur, sit sacrilegus, sit flagitiorum omnium vitiorumque princeps.** (p. 57, lines 30-1)
*Granted he's a thief, he's a temple-robber, he's the ring-leader in all manner of immoral acts and vices.*

## 4. Asyndeton

Asyndeton, the omission of conjunctions to link related words, phrases or clauses, is a notable feature of Cicero's style. The staccato effect produces a heightened impact, e.g.

**feci ut postea cotidie praesentem me viderent, habitavi in oculis, pressi forum.** (p. 11, lines 24-5)
*I made sure that after that they saw me in person, I lived in the public eye (and) I haunted the forum.*

**invitat Canius postridie familiares suos, venit ipse mature, scalmum nullum videt.** (p. 179, lines 21-2)
*Next day Canius invited his friends, came early himself, (but) saw not a single boat.*

# C. RHYTHMIC ENDINGS

Cicero's prose-style, especially in the speeches, often involves elaborately constructed sentences or 'periods' into which he weaves several subordinate clauses. The concluding phrases (**clausulae**) of these 'periods' (and sometimes of the clauses within them) often have rhythmic metrical patterns of long (–) and short (∪) syllables as in Latin poetry. The **clausulae** most favoured by Cicero include:

(a) Dactyl (–∪∪) and double trochee (– ∪ – ∪), e.g.

–∪∪ – ∪ – ∪
**libidinis esse posset** (p. 67, lines 96-7)

N.B. As in Latin poetry, the final syllable in a metrical unit may be long (—) or short (∪).

(b) Double cretic (– ∪ – – ∪ –), e.g.

– ∪ – – ∪–
**indigna direptio** (p. 69 line 115)

(c) Double dactyl (– ∪ ∪ – ∪ ∪), e.g.

– ∪ ∪– ∪ ∪
**conviviis muliebribus** (p. 69, line 110)

(d) Cretic (– ∪ –) and trochee (– ∪), e.g.

– ∪ ∪ ∪– ∪
**esse videatur** (p. 83, line 69)

Note that in this example the second long syllable of the cretic (–) has been resolved into a double short syllable (∪ ∪).

The use of these rhythmic patterns would naturally heighten the pleasure of those listening to Cicero and illustrates the importance of sound in the Latin language. Quintilian (c.AD 35-95), Rome's distinguished literary critic and 'professor' of oratory, makes the following comment in his work *The Training of the Orator*:

*I knew some men who reckoned that they had beautifully expressed the characteristic style of this man* (i.e. Cicero) *who was heaven-inspired in his oratory, if they had put* **esse videatur** *in a clausula.* (Quintilian, *Institutio Oratoria*, X.ii.18)

**Note:** Although many of the rhetorical and linguistic techniques used by Cicero have been explained and illustrated separately in this Appendix, there can, of course, be some overlap. For example, 'Humour' could involve 'Sarcasm', 'Invective' or 'Exaggeration'.

Appendix 2

# Geographical Index

(Numbers refer to pages.)

**Puteoli, -orum** (*m.pl*), spa on the Bay of Naples (7, 229)

**Rhodus, -i** (*f*), Rhodes, an island in the eastern Mediterranean (17, 70, 144)
**Roma, -ae** (*f*), Rome (iii, xvi, 17, 18, 70, 95, 133, 157, 229)
**Rostra, -orum** (*n.pl*), speakers' platform in Rome (xvi)
**Rubico, -onis** (*m*), River Rubicon, boundary between Umbria and Cisalpine Gaul (157)

**Segesta, -ae** (*f*), town in the west of Sicily (38)
**Sicilia, -ae** (*f*), Sicily (7, 17, 38, 70)
**Synnada, -ae** (*f*), town in Phrygia, Asia Minor (145)
**Syracusae, -arum** (*f.pl*), Syracuse, chief town of Sicily (7, 38, 67)
**Syria, -ae** (*f*), province in eastern Mediterranean (iii, 144)

**Tarentum, -i** (*n*), sea-port in the heel of Italy (157)
**Tarsus, -i** (*f*), capital of Cilicia, Asia Minor (145)
**Tauri Pylae**, a gorge in the Taurus Mountains, Asia Minor (145)
**Temple of Concord**, in Rome (xvi)
**Temple of Jupiter Stator**, in Rome (xvi)
**Temple of Ops**, in Rome (xvi)
**Theatre of Pompey**, in Rome (xvi, 18)
**Thessalonica, -ae** (*f*), town in northern Greece (133, 145)
**Tiberis, -is** (*m*), River Tiber, on which Rome stands (xvi, 18)
**Tibur, -uris** (*n*), (now Tivoli), town in Latium, east of Rome (95, 157),
**Transalpinus, -a, -um**, across the Alps
**Transpadanus, -a, -um**, Transpadane, across the River Po
**Tres Tabernae**, a place on the Appian Way south of Rome (95)
**Troia, -ae** (*f*), Troy, an ancient city in the north-west of Asia Minor (145)
**Tusculum, -i** (*n*), town in Latium, east of Rome, where Cicero had a villa (229)

**Venusia, -ae** (*f*), town in Apulia, on the Appian Way (157)
**Via Appia**, Appian Way, road leading from Rome to Brundisium (xvi, 157, 229, 18)
**Via Aurelia**, Aurelian Way, which ran up the west coast north of Rome (18, 157)
**Via Flaminia**, Flaminian Way, which ran north-east from Rome to the Adriatic (xvi, 18, 157)
**Via Latina**, Latin Way, which ran south-east from Rome (18, 229)
**Via Sacra**, Sacred Way, which ran through the Forum up to the Capitol (18)

# Select Vocabulary

**a, ab** (+ abl.), by, from, away from
**abeo, -ire, -ii, -itum**, to go away, leave
**abicio** (3), **-ieci, -iectum**, to throw away, throw down, reject
**absens, -entis**, absent, far away, away from
**absum, -esse, afui**, to be absent, be missing, be far (from), fall short
**ac**, and, moreover
**accedo** (3), **-cessi, -cessum**, to go/come to, approach, reach, be added to
**huc accedit**, added to this is the fact
**accidit**, it happens, happened, turns out
**accipio** (3), **-cepi, -ceptum**, to receive, accept, welcome, hear, learn
**accusatio, -onis** (*f*), prosecution
**accusator, -oris** (*m*), prosecutor
**accuso** (1), to accuse, prosecute
**acer, acris, acre**, spirited, fierce, keen, lively, alert, vigorous, extreme, bitter
**acerbus, -a, -um**, bitter, harsh, painful, cruel
**acerrime**, very energetically
**ad** (+ acc.), to, towards, at, near
**adduco** (3), **-duxi, -ductum**, to lead to, take to, induce, prompt, persuade
**adfero**, (see **affero**)
**adhuc**, still, so far, as yet, until now
**adiuvo** (1), **-iuvi, -iutum**, to help
**adsum, -esse, -fui**, to be present, appear
**adulescens, -entis** (*m*), young man
**adulter, -eri** (*m*), adulterer
**adventus, -us** (*m*), arrival, approach
**aetas, -atis**, (*f*), age, age-group
**affero, -ferre, attuli, allatum**, to bring, bring forward, bring to court, assert
**ager, agri** (*m*), land, territory
**ago** (3), **egi, actum**, to do, act, drive, carry out, fare, achieve, deal, discuss
**aliquando**, at last, eventually, now at long last, some day
**aliqui, aliqua, aliquod**, some, any
**aliquis, -quid**, some, someone/thing
**alius, alia, aliud**, other, another
**alii ... alii ...**, some ... others ...
**alter, -a, -um**, the other, another, the second
**alter ... alter ...**, the one ... the other
**altus, -a, -um**, high, deep
**amicitia, -ae** (*f*), friendship, love
**amicus, -i** (*m*), friend
**amitto** (3), **-misi, -missum**, to lose
**amo** (1), to love
**amor, -oris** (*m*), love, affection
**an**, whether (... or)
**animadverto** (3), **-verti, -versum**, to notice
**animus, -i** (*m*), mind, attitude, spirit, heart, intention, passion, courage
**annus, -i** (*m*), year
**ante** (+ acc.), before, in front of, previously
**antea**, before, previously, earlier
**antiquus, -a, -um**, ancient, old-fashioned
**apertus, -a, -um**, open
**appello** (1), to call upon, appeal to
**apud** (+ acc.), among, at the house of
**arbitror** (1), to think, suppose, consider
**ardens, -entis**, blazing
**arma, -orum** (*n.pl*), arms
**armatus, -a, -um**, armed
**ars, artis** (*f*), skill, knowledge
**aspicio** (3), **-spexi, -spectum**, to look at, see, view, gaze at, watch, regard

**at**, but, yet, moreover
**atque**, and, and also, and yet, furthermore
**auctoritas, -atis** (*f*), authority, influence, will, standing, validity
**audacia, -ae** (*f*), daring, audacity, boldness, courage, effrontery
**audax, -acis**, bold, daring, rash, foolhardy
**audeo** (2), **ausus sum**, to dare
**audio** (4), to hear, hear of, listen to
**aufero, -ferre, abstuli, ablatum**, to carry away, remove, withdraw
**auspicia, -orum** (*n.pl*), auspices, omens
**aut**, or
**aut ... aut ...**, either ... or ...
**autem**, however, but, and moreover, now, whereas, on the other hand
**auxilium, -i** (*n*), help; (*pl*) auxiliary troops
**auxilio esse**, to be helpful, be a help

**barbarus, -a, -um**, barbarian, uncivilised
**basis, -is** (*f*), base, pedestal (of statue)
**bellum, -i** (*n*), war, warfare, battle
**bene**, well
**bonus, -a, -um**, good, loyal
**boni, -orum** (*m.pl*), loyal citizens

**C.**, Gaius
**Cn.**, Gnaeus
**caedes, -is** (*f*), murder, bloodshed
**caelum, -i** (*n*), heaven, sky
**capio** (3), **cepi, captum**, to take, capture, arrest, hold, keep, adopt
**caput, -itis** (*n*), head, one's person
**careo** (2) (+ abl.), to miss, lack, do without
**caritas, -atis** (*f*), dearness, affection
**castra, -orum** (*n.pl*), camp
**causa, -ae** (*f*), cause, reason, case, trial
**causam agere**, to plead a case
**causa** (+ gen.), for the sake of
**caveo** (2), **cavi, cautum**, to beware of, be on one's guard against
**cave ne** (+ subjunctive), take care that you don't
**cedo** (3), **cessi, cessum**, to yield, give in, withdraw, retreat
**celebro** (1), to celebrate, honour, hail
**celeritas, -atis** (*f*), speed
**celeriter**, quickly
**celerius**, more quickly
**cena, -ae** (*f*), dinner
**censeo** (2), **-ui, censum**, to think, believe
**centurio, -onis** (*m*), centurion
**certe**, certainly, surely, at least
**certus, -a, -um**, certain, definite, reliable, regular, specific, particular
**certiorem facere**, to inform
**certior fieri**, to be informed
**ceteri, -ae, -a**, the rest, the others
**circum** (+ acc.), round, around
**citerior, -oris**, nearer
**civilis, -is, -e**, civil, concerning citizens, concerned with public life
**civis, -is** (*m*), citizen
**civitas, -atis** (*f*), city, community, state, district, country, nation
**clamo** (1), to shout, cry
**clamor, -oris** (*m*), shout, shouting, noise
**clarus, -a, -um**, famous, distinguished, illustrious, brilliant, well-known
**classis, -is** (*f*), fleet
**coactus, -a, -um**, (see **cogo**)
**coepi, -isse**, I began, have begun
**cogito** (1), to consider, think about, reflect upon, have in mind
**cogo** (3), **coegi, coactum**, to force, compel
**cognosco** (3), **-novi, -nitum**, to learn, find out, realise, get to know
**cohors, -ortis** (*f*), cohort, battalion
**collega, -ae** (*m*), colleague, fellow-consul
**colligo** (3), **-legi, -lectum**, to collect, gather
**colo** (3), **colui, cultum**, to cultivate, study, worship

**comitium, -i** (*n*), assembly
**committo** (3), **-misi, -missum**, to bring about, entrust, commit, expose, do
**commodum, -i** (*n*), interest, advantage, convenience, good-will; (*pl*) goods
**commoveo** (2), **-movi, -motum**, to move, cause concern to, upset
**comparo** (1), to prepare, get ready, provide, hire, plan, plot, compare
**complexus, -us** (*m*), embrace
**comprehendo** (3), **-hendi, -hensum**, to put together, understand, express
**concedo** (3), **-cessi, -cessum** (+ dat.), to give, grant, allow, agree to
**concido** (3), **-cidi**, to fall, collapse
**concursus, -us** (*m*), gathering, flocking together, assembly, large crowd
**confero, -ferre, -tuli, collatum**, to bring together, compare, direct
**conficio** (3), **-feci, -fectum**, to finish, complete, consume, overcome
**confirmo** (1), to establish, assure, declare, strengthen, justify
**confligo** (3), **-flixi, -flictum**, to fight, contend, be in conflict with
**conicio** (3), **-ieci, -iectum**, to drive, hurt, guess, conjecture, predict
**conor** (1), to try, attempt
**conscriptus**, (see **patres conscripti**)
**consequor** (3), **-secutus sum**, to catch up, pursue, overtake, achieve, win
**conservo** (1), to save, keep safe, preserve
**considero** (1), to consider, reflect
**consilium, -i** (*n*), plan, plan of action, strategy, intention, wisdom, advice
**constituo** (3), **-ui, -utum**, to decide, confirm, declare, set up, establish
**consuetudo, -inis** (*f*), custom, tradition, style, habit, familiarity, surroundings
**consul, -ulis** (*m*), consul
**consulatus, -us** (*m*), consulship
**consulo** (3), **-ui, -ultum**, to consult, plan; (+ dat.) consult the interests of
**contemno** (3), **-tempsi, -temptum**, to spurn, despise, scorn, minimise
**contendo** (3), **-tendi, -tentum**, to fight, hasten, urge, insist, compete
**contentio, -onis** (*f*), contest, striving, struggle, effort, straining, rivalry
**contra** (+ acc.), against, contrary to
**contra** (adverb), on the other hand
**convenio** (4), **-veni, -ventum**, to meet, gather, flock round, assemble
**conventus, -us** (*m*), gathering, crowd, assembled company, assembly
**convivium, -i** (*n*), banquet, feasting
**convoco** (1), to call together, summon
**copia, -ae** (*f*), abundance, supply, quantity, opportunity; (*pl*) forces
**corpus, -oris** (*n*), body
**corruptor, -oris** (*m*), corrupter
**credo** (3), **-didi, -ditum** (+ dat.), to believe, suppose, trust, imagine
**crudelitas, -atis** (*f*), cruelty, brutality
**cum** (+ abl.), with
**cum**, when, since, although, whenever
**cum ... tum ...**, both ... and, not only ... but also, while ... also
**cupiditas, -atis** (*f*), (covetous) desire, craving, longing, lust, greed
**cupio** (3), **-ivi, -itum**, to want, desire, wish, long for, be keen to
**cur**, why
**curo** (1), to look after, see to, attend to
  **cura ut** (+ subj.), see to it that ...
**curro** (3), **cucurri, cursum**, to run

**D.** = **datum** or **data**, handed over, dated
**de** (+ abl.), down, down from, about, concerning
**debeo** (2), to owe, ought; (*passive*) to be due
**decedo** (3), **-cessi, -cessum**, to depart from, leave, leave a province
**decem**, ten
**December, -bris, -bre**, (of) December
**deduco** (3), **-duxi, -ductum**, to lead down, bring, escort, lead away from

**defendo** (3), **-endi, -ensum**, to defend
**defensio, -onis** (*f*), defence, justification
**defensor, -oris** (*m*), defender, champion
**defero, -ferre, -tuli, -latum**, to bring, lay before, entrust, offer, report
**dein**, then, next
**deinde**, then, next, secondly
**delectus, -a, -um**, chosen, selected
**deleo** (2), **-evi, -etum**, to destroy, remove
**deligo** (3), **-legi, -lectum**, to choose, select
**demolior** (4), to dismantle, take down
**demonstro** (1), to point out, show
**denique**, in short, at length, finally
**deprecor** (1), to beg, plead for
**desero** (3), **-serui, -sertum**, to desert, abandon
**desidero** (1), to long for, desire, need, miss, find wanting
**desisto** (3), **-stiti, -stitum**, to stop, stop doing, cease, desist from
**desum, deesse, defui** (+ dat.), to be lacking, fail, disappoint
**detraho** (3), **-traxi, -tractum** (+ dat.), to take away (from)
**deus, -i** (*m*), god
**dexter, -tra, -trum**, right
**dico** (3), **dixi, dictum**, to say, tell, speak, mention, utter
**dies, diei** (*m*), day
**difficilis, -is, -e**, difficult
**dignus, -a, -um** (+ abl.), worthy (of), deserving (of), in keeping (with)
**diligenter**, carefully, conscientiously
**diligentia, -ae** (*f*), diligence, hard work, thoroughness, vigilance
**discedo** (3), **-cessi, -cessum**, to depart, leave, go away, withdraw
**disciplina, -ae** (*f*), training, teaching, science, discipline, education
**dispersus, -a, -um**, scattered
**dissimulo** (1), to pretend not to, conceal, disguise, hide one's feelings
**diu**, for a long time
**divinus, -a, -um**, divine, sacred, god-like, superhuman, divinely inspired
**divinus, -i** (*m*), soothsayer
**do** (1), **dedi, datum**, to give
**dolor, -oris** (*m*), grief, pain, suffering
**dolus, -i** (*m*), guile, fraud, trickery, treachery
**domesticus, -a, -um**, of a home, within the family (or country), national, internal, civil
**domus, -us** (*f*), house, home
  **domi**, at home
  **domo**, from home
  **domum**, to home, homewards
**dubius, -a, -um**, doubtful, uncertain, critical, ambiguous
**dum**, while, until
**duo, duae, duo**, two
**dux, ducis** (*m*), leader, general, guide

**e** or **ex** (+ abl.), out of, from
**educo** (3), **-duxi, -ductum**, to lead out
**efficio** (3), **-feci, -fectum**, to cause, create, produce, achieve
**egeo** (2), **-ui** (+ abl.), to want, need, lack, be without, be in need of
**egestas, -atis** (*f*), need, extreme poverty
**ego**, I
**egredior** (3), **-gressus sum**, to go out, leave
**egregius, -a, -um**, outstanding, eminent, distinguished
**eicio** (3), **eieci, eiectum**, to throw out, cast out, drive out, banish
**eloquentia, -ae** (*f*), eloquence
**emo** (3), **emi, emptum**, to buy
**enim**, for
**eo** (adverb), to that place
**eo, ire, ivi, itum**, to go
**equidem**, I certainly, I for my own part
**equites, -um** (*m.pl*), horsemen, cavalry, knights, the business class
**ergo**, therefore, then, well then
**eripio** (3), **-ripui, -reptum** (+ dat.), to snatch away (from)

**et**, and, also
**et ... et ...**, both ... and ...
**etenim**, for, for in fact, indeed
**etiam**, also, even, yet, still
**etiam mehercule**, ah yes, upon my word
**etsi**, even if, although
**exclamo** (1), to call out, exclaim
**exemplum, -i** (*n*), example, model
**exeo, -ire, -ii, -itum**, to go out, go forth, leave, spread, be quoted
**exercitus, -us** (*m*), army
**existimo** (1), to think, consider, believe
**exitus, -us** (*m*), end, conclusion, death
**expono** (3), **-posui, -positum**, to set out, display, mention
**exporto** (1), to carry out, carry away from
**exsilium, -i** (*n*), exile
**exspectatio, -onis** (*f*), expectation, suspense, waiting time, interest
**exspecto** (1), to wait for, expect, look for
**exstinguo** (3), **-stinxi, -stinctum**, to snuff out, quench
**extra** (+ acc.), outside, outwith
**extremus, -a, -um**, last, latest, end of

**facilis, -is, -e**, easy
**facio** (3), **feci, factum**, to do, make
**fac ut** (+ subjunct.), see to it that
**factum est ut** (+ subjunct.), it happened that, the result was that
**factum, -i** (*n*), deed, action, act
**fallo** (3), **fefelli, falsum**, to fail, deceive
**falsus, -a, -um**, false, insincere
**familia, -ae** (*f*), family, household, the slaves of the household
**familiaris, -is, -e**, of the family, private
**familiaris, -is** (*m*), friend, henchman
**fasti, -orum** (*m.pl*), public records
**fatum, -i** (*n*), fate
**Februarius, -a, -um**, (of) February
**fera, -ae** (*f*), wild beast
**fero, ferre, tuli, latum**, to bear, endure, tolerate, withstand, accept
**ferrum, -i** (*n*), iron, sword, dagger
**fides, -ei** (*f*), good faith, trust, honesty, trustworthiness, loyalty, honour
**filius, -i** (*m*), son
**fio, fieri, factus sum**, to be done, happen, become, take place
**flagitium, -i** (*n*), shameful deed, outrageous behaviour, immorality
**flamma, -ae** (*f*), flame, fire
**fluo** (3), **fluxi, fluxum**, to flow, overflow
**fore = futurus esse**, (fut.infin. of **esse**)
**forensis, -is, -e**, in the law courts
**forte**, by chance
**fortis, -is, -e**, brave, strong, vigorous
**fortuna, -ae** (*f*), fortune, good or bad luck; (*pl*) property, possessions
**fortunatus, -a, -um**, fortunate, lucky
**forum, -i** (*n*), forum, market-place, court
**frango** (3), **fregi, fractum**, to break
**frater, -tris** (*m*), brother
**frequens, -entis**, constant(ly), regular(ly)
**fructus, -us** (*m*), fruit, profit, source of income, prosperity, reward, enjoyment
**frumentum, -i** (*n*), corn
**fugio** (3), **fugi**, to flee, run away from
**futurus, -a, -um**, future, about to be, likely to be

**gaudeo** (2), **gavisus sum**, to rejoice, be glad
**gens, gentis** (*f*), tribe, clan, race, nation
**genus, -eris** (*n*), type, kind, family, nature, birth, social rank
**geometria, -ae** (*f*), earth-measuring, geometry
**gero** (3), **gessi, gestum**, to do, wage, wear, fight, undertake
**gladiator, -oris** (*m*), gladiator
**gladius, -i** (*m*), sword
**gloria, -ae** (*f*), glory, fame, distinction

**gratulatio, -onis** (*f*), thanks, rejoicing, congratulation, public thanksgiving
**gratus, -a, -um**, pleasing, popular
**gravis, -is, -e**, heavy, serious, important, authoritative, dignified
**graviter**, heavily, seriously

**habeo** (2), to have, hold, consider
**haruspex, -icis** (*m*), soothsayer
**heri**, yesterday
**hesterno die**, yesterday
**hiberna, -orum** (*n.pl*), winter-quarters
**hic**, here
**hic, haec, hoc**, this; he, she, it
**hiems, hiemis** (*f*), winter, stormy weather
**hieme summa**, in the depths of winter
**hodie**, today
**homo, -inis** (*m*), man, fellow, person
**honestus, -a, -um**, honourable, not corrupt, respectable, respected,
**honos (honor), -oris** (*m*), honour, respect, distinction, public office
**hortus, -i** (*m*), garden
**hostis, -is** (*m*), enemy (of the state)
**humanitas, -atis** (*f*), kindness, refinement
**humanus, -a, -um**, human

**iaceo** (2), to lie, lie prostrate, be situated
**iam**, already, now
**iam vero**, turning now to, moreover
**Ianuarius, -a, -um**, (of) January
**ibi**, there
**idem, eadem, idem**, same
**idem quod**, the same as
**Idus, -uum** (*f.pl*), the Ides (13th or 15th day of the month)
**igitur**, therefore
**ignoro** (1), to be ignorant of, be unaware of, disregard
**ignosco** (3), **-novi, -notum** (+ dat.), to pardon, forgive
**ille, illa, illud**, that; that person or thing
**immortalitas, -atis** (*f*), immortality
**impedio** (4), to hinder, frustrate, prevent, affect adversely
**imperator, -oris** (*m*), general
**imperatorius, -a, -um**, of a general, due to a general
**imperium, -i** (*n*), (supreme) power, command, supremacy, empire
**impero** (1), to order, demand, requisition
**impetus, -us** (*m*), attack, power,
**impono** (3), **-posui, -positum**, to impose
**improbus, -a, -um**, wicked, shameful, shameless, villainous, disloyal
**impunitas, -atis** (*f*), impunity, recklessness
**in** (+ abl.), in, on
**in** (+ acc.), into, against
**incendo** (3), **-endi, -ensum**, to burn
**incido** (3), **-cidi, -casum**, to fall into
**incido** (3), **-cidi, -cisum**, to cut into, inscribe
**incolumis, -is, -e**, safe, unharmed
**incredibilis, -is, -e**, incredible, beyond belief, extraordinary
**inde**, from there
**indignus, -a, -um** (+ abl.), unworthy (of), undeserved, shameful
**infimus, -a, -um**, lowest
**ingenium, -i** (*n*), intelligence, intellect, talent, ability, genius, flair
**ingens, -entis**, huge
**ingredior** (3), **-gressus sum**, to go in (on), enter, embark upon
**inimicus, -a, -um**, enemy, hostile
**initium, -i** (*n*), beginning, origin
**innocens, -entis**, innocent, upright
**innocentia, -ae** (*f*), innocence, blamelessness
**inquam, inquit**, I say, he/she says
**insidiae, -arum** (*f.pl*), ambush, plot
**insidiator, -oris** (*m*), one who lies in ambush
**insignis, -is, -e**, distinguished, eminent
**intellego** (3), **-lexi, -lectum**, to realise, understand, recognise, know

**inter** (+ acc.), between, among
**interficio** (3), **-feci, -fectum**, to kill, murder
**intra** (+ acc.), within, inside
**inutilis, -is, -e**, useless
**invenio** (4), **-veni, -ventum**, to find
**invito** (1), to invite
**ipse, -a, -um**, -self, that very person/thing
**is, ea, id**, that; he, she, it
**iste, ista, istud**, that (of yours), that man, the accused
**ita**, so, so much, in such a way, in this way
**itaque**, therefore
**item**, also, likewise
**iter, itineris** (*n*), journey, march, track
**iubeo** (2), **iussi, iussum**, to order
**iudices, -um** (*m.pl*), judges, jurors, jury, members of the jury
**iudicium, -i** (*n*), law court
**ius, iuris** (*n*), right, law, duty, judgement
**Kalendae, -arum** (*f.pl*), Kalends, first day of the month

**L.**, Lucius
**labor, -oris** (*m*), labour, hard work, exertion, hardship, trouble
**laboro** (1), to work, work at, be struggling, be in difficulties
**lacrima, -ae** (*f*), tear
**laetor** (1), to rejoice in/over, take pleasure in
**lamentatio, -onis** (*f*), cry of grief, wailing
**latro, -onis** (*m*), robber, gangster, thug, bandit
**laudo** (1), to praise
**laus, laudis** (*f*), praise, glory, renown, fame, honour, reputation
**legatus, -i** (*m*), ambassador, envoy, legate, deputy, lieutenant
**legio, -onis** (*f*), legion
**lenitas, -atis** (*f*), leniency
**lex, legis** (*f*), law, rule, convention, condition
**liber, -era, -erum**, free
**liberator, -oris** (*m*), one who frees
**libero** (1), to free, set free
**libertas, -atis** (*f*), freedom, liberty
**libido, -inis** (*f*), lust, debauchery
**licet** (2), **licuit**, it is allowed, it is permitted
**littera, -ae** (*f*), letter (of the alphabet); (*pl*) letter, dispatch(es), literature, records, literary ability
**locus, -i** (*m*), place, location, situation, vantage-point, topic, connection
**longitudo, -inis** (*f*), length
**longus, -a, -um**, long
**loquor** (3), **locutus sum**, to speak, say, talk

**M.**, Marcus
**M'.**, Manius
**magis**, more, rather
**magister, -tri** (*m*), master, teacher, leader
**magistratus, -us** (*m*), magistrate
**magnitudo, -inis** (*f*), size, bigness
**magnus, -a, -um**, great, big, large
**maior, maius**, greater, bigger
**maiores, -um** (*m.pl*), ancestors, older men
**Maius, -a, -um**, (of) May
**Martius, -a, -um**, (of) March, of Mars
**malum, -i** (*n*), evil, misfortune, calamity
**manus, -us** (*f*), hand, band, company
**mare, maris** (*n*), sea
**maritimus, -a, -um**, of the sea, at sea
**maxime**, most, especially, greatly
**maximus, -a, -um**, greatest, very big
**mecum**, with me
**medius, -a, -um**, middle (of)
**mehercule!**, by Hercules, heavens above, upon my word
**melior, -ius**, better
**melius** (adverb), better
**memoria, -ae** (*f*), memory, recollection
**mens, mentis** (*f*), mind, sense, intention
**mercator, -oris** (*m*), merchant, trader

**metuó** (3), **-ui, -utum**, to fear, dread
**metus, -us** (*m*), fear, apprehension
**meus, -a, -um**, my
**miles, -itis** (*m*), soldier
**militaris, -is, -e**, military
**res militaris**, warfare, military service, military prowess
**minimus, -a, -um**, smallest, least
**minor** (1) (+dat.), to threaten
**misceo** (2), **miscui, mixtum**, to mix
**miser, -era, -erum**, unhappy, poor
**me miserum!**, o dear me!
**mitto** (3), **misi, missum**, to send
**modo**, only
**modus, -i** (*m*), way, manner, kind, limit, moderation, tone, melody
**monumentum, -i** (*n*), memorial, reminder
**mortuus, -a, -um**, dead
**moror** (1), **moratus sum**, to delay, stay
**mors, mortis** (*f*), death
**moveo** (2), **movi, motum**, to move
**mulier, -eris** (*f*), woman
**multitudo, -inis** (*f*), crowd, mob, great number
**multo** (+ comparative), much
**multus, -a, -um**, much; (*pl*) many
**musicus, -i** (*m*), musician
**muto** (1), to change, reverse, transform
**mutue**, mutually, reciprocally

**nam**, for
**nascor** (3), **natus sum**, to be born
**natio, -onis** (*f*), nation, tribe, people
**natura, -ae** (*f*), nature, disposition
**navigo** (1), to sail
**navis, -is** (*f*), ship
**-ne**, *indicates a question*
**ne** + subjunctive, lest, so that ... not
**nec**, and ... not, nor
**nec ... nec ...**, neither ... nor ...
**ne ... quidem**, not even
**necessarius, -a, -um**, necessary, inevitable
**neco** (1), to kill, execute, murder, slaughter
**nefarius, -a, -um**, abominable, loathsome, heinous, despicable, wicked
**negotium, -i** (*n*), business, operation, task, difficulty, problem, campaign
**nemo, nullius**, no, no one
**neque**, and not
**neque ... neque (nec)**, neither ... nor
**nihil**, nothing
**nimis**, too much
**nisi**, unless, if ... not, except
**nobilis, -is, -e**, noble, high-ranking, well-known
**nocturnus, -a, -um**, by night, of the night
**nolo, nolle, nolui**, to be unwilling, not to wish, to refuse, decline
**noli** (+ infinitive), do not ... !
**nomen, -inis** (*n*), name, reputation
**non**, not
**Nonae, -arum** (*f.pl*), the Nones (5th or 7th day in the month)
**nonne?** Surely ... ?
**nonnullus, -a, -um**, some
**nos**, we, us
**noster, -tra, -trum**, our
**notus, -a, -um**, known, well-known
**November, -bris, -bre**, (of) November
**novi, novisse**, to know
**novus, -a, -um**, new, new-fangled
**nox, noctis** (*f*), night, darkness
**nudus, -a, -um**, naked, bare
**nullus, -a, -um**, no, none
**num** (*asks a question*), whether, surely ... not
**numerus, -i** (*m*), number, quantity
**numquam**, never
**nunc**, now, as things stand
**nuntio** (1), to announce, report, bring news
**nuntius, -i** (*m*), messenger, message, news

**obeo, -ire, -ii, -itum**, to go to, inspect
**obtuli**, (see **offero**)
**October, -bris, -bre**, (of) October
**oculus, -i** (*m*), eye

**offendo** (3), **-fendi, -fensum**, to give offence to, displease, vex, make a mistake
**offero, -ferre, obtuli, oblatum**, to offer, expose, present, force oneself on
**officium, -i** (*n*), duty, sense of duty, devotion to duty, loyalty, obligation
**omnino**, altogether, entirely, at all events, utterly, absolutely
**omnis, -is, -e**, all, every
**operam dare** (**ut** + subjunctive), to make an effort (to)
**opinio, -onis** (*f*), opinion, belief, feeling
**oportet** (+ infinitive), one ought (to), it is necessary
**te oportet**, you ought
**oppidum, -i** (*n*), town, township
**oppono** (3), **-posui, -positum**, to oppose, set against, put in one's way
**optime**, best, very well
**optimus, -a, -um**, very good, excellent
**opto** (1), to wish for, long for, desire
**opus, operis** (*n*), work, task, skill
**opus est** (+ abl.), there is need (of), it is necessary
**oratio, -onis** (*f*), speech, words, account, utterance, eloquence
**orator, -oris** (*m*), orator, public speaker
**ordo, -inis** (*m*), order, rank, social class
**ornatus, -a, -um**, decorated, ornate, florid, illustrious, accomplished
**ostendo** (3), **-tendi, -tentum**, to show, display, reveal, offer
**otium, -i** (*n*), leisure, peace, calm

**P.**, Publius
**palam**, openly, in public
**parens, -entis** (*m/f*), parent, father, mother
**paro** (1), to prepare, make ready
**pars, partis** (*f*), part, side, some
**patefacio** (3), **-feci, -factum**, to lay open, expose, reveal, uncover
**pater, patris** (*m*), father
**patior** (3), **passus sum**, to suffer, allow
**patria, -ae** (*f*), native land, homeland
**pauci, -ae, -a**, few, a few
**pax, pacis** (*f*), peace
**pecunia, -ae** (*f*), money
**penuria, -ae** (*f*), scarcity, shortage
**per** (+ acc.), through, by
**percipio** (3), **-cepi, -ceptum**, to receive, perceive, experience, gain
**perditus, -a, -um**, abandoned, corrupt, lost, criminal, ruined, desperate
**perdo** (3), **-didi, -ditum**, to lose, waste, ruin, squander, destroy
**pereo, -ire, -ii, -itum**, to perish, be lost, die
**perfero, -ferre, -tuli, -latum**, to carry, bring news, endure
**perficio** (3), **-feci, -fectum**, to finish, bring about, achieve, accomplish
**periculum, -i** (*n*), danger, risk
**perpetuus, -a, -um**, perpetual, continuous, permanent, for life
**persequor** (3), **-secutus sum**, to pursue, follow up, escort, avenge
**pertimesco** (3), **-timui**, to become very afraid, fear greatly, become alarmed
**peto** (3), **petivi, petitum**, to seek, ask, make for, request, seek election
**philosophia, -ae** (*f*), philosophy
**philosophus, -i** (*m*), philosopher
**piscis, -is** (*m*), fish
**piscor** (1), to fish
**plane**, clearly, entirely, definitely
**plures, plura**, more, several
**plus, pluris**, more
**polliceor** (2), **pollicitus sum**, to promise
**pono** (3), **posui, positum**, to place, mention, put before
**populus, -i**, (*m*), people
**porta, -ae** (*f*), gate
**possum, posse, potui**, to be able

**post** (adverb), afterwards, later
**post** (+ acc.), after, behind
**postea**, afterwards, later
**postquam** (conjunction), after
**postridie**, on the following day, on the next day
**potestas, -atis** (*f*), power, authority, control, opportunity
**potius**, rather
**praeclarus, -a, -um**, famous, excellent, exceptional, distinguished, splendid
**praesens, -entis**, present, in person
**praesertim**, especially
**praesidium, -i** (*n*), garrison, stronghold, protection, bodyguard, defence
**praeter** (+ acc.), beyond, besides, except for, to a greater degree than
**praeterea,** besides, in addition
**praetor, -oris** (*m*), praetor
**praetura, -ae** (*f*), praetorship
**premo** (3), **pressi, pressum**, to press, burden, weigh down, persecute
**pridie**, on the previous day
**primo**, at first
**primum**, first, firstly, for the first time
**primus, -a, -um**, first, earliest, early
**princeps, -cipis** (*m*), leading citizen, instigator, proposer (of a bill)
**privatus, -a, -um**, private
**pro** (+ abl.), on behalf of, for the sake of, in defence of
**proficiscor** (3), **-fectus sum**, to start, set out, leave
**propter** (+ acc.), on account of, thanks to
**propterea quod**, especially because, for the very reason that
**prosequor** (3), **-secutus sum**, to pursue, escort
**provideo** (2), **-vidi, -visum**, to plan ahead, see to it, take precautions
**provincia, -ae** (*f*), province, command
**proximus, -a, -um**, nearest, very near, next, latest, last, most recent
**prudens, -entis**, wise, shrewd
**prudentia, -ae** (*f*), foresight, wisdom, commonsense, discretion, judgment
**publicus, -a, -um**, public
**puer, -i** (*m*), boy
**pueritia, -ae** (*f*), boyhood
**pugna, -ae** (*f*), fight
**pugno** (1), to fight, take up arms against
**pulcher, -chra, -chrum**, beautiful, splendid, fine, noble, glorious
**puto** (1), to think, consider

**Q.**, Quintus
**quaero** (3), **quaesivi, quaesitum**, to seek, ask, try to find, investigate
**quaestor, -oris** (*m*), quaestor
**quaestura, -ae** (*f*), quaestorship
**qualis, -is, -e**, what sort of
**quam**, than
**quam!**, how!
**quam primum**, as soon as possible
**quamquam**, although
**quando**, when
**quantus, -a, -um?**, how great?, how much?
**quare**, why, therefore
**quasi**, as if, like, as it were
**quattuor**, four
**-que**, and
**quemadmodum**, how, as, just as, so
**qui, quae, quod**, who, which, that
**quid?**, what?, why?, well then, again (*adding another point*)
**quidam, quaedam, quoddam**, a certain, a kind of, a
**quidem**, indeed, in fact, really, certainly, but, at least, admittedly
**quinque**, five
**Quirites, -ium** (*m.pl*), citizens of Rome
**quis? quid?**, who?, what?
**quis, quid**, anyone, anything, someone, something
**quisquam, quaequam, quicquam**, anyone, anything
**quisque, quaeque, quodque**, each

**quo?**, where to?
**quo**, to which place
**quodsi**, and if, but if
**quoniam**, since

**ratio, -onis** (*f*), reason, reasoning ability, intellect, method, means, plan, judgement, argument, style, principle
**recipio** (3), **-cepi, -ceptum**, to take back, receive, accept, undertake
**recte**, rightly, properly, justly, reliably
**recupero** (1), to recover, regain, redeem
**reddo** (3), **-didi, -ditum**, to give back, return, hand over, change into
**redeo, -ire, -ii, -itum**, to go back, return
**reditus, -us** (*m*), return
**regno** (1), to reign, rule, rule as a king
**regnum, -i** (*n*), kingdom, kingly power, title of king, kingship
**religio, -onis** (*f*), holiness, religious awe, religious practice, object of worship
**relinquo** (3), **-liqui, -lictum**, to leave, leave behind, abandon
**reliquus, -a, -um**, remaining, the rest, other
**remitto** (3), **-misi, -missum**, to release
**removeo** (2), **-movi, -motum**, to remove, withdraw
**repono** (3), **-posui, -positum**, to put back
**reporto** (1), to bring back, carry off
**requiro** (3), **-quisivi, -quisitum**, to ask, request, reclaim, miss, lack, need
**res, rei** (*f*), thing
**res familiaris**, private property
**res gestae**, achievements, exploits
**res militaris**, warfare, military service, military prowess
**res publica, rei publicae** (*f*), state, the interests of the state, republic
**respondeo** (2), **-spondi, -sponsum**, to reply, answer
**retorqueo** (2), **-torsi, -tortum**, to turn back
**revoco** (1), to recall, call back
**rex, regis** (*m*), king, monarch

**S.**, Sextus
**saepe**, often
**Sal. = salutem**, greetings
**salus, -utis** (*f*), safety, well-being, welfare, security, greetings
**saluto** (1), to greet, welcome
**salvus, -a, -um**, safe, safe and sound, unharmed, well, surviving
**sane**, very, truly, really, certainly
**satis**, enough, sufficient, quite, clearly
**scelus, -eris** (*n*), crime, wickedness, villainy, criminal act
**scientia, -ae** (*f*), knowledge
**scio** (4), to know (how to)
**scito! scitote!** (imperative), know, let me tell you, let me assure you
**scribo** (3), **scripsi, scriptum**, to write
**se** or **sese**, himself, herself, themselves
**sed**, but
**sedeo** (2), **sedi, sessum**, to sit, be seated, stay seated
**semper**, always
**senator, -oris** (*m*), senator
**senatus, -us** (*m*), senate
**senectus, -utis** (*f*), old age
**sensus, -us** (*m*), sense(s), feeling, sensation
**sententia, -ae** (*f*), thought, opinion, view, policy, advice
**sentio** (4), **sensi, sensum**, to feel, notice, perceive, realise, think, experience
**September, -bris, -bre**, (of) September
**septimus, -a, -um**, seventh
**sequor** (3), **secutus sum**, to follow
**servio** (4) (+ dat.), to serve, be a slave, be subservient, devote oneself
**servo** (1), to save, keep, preserve
**servus, -i** (*m*), slave
**sese = se**
**severitas, -atis** (*f*), severity, strictness

**sex**, six
**Sextilis, -is, -e**, (of) August, the sixth month
**si**, if
**sic**, thus, so, in this way, as follows
**signum, -i** (*n*), statue, (military) standard
**silentium, -i** (*n*), silence
**simulacrum, -i** (*n*), statue, image, shrine
**simulo** (1), to pretend
**sin**, but if
**sine** (+ abl.), without
**singularis, -is, -e**, exceptional, remarkable, unusual, unique
**socius, -i** (*m*), ally, companion, accomplice
**soleo** (2), **solitus sum**, to be in the habit (of), accustomed (to), be customary
**solum**, only
**solus, -a, -um**, alone
**Sp.**, Spurius
**spero** (1), to hope (for)
**spes, spei** (*f*), hope
**statim**, immediately
**statua, -ae** (*f*), statue
**studium, -i** (*n*), study, enthusiasm, keenness, determination, efforts
**subito**, suddenly
**suffero, -ferre, sustuli, sublatum**, to suffer, endure
**sum, esse, fui**, to be
**summus, -a, -um**; greatest, excellent, top, outstanding, main, total
**superior, -oris**, more exalted, previous
**supplicium, -i** (*n*), punishment
**supra**, above, over, before
**suscipio** (3), **-cepi, -ceptum**, to adopt, undertake, receive, undergo, uphold
**suspicio, -onis** (*f*), suspicion, uneasiness
**sustineo** (2), **-tinui, -tentum**, to sustain, support, shoulder, face, keep going
**suus, -a, -um**, his/her own, their own
**talis, -is, -e**, such, of such a kind, of such ability, of such quality
**talis ... qualis ...**, as much ... as, as ... as
**tam**, so
**tamen**, however
**tamquam**, as if, as though
**tandem**, at length, at last; (*in a question*) pray tell me
**tantus, -a, -um**, so much, so big, so strong
**tectum, -i** (*n*), roof, home, dwelling-house
**templum, -i** (*n*), temple, sacred area
**tempto** (1), to try, test
**tempus, -oris** (*n*), time, age, occasion, timing, opportunity
**teneo** (2), **-ui, tentum**, to hold, control, detain, hold in check, trap
**terra, -ae** (*f*), land
**tertius, -a, -um**, third
**timeo** (2), to fear
**timidus, -a, -um**, timid, afraid
**tollo** (3), **sustuli, sublatum**, to lift, pick up, remove, carry off, banish
**tot**, so many
**totus, -a, -um**, all, (the) whole, entire
**trado** (3), **-didi, -ditum**, to hand over, hand down, surrender
**trans** (+ acc.), across
**transeo, -ire, -ii, -itum**, to cross
**tres, tres, tria**, three
**tribunus plebis**, tribune of the plebs
**triumphus, -i** (*m*), triumph
**tu**, you (singular)
**tueor** (2), **tuitus sum**, to protect, defend
**tum**, then, on that occasion, at that time
**tum ... cum ...**, at a time when
**cum ... tum ...**, both ... and ...
**tunica, -ae** (*f*), tunic
**turpis, -is, -e**, shameful, disgraceful, loathsome, humiliating
**tutus, -a, -um**, safe
**tuus, -a, -um**, your
**tyrannus, -i** (*m*), tyrant

**ubi**, where, when
**ullus, -a, -um**, any
**umquam**, ever
**unde**, where from, from which
**unus, -a, -um**, one, single
**urbs, urbis** (*f*), city, township
**ut** (+ indicative), when, as, just as, from the time when, ever since
**ut** (+ subjunctive), in order that, so that, how
**uti = ut**
**utilis, -is, -e**, useful, advantageous
**utinam** (+ subjunctive), I wish that, would that
**utor** (3), **usus sum** (+ abl.), to use, adopt, accept, play
**uxor, -oris** (*f*), wife

**valde**, very, really, utterly
**valeo** (2), to be well, keep well
**vale! valete!**, farewell!, goodbye!
**valetudo, -inis** (*f*), sickness, disease, health, state of health
**vehementer**, violently, vehemently, greatly, strongly, very much
**vel**, or, certainly
**vel ... vel ...**, either ... or ...
**vendo** (3), **didi, -ditum**, to sell
**venio** (4), **veni, ventum**, to come
**verbum, -i** (*n*), word
**vereor** (2), **veritus sum**, to fear, be afraid
**vero**, truly, indeed, in fact, certainly, but
**versor** (1), to turn, move about among, be, be involved, be engaged in, be found, happen, live, spend time
**verum**, but
**verus, -a, -um**, true, real, genuine, correct
**vester, -tra, -trum**, your
**vetus, veteris**, old, ancient, former
**via, -ae** (*f*), road, street, way, line
**victor, -oris** (*m*), victor
**victoria, -ae** (*f*), victory
**video** (2), **vidi, visum**, to see, look at, consider, reflect upon
**videor** (2), **visus sum**, to seem
**vigilantia, -ae** (*f*), vigilance, alertness, watchfulness
**vigilo** (1), to keep watch, be vigilant
**viginti**, twenty
**villa, -ae** (*f*), villa, country house
**vinco** (3), **vici, victum**, to conquer, defeat, overcome, surpass, upset
**violo** (1), to violate, infringe
**vir, viri** (*m*), man
**viri boni**, loyal citizens
**virgo, -inis** (*f*), maiden
**virtus, -utis** (*f*), virtue, courage, bravery, valour, merit, ability, excellence, goodness, brilliance, quality, integrity, uprightness
**vis, vim** (acc.), **vi** (abl.) (*f*), force, strength, act of violence
**vita, -ae** (*f*), life, life-style
**vivo** (3), **vixi, victum**, to live, be alive
**voco** (1), to call, summon, bring
**volo, velle, volui**, to wish, be willing, resolve
**vos**, you
**vox, vocis** (*f*), voice
**vulnus, -eris** (*n*), wound

CPSIA information can be obtained
at www.ICGtesting.com
Printed in the USA
LVOW05s1941220817
545961LV00015B/268/P